PAXEN

Melbourne, Florida
www.paxen.com

Acknowledgments

For each of the selections and images listed below, grateful acknowledgment is made for permission to excerpt and/or reprint original material, as follows:

Text

2 Used with the permission of THE ATLANTIC © 2008 **5** From American Rhetoric, www.americanrhetoric.com **4** Used with the permission of NATIONAL PARKS MAGAZINE. "While They Were Sleeping" by Tom Clynes, originally published in National Parks Magazine © 2008; Used with the permission of THE ATLANTIC © 2008 **5** Excerpts from ECOLOGY OF A CRACKER CHILDHOOD by Janisse Ray (Minneapolis: Milkweed Editions, 1999) © 1999 by Janisse Ray. Reprinted with permission from Milkweed Editions. www.milkweed.org **8** From American Rhetoric, www.americanrhetoric.com "Inaugural Address" by John F. Kennedy ©1961; From American Rhetoric, www.americanrhetoric.com; From American Rhetoric, www.americanrhetoric.com "Checkers" by Richard M. Nixon © 1952 **10** From American Rhetoric, www.americanrhetoric.com "Let Us Continue" by Lyndon Baines Johnson © 1963 **11** Used with the permission of Elie Wiesel © 1999 **12** Excerpts reprinted with permission by CAR AND DRIVER **14** From THE NEW YORK TIMES, September 9 © 1975 The New York Times All rights reserved. Used by permission and protected by the Copyright Laws of the United States. The printing, copying, redistribution, or retransmission of the Material without express written permission is prohibited. **15** "School vs. Education" by Russell Baker, from THE NEW YORK TIMES, 9/9/1975 © 1975 The New York Times. All rights reserved. Used by permission and protected by the Copyright Laws of the United States. The printing, copying, redistribution, or retransmission of this Content without express written permission is prohibited. **17** Reprinted by permission of Don Congdon Associates, Inc. © 1968 by Edward Abbey, renewed 1996 by Clarke Abbey **18** From SAVAGE INEQUALITIES: CHILDREN IN AMERICA'S SCHOOLS by Jonathan Kozol © 1991 by Jonathan Kozol. Used by permission of Crown Books, an imprint of the Crown Publishing Group, a division of Random House LLC. All rights reserved **19** Reprinted by permission of Don Congdon Associates, Inc. © 1968 by Edward Abbey, renewed 1996 by Clarke Abbey **20** From www.historyofvaccines.org, accessed 2013 **21** From SAVAGE INEQUALITIES by Jonathan Kozol © 1991 by Jonathan Kozol. Used by permission of Crown Publishers, a division of Random House, Inc. **22** Used by permission of The YGS Group. **23** From THE NEW YORK TIMES, July 24 © 2008 The New York Times All rights reserved. Used by permission and protected by the Copyright Laws of the United States. The printing, copying, redistribution, or retransmission of the Material without express written permission is prohibited. **24** From THE NEW YORK TIMES, August 30 © 2005 The New York Times All rights reserved. Used by permission and protected by the Copyright Laws of the United States. The printing, copying, redistribution, or retransmission of the Material without express written permission is prohibited. **25** USA TODAY, October 24, 2008. Reprinted with Permission **26** Used with the permission of the University of New Mexico. "The Way to Rainy Mountain" by N. Scott Momaday, originally published in THE WAY TO RAINY MOUNTAIN © 1969 **29** From Tom Jackson's BLACK BEARS, © 2008. All rights reserved. Reprinted by permission of Children's Press, an imprint of Scholastic Library Publishing, Inc. **32** From THE NEW YORK TIMES, October 7 © 1960 The New York Times All rights reserved. Used by permission and protected by the Copyright Laws of the United States. The printing, copying, redistribution, or retransmission of the Material without express written permission is prohibited. **33** From NEWSWEEK, December 11 © 2007 Newsweek, Inc. All rights reserved. Used by permission and protected by the Copyright Laws of the United States. The printing, copying, redistribution, or retransmission of the Material without express written permission is prohibited. **34** From AS THEY WERE by M.F.K. Fisher, © 1982 by M.F.K. Fisher. Used by permission of Alfred A. Knopf, a division of Random House, Inc. **35** From THE NEW YORK TIMES, December 20 © 1995 The New York Times All rights reserved. Used by permission and protected by the Copyright Laws of the United States. The printing, copying, redistribution, or retransmission of the Material without express written permission is prohibited. **38** Reprinted by permission of International Creative Management, Inc. © 1990 by Barbara Ehrenreich **40** Albert A. Gore's Nobel Lecture © The Nobel Foundation (Oslo, December 10, 2007) **41** William Faulkner's Nobel Lecture © The Nobel Foundation (Oslo, December 10, 1950) **42** From THE NEW YORK TIMES, June 29 © 2008 The New York Times All rights reserved. Used by permission and protected by the Copyright Laws of the United States. The printing, copying, redistribution, or retransmission of the Material without express written permission is prohibited. **43** From "For Girls' Schools and Women's Colleges, Separate is Better," Originally published in THE NEW YORK TIMES, June 12 © 1994 Used with the permission of Susan Estrich **44** From businessweek.com, "Working Remotely or Remotely Working?" © 2008 **45** From "For Girls' Schools and Women's Colleges, Separate is Better," Originally published in THE NEW YORK TIMES, June 12 © 1994 Used with the permission of Susan Estrich **47** Reprinted with permission from MayoClinic.com **48** From cnn.com "Reduce Poverty by Promoting Schools, Families" © 2013 **49** From the huffingtonpost.com article THE AFFORDABLE CARE ACT: GOOD NEWS FOR FORMER FOSTER YOUTH by Michael Piraino, CEO, National Court Appointed Special Advocate Association (CASA for Children) **55** Excerpt from INSIDE THE CRIMINAL MIND by Stanton Samenow, 1984 by Stanton E. Samenow. Used by permission of Times Books, an imprint of Random House LLC. All Rights Reserved. **57** From nationalzoo.si.edu, "Monarch Butterfly Migration Underway," accessed 2013. Used with permission from the National Zoo **60** From www.nationalgeographic.

© 2014 by Paxen Publishing LLC. All rights reserved.

No part of this work may be reproduced or transmitted in any form or by any means, electronic or mechanical, including photocopying or recording, or by any information storage or retrieval system, without the prior written permission of the copyright owner, unless such copying is expressly permitted by federal copyright law. Requests for permission to make copies of any part of the work should be addressed to Paxen Publishing LLC, 710 Atlantis Road, Melbourne, FL 32904.

ISBN: 978-1-934350-59-1

1 2 3 4 5 6 7 8 9 10   1689   20 19 18 17 16 15 14   Printed in the U.S.A.

4500508872

com, "Apollo Anniversary: Moon Landing Inspired World," by John Roach ˝ 2004 accessed 2013 **61** North Dakota Parks and Recreation Department. No Date. North Dakota Prairie: Our Natural Heritage. North Dakota Parks and Recreation Department, U.S. Department of the Interior, U.S. Fish and Wildlife Service. Jamestown, ND: Northern Prairie Wildlife Research Center Online http://www.npwrc.usgs.gov/resource/habitat/heritage/index.htm (Version 05MAY99). **62** From THE NEW YORK TIMES, August 7 © 2008 The New York Times All rights reserved. Used by permission and protected by the Copyright Laws of the United States. The printing, copying, redistribution, or retransmission of the Material without express written permission is prohibited. **63** From THE NEW YORK TIMES, June 10 © 2008 The New York Times All rights reserved. Used by permission and protected by the Copyright Laws of the United States. The printing, copying, redistribution, or retransmission of the Material without express written permission is prohibited. **64** From THE NEW YORK TIMES, August 11 © 2008 The New York Times All rights reserved. Used by permission and protected by the Copyright Laws of the United States. The printing, copying, redistribution, or retransmission of the Material without express written permission is prohibited. **65** From THE NEW YORK TIMES, January 3 © 1981 The New York Times All rights reserved. Used by permission and protected by the Copyright Laws of the United States. The printing, copying, redistribution, or retransmission of the Material without express written permission is prohibited. **66** From THE NEW YORK TIMES, July 26 © 2008 The New York Times All rights reserved. Used by permission and protected by the Copyright Laws of the United States. The printing, copying, redistribution, or retransmission of the Material without express written permission is prohibited. **67** From Barbara Jordan's Keynote Speech at the 1976 Democratic National Convention, © 1976, Barbara Jordan Archives, Texas Southern University **68** From American Rhetoric, www.americanrhetoric.com. "A Time for Choosing" Ronald Reagan © 1965 **69** From American Rhetoric, www.americanrhetoric.com. "Duty, Honor, Country" by Douglas MacArthur © 1962 **71** From American Rhetoric, www.americanrhetoric.com. "A Time for Choosing" by Ronald Reagan © 1965 **72** Used with the permission of Malcolm Gladwell. "Annals of Public Policy: Troublemakers." Originally published in The New Yorker ©2006 **74** Used with permission of The Associated Press © 2007 **75** From NEWSWEEK, August 9 © 2008 Newsweek, Inc. All rights reserved. Used by permission and protected by the Copyright Laws of the United States. The printing, copying, redistribution, or retransmission of the Material without express written permission is prohibited **90** Excerpt from "The Lecture" from THE SÉANCE AND OTHER STORIES by Isaac Bashevis Singer © 1968 by Isaac Bashevis Singer. Reprinted by permission of Farrar, Straus and Giroux, LLC. **92** Used with the permission of the Estate of Martha Gellhorn "Miami-New York" by Martha Gellhorn © 1948 **93** © 1961 Tillie Olsen from TELL ME A RIDDLE, reprinted by permission of the Frances Goldin Literary Agency. **94** Used with the permission of James A. McPherson. Originally published in Elbow Room © 1972 **95** From "The Doll's House" by Katherine Mansfield, ˝ © 1922. **96** Used with the permission of James A. McPherson. Originally published in Elbow Room © 1972 **97** © 1961 Tillie Olsen from TELL ME A RIDDLE, reprinted by permission of the Frances Goldin Literary Agency. **108** Used with the permission of Pam Durban. Originally published in The Southern Review © 1996 **109** "Criers and Kibitzers, Kibitzers and Criers" by Stanley Elkin © 1965 by Stanley Elkin. Reprinted by permission of Georges Borchardt, Inc., on behalf of the Estate of Stanley Elkin. **111** Used with the permission of Pam Durban. Originally published in The Southern Review © 1996 **112** "Criers and Kibitzers, Kibitzers and Criers" by Stanley Elkin © 1965 by Stanley Elkin. Reprinted by permission of Georges Borchardt, Inc., on behalf of the Estate of Stanley Elkin. **113** © 1970 Ontario Review, Inc. Reprinted by permission of John Hawkins & Associates, Inc. **114** Excerpt from "the Circling Hand" from ANNIE JOHN by Jamaica Kincaid © 1985 by Jamaica Kincaid. Reprinted by permission of Farrar, Straus and Giroux, LLC **117** Except from "The German Refugeee" from IDIOTS FIRST by Bernard Malamud © 1963 by Bernard Malamud and renewed 1991 by Ann Malamud. Reprinted by permission of Farrar, Straus and Giroux, LLC **119** Reprinted by permission of International Creative Management, Inc. © 1988 by Bobbie Ann Mason. **122** Reprinted by permission of International Creative Management, Inc. © 1988 by Bobbie Ann Mason **124** Reprinted by permission of International Creative Management, Inc. © 1940 by Walter Van Tilburg Clark **127** Excerpt from "Death of a Traveling Salesman" in A CURTAIN OF GREEN AND OTHER STORIES, © 1941 and renewed 1969 by Eudora Welty, reprinted by permission of Houghton Mifflin Harcourt Publishing Company **128** You Were Perfectly Fine," from THE PORTABLE DOROTHY PARKER by Dorothy Parker, edited by Marion Meade, ©1928, renewed © 1956 by Dorothy Parker; © 1973, 2006 by The National Assoc. for the Advancement of Colored People. Used by permission of Viking Penguin, a division of Penguin Group (USA) Inc. **130** "You'll Never Know, Dear, How Much I Love You," from PIGEON FEATHERS AND OTHER STORIES by John Updike © 1962, copyright renewed 1990 by John Updike. Used by permission of Alfred A. Knopf, an imprint of the Knopf Doubleday Publishing Group, a division of Random House LLC. All rights reserved. **131** From O HOW SHE LAUGHED, © 1934, 1962 by Conrad Aiken. Reprinted by permission of Brandt & Hochman Literary Agents, Inc. All rights reserved. **132** Used with the permission of J. F. Powers. "The Valiant Woman" by J.F Powers © 1937 **133** © 1952 by the James Agee Trust, reprinted with permission of The Wylie Agency LLC. **134** Excerpt from "The Interior Castle" from COLLECTED STORIES by Jean Stafford © 1969 by Jean Stafford. Reprinted by permission of Farrar, Straus and Giroux, LLC. **135** Reprinted by permission of Don Congdon Associates, Inc. © 1950 by Crowell Collier Publishing, renewed 1977 by Ray Bradbury **136** Excerpt from "The Interior Castle" from COLLECTED STORIES by Jean Stafford © 1969 by Jean Stafford. Reprinted by permission of Farrar, Straus and Giroux, LLC. **139** © by 1974 by Alice Munro. Reprinted by permission of William Morris Agency, LLC on behalf of the Author **145** "Edie: A Life" first appeared in Epoch, 1988. Published in The Tiger in the Grass by Viking Adult © 1995. Used with permission of Martha Toppin and the Harriet Doerr Papers at Stanford University **147** "Pie Dance" from ROUGH TRANSLATIONS by Molly Giles. Originally published by The University of Georgia Press, © 1985 **148** "In the Gloaming" by Alice Elliott Dark, THE NEW YORKER © 1993 Alice Elliott Dark. Reprinted with permission by Dunow, Carlson & Lerner Literary Agency **149** © 1989 by Joy Williams. Used by permission of Grove/Atlantic, Inc. **150** Excerpt from "The Legacy" in A HAUNTED HOUSE AND OTHER SHORT STORIES by Virginia Woolf, ©1944 and renewed 1972 by Harcourt, Inc., reprinted by permission of the publisher **151** Excerpt from "Yonder Peasant, Who Is He?" in MEMORIES OF A CATHOLIC GIRLHOOD, ©1948 and renewed 1975 by Mary McCarthy, reprinted by permission of Houghton Mifflin Harcourt Publishing Company **152** "In the Gloaming" by Alice Elliott Dark, THE NEW YORKER © 1993 Alice Elliott Dark. Reprinted with permission by Dunow, Carlson & Lerner Literary Agency **154** From "Healthy Landscape with Dormouse" by Sylvia Townsend Warner **155** Used with the permission of Eileen Goudge **156** From "Healthy Landscape with Dormouse" by Sylvia Townsend Warner **158** Used with the permission of the Estate of W. S. Maugham. Copyright © 1929 by W. Somerset Maugham **165** © 1940 by Ogden Nash, renewed. Reprinted by permission of Curtis Brown, Ltd.; "One Perfect Rose", copyright 1926, renewed © 1954 by Dorothy Parker, from THE PORTABLE DOROTHY PARKER by Dorothy Parker, edited by Marion Meade. Used by permission of Viking Penguin, a division of Penguin Group (USA) Inc. **166** "Song" by W.H. Auden **167** © 1954, 1982 by Norma Millay Ellis. Reprinted by permission of Elizabeth Barnett, Literary Executor, The Millay Society **172** From MOUNTAINS AND MOLEHILLS by Frances Cornford © 1934. Reprinted by permission of Cambridge University Press **177** "Once by the Pacific" from the book THE POETRY OF ROBERT FROST edited by Edward Connery Lathem © 1956 by Henry Holt and Company LLC. All rights reserved. **179** "My Papa's Waltz," © 1942 by Hearst Magazine, Inc.; from COLLECTED POEMS OF THEODORE ROETHKE by Theodore Roethke. Used by permission of Doubleday, an imprint of the Knopf Doubleday Group, a division of Random House LLC All rights reserved. **181** "Harlem (2) ["What happens to a dream deferred…"]", from THE COLLECTED POEMS OF LANGSTON HUGHES by Langston Hughes, edited by Arnold Rampersad with David Roessel, Associate Editor, © 1994 by the Estate of Langston Hughes. Used by permission of Alfred A. Knopf, a division of Random House, Inc. **182** "The Parade" from NINE HORSES by Billy Collins © 2002 by Billy Collins. Used with the permission of Random House, Inc. **188** "For a Five-Year-Old" by Fleur Adcock, originally published in POEMS 1960-2000, Bloodaxe Books, 2000 **189** Naomi Shihab Nye, "Hidden" from FUEL © 1998 by Naomi Shihab Nye. Reprinted by permission of The Permission Company, Inc., on behalf of BOA Editions, Ltd., www.BOAEditions.org **191** © 1999 by Wendell Berry from THE SELECTED POEMS OF WENDELL BERRY. Reprinted by permission of Counterpoint **196** "Awake to a Smile" by Robert Service **197** "Happiness" from WHERE WATER COMES TOGETHER WITH OTHER WATER by Raymond Carver © 1984, 1985 by Raymond Carver. Used by permission of Random House, Inc. **198** "To a Daughter Leaving Home," from CARNIVAL EVENING: New and Selected Poems 1968–1998 by Linda Pastan © 1998 by Linda Pastan. Used by permission of W. W. Norton & Company, Inc.

Images

(front cover) Daniel Aguilera/Getty Images . **vi** iStockphoto. **vii** iStockphoto. **xi** Jamie Carrol/iStockphoto.

High School Equivalency Test Preparation

Reading Student Book

Table of Contents

About High School Equivalency Tests v
About *High School Equivalency Test Preparation* vii
About *High School Equivalency Test Preparation: Reading* viii
Test-Taking Tips ix
Study Skills x
Before You Begin: Using Logic and Making Assumptions xi

UNIT 1 *Non-Fiction* xii

Frequently Misspelled Words 1

LESSON
 1: Main Idea and Details 2
 2: Summarize 7
 3: Categorize 12
 4: Sequence 17
 5: Cause and Effect 22
 6: Compare and Contrast 27
 7: Distinguish Fact from Opinion 32
 8: Make Inferences 37
 9: Draw Conclusions 42
 10: Determine Author's Purpose 47
 11: Analyze Elements of Persuasion 52
 12: Identify Evidence 57
 13: Determine Point of View 62
 14: Style and Tone 67
 15: Generalize 72

Unit 1 Review 77

UNIT 2 *Fiction* 81

Glossary 82

LESSON
 1: Context Clues 83
 2: Cause and Effect 88
 3: Compare and Contrast 93
 4: Plot Elements 98
 5: Characters 103
 6: Motivation 108
 7: Point of View 113
 8: Theme 118
 9: Setting 123
 10: Tone 128
 11: Figurative Language 133
 12: Symbols and Imagery 138
 13: Make Inferences 143
 14: Draw Conclusions 148
 15: Apply Ideas 153

Unit 2 Review 158

UNIT 3 *Poetry* 162

Frequently Confused Words 163

LESSON
 1: Rhythm and Rhyme 164
 2: Analogies 169
 3: Figurative Language 174
 4: Symbols and Imagery 179
 5: Make Inferences 184
 6: Restatement 189
 7: Theme 194

Unit 3 Review 199

ANNOTATED ANSWER KEY 203
INDEX 227

About High School Equivalency Tests

Simply by turning to this page, you've made a decision that will change your life for the better. Each year, thousands of people just like you decide to pursue a high school equivalency certificate. Like you, they left school for one reason or another. And now, just like them, you've decided to continue your education by studying for and taking the high school equivalency tests.

However, these tests are no easy task. The tests, five in all, are spread across the subject areas of Language Arts/Reading, Language Arts/Writing, Mathematics, Science, and Social Studies. Preparation for the tests can involve extensive study and review. The payoff, however, is significant: more and better career options, higher earnings, and the sense of achievement that comes with a high school equivalency certificate. Employers and colleges and universities accept the certificate as they would a high school diploma. On average, certificate recipients earn $10,000 more per year than do employees without a high school diploma or an equivalency certificate.

High school equivalency tests are designed to mirror a high school curriculum. Although you will not need to know all of the information typically taught in high school, you will need to answer a variety of questions in specific subject areas. In Language Arts/Writing, you will need to write an essay.

In all cases, you will need to effectively read and follow directions, correctly interpret questions, and critically examine answer options. The table below details the five subject areas. Since different states have different requirements for the number of tests you may take in a single day, you will need to check with your local adult education center for requirements in your state or territory.

SUBJECT AREA TEST	CONTENT AREAS
Language Arts/Reading	Literary Texts Informational Texts
Language Arts/Writing (Editing)	Organization of Ideas Language Facility Writing Conventions
Language Arts/Writing (Essay)	Development and Organization of Ideas Language Facility Writing Conventions
Mathematics	Numbers and Operations on Numbers Data Analysis/Probability/Statistics Measurement/Geometry Algebraic Concepts
Science	Life Science Earth/Space Science Physical Science
Social Studies	History Civics/Government Economics Geography

Three of the subject-area tests—Language Arts/Reading, Science, and Social Studies—will require you to answer questions by interpreting passages. The Science and Social Studies tests also require you to interpret tables, charts, graphs, diagrams, timelines, political cartoons, and other visuals. In Language Arts/Reading, you also will need to answer questions based on workplace and consumer texts. The Mathematics Test will require you to use basic computation, analysis, and reasoning skills to solve a variety of word problems, many of them involving graphics. On all of the tests, questions will be multiple-choice with five answer options. An example follows:

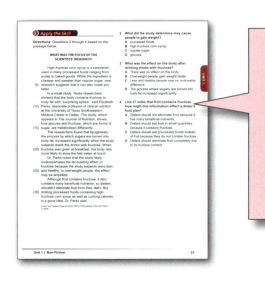

On the Mathematics Test, you will have four or five answer options for each multiple choice question.

As the table on page v indicates, the Language Arts/Writing Test contains two parts, one for editing, the other for essay. In the editing portion of Language Arts/Writing, you will be asked to identify and correct common errors in various passages and texts while also deciding on the most effective organization of a text. In the essay portion, you will write an essay that analyzes texts or provides an explanation or an opinion on a single topic of general knowledge.

So now that you understand the task at hand—and the benefits of a high school equivalency certificate—you must prepare for the tests. In the pages that follow, you will find a recipe of sorts that, if followed, will help guide you toward successful completion of your certificate. So turn the page. The next chapter of your life begins right now.

About *High School Equivalency Test Preparation*

Along with choosing to pursue your high school equivalency certificate, you've made another smart decision by selecting this program as your main study and preparation tool. Simply by purchasing *High School Equivalency Test Preparation*, you've joined an elite club with thousands of members, all with a common goal—earning their high school equivalency certificates. In this case, membership most definitely has its privileges.

For more than 70 years, high school equivalency tests have offered a second chance to people who need it most. To date, more than 17 million Americans like you have studied for and earned high school equivalency certificates and, in so doing, jump-started their lives and careers. Benefits abound for certificate holders: Recent studies have shown that people with certificates earn more money, enjoy better health, and exhibit greater interest in and understanding of the world around them than do those without.

In addition, many certificate recipients plan to further their educations, which will provide them with more and better options. As if to underscore the point, the U.S. government's Division of Occupational Employment Projections estimates that through 2022, about 3.1 million new jobs will require a bachelor's degree for entry.

Your pathway to the future—a *brighter* future—begins now, on this page, with *High School Equivalency Test Preparation*. Unlike other programs, which take months to teach through a content-based approach, *High School Equivalency Test Preparation* gets to the heart of the tests—and quickly—by emphasizing *concepts*. At their core, the majority of the tests are reading-comprehension exams. Test-takers must be able to read and interpret excerpts, passages, and various visuals—tables, charts, graphs, timelines, and so on—and then answer questions based upon them.

High School Equivalency Test Preparation shows you the way. By emphasizing key reading and thinking concepts, *High School Equivalency Test Preparation* equips learners like you with the skills and strategies you'll need to correctly interpret and answer questions on the tests. Five-page lessons in each student book provide focused and efficient instruction, while callout boxes, sample exercises, and test-taking and other thinking strategies aid in understanding complex concepts.

Unlike other high school equivalency test preparation materials, which were designed *for* the classroom, these materials were designed *from* the classroom, using proven educational theory and cutting-edge classroom philosophy. For learners who have long had the deck stacked against them, the odds are finally in their favor. And yours.

HIGH SCHOOL EQUIVALENCY TESTS—FAST FACTS

- About 800,000 people take high school equivalency exams each year.
- Workers with a high school equivalency certificate earn an average of $10,000 a year more than people without a high school diploma or its equivalent.
- Over 3,000,000 students drop out of high school each year.
- Over 85% of Americans have a high school diploma or its equivalent.
- High school dropouts are not eligible for 90% of U.S. jobs.

About *High School Equivalency Test Preparation: Reading*

For those who think the high school equivalency tests for Language Arts/Reading are a breeze, think again. The test is a rigorous exam that will assess your ability to understand and interpret subject-specific passages. You will answer questions organized across four main content areas: Non-fiction and Fiction and Poetry. Material in *High School Equivalency Test Preparation: Reading* has been organized with these content areas in mind.

High School Equivalency Test Preparation: Reading helps deconstruct the different elements of the test by helping learners like you to build and develop key reading and thinking skills. A combination of targeted strategies, informational call-outs and sample questions, assorted tips and hints (including Test-Taking Tips, Using Logic, and Making Assumptions), and ample assessment help to clearly focus study efforts in needed areas, all with an eye toward the end goal: Success on high school equivalency tests.

As on the social studies and science tests, the language arts/reading test uses the thinking skills of *comprehension*, *application*, *analysis*, and *synthesis*. Certain questions on the test ask you to take information from the text and apply it to a different situation. *High School Equivalency Test Preparation: Reading* provides a number of questions of this type for practice.

The Learn the Skill section defines and provides additional information about the skill to be studied.

Callouts provide strategies and information that you may use to understand and interpret various passages or graphics.

Numbers in parentheses let you know the number of lines in the excerpts.

Making Assumptions guides you to making smart, rational assumptions that will help you answer multiple-choice questions.

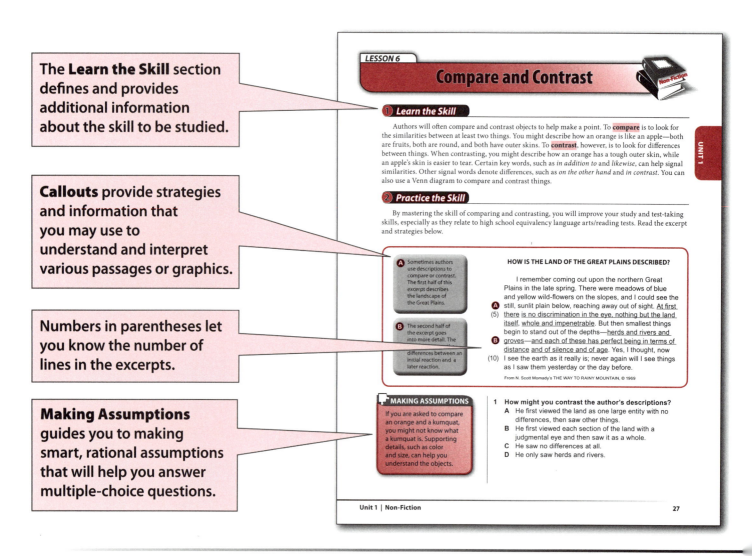

Test-Taking Tips

High school equivalency tests include questions across the five subject-area exams of Language Arts/Reading, Language Arts/Writing, Mathematics, Science, and Social Studies. In each test, you will need to apply some amount of subject-area knowledge. However, because all of the questions are multiple-choice items largely based on text or visuals (such as tables, charts, or graphs), the emphasis in *High School Equivalency Test Preparation* is on helping learners like you build and develop core reading and thinking skills. As part of the overall strategy, various test-taking tips are included below and throughout the book to help you improve your performance on the tests. For example:

◆ **Always thoroughly read the directions so that you know exactly what to do.** For example, on many tests direction lines explicitly state which questions are to be answered using information in a passage, visual, map, or chart. Pay attention to these directions in order to make sure you are correctly matching up these test elements.

◆ **Read each question carefully so that you fully understand what it is asking.** Some questions, for example, may present more information than you need to correctly answer them.

◆ **Manage your time with each question.** Because the tests are timed exams, you'll want to spend enough time with each question, but not *too* much time. You can save time by first reading each question and its answer options before reading the passage or examining the graphic. Once you understand what the question is asking, review the passage or visual for the appropriate information.

◆ **Note any unfamiliar words in questions.** First, attempt to reread the question by omitting the unfamiliar word(s). Next, try to substitute another word in its place.

◆ **Answer all questions, regardless of whether you know the answer or are guessing at it.** There is no benefit in leaving questions unanswered. Keep in mind the time that you have for each test and manage it accordingly. For time purposes, you may decide to initially skip questions. However, note them with a light mark beside the question and try to return to and answer them before the end of the test.

◆ **Narrow answer options by rereading each question and the text or graphic that goes with it.** Although all answer choices are *possible*, keep in mind that only one of them is *correct*. You may be able to eliminate one or two answers immediately; others may take more time and involve the use of either logic or assumptions. In some cases, you may need to make your best guess between two options. If so, keep in mind that test makers often avoid answer patterns; that is, if you know the previous answer is **B** and are unsure of the answer to the next question but have narrowed it to options **B** and **D**, you may want to choose **D**.

◆ **Read all answer choices.** Even though the first or second answer choice may appear to be correct, be sure to thoroughly read all answer choices. Then go with your instinct when answering questions. For example, if your first instinct is to mark **A** in response to a question, it's best to stick with that answer unless you later determine that answer to be incorrect. Usually, the first answer you choose is the correct one.

◆ **Correctly complete your answer sheet by marking one lettered space on the answer sheet beside the number that corresponds to it.** Mark only one answer for each item; multiple answers will be scored as incorrect. If time permits, double-check your answer sheet after completing the test to ensure that you have made as many marks—no more, no less—as there are questions.

Study Skills

You've already made two very smart decisions in trying to earn your high school equivalency certificate and in purchasing *High School Equivalency Test Preparation* to help you to do so. The following are additional strategies to help you optimize your success on the tests.

3 weeks out...

- Set a study schedule. Choose times in which you are most alert, and places, such as a library, that provide the best study environment.
- Thoroughly review all material in *High School Equivalency Test Preparation*.
- Make sure that you have the necessary tools for the job: sharpened pencils, pens, paper, and, for mathematics, a calculator.
- Keep notebooks for each of the subject areas that you are studying. Folders with pockets are useful for storing loose papers.
- When taking notes, restate thoughts or ideas in your own words rather than copying them directly from a book. You can phrase these notes as complete sentences, as questions (with answers), or as fragments, provided you understand them.

1 week out...

- Take the pretests, noting any troublesome subject areas. Focus your remaining study around those subject areas.
- Prepare the items you will need for the test day: admission ticket (if necessary), acceptable form of identification, some sharpened No. 2 pencils (with erasers), a watch, eyeglasses (if necessary), a sweater or jacket, and a high-protein snack to eat during breaks.
- Map out the course to the test center, and visit it a day or two before your scheduled exam. If you drive, find a place to park at the center.
- Get a good night's sleep the night before the tests. Studies have shown that learners with sufficient rest perform better in testing situations.

The day of...

- Eat a hearty breakfast high in protein. As with the rest of your body, your brain needs ample energy to perform well.
- Arrive 30 minutes early to the testing center. This will allow sufficient time in the event of a change to a different testing classroom.
- Pack a sizeable lunch, especially if you plan to be at the testing center most of the day.
- Focus and relax. You've come this far, spending weeks preparing and studying for the tests. It's your time to shine.

Before You Begin: Using Logic and Making Assumptions

At several hours in length, the high school equivalency tests are to testing what marathons are to running. Just like marathons, though, you may train for success on the tests. As you know, the exams test your ability to interpret and answer questions about various passages and visual elements. Your ability to answer such questions involves the development and use of core reading and thinking skills. Chief among these are the skills of reasoning, logic, and assumptions.

Reasoning involves the ability to explain and describe ideas. **Logic** is the science of correct reasoning. Together, reasoning and logic guide our ability to make and understand assumptions. An **assumption** is an idea that we know to be true and which we use to understand the world around us.

You use logic and make assumptions every day, sometimes without even knowing that you're doing so. For example, you might go to bed one night knowing that your car outside is dry; you might awaken the next morning to discover that your car is wet. In that example, it would be *reasonable* for you to *assume* that your car is wet because it rained overnight. Even though you did not see it rain, it is the most *logical* explanation for the change in the car's appearance.

When thinking logically about items on the tests, you identify the consequences, or answers, from text or visuals. Next, you determine whether the text or visuals logically and correctly support the consequences. If so, they are considered valid. If not, they are considered invalid. For example, read the following passages and determine whether each is valid or invalid:

Passage A

High school equivalency tests assess a person's reading comprehension skills. Ellen enjoys reading. Therefore, Ellen will do well on the tests.

Passage B

High school equivalency tests cover material in five different subject areas. Aaron has geared his studies toward the tests, and he has done well on practice tests. Therefore, Aaron may do well on the actual tests.

Each of the above situations has a consequence: *Ellen will* or *Aaron may* do well on the tests. By using reasoning and logic, you can make an assumption about which consequence is valid. In the example above, it is *un*reasonable to assume that Ellen *will* do well on the tests simply because she likes to read. However, it *is* reasonable to assume that Aaron *may* do well on the tests because he has studied for the tests and has done well on the practice tests in each of the five subject areas.

Use the same basic principles of reasoning, logic, and assumptions to determine which answer option logically and correctly supports a question on the science test. You may find occasions in which you have narrowed the field of possible correct answers to two, from which you must make a best, educated guess. In such cases, weigh both options and determine the one that, reasonably, makes the most sense.

Reading Student Book | Before You Begin: Using Logic and Making Assumptions

Unit 1

Unit Overview

Whether at work, at home, or places in-between, you likely read various newspaper, magazine, and Web articles every day. Odds are that most of these articles are non-fiction pieces whose primary purpose is to inform and educate. At work, for example, you may need to read an employee manual to better understand a job-related policy. At home, you may need to read instructions to successfully use your new media device.

Similarly, non-fiction pieces play a vital role in the High-School Equivalency Language Arts/Reading Test. As with other areas of the tests, questions about non-fiction works will test your ability to read and interpret passages through the use of various reading skills. In Unit 1, the introduction of skills such as summarizing, categorizing, sequencing, and generalizing will help you prepare for the High-School Equivalency Language Arts/Reading Test.

Table of Contents

Lesson 1: Main Idea and Details 2
Lesson 2: Summarize 7
Lesson 3: Categorize. 12
Lesson 4: Sequence 17
Lesson 5: Cause and Effect 22
Lesson 6: Compare and Contrast 27
Lesson 7: Distinguish Fact from Opinion 32
Lesson 8: Make Inferences. 37
Lesson 9: Draw Conclusions 42
Lesson 10: Determine Author's Purpose 47
Lesson 11: Analyze Elements of Persuasion 52
Lesson 12: Identify Evidence. 57
Lesson 13: Determine Point of View 62
Lesson 14: Style and Tone 67
Lesson 15: Generalize. 72
Unit 1 Review 77

Non-Fiction

Frequently Misspelled Words

A
a lot
absence
accept
accident
accommodate
address
again
agree
all right
almost
already
although
always
appear
argue
attention
author
awful

B
beautiful
because
beginning
being
believe
benefit
bicycle
borrow
business

C
captain
career
chief
college
congratulate
curiosity

D
daily
daughter

definitely
delicious
describe
difference
different
discover
disease
distance
dollar
doubt

E
easy
education
effect
either
embarrass
emergency
enough
environment
equipment
especially
excellent
except
exercise
extreme

F
familiar
financial
foreign
former
friend
further

G
general
genius
government
governor
grateful
great
grocery

guard
guess

H
happiness
healthy
heard
heavy
height
heroes
holiday
hopeless
hospital

I
immediately
increase
independence
instead
interrupt
invitation
island

K
kitchen
knowledge

L
language
laugh
library
license
light
likely
loyal

M
maintenance
medicine
muscle
mystery

N
natural
necessary

neighbor

O
occasion
ocean
operate
opinion

P
particular
patience
people
perfect
permanent
picture
piece
positive
prepare
probably
produce
professional
profit
promise

Q
quality
quiet

R
raise
reason
receive
recipe
recognize
recommend
relieve
right
roommate

S
sandwich
scene
schedule
season

sense
separate
service
several
similar
since
soldier
soul
source
special
stomach
strength
stretch
succeed
successful
surprise
sympathy

T
technical
though
through
together
tomorrow
toward
tragedy

U
unnecessary
unusual
usual

V
valuable
variety
view
voice

W
weather
whether
while

UNIT 1

LESSON 1

Main Idea and Details

① Learn the Skill

The **main idea** of a text is the most important point of the passage. The main idea is usually found in the topic sentence of a paragraph and may be in the beginning, middle, or end of a passage. **Supporting details** provide additional information about the main idea. These details can include facts, statistics, examples, or descriptions.

② Practice the Skill

By mastering the skill of identifying the main idea and supporting details, you will improve your study and test-taking skills, especially as they relate to high school equivalency language arts/reading tests. Read the excerpt and strategies below.

A By reading the underlined text, you know that the main idea of this passage is the effectiveness of teachers trained by Teach for America.

B The second sentence provides supporting details, giving the reader additional information about the main idea.

WHY DID RESEARCHERS PERFORM THE STUDY?

A However, the first study to examine Teach for America at the secondary-school level, recently released by the Urban Institute, <u>finds that its teachers are in fact more effective than those with traditional training</u>—at all levels (5) of experience. <u>The study measured performance on state exams and found that students of Teach for America</u> **B** <u>instructors did significantly better in all subject areas tested, and especially in math and science</u>. The authors found that even though the program's teachers are (10) assigned to "the most demanding classrooms," they're able to compensate for their lack of experience with better academic preparation and motivation.

From The Atlantic's, THE KIDS ARE ALRIGHT, © 2008

USING LOGIC

Questions will often indirectly ask you to find the main idea or supporting detail of a passage or paragraph. For example, you may be asked "What is the author trying to say?"

1. Which line from the text contains a detail that supports the idea that the Teach for America program trains valuable teachers?
   A "The study measured performance on state exams... ."
   B "...the program's teachers are assigned to 'the most demanding classrooms'... ."
   C "…the first study to examine Teach for America at the secondary-school level."
   D "…finds that its teachers are in fact more effective than those with traditional training."

Apply the Skill

Directions: Questions 2 and 3 are based on the memo below.

WHAT IS THE MAIN IDEA OF THE MEMO?

Redlands Community College

To: Redlands Community College Department Heads
From: Marissa Vega, Human Resources Director
Date: May 8
(5) Memo: Guidelines for Appropriate Summer Attire

Each employee of Redlands Community College is responsible for reporting to work in a clean, neat manner. Proper attire has a positive image on Redlands, fostering public confidence and a professional environment.

As we approach the summer season, I would like to review the "summer business casual" dress
(10) code. As a reminder, the Personnel Dress Code in the Redlands Employee Handbook states:

Department heads shall determine appropriate attire for the employees under their supervision. Employees are expected to wear clothing suitable to their job and work site.

Department heads should use their discretion in determining how the employees in their departments may adapt to summer weather with more casual clothing. However, the following are
(15) clearly not acceptable at Redlands Community College:

• Tight-fitting or transparent clothing
• Shirts with potentially offensive words or logos
• Clothing that shows the midriff, such as low jeans or short shirts

If an employee's clothing fails to meet department standards, the supervisor should clarify why the
(20) item is inappropriate and instruct the individual to not wear it again.

---

2. Why is the human resources director distributing this memo?
   A She hopes to suggest alternative summer attire.
   B She intends to discipline department heads.
   C She needs to introduce a new dress code policy.
   D She wants to clarify the summer dress code policy.

3. Based on this memo, when would it be appropriate for department heads to ask an employee to not wear an item of clothing to work at a community college?
   A It is never appropriate.
   B Department heads could instruct employees not to wear shirts with rude slogans.
   C Department heads should ask employees to avoid wearing pins with political statements.
   D Employees should be advised if they wear cheaply made brands.

Unit 1 | Non-Fiction

Directions: Questions 4 and 5 are based on the passage below.

HOW DOES THE AUTHOR DESCRIBE ANIMALS IN WINTER?

Take a solitary walk through any of America's national parks in winter, and you may get the impression that you're the sole wakeful presence in an otherwise sleeping
(5) world. For the most part, you'd be right. Although some predators are able to find food in wintertime, animals that don't migrate generally spend the coldest months in a deep slumber, conserving energy.
(10) The seasonal state of inactivity we call hibernation is characterized by decreased metabolism, lowered body temperatures, and slowed breathing rates. Once food becomes sparse, hibernating mammals seek out or
(15) excavate den sites that are, preferably, below the frost line and predator-proof.
Mammals can delay or even forego hibernation to adapt to local conditions. But reptiles have no control over the timing of their
(20) winter inactive phase, called brumation.

From Tom Clynes's WHILE THEY WERE SLEEPING, © 2008

4 This passage discusses reasons why animals hibernate. What is one reason listed?

Animals hibernate to
A ward off predators.
B conserve energy.
C adapt to local conditions.
D increase their metabolism.

5 What is the main point the author tells readers about hibernation?
A Animals hibernate once food becomes sparse.
B Mammals create dens to hibernate.
C Hibernation is the seasonal state of inactivity.
D Hibernation causes decreased metabolism.

Directions: Questions 6 and 7 are based on the excerpt below.

HOW DO TURTLES CHOOSE THEIR MATES?

Tortoises mate in spring after elaborate courtships that involve visits by head-bobbing males to female burrows. The female decides when she's interested. Several weeks after
(5) mating, female tortoises deposit three to fifteen eggs in the sand mounds in front of their burrows or some other nearby sandy flat. Incubation depends on climate and varies from seventy to one hundred days up the length
(10) of the tortoise range. Usually the female lays one clutch per year, but often raccoons, foxes, armadillos, skunks, and fire ants raid the eggs, so that only one nest in ten survives.

From Janisse Ray's ECOLOGY OF A CRACKER CHILDHOOD, © 1999

6 What is the main idea of the excerpt?
A Male tortoises choose their mates.
B Male tortoises will only mate in spring.
C Tortoises have well-defined habits.
D A female tortoise deposits three to fifteen eggs.

7 In lines 3 and 4, the author says, "Several weeks after mating, female tortoises deposit three to fifteen eggs." What is this statement's role in the passage? This statement is
A an explicit main idea.
B the beginning of a topic sentence.
C an implied main idea.
D a supporting detail.

Directions: Questions 8 through 11 are based on the excerpt below.

WHAT MIGHT BE THE AUTHOR'S GOAL IN WRITING THIS PIECE?

Their ancestors were one of at least twenty-three species of land tortoises that originated in western North America some sixty million years ago. Along with scrub
(5) jays and burrowing owls, they were part of a savanna fauna that migrated to the Southeast. Of four species of land tortoises remaining in North America, gopher tortoises are unique in their occurrence east of the Mississippi River.
(10) Some people, because of the inhospitable climate, refer to gopher tortoise habitat as the "southeastern desert."

During winter, tortoises hibernate, although on warm afternoons they trudge to the surface
(15) to sun on patios of their burrows. During warmer months they stay underground during the heat of the day, coming out at dawn and dusk to feed.

The gopher tortoise has been broadsided
(20) by the absence of regenerative burning in pine forests. Because it relies upon herbaceous plants for food, it is confounded by dense understory vegetation—gallberry, blackberry brambles, sumac, turkey oak—which take
(25) over in the absence of fire. Food for tortoises becomes scarce.

From Janisse Ray's ECOLOGY OF A CRACKER CHILDHOOD, © 1999

8 What is the purpose of the first paragraph in this excerpt?
   A to discuss the other animals that are part of the savannah fauna, like the gopher tortoise
   B to discuss the slang terms used for the tortoise's habitat
   C to discuss the tortoise's ancestry and habitat
   D to demonstrate how old the tortoise is

9 What detail demonstrates the tortoise's summer behavior? Tortoises
   A stay underground during the heat of the day.
   B come out of their burrows for food during any point of the day.
   C hibernate during the summer instead of the winter to keep warm.
   D make patios on top of their burrows to stay cool.

10 What is the main idea of the third paragraph?
   A Forest fires are not common in the pine forests where the gopher tortoises live.
   B Gopher tortoises' food supplies have been reduced.
   C Gopher tortoises eat a variety of plants.
   D Food supplies for gopher tortoises have not changed in any way.

11 Based on this excerpt, which of the following presents the greatest problem for gopher tortoises?
   A the desert habitat
   B burrowing owls
   C lack of water
   D reduction in vegetation

Directions: Questions 12 through 16 are based on the excerpt below.

WHY IS THE AUTHOR WRITING THIS LETTER?

I need hardly say how heartily I sympathize with the purposes of the Audubon Society. I would like to see all harmless wild things, but especially all birds protected in every way. I do
(5) not understand how any man or woman who really loves nature can fail to try to exert all influence in support of such objects as those of the Audubon Society. Spring would not be spring without bird songs, any more than it
(10) would be spring without buds and flowers, and I only wish that besides protecting the songsters, the birds of the grove, the orchard, the garden and the meadow, we could also protect the birds of the sea shore and of the
(15) wilderness. The loon ought to be, and, under wise legislation, could be a feature of every Adirondack lake; ospreys, as everyone knows, can be made the tamest of the tame; and terns should be as plentiful along our shores as
(20) swallows around our barns.... When I hear of the destruction of a species I feel just as if all the works of some great writer had perished...

From Theodore Roosevelt's "LETTER TO FRANK MICHLER CHAPMAN," © 1899

12 What is the main idea of this letter?
  A The speaker is sympathetic to the purpose of the Audubon Society.
  B People who love nature should protect it.
  C All harmless wildlife, especially birds, should be protected.
  D The seasons would not seem right without the appropriate songs of birds.

13 With whom does the author sympathize in the letter?
  A people who fish in Adirondack lakes
  B members of a nature conservancy group
  C farmers storing hay in barns
  D workers tending to orange groves

14 Based on this excerpt, which of the following might the author enjoy doing in his spare time?
  A skiing
  B painting
  C gardening
  D hiking

15 Which of the following details best supports the main idea?
  A "I would like to see all harmless wild things, but especially all birds protected in every way." (lines 2–4)
  B "I do not understand how any man or woman who really loves nature can fail to try to exert all influence…" (lines 4–7)
  C "Spring would not be spring without bird songs, any more than it would be spring without buds and flowers…" (lines 8–10)
  D "…I only wish that besides protecting the songsters, the birds of the grove, the orchard, the garden and the meadow…" (lines 11–13)

16 Based on this information, for which of the following would the author most likely vote?
  A a bill to allow off-shore drilling
  B a bill to lessen restrictions on hunting wild animals
  C a bill to increase funding for community parks
  D a bill to introduce more restrictions on hunting in national parks

LESSON 2

Summarize

① Learn the Skill

When you **summarize** a text, you are restating the main points of the piece in your own words. The first step to summarizing is to locate the main ideas. A summary should include all of the main ideas, assertions, or findings, as well as other significant information the author provides. Questions that begin with *who, what, when, where, why*, and *how* can help you identify ideas that should be included.

② Practice the Skill

By mastering the skill of summarizing, you will improve your study and test-taking skills, especially as they relate to high school equivalency language arts/reading tests. Read the excerpt and strategies below.

A A summary should give the most important information. In this passage, we learn important information about the main character, Bruce Wayne.

B Pay close attention to the words the author uses. A summary should not include the author's point of view. This author explains one result of an event without bias.

WHY IS BATMAN'S HISTORY IMPORTANT?

The Batman franchise adds to its chronicles with its 2005 release of the prequel *Batman Begins*. **A** <u>The movie gives its audience a taste of its main character, Bruce Wayne, prior to his becoming the caped crusader of Gotham. As Batman he is trying to avenge the death of his parents</u>. Before Batman puts on his bat suit and drives off in the batmobile equipped with fancy gadgets, the audience learns about Bruce Wayne the boy and young man. **B** <u>As a boy, Bruce falls into a well full of bats. This event scares him and comes to represent his biggest fears</u>. Later as a rich Ivy Leaguer, he decides to leave Princeton to take a journey to the Himalayas. There he is trained in martial arts in order to gain the strength that will eventually turn him into Batman.

(5)

(10)

✓ TEST-TAKING TIPS

This review is a summary of a movie. The author identified the important parts of the movie and described them briefly, without judgment. Think about how you might summarize your favorite movie.

1 What does the summary tell us about Bruce Wayne?
   Bruce Wayne
   A only goes to an Ivy League school because he is rich
   B would rather contemplate his past than focus on his future
   C is very content as a student at Princeton
   D would rather seek his education outside the walls of Princeton

3 Apply the Skill

Directions: Questions 2 and 3 are based on the speech below.

HOW DOES THE SPEAKER FEEL ABOUT HIS COUNTRY?

In the long history of the world, only a few generations have been granted the role of defending freedom in its hour of maximum danger. I do not shrink from this
(5) responsibility —I welcome it. I do not believe that any of us would exchange places with any other people or any other generation. The energy, the faith, the devotion which we bring to this endeavor will light our country and all
(10) who serve it. And the glow from that fire can truly light the world.
    And so, my fellow Americans, ask not what your country can do for you; ask what you can do for your country.
(15)   My fellow citizens of the world, ask not what America will do for you, but what together we can do for the freedom of man.

From John F. Kennedy's INAUGURAL ADDRESS, © 1961

2 What responsibility does the speaker welcome in lines 3 through 5?
   A govern a country with energy and faith
   B help bring light to the rest of the world
   C speak to other citizens of the world
   D defend freedom in its hour of danger

3 What is the speaker's main point in lines 11 through 13?
   A Americans should be willing to work for their country.
   B Americans should allow their country to work for them.
   C Americans should not question their government.
   D Americans should rely on themselves, not on their government.

Directions: Questions 4 and 5 are based on the speech below.

WHAT DOES THE SPEAKER FEEL IS HIS BEST OPTION?

I come before you tonight as a candidate for the Vice Presidency and as a man whose honesty and integrity has been questioned.
    Now, the usual political thing to do when
(5) charges are made against you is to either ignore them or to deny them without giving details. I believe we've had enough of that in the United States, particularly with the present Administration in Washington, D.C.
(10) To me the office of the Vice Presidency of the United States is a great office, and I feel that the people have got to have confidence in the integrity of the men who run for that office and who might obtain it.

From Richard M. Nixon's CHECKERS, © 1952

4 In lines 1 through 3, the speaker says his honesty and integrity have been questioned. According to him, what is the usual political thing to do when charges are made?
   A question those charges
   B refute those charges
   C explain the merit of the charges
   D ignore or deny those charges

5 Which of the following best summarizes the passage?
   A The speaker says that his honor has been upheld.
   B The speaker wants people to forget about voting.
   C The speaker believes that people should have faith in him.
   D The speaker believes he has been justly accused of wrongdoing.

Directions: Questions 6 through 8 are based on the passage below.

HOW DOES THE AUTHOR FEEL ABOUT THE SEPARATION OF NORTHERN AND SOUTHERN STATES?

If we could just know where we are and whither we appear to be tending, we could all better judge of what to do, and how to do it. We are now well into our fifth year since a
(5) policy was initiated with the avowed object and confident purpose of putting an end to slavery agitation.

However, under the operation of that policy, that agitation has not only not ceased,
(10) but has constantly augmented. In my opinion, it will not cease until a crisis shall have been reached and passed. "A house divided against itself cannot stand."

I believe this government cannot endure
(15) permanently half slave and half free. I do not expect the Union to be dissolved—I do not expect the house to fall—but I do expect it will cease to be divided. It will become all one thing, or all the other. Either the opponents of
(20) slavery will arrest this further spread and place it where the public mind shall rest in the belief that it is on a course of ultimate extinction; or its advocates shall press it forward, until it shall become alike lawful in all of the States, old as
(25) well as new, North as well as South.

From Abraham Lincoln's A HOUSE DIVIDED, © 1858

6. **The author delivered this speech to Congress in 1858. The main idea in the first paragraph is stated in lines 4 through 7. How could this main idea be summarized?**
   A Congress should know where the country is heading with regards to slavery
   B Congress should be a better judge on the issues at hand
   C Congress should know how to vote regarding slavery
   D a policy was issued five years prior with the purpose of ending slavery agitation

7. **What does the author mean when he says, "A house divided against itself cannot stand" (lines 12–13)?**
   A If Congress is divided, then the United States' government will succeed.
   B If the country disagrees on the issue of slavery, then the states will no longer remain united as a country.
   C If the North and South are divided, each will operate under its own governments.
   D When people disagree, they end up alone.

8. **In paragraph three, the author explains his thoughts about the issue of slavery. How can the author's thoughts be summarized?**
   A The government will go on enduring the trials between free states and slave states.
   B The union will not dissolve.
   C Opponents of slavery will ensure that all the states are free states.
   D The nation will stop being divided as all states will either be slave states or free states.

Directions: Questions 9 through 12 are based on the passage below.

FOR WHAT IS THE AUTHOR ASKING THE PEOPLE OF THE UNITED STATES?

For 32 years Capitol Hill has been my home. I have shared many moments of pride with you, pride in the ability of the Congress of the United States to act, to meet any crisis,
(5) to distill from our differences strong programs of national action. An assassin's bullet has thrust upon me the awesome burden of the Presidency. I am here today to say I need your help. I cannot bear this burden alone. I need
(10) the help of all Americans, and all America.

This nation has experienced a profound shock, and in this critical moment, it is our duty, yours and mine, as the Government of the United States, to do away with uncertainty
(15) and doubt and delay, and to show that we are capable of decisive action; that from the brutal loss of our leader we will derive not weakness, but strength; that we can and will act and act now.

(20) From this chamber of representative government, let all the world know and none misunderstand that I rededicate this Government to the unswerving support of the United Nations, to the honorable and
(25) determined execution of our commitments to our allies, to the maintenance of military strength second to none, to the defense of the strength and the stability of the dollar, to the expansion of our foreign trade, to the
(30) reinforcement of our programs of mutual assistance and cooperation in Asia and Africa, and to our Alliance for Progress in this hemisphere.

On the 20th day of January, in 19 and
(35) 61, John F. Kennedy told his countrymen that our national work would not be finished "in the first thousand days, nor in the life of this administration, nor even perhaps in our lifetime on this planet." "But," he said, "let us begin."

(40) Today in this moment of new resolve, I would say to all my fellow Americans, let us continue.

From Lyndon Baines Johnson's LET US CONTINUE, © 1963

9. **For what does the author ask in the first paragraph?**
   A for Capitol Hill to become his home
   B for the help of all Americans
   C for the gift of pride
   D to distill strong programs of national action

10. **The author acknowledges the nation has "experienced a profound shock" (lines 11–12). How does he suggest the nation move on?**
    A move on with dignity
    B mourn its brutal loss
    C gather and act upon its strength
    D show its side of weakness

11. **The author uses the word "rededicate" and then lists important concepts (line 22). Which of the following might be another example of the meaning of *rededicate*?**
    A to sign a contract renewal
    B to accept a prize again
    C to fight another war
    D to re-establish trade with another country

12. **What is the author's overall message in this speech?**
    A to start over as a nation
    B to grieve and to mourn a lost President
    C to silence the voices and actions of the United States
    D to demonstrate new persistence and move forward as a nation

Directions: Questions 13 through 16 are based on the passage below.

TO WHAT PROBLEM IS THE AUTHOR DRAWING ATTENTION?

Over there, behind the black gates of Auschwitz, the most tragic of all prisoners were the "Muselmanner," as they were called. Wrapped in their torn blankets, they would
(5) sit or lie on the ground, staring vacantly into space, unaware of who or where they were—strangers to their surroundings. They no longer felt pain, hunger, thirst. They feared nothing. They felt nothing. They were dead and did not
(10) know it.

Rooted in our tradition, some of us felt that to be abandoned by humanity then was not the ultimate. We felt that to be abandoned by God was worse than to be punished by Him...
(15) In a way, to be indifferent to that suffering is what makes the human being inhuman. Indifference, after all, is more dangerous than anger and hatred. Anger can at times be creative. One writes a great poem, a great
(20) symphony. One does something special for the sake of humanity because one is angry at the injustice that one witnesses. But indifference is never creative. Even hatred at times may elicit a response. You fight it. You denounce it. You
(25) disarm it.

Indifference elicits no response. Indifference is not a response. Indifference is not a beginning; it is an end. And, therefore, indifference is always the friend of the enemy,
(30) for it benefits the aggressor—never his victim, whose pain is magnified when he or she feels forgotten. The political prisoner in his cell, the hungry children, the homeless refugees—not to respond to their plight, not to relieve their
(35) solitude by offering them a spark of hope is to exile them from human memory. And in denying their humanity, we betray our own.

Indifference, then, is not only a sin, it is a punishment.
(40) And this is one of the most important lessons of this outgoing century's wide-ranging experiments in good and evil.

From Elie Wiesel's THE PERILS OF INDIFFERENCE, © 1999

13 Why were the prisoners who were called "Muselmanner" (line 3) considered the most tragic?
 A because they only had torn blankets
 B because they were prisoners of Auschwitz
 C because they could not see
 D because they feared and felt nothing, they were dead but did not yet know it

14 According to the author, of whom is indifference a friend?
 A everyone
 B apathetic people
 C the enemy
 D victims

15 What is the author saying in lines 34 through 36?
 A to give no hope to those who are in a plight
 B offering hope to those who suffer does them no good
 C by not offering hope to those in need, people are working to benefit humanity
 D by not offering hope to those in need, people are choosing indifference and betraying humanity

16 How does the author view indifference?
 A indifference can be good as well as evil
 B indifference acts as punishment and sin against those who demonstrate it
 C indifference can lead the helpless out of a long and suffering plight
 D indifference has many definitions; some are beneficial while others are hazardous

LESSON 3

Categorize

1 Learn the Skill

Categorizing can help you organize information into groups. You can sort many elements, such as people, events, places, and even texts, into groups based on their similarities or differences. Categories are typically broad, such as *Regions of the United States* or *Animals of Asia*.

2 Practice the Skill

By mastering the skill of categorizing, you will improve your study and test-taking skills, especially as they relate to high school equivalency language arts/reading tests. Read the excerpt and strategies below.

Ⓐ The first line in this excerpt names a car company and refers to "car buyers." From this information, you know that you will be categorizing cars.

Ⓑ The word "sedan" at the beginning of sentence and the term "mid-size segment" at the end let you know to categorize kinds of car models.

WHY DID MAZDA REDESIGN THE MAZDA 6?

Ⓐ Executives from Mazda are betting that car buyers looking for a new sedan who might ordinarily lean towards the Toyota Camry or Honda Accord will give serious consideration to the new 2009 Mazda 6, which has been
(5) designed specifically to match up with those rivals in the mid-size segment. **Ⓑ**
　"This is the most important new vehicle Mazda has launched in a decade," said Mazda North America CEO Jim O'Sullivan.
(10)　The first new Mazda 6s rolled off the assembly line at the Auto Alliance Plant in Flat Rock, Michigan, this week and O'Sullivan couldn't be happier. "We think sales of 100,000 units are within our grasp," says O'Sullivan, acknowledging that the old version of the Mazda 6
(15) had dropped off the shopping lists prepared by a lot of consumers.

From Joseph Szczesny's 2009 MAZDA 6 A CRUCIAL LAUNCH, © 2008

USING LOGIC

While categorizing, you may come across an object that you think should be put into a category, but you might not know what category. Clues from the sentence in which the object appears can indicate the correct category for that object.

1 Into which size group is the author categorizing the 2009 Mazda 6?
　A SUV
　B compact
　C luxury
　D mid-size

Apply the Skill

Directions: Questions 2 and 3 are based on the letter below.

WHAT OPTIONS ARE PROVIDED FOR MR. JACKSON?

Eric Jackson
Jackson Homes
330 Plum Street
Sioux City, IO 51101

(5) Dear Mr. Eric Jackson,

Thank you for your interest in a line of credit with Greenville Bank. We currently have a variety of options available for our business customers. These options are listed below.

Option 1: $250,000 credit line with 6.9% APR for members who have an annual income of $75,000 or more.

(10) Option 2: $250,000 credit line with 7.9% APR for members who have an annual income between $50,000 and $75,000.

Option 3: $250,000 credit line with 8.9% APR for members who have an annual income under $50,000.

These options do not include conditions that may lower your monthly payments, such as down
(15) payments, collateral, and co-signees. If you would like to consider options that do include such conditions, please schedule an appointment with a Greenville Bank Credit Specialist at your earliest convenience.

Greenville Bank has a long-standing history of quality customer care and excellent service. We appreciate your interest in our banking services, and look forward to hearing from you.

(20) Thank you,

George Sanders
Credit Specialist
Greenville Bank

---

2 Mr. Jackson currently has an annual salary of $63,000. Based on this information, into which category might he fall?
  A approved for option 1
  B approved for option 2
  C approved for option 3
  D not approved

3 Based on this letter, how might a person with a down payment be categorized?
  A He or she may be ineligible for a credit line.
  B He or she may get a higher APR.
  C He or she would not need a credit line.
  D He or she may get a lower monthly payment.

Unit 1 | Non-Fiction

Directions: Questions 4 through 7 are based on the following excerpt.

WHAT HAPPENS WHEN LEAVES ABSORB WATER?

In tree infancy the nursing leaves take oxygen from the air, and through its influence the starch in the nursing leaves is transmuted into a tree baby-food, called dextrine, which
(5) is conveyed by the water absorbed during germination to the young rootlet and to the gemmule and also to the first aerial leaf. So fed, this leaf expands, and remains on the stem all summer. The nursing leaves die when
(10) the aerial leaves have taken their food away, and then the first stage of oakhood has begun. It has subterranean and superterranean organs, the former finding plant-food in the earth, and the latter gathering it in the air, the
(15) sunlight, and the storm. The rootlets in the dark depths of soil, the foliage in the sunlit air, begin now their common joint labor of constructing a majestic oak. Phosphates and all the delicacies of plant-food are brought in from the
(20) secret stores of the earth by the former, while foliage and twig and trunk are busy in catching sunbeams, air, and thunderstorms, to imprison in the annual increment of solid wood. There is no light coming from your wood, corncob, or
(25) coal fire which some vegetable Prometheus did not, in its days of growth, steal from the sun and secrete in the mysteries of a vegetable organism.

From J. Sterling Morton's ABOUT TREES, © 1893

4 The author is describing oak trees in this passage. What part of an oak tree is the author categorizing?
   A roots
   B trunk
   C leaves
   D branches

5 What items are described as "catching sunbeams, air, and thunderstorms" (lines 21–22)?
   A nursing leaves and aerial leaves
   B foliage, twig, and trunk
   C soil, rootlet, and gemmule
   D subterranean and superterranean organs

6 The author discusses leaves taking oxygen from the air (lines 1–3). How might this process be described in a different context?
   A leaves turning colors
   B babies feeding from a bottle
   C birds molting
   D cows producing milk

7 Based on the information in lines 18 through 20, you know that phosphates are important to a plant's life-cycle. Into which of the following categories would you place phosphates?
   A bone development
   B waste production
   C blood transfusions
   D nutrient gathering

Directions: Questions 8 through 11 are based on the following passage.

WHAT DOES THE AVERAGE CHILD LEARN DURING FORMAL EDUCATION?

By the age of six the average child will have completed the basic American education and be ready to enter school. If the child has been attentive in these preschool years, he or
(5) she will already have mastered many skills.

From television, the child will have learned how to pick a lock, commit a fairly elaborate bank holdup, prevent wetness all day long, get the laundry twice as white, and kill people with
(10) a variety of sophisticated armaments....

During formal education, the child learns that life is for testing. This stage lasts twelve years, a period during which the child learns that success comes from telling testers what
(15) they want to hear.

Early in this stage, the child learns that he is either dumb or smart. If the teacher puts intelligent demands upon the child, the child learns he is smart. If the teacher expects little
(20) of the child, the child learns he is dumb and soon quits bothering to tell the testers what they want to hear....

At this stage of education, a fresh question arises for everyone. If the point of lower
(25) education was to get into college, what is the point of college? The answer is soon learned. The point of college is to prepare the student—no longer a child now—to get into graduate school. In college the student learns that it is
(30) no longer enough simply to tell the testers what they want to hear. Many are tested for graduate school; few are admitted.

Those excluded may be denied valuable certificates to prosper in medicine, at the bar,
(35) in the corporate boardroom. The student learns that the race is to the cunning and often, alas, to the unprincipled.

Thus, the student learns the importance of destroying competitors and emerges richly
(40) prepared to play his role in the great simmering melodrama of American life.

Afterward, the former student's destiny fulfilled, his life rich with Oriental carpets, rare porcelain, and full bank accounts, he may
(45) one day find himself with the leisure and the inclination to open a book with a curious mind, and start to become educated.

From The New York Times, 9/9/1975 © 1975 The New York Times. All rights reserved. Used by permission and protected by the Copyright Laws of the United States. The printing, copying, redistribution, or retransmission of this Content without express written permission is prohibited.

8 Which does the speaker categorize in lines 6 through 10 of the excerpt?
  A basic American education
  B knowledge of products by a child
  C a child's knowledge from preschool class
  D skills learned from television by a preschooler

9 Baker states, "During formal education, the child learns that life is for testing" (lines 11–12). How would the author categorize this period?
  A do what they're told
  B learn that success is based on doing well on tests
  C learn the importance of a good education
  D do not learn the importance of taking tests

10 How might the author describe those students not getting into graduate school?
  A as poor test takers
  B as knowing how to work the educational system
  C as future professionals
  D as intelligent test takers

11 How would the author categorize the person in the last paragraph (lines 42–47)?
  A wealthy and successful
  B one with worldly possessions
  C rich with things but not with education
  D one who benefited from a strong education

Directions: Questions 12 through 15 are based on the following passage.

VOTING TRENDS IN THE UNITED STATES

The Census Bureau, as well as private polls and studies, tracks voting trends in the United States. One discovery—not at all surprising—is that older citizens, particularly those over 65,
(5) vote more regularly than younger citizens in the 18–29 age range. One reason is mobility—or, conversely, stability. Voter registration in the United States is tied to voter residence. Because older voters change residences
(10) less frequently than younger voters do, voter registration for older citizens remains the same. They are permanently registered at the same address and do not have to think about registering before an election.
(15) Younger voters, on the other hand, tend to move more often. Whether they join the military, go away to college, move to another election district or to another state, they tend not to remain in one place as long as older voters do.
(20) Therefore, younger voters must think about obtaining absentee ballots or registering in their new place of residence. If the state does not have election-day registration, new residents may not register within the appropriate time
(25) frame and, thus, not register at all. When attributing causes of low election-day turnout among younger voters, researchers and pollsters should consider that the residence-based voter registration system is in some part
(30) responsible for this situation.

12 What key categories are being described or compared in lines 1 through 5 of the passage?
  A whom voters elect
  B bureaus that track voting trends
  C older and younger citizens
  D types of voter registrations

13 To which other category is the age of a voter related?
  A interest in politics
  B mobility
  C free time
  D place of residence

14 How might the author describe those voters who do not have to think about voter registration before every election?
  A as living in one place for a long time
  B as having excellent memories
  C as caring about elections a great deal
  D as having a longer habit of voting

15 How does the second paragraph relate to the first paragraph? In the second paragraph, the author
  A provides exact details about the registration process.
  B gives examples of other categories of voters.
  C explains the situations of voters categorized as younger.
  D defines the category of voter ages.

LESSON 4
Sequence

1 Learn the Skill

A passage's **sequence** is the order in which events occur. Often when reading non-fiction writing, identifying the sequence of events in chronological order is important to help you understand the relationships between events. For example, if you understand the sequence of a newspaper story, you will be better able to analyze how one event in the story may have led to another. If an author does not use dates, he or she may use signal words. These signal words, such as *first*, *next*, *then*, and *finally*, will help you determine the sequence.

2 Practice the Skill

By mastering the skill of identifying sequence, you will improve your study and test-taking skills, especially as they relate to high school equivalency language arts/reading tests. Read the excerpt and strategies below.

A When you read a story, it may help to create a time line sequence. This piece organizes events by days of the week.

B Progression is the way in which a story moves forward. This story progresses by the passing of days.

WHAT IS THE AUTHOR'S ROUTINE?

(A) For me the work week begins on Thursday, which I usually spend in patrolling the roads and walking out the trails. On Friday I inspect the campgrounds, haul firewood, and distribute toilet paper. Saturday and Sunday are my
(5) busy days as I deal with the influx of weekend visitors and campers, answering questions, pulling cars out of the sand, lowering children down off the rocks, tracking lost grandfathers and investigating picnics. **(B)** My Saturday night campfire talks are brief and to the point. "Everything all
(10) right?" I say, badge and all, ambling up to what looks like a cheerful group. "Fine," they'll say; "how about a drink?" "Why not?" I say.

From Edward Abbey's INDUSTRIAL TOURISM AND NATIONAL PARKS, © 1968

✓ TEST-TAKING TIPS

Instructional and business writings are often the easiest pieces of writing in which to determine the sequence. Instructions will tell you the order in which steps must be done. Business writing will often explain how a business transaction occurred.

1 Which line from the excerpt best describes what the author does first in his work week?
  A "...I inspect the campgrounds."
  B "...I deal with the influx of weekend visitors and campers."
  C "...I usually spend in patrolling the roads and walking out the trails."
  D "...haul firewood, and distribute toilet paper."

Apply the Skill

Directions: Questions 2 through 5 are based on the excerpt below.

HOW DOES THE AUTHOR FEEL ABOUT THE SCHOOL SYSTEM?

I had begun to teach in 1964 in Boston in a segregated school so crowded and so poor that it could not provide my fourth grade children with a classroom. We shared an
(5) auditorium with another fourth grade and the choir and a group that was rehearsing, starting in October, for a Christmas play that, somehow, never was produced. In the spring I was shifted to another fourth grade that had
(10) a string of substitutes all year. The 35 children in the class hadn't had a permanent teacher since they entered kindergarten. That year, I was their thirteenth teacher.

The results were seen in the first tests I
(15) gave. In April, most were reading at the second grade level. Their math ability was at the first grade level.

In an effort to resuscitate their interest, I began to read them poetry I liked. They were
(20) drawn especially to poems of Robert Frost and Langston Hughes. One of the most embittered children in the class began to cry when she first heard the words of Langston Hughes. ...

The next day, I was fired. There was, it
(25) turned out, a list of "fourth grade poems" that teachers were obliged to follow but which, like most first-year teachers, I had never seen.

From Jonathan Kozol's SAVAGE INEQUALITIES: CHILDREN IN AMERICA'S SCHOOLS, © 1991

2. What was the author doing in the spring of 1965?
   A sharing an auditorium for a classroom
   B reading poetry to a new fourth grade class
   C working with students for a Christmas play that never was produced
   D being fired for teaching poetry

3. Which action led to the author being fired from his job?
   A teaching a text that was not approved
   B encouraging student interest in the lessons
   C never producing a Christmas play
   D teaching students to read on a second grade level

4. Which meaning does the author intend when he writes that "the results were seen in the first tests I gave" (lines 14–15)?
   A The students were very well prepared for their tests.
   B The constant changing of teachers had not prepared students for the tests.
   C The students' test results were strong.
   D The students could read and do math.

5. Based on the excerpt, which of the following most likely happened next?
   A The author went to work for the city government.
   B Poems by Robert Frost and Langston Hughes were approved to be taught to fourth graders.
   C The author began to teach at another school.
   D The Christmas play was produced.

Directions: Questions 6 through 8 are based on the passage below.

WHAT HAPPENS THAT UPSETS THE AUTHOR?

I'd been warned. On the very first day Merle and Floyd had mentioned something about developments, improvements, a sinister Master Plan. Thinking that *they* were the
(5) dreamers, I paid little heed and had soon forgotten the whole ridiculous business. But only a few days ago something happened which shook me out of pleasant apathy.

I was sitting out back on my 33,000-acre
(10) terrace, shoeless and shirtless, scratching my toes in the sand and sipping on a tall iced drink, watching the flow of evening over the desert. Prime time: the sun very low in the west, the birds coming back to life, the
(15) shadows rolling for miles over rock and sand to the very base of the brilliant mountains. I had a small fire going near the table—not for heat or light but for the fragrance of the juniper and the ritual of the clear flames. For symbolic
(20) reasons. For ceremony. When I heard a faint sound over my shoulder I looked and saw a file of deer watching from fifty yards away, three does and a velvet-horned buck, all dark against the sundown sky....Smiling thoroughly
(25) at peace, I turned back to my drink, the little fire, the subtle transformations of the immense landscape before me. On the program: rise of the full moon.

It was then I heard the discordant note,
(30) the snarling whine of a jeep in low range and four-wheel-drive, coming from an unexpected direction, from the vicinity of the old foot and horse trail that leads from Balanced Rock down toward Courthouse Wash and
(35) on to park headquarters near Moab....Now operating a motor vehicle of any kind on the trails of a national park is strictly forbidden, a nasty bureaucratic regulation which I heartily supported.

From Edward Abbey's INDUSTRIAL TOURISM AND THE NATIONAL PARKS, © 1968

6 Based on the events of this excerpt, which of the following events most likely happened after the last paragraph?
  A The author went inside his house so he would not hear the noise.
  B The driver pulled up to the author's house and asked for directions.
  C The author continued to sit on his porch and enjoy the evening.
  D The author called the park rangers to report the motor vehicle on the trail.

7 Given the details of the excerpt, which of the following would best describe the author's feelings in the second paragaph?
  A irritated
  B restless
  C chaotic
  D peaceful

8 The author states, "But only a few days ago something happened which shook me out of pleasant apathy" (lines 6–8). From these lines, in what order is the author telling his story? The author is telling his story
  A from that moment forward
  B in chronological order
  C in reverse chronological order
  D with no direction (his narrative jumps around)

Directions: Questions 9 through 12 are based on the passage below.

THE DISCOVERY OF THE SMALLPOX VACCINE

Edward Jenner, born in England in 1749, is one of the most famous physicians in medical history. Jenner tested the hypothesis that infection with cowpox could protect a person
(5) from smallpox infection. …

Jenner is said to have been interested in the observation of a dairymaid. She told him, "I shall never have smallpox, for I have had cowpox. I shall never have an ugly pockmarked
(10) face." And many other dairy workers commonly believed that infection with cowpox protected them from smallpox. …

Jenner scratched some material from a cowpox sore on the hand of a milkmaid into the
(15) arm of eight-year-old James Phipps, the son of Jenner's gardener. Young Phipps felt poorly for several days, but made a full recovery.

A short time later, Jenner scratched some matter from a fresh human smallpox sore into
(20) Phipps's arm in an attempt to make him ill with smallpox. Phipps, however, did not contract smallpox. Jenner went on to test his idea on other humans and published a report of his findings.

From historyofvaccines.org, accessed 2013

9 What was the first step in Jenner's investigation?
- **A** He became famous in medical history.
- **B** A dairymaid told him why she would never have smallpox.
- **C** Young Phipps made a full recovery from cowpox.
- **D** People who had cowpox did not become ill with smallpox.

10 What did Jenner do to test his hypothesis that cowpox protects against smallpox?
- **A** He interviewed many dairy workers.
- **B** He infected Phipps with cowpox.
- **C** He found Phipps feeling ill.
- **D** He tested his idea on many humans.

11 Jenner waited until Phipps recovered before infecting him with smallpox. Why was the waiting period between steps important?
- **A** He first had to get the smallpox sample.
- **B** He was testing his idea on other humans.
- **C** He wanted to allow time for the vaccine to work.
- **D** He waited until Phipps had recovered from smallpox.

12 What happens last in this passage when Jenner discovered the smallpox vaccine?
- **A** Jenner became a physician.
- **B** Jenner worried about pockmarked faces.
- **C** Jenner let others know by publishing a report.
- **D** Jenner made sure Phipps was ill only for a few days.

Directions: Questions 13 through 16 are based on the passage below.

WHAT INEQUALITIES ARE DESCRIBED?

Since October 1987, when the city's garbage pickups ceased, the backyards of residents have been employed as dump sites. In the spring of 1988 a policeman tells a visitor
(5) that 40 plastic bags of trash are waiting for removal from the backyard of his mother's house. Public health officials are concerned the garbage will attract a plague of flies and rodents in the summer. The policeman speaks
(10) of "rats as big as puppies" in his mother's yard. They are known to residents, he says as, "bull rats." Many people have no cars or funds to cart the trash and simply burn it in their yards. The odor of smoke from burning garbage, says
(15) the *Post-Dispatch*, "has become one of the scents of spring" in East St. Louis….

In March of 1989, a task force appointed by Governor James Thompson notes that the city was in debt by more than $40 million,
(20) and proposed emergency state loans to pay for garbage collection and to keep police and fire departments in continued operation. The governor, however, blamed the mayor and his administrators, almost all of whom were
(25) black, and refused to grant loans unless the mayor resigned. Thompson's response, said a Republican state legislator, "made my heart feel good….It's unfortunate, but the essence of the problem in East St. Louis is the people"
(30) who are running things….

The dangers of exposure to raw sewage, which backs up repeatedly into homes of residents of East St. Louis, were first noticed, in the spring of 1989, at a public housing
(35) project, Villa Griffin. Raw sewage, says the *Post-Dispatch*, overflowed into a playground just behind the housing project, which is home to 187 children, "forming an oozing lake of… tainted water." Two schoolgirls, we are told,
(40) "experienced hair loss since raw sewage flowed into their homes."

From Jonathan Kozol's SAVAGE INEQUALITIES: CHILDREN IN AMERICA'S SCHOOLS, © 1999

13 How is the order of events listed in this excerpt?
  A by season
  B by date
  C by using signal words
  D by the stories of the Post-Dispatch

14 The first event listed from the excerpt was the elimination of the city's garbage pickups (lines 1–2). How did this event prove hazardous?
  A The poor residents had to spend money to have garbage hauled to a dump.
  B Residents had to do without basic necessities to avoid having extra waste.
  C Residents were forced to move.
  D Residents stock piled garbage in their yards which concerned public health officials.

15 How does the author report the events taking place in East St. Louis?
  A without hope for improvements
  B by providing his reader with alarming stories based on interviews and news accounts
  C as an insider
  D in a tone of disgust toward the residents of East St. Louis

16 The description of an event that happened in 1989 warns of dangers of exposure to raw sewage (lines 35–42). Who seems most at risk to this exposure? Those most at risk
  A were the health inspectors investigating the situation.
  B the people living in the apartments across town.
  C the children who lived in the nearby apartments and played on an infested playground.
  D the reporters reporting the situation.

LESSON 5

Cause and Effect

① Learn the Skill

A traffic accident blocks the road you travel to get to work. You choose to take another route. This is an example of cause and effect in action. A **cause** is an action that makes another event happen. Many times, a cause will be directly stated in a text, although sometimes it will be implied. An **effect** is something that happens as the result of a cause. In the example above, the traffic accident is the cause, and having to find a new route is the effect. In a non-fiction text, signal words such as *accordingly*, *because*, *consequently*, *as a result*, *therefore*, *so*, *then*, and *to this end* can help you determine a cause and its effect.

② Practice the Skill

By mastering the skill of identifying causes and their effects, you will improve your study and test-taking skills, especially as they relate to high school equivalency language arts/reading tests. Read the excerpt and strategies below.

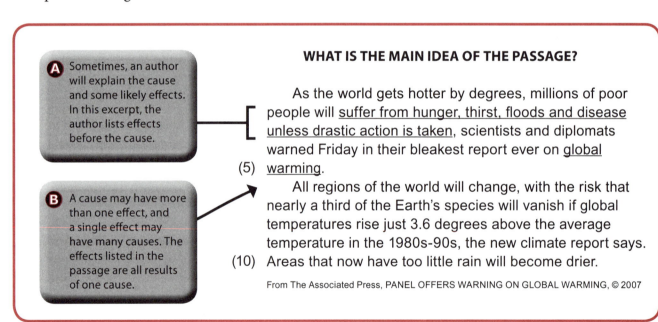

A Sometimes, an author will explain the cause and some likely effects. In this excerpt, the author lists effects before the cause.

B A cause may have more than one effect, and a single effect may have many causes. The effects listed in the passage are all results of one cause.

WHAT IS THE MAIN IDEA OF THE PASSAGE?

As the world gets hotter by degrees, millions of poor people will suffer from hunger, thirst, floods and disease unless drastic action is taken, scientists and diplomats warned Friday in their bleakest report ever on global warming.
(5) All regions of the world will change, with the risk that nearly a third of the Earth's species will vanish if global temperatures rise just 3.6 degrees above the average temperature in the 1980s-90s, the new climate report says.
(10) Areas that now have too little rain will become drier.

From The Associated Press, PANEL OFFERS WARNING ON GLOBAL WARMING, © 2007

USING LOGIC

Signal words can appear to guide your reading for cause and effect, but sometimes they do not. In some instances, you can find the cause or the effect by connecting key ideas or details to one another.

1. Based on this excerpt, what will cause millions of people to suffer from hunger?
   A cooling weather
   B floods
   C disease
   D global warming

③ Apply the Skill

Directions: Questions 2 through 4 based on the passage below.

WHAT WAS THE FOCUS OF THE SCIENTISTS' RESEARCH?

High-fructose corn syrup is a sweetener used in many processed foods ranging from sodas to baked goods. While the ingredient is cheaper and sweeter than regular sugar, new
(5) research suggests that it can also make you fatter.

In a small study, Texas researchers showed that the body converts fructose to body fat with "surprising speed," said Elizabeth
(10) Parks, associate professor of clinical nutrition at the University of Texas Southwestern Medical Center in Dallas. The study, which appears in The Journal of Nutrition, shows how glucose and fructose, which are forms of
(15) sugar, are metabolized differently. …

The researchers found that lipogenesis, the process by which sugars are turned into body fat, increased significantly when the study subjects drank the drinks with fructose. When
(20) fructose was given at breakfast, the body was more likely to store the fats eaten at lunch.

Dr. Parks noted that the study likely underestimates the fat-building effect of fructose because the study subjects were lean
(25) and healthy. In overweight people, the effect may be amplified.

Although fruit contains fructose, it also contains many beneficial nutrients, so dieters shouldn't eliminate fruit from their diets. But
(30) limiting processed foods containing high-fructose corn syrup as well as curbing calories is a good idea, Dr. Parks said.

From Tara Parker-Pope's DOES FRUCTOSE MAKE YOU FATTER?, © 2008

2. **What did the study determine may cause people to gain weight?**
   A   processed foods
   B   high-fructose corn syrup
   C   regular sugar
   D   glucose

3. **What was the effect on the body after drinking drinks with fructose?**
   A   There was no effect on the body.
   B   Overweight people gain weight faster.
   C   Lean and healthy people saw no noticeable difference.
   D   The process where sugars are turned into body fat increased significantly.

4. **Line 27 notes that fruit contains fructose. How might this information effect a dieter's food plan?**
   A   Dieters should not eliminate fruit because it has many beneficial nutrients.
   B   Dieters should eat fruit in small quantities because it contains fructose.
   C   Dieters should eat processed foods instead of fruit because they do not contain fructose.
   D   Dieters should eliminate fruit completely due to its fructose content.

Directions: Questions 5 and 6 are based on the passage below.

WHAT EFFECTS MIGHT VIOLENT VIDEO GAMES HAVE ON CHILDREN?

Republicans and Democrats alike screamed government waste last March when a group of senators suggested spending $90 million to study how video games "and
(5) other electronic media" influenced children's behavior. Surely an important question, critics of the plan said, but $90 million?

Some believe that, in any case, the verdict is already in. This month, the American
(10) Psychological Association called for a reduction of violence in all video games, saying the evidence from 20 years of research on the subject was clear. They based their conclusion largely on the work of Kevin M. Kieffer, a
(15) psychologist at St. Leo University near Tampa, Fla., who prepared an analysis of dozens of relevant studies.

He found that, in general, children exposed to virtual bloodshed showed greater "short-
(20) term" increases in hostility toward peers and authority figures than those exposed to more benign games. And many of the studies included in the analysis were randomized, rebutting the notion that aggressive people
(25) are simply drawn to violent games, Dr. Kieffer found….

In the end, the study's findings may be more in line with public opinion. On the day its findings were announced, a jury in Alabama
(30) reached a guilty verdict in the case of Devin Moore, who killed three people when he was 18 and as his defense blamed the video game "Grand Theft Auto."

Studies generally show that violent video
(35) games can have short-term, or momentary, effects on children, but there is little evidence of long-term changes.

From Anahad O'Connor's THE CLAIM: VIOLENT VIDEO GAMES MAKE YOUNG PEOPLE AGGRESSIVE, © 2005

5. What did Republicans and Democrats believe would be a likely result of spending $90 million on a video game study?
   A. The money spent would be wasted.
   B. There would be a well-defined plan of studying video games and violence.
   C. The study of video games and violence was worth the monetary spending.
   D. The topic was not worth investigating.

6. The excerpt states, "[The American Psychological Association] based their conclusion largely on the work of Kevin M. Kieffer, a psychologist at St. Leo University near Tampa, Fla., who prepared an analysis of dozens of relevant studies" (lines 13–17). What did these studies find?
   A. a variety of conclusions from many noted psychologists
   B. conclusions were reached largely by the work of Kevin M. Kieffer
   C. increased "short-term" hostility in children exposed to more violent video games
   D. increased "short-term" hostility in children exposed to all video games

Directions: Questions 7 through 10 are based on the passage below.

WHAT EFFECTS MIGHT GOING GREEN HAVE ON EDUCATION?

Classrooms are slowly going green, prodded by rising energy bills, public health concerns and a general desire to adopt eco-friendly principles. Green schools
(5) cost a little more to build—generally 1% to 2% extra—than conventional schools but promise payback through lower utility bills and, some studies suggest, better student achievement….
(10) Ohio has been a leader in the green school movement, Gutter said. Using money received through a legal settlement with tobacco companies, they are planning to build 250 green schools over the next two
(15) years. The state expects to save $1.4 billion in energy costs over the next 40 years thanks to the program….
Studies in 1999 and 2003 by the Heschong Mahone Group, a California
(20) consulting firm that promotes energy-efficient design, found that children generally fared better on math and reading tests in schools where natural light was more prevalent because it improved student focus and
(25) achievement. "Daylighting," as it's called, is encouraged because it cuts down on energy bills by reducing the need for artificial lighting.

From Ledyard King's COSTS, CONCERNS PUSH SCHOOLS TO USE ECO-FRIENDLY ELEMENTS, © 2008

7 Why are classrooms "going green" (line 1)?
  A because the construction on green schools is less expensive
  B to educate more people about eco-friendly environments
  C because of the rise of energy bills and public health concerns
  D because the government is forcing new schools to go green

8 According to the passage, what is an effect of daylighting on students?
  A Students are more focused and achieve better scores because of the natural light.
  B Students pay less for their school materials because of lower energy fees.
  C Students become more aware of the impact they have on the environment.
  D Students are studied more to determine how artificial light affects test scores.

9 What is an implied effect of Ohio schools going green on the performance of Ohio students?
  A They may become the top students in the United States.
  B They may achieve better test scores in reading and math.
  C They may become the leaders of the green school movement.
  D They may have to pay more for the new schools to be built.

10 What is a main cause of Ohio's building 250 green schools in just two years?
  A to increase students' test scores on achievement tests
  B to use money from a legal settlement with tobacco companies
  C to become a leader in the green school movement
  D to save more than a billion dollars over forty years

Directions: Questions 11 through 15 are based on the passage below.

ABOUT POISON IVY

Many people look forward to summer because they love camping, hiking, picnicking, and just spending time outdoors. Summers can be a fun time of the year, but a few outdoors
(5) plants can spoil a sunny day. One is a common weed known as poison ivy.

Poison ivy is a toxic plant with an oily sap called urushiol. Urushiol can cause itching and a painful rash in many people who touch
(10) poison ivy or who come in contact with this oily substance on pets, clothing, tools, or equipment. Touching anything with urushiol and then touching other parts of the body can spread the rash.

(15) Urushiol sticks to the skin, forming red bands of inflammation at the areas of contact. These bands of swelling often grow into bumps and blisters. The greater the contact, the more urushiol sticks to a person's skin, causing a
(20) more severe rash. Scratching the itchy rash can break the blisters open. This becomes a problem when the bacteria from someone's fingers results in a skin infection that requires a doctor's care.

(25) When someone realizes he or she has had contact with poison ivy or its sap, doctors recommend immediate washing of the contact area with soap and water to eliminate as much of the urushiol as possible. They also
(30) advise campers and hikers to clean their boots, clothing, and backpacks. If swelling and redness are followed by a rash and blistering, there are lotions to help ease the itching. If an infection sets in, doctors can prescribe
(35) antibiotics to kill the bacteria.

The question that many people have is how to avoid getting poison ivy in the first place. Experts suggest people learn to recognize this plant on sight in order to avoid it. Poison ivy
(40) has almond-shaped leaves that are in groups of three. A helpful rhyme is "Leaves of three? Let them be!" Because poison ivy has fruit in the form of white berries, another is "Berries white? Run in fright!"

11 What causes the poison ivy rash?
  A direct contact with three-leafed plants
  B urushiol from the poison ivy plant
  C blisters that cause urushiol to spread
  D inhaling smoke from burning plants

12 A large amount of urushiol on the skin may cause
  A effective protection from poison ivy.
  B less susceptibility to bacterial infection.
  C more blisters but less redness and swelling.
  D more severe cases of poison ivy.

13 What causes the poison ivy rash to spread to other parts of the body?
  A pus from broken blisters
  B brushing against a cat or dog
  C touching items contaminated by urushiol
  D direct contact with a person who has poison ivy

14 What is one possible effect of scratching a poison ivy rash?
  A Blisters can burst and spread from one area to another.
  B Skin can become infected from bacteria.
  C Urushiol can spread, causing fever and swelling.
  D Lungs and nasal passages may become irritated.

15 On the basis of what causes poison ivy, washing thoroughly immediately after contact with the poison ivy plant might help
  A get rid of urushiol on the skin.
  B prevent the spread of infection.
  C keep the skin clean.
  D lubricate areas of dry skin.

LESSON 6
Compare and Contrast

① Learn the Skill

Authors will often compare and contrast objects to help make a point. To **compare** is to look for the similarities between at least two things. You might describe how an orange is like an apple—both are fruits, both are round, and both have outer skins. To **contrast**, however, is to look for differences between things. When contrasting, you might describe how an orange has a tough outer skin, while an apple's skin is easier to tear. Certain key words, such as *in addition to* and *likewise*, can help signal similarities. Other signal words denote differences, such as *on the other hand* and *in contrast*. You can also use a Venn diagram to compare and contrast things.

② Practice the Skill

By mastering the skill of comparing and contrasting, you will improve your study and test-taking skills, especially as they relate to high school equivalency language arts/reading tests. Read the excerpt and strategies below.

> **A** Sometimes authors use descriptions to compare or contrast. The first half of this excerpt describes the landscape of the Great Plains.
>
> **B** The second half of the excerpt goes into more detail. The author contrasts the differences between an initial reaction and a later reaction.

HOW IS THE LAND OF THE GREAT PLAINS DESCRIBED?

I remember coming out upon the northern Great Plains in the late spring. There were meadows of blue and yellow wild-flowers on the slopes, and I could see the still, sunlit plain below, reaching away out of sight. **(A)** At first (5) there is no discrimination in the eye, nothing but the land itself, whole and impenetrable. But then smallest things begin to stand out of the depths—herds and rivers and **(B)** groves—and each of these has perfect being in terms of distance and of silence and of age. Yes, I thought, now (10) I see the earth as it really is; never again will I see things as I saw them yesterday or the day before.

From N. Scott Momady's THE WAY TO RAINY MOUNTAIN, © 1969

MAKING ASSUMPTIONS

If you are asked to compare an orange and a kumquat, you might not know what a kumquat is. Supporting details, such as color and size, can help you understand the objects.

1 How might you contrast the author's descriptions?
  A He first viewed the land as one large entity with no differences, then saw other things.
  B He first viewed each section of the land with a judgmental eye and then saw it as a whole.
  C He saw no differences at all.
  D He only saw herds and rivers.

Unit 1 | Non-Fiction

Directions: Questions 2 and 3 are based on the memo below.

WHAT NEW POLICY IS OUTLINED IN THE MEMO?

Memo
To: WaveLength Team Members and Contractors
From: WaveLength Security Department
Date: November 9
(5) Subject: New Badge Policy

Currently, WaveLength employees and contractors may gain access into the buildings on the WaveLength campus by showing a number of types of photo identification. To avoid miscommunications and other security issues, the following badge policy will be in effect beginning Monday, November 15. This policy is mandatory, and **no exceptions** will be made.

(10)   New WaveLength Facility Badge Policy

- All employees and contractors must wear their WaveLength badges AT ALL TIMES while in the facility. Previous policy required that badges or IDs be shown only at point of entry.
- Badges must be clearly VISIBLE at all times. Clothing should not obstruct a clear view of the badge. Employees customarily have worn badges on shirt pockets, where they could be obscured
(15) by jackets or sweaters. Please note the change.
- Employees and contractors MUST swipe their badges at the door, even if the door is already open. Previously, employees entering open doors with groups of people have held up cards to show them to security guards.
- Employees and contractors who do not have badges upon arrival at work MUST enter the building through
(20) the main doors to obtain a temporary badge. Security guards will no longer be allowed to gain authorization from department heads or other supervisor.
- If you observe ANYONE in the building not wearing a badge, escort that person IMMEDIATELY to the front desk.

2 Based on the information in this memo, how does the new badge policy compare with the previous policy?
   A The new policy applies only to contractors, not to employees.
   B The new policy is more strict than the old policy was.
   C The old policy allowed access only to people with badges.
   D The old policy required all employees to enter by the front desk.

3 What type of business might consider making changes suggested in this memo?
   A a sports arena
   B a farmer's market
   C a shopping center
   D a child care facility

Directions: Questions 4 through 7 are based on the passage below.

HOW ARE BROWN BEARS AND GRIZZLY BEARS RELATED?

Black bears can be found throughout North America. They usually live in forests, away from human beings. They eat grass, shrubs, berries, and nuts. They also eat insects, fish,
(5) frogs, and small mammals.

True to their name, black bears are usually black in color. But in some areas of North America they are blue-gray or even brown. Black bears are smaller than brown grizzly
(10) bears, and black bears usually have a pale snout. They also have longer, less furry ears than brown bears. ...

Bears are the largest hunting mammals in the world. Although still intimidatingly large,
(15) black bears are smaller cousins of the real American giants: the grizzly bear and polar bear. A male grizzly bear weighs about 700 pounds (320 kg). ...But a male black bear—sometimes called a boar—weighs about 375
(20) pounds (170 kg).

From Tom Jackson's BLACK BEARS, © 2008. All rights reserved. Reprinted by permission of Children's Press, an imprint of Scholastic Library Publishing, Inc.

4 How are grizzly bears and black bears different?
  A Grizzly bears eat insects, fish, frogs, and small mammals.
  B Grizzly bears are much larger than black bears.
  C Grizzly bears live in forests, away from human beings.
  D Grizzly bears have longer, less furry ears.

5 Based on this excerpt, what can you assume about bears?
  A Polar bears are found all over North America.
  B Black bears are among the smallest kinds of bears.
  C Grizzly bears eat less food than black bears.
  D Polar bears likely weigh as much or more than grizzly bears.

6 How does the author use structure to compare and contrast the black bear and the grizzly bear?
  A He gives most of the facts about the black bear first, and then he gives the facts about the grizzly bear.
  B He gives all the similarities of the two kinds of bears first, and then he gives all the differences between them.
  C He gives all the differences between the two kinds of bears, and then he gives all their similarities.
  D He gives a similarity of the two kinds of bears, then a difference between them, followed by another similarity and another difference throughout the passage.

7 According to this passage, how are grizzly bears similar to polar bears?
  A Both kinds of bears are not afraid to live near human beings.
  B Both grizzly bears and polar bears do not have a lot of fur on their ears.
  C Both grizzly bears and polar bears are sometimes called a boar.
  D Both kinds of bears are giants among the North American bears.

Directions: Questions 8 through 9 are based on the passage below.

REBUILDING A NATION

As the Civil War came to a close, President Abraham Lincoln began to consider how the United States should be rebuilt. In his second inaugural address, he summed up the ideas
(5) on which he based his plan, saying "… let us strive on to finish the work we are in; to bind up the nation's wounds.…" He hoped to heal the nation with as little animosity as possible between the North and the South. In his plan,
(10) former Confederates who agreed to support the Constitution and the United States would be offered pardons. Confederate states could rejoin the Union if they established anti-slavery governments. Moreover, after rejoining,
(15) southern states would be allowed to elect former Confederates to Congress.

Radical Republicans in Congress, on the other hand, had a different view. In an explanation of the radical Republicans' stance,
(20) Congressman Thaddeus Stevens stated, "Our fathers … proclaimed the equality of men before the law. Upon that they created a revolution and built the Nation. It is our duty to complete their work." Under their plan,
(25) former Confederates would be banned from Congress, and southern states placed under military rule. The radical Republicans also expected states to allow former slaves some rights afforded white citizens.

8 **The Reconstruction plans of Lincoln and the radical Republicans**
 A aimed to rebuild the nation as quickly as possible.
 B featured different objectives for the process of Reconstruction.
 C delegated much responsibility for Reconstruction to the states.
 D imposed similarly harsh penalties on the Confederacy.

9 **In contrast to the radical Republicans' plan for Reconstruction, how is Lincoln's plan best described?**
 A forgiving
 B harsh
 C bold
 D ambitious

Directions: Questions 10 through 13 are based on the passage below.

THE ARTICLES OF CONFEDERATION AND THE U.S. CONSTITUTION

After declaring independence from Britain, the American colonies set forth to govern themselves. In 1776 and 1777, colonial leaders wrote the Articles of Confederation, designed
(5) to limit the national government's power to make and enforce laws. The Articles were adopted by Congress on November 15, 1777, and fully ratified by all states on March 1, 1781.

Although some important achievements
(10) occurred under the Articles, including a plan for new states in the Northwest Ordinance of 1787, the weak central government made it difficult for the states to function as one nation. In particular, the national government was
(15) unable to tax or regulate trade between states.

Therefore, in the summer of 1787, a group of 55 delegates attended the Constitutional Convention in Philadelphia to draft a more effective governing document. The Constitution
(20) they submitted for ratification in September established a strong national government, with a president, a bicameral instead of a unicameral legislature, and a supreme court, which could settle disputes between states.
(25) The legislature was a mixture of equal and proportional representation. All three branches of government were powerful but checked one another.

Other differences between the Articles
(30) of Confederation and the U.S. Constitution involved levying taxes, admitting new states, adding amendments, and coining money. Under the Articles, the states collected taxes, but under the Constitution, only the
(35) national government collected taxes. Under the Articles, new states were admitted by agreement of at least nine states. Under the Constitution, new states were admitted through agreement by Congress. The Articles could be
(40) amended only by agreement of all states; the Constitution could be amended by agreement of three fourths of the states. The Constitution removed the states' power to coin money.

At the time of ratification, the U.S.
(45) Constitution had no provisions protecting personal freedoms. Although states were concerned about a strong national government that did not secure freedoms, the U.S. Constitution became law when ratified by nine
(50) states in 1788. The Bill of Rights was added in 1791.

10 According to the passage, both the Articles of Confederation and the U.S. Constitution were
  A ratified by all states.
  B signed by 55 representatives.
  C written to govern the original states.
  D amendments to the Northwest Ordinance.

11 Unlike the U.S. Constitution, the Articles of Confederation
  A created a plan for admitting new states.
  B gave states more power than the national government.
  C established three branches of government.
  D contained a Bill of Rights to protect individual freedoms.

12 One difference between the legislative branch in the Articles of Confederation and the U.S. Constitution is that the Articles
  A provided for two houses of Congress, but the Constitution provided for one.
  B established the presidency, but the Constitution provided for a supreme court.
  C had three legislative branches, but the Constitution had a single legislative branch.
  D had a single legislature, but the Constitution provided for two legislative houses.

13 Which act would have been possible under the Articles of Confederation only?
  A Members of the Senate levied a tax.
  B Ten states ratified a constitutional amendment.
  C Pennsylvania elected two representatives more than Virginia.
  D The state of New Hampshire collected taxes.

LESSON 7

Distinguish Fact from Opinion

1 Learn the Skill

When reading a passage of non-fiction text, it is important to determine what is fact and what is opinion. Some texts are based on facts, such as a piece of scientific writing that includes figures like "two-thirds of the planet is covered in water." A **fact** is a piece of information that can be proven true or untrue. Other texts are based on opinions, such as an editorial in a newspaper. An **opinion** is a person's view or judgment and cannot be proven true or untrue.

2 Practice the Skill

By mastering the skill of determining facts from opinions, you will improve your study and test-taking skills, especially as they relate to high school equivalency language arts/reading tests. Read the excerpt and strategies below.

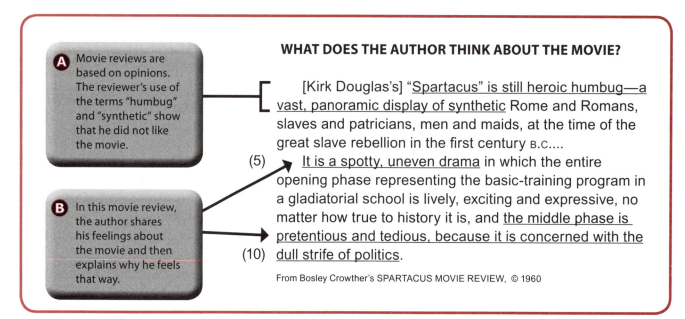

WHAT DOES THE AUTHOR THINK ABOUT THE MOVIE?

A. Movie reviews are based on opinions. The reviewer's use of the terms "humbug" and "synthetic" show that he did not like the movie.

B. In this movie review, the author shares his feelings about the movie and then explains why he feels that way.

[Kirk Douglas's] "Spartacus" is still heroic humbug—a vast, panoramic display of synthetic Rome and Romans, slaves and patricians, men and maids, at the time of the great slave rebellion in the first century B.C....

(5) It is a spotty, uneven drama in which the entire opening phase representing the basic-training program in a gladiatorial school is lively, exciting and expressive, no matter how true to history it is, and the middle phase is pretentious and tedious, because it is concerned with the
(10) dull strife of politics.

From Bosley Crowther's SPARTACUS MOVIE REVIEW, © 1960

MAKING ASSUMPTIONS

To determine if a piece is based on fact or opinion, you might make assumptions based on the language the author uses. Look for words or phrases that sound unscientific or sensational, such as "a great book" or "a miserable experience." These phrases cannot be proven true or untrue.

1. Which line best represents an opinion from the excerpt?
   A "...Rome and Romans, slaves and patricians, men and maids..."
   B "...no matter how true to history it is..."
   C "...basic training program in a gladiatorial school is lively, exciting, and expressive..."
   D "...the entire opening phase..."

③ Apply the Skill

Directions: Questions 2 through 4 are based on the passage below.

WHAT ISSUE IS THE AUTHOR PRESENTING?

This is the real world of eating and nutrition in the rural United States. Forget plucking an apple from a tree, or an egg from under a chicken. "The stereotype is everyone in rural
(5) America lives on a farm, which is far from the truth," says Jim Weill, president of the nonprofit Food Research and Action Center (FRAC). New research from the University of South Carolina's Arnold School of Public Health
(10) shows just how unhealthy the country life can be. The study, which examined food-shopping options in Orangeburg County (1,106 square miles, population 91,500) found a dearth of supermarkets and grocery stores. Of the 77
(15) stores that sold food in Orangeburg County in 2004, when the study was done, 57— nearly 75 percent—were convenience stores. Grocery stores, which stock far more fruits and vegetables than convenience stores, are often
(20) too far away, says University of South Carolina epidemiologist Angela Liese, lead author of the study, which appeared in last month's Journal of the American Dietetic Association. "Oftentimes a nutritionist will just say, 'Buy
(25) more fruits and vegetables,' when, in fact, the buying part is not simple."
  Like other rural areas (and some inner-city ones), Orange County is an isolated "food desert." "You are pretty much at the mercy
(30) of what's in your neighborhood," says Adam Drewnowski, director of the center for obesity research at the University of Washington. Although only 28 percent of all the stores in Orangeburg County carried any of the fruits
(35) and vegetables—apples, cucumbers, oranges, tomatoes—that were part of the survey, Liese and her colleagues found plenty of healthy foods in the county's 20 supermarkets and grocery stores. The situation in the
(40) convenience stores was decidedly grimmer.

From Karen Springen's JUNK FOOD COUNTY, © 2007

2. **Why is the author writing about this topic?**
   A to show the benefits of country living
   B to demonstrate the kinds of eating habits associated with country living
   C to discuss numerous nutrition studies
   D to prove that people in the country shop mainly at grocery stores

3. **How does the author present information in this piece?**
   A by using supporting statistics and studies
   B by presenting a list of pros and cons for country living
   C by posing her opinion about rural areas
   D by critically judging the studies done on food buying

4. **Which fact supports the idea that rural areas are considered "an isolated 'food desert'" (lines 28–29)?**
   A People's food choices are limited to what they can grow.
   B Rural areas are isolated from people just as some inner-city areas are.
   C People often have to travel great distances for any kind of food.
   D People are limited to the foods and stores available in their neighborhoods.

Directions: Questions 5 through 8 are based on the passage below.

HOW DOES THE AUTHOR VIEW THE RESTAURANT?

It is one of the most amazing public dining rooms I have ever seen, or even imagined. The ceiling is very high and elaborate. The windows are tall, looking on one side upon a goodly part
(5) of Paris, and then to the right into and under the endless stretch of grey glass roof over all the tracks that come to a dead stop below ... Switzerland, Italy, Spain, the Near East, all France to the south. ...
(10) The Walls, between and above the great lace-hung windows, are covered with more than forty huge murals of every possible scenic delight that the Paris-Lyon-Mediterranean trains could offer their travelers at the turn of
(15) the century....

In 1967 or whenever that was, I felt dismal about the state of bread in Paris, and had not yet found that it would be almost as bad everywhere, and I decided then that the
(20) fresh loaf served at the Gare de Lyon was the best I had tasted since before World War II. (It still is.) The butter was impeccable, not something from a tinfoil wrapping ... The ham was genuine, perhaps tasting of violets on the
(25) wishful tongue. The champagne seemed one of the best I had ever drunk. ...

The next time that I cannily arranged to be in Paris so that I would have to take the Mistral again, I went somewhat earlier to the station.
(30) I forget whether there were only two waiters that morning, or whether it was later on, when I suddenly looked up from my habitual little meal and saw four or five of them drifting around the table.

From M.F.K. Fisher's GARE DE LYON, © 1982

5 In the first paragraph, which line best represents the author's opinion?
 A "The windows are tall..."
 B "...over all the tracks that come to a dead stop below..."
 C "It is one of the most amazing public dining rooms I have ever seen..."
 D "The ceiling is very high and elaborate."

6 Based on the excerpt, which of the following most likely affected the author's opinion of the food?
 A The proof that it was the best food ever made.
 B The food the author had eaten previously was not very good.
 C The chef who prepared the food had been voted the best chef in Paris.
 D The food at the restaurant was very fresh.

7 In the third paragraph, the author discusses her meal. What opinion does she have of the food at Gare de Lyon? She thinks the food is
 A fantastic.
 B mediocre.
 C decent for a meal at a train station.
 D horrendous.

8 Based on the excerpt, how might the author compare the Gare de Lyon to a restaurant in an American airport terminal? She would view the American restaurant as
 A equally elegant as the Gare de Lyon.
 B a better restaurant than the Gare de Lyon.
 C slightly less appealing than the Gare de Lyon.
 D a restaurant that could not even be compared to the Gare de Lyon.

Directions: Questions 9 through 11 are based on the passage below.

HOW DOES THE AUTHOR VIEW THE WORK OF RALPH ELLISON?

If truth be told, Ralph Ellison, whose novel "Invisible Man" is one of the indisputable classics of American literature, has faded from the public mind, occupying what might
(5) be called a highly respected position on the sidelines of the general consciousness. This is a shame, as any reader of this new and elegant collection of his nonfiction articles will immediately see. And yet, paradoxically
(10) [ironically], the collection serves contradictory purposes. It reminds us just how subtle, deeply cultivated and searching Mr. Ellison's mind was. At the same time, it suggests why that mind seems, sadly, to be underappreciated
(15) these days.
    Mr. Ellison, who was born in Oklahoma City in 1914 and died in New York in 1994, always identified himself as an "American Negro writer." The essays in this collection
(20) represent a sustained, lifelong reflection on issues that are still so much with us: race, racism and African-American identity. But while Mr. Ellison clearly took the oppression of blacks as an essential and irreducible fact
(25) of American life, he also waged an untiring intellectual war against those "who regard blackness as an absolute, and who see in it a release from the complications of the real world."

From Richard Bernstein's BOOKS OF THE TIMES; BLACK IDENTITY, RACISM, AND A LIFETIME OF REFLECTION, © 1995

9 Which line from the excerpt states a fact?
  A "It reminds us just how subtle, deeply cultivated and searching Mr. Ellison's mind was."
  B "...the collection serves contradictory purposes."
  C "Mr. Ellison, who was born in Oklahoma City in 1914 and died in New York in 1994..."
  D "...Ralph Ellison, whose novel Invisible Man is one of the indisputable classics of American literature..."

10 Based on the first paragraph, what is the author's opinion?
  A An intellectual mind is underappreciated in today's society.
  B People today appreciate an author with a great cultivated mind.
  C Ralph Ellison is a widely popular author.
  D Ralph Ellison reserved his thoughts only for his books.

11 Ralph Ellison wrote a novel called *Invisible Man.* Based on the information about Mr. Ellison provided in the excerpt, which of the following most likely describes the subject of *Invisible Man*?
  A a fantasy piece about a man who cannot be seen
  B about a person who wishes he was invisible
  C examining the problems of identity for African-Americans
  D stating that men should attempt to "be seen and not heard"

Directions: Questions 12 and 13 are based on the passage below.

HOW DOES THE AUTHOR VIEW THE PRODUCTION OF PLAY?

The Broadway production of *The Phantom of the Opera* passed its 6,000 performance, a feat only accomplished by *Cats, Les Miserables,* and *A Chorus Line.* Although the
(5) cast is not its original, the current performers are very memorable. The character of the Phantom is played by Howard McGillin. He is an exciting lead character. His singing and acting are wonderful throughout his
(10) performance. Adrienne McEwan, who plays the alternate Christine, also delivers an excellent performance. The rest of the cast is composed of mostly strong, funny, and talented actors and singers. Additionally, the
(15) sets, lighting, make-up, and wardrobe are quite impressive. These things combined create an overall positive play-going experience.

12 Based on the description of the actor that plays the Phantom, what is the author's opinion about the actor who plays the Phantom?
 A extremely talented
 B the second best performer in the cast
 C not a good performer
 D only mediocre

13 What activity would the author most likely enjoy?
 A going to the beach
 B singing in a choir
 C traveling abroad
 D watching a movie

Directions: Questions 14 and 15 are based on the passage below.

HOW DOES THE AUTHOR VIEW THE PERFORMANCE?

The New York Youth Symphony is mostly composed of high school and college-aged musicians. Under the direction of their young conductor, 27 year old Ryan McAdams, they
(5) played a skilled performance of Braham's First Symphony at Carnegie Hall. The youth symphony and their conductor were extremely remarkable. The piece was played with great technical poise, but was made even more
(10) pleasing due to the fresh eagerness of the players. Though the piece is widely known, it did not seem dull. This is owed to the fact that the orchestra playing it was made up of such talented young musicians. Mr. McAdams led
(15) the youth orchestra through other pieces as well, and is indeed doing notable and highly credible work.

14 Which item from the review best indicates the author's opinion?
 A The New York Youth Symphony performed at Carnegie Hall.
 B The New York Youth Symphony performed Braham's First Symphony.
 C The conductor led the symphony through other pieces.
 D The New York Youth Symphony delivered a lively performance.

15 Which of the following would most likely be a hobby of the conductor's?
 A join a reading group
 B take part in a jogging club
 C volunteer at a summer camp
 D lead nature hikes

LESSON 8

Make Inferences

1 Learn the Skill

Occasionally when reading non-fiction, details that are necessary to understanding the piece are only suggested, or implied. To understand what the author is saying, you must use the stated, or explicit, information as well as the implied information to **make an inference**. An inference is an idea that is supported by facts that are presented in a passage. Readers make inferences when they use suggestions, clues, or facts presented in a text to figure out what an author is saying.

2 Practice the Skill

By mastering the skill of making inferences, you will improve your study and test-taking skills, especially as they relate to high school equivalency language arts/reading tests. Read the excerpt and strategies below.

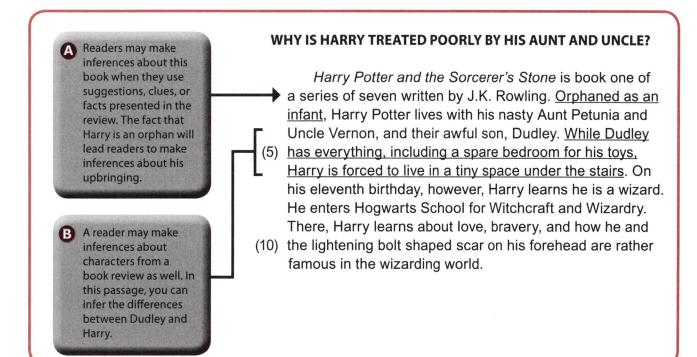

A Readers may make inferences about this book when they use suggestions, clues, or facts presented in the review. The fact that Harry is an orphan will lead readers to make inferences about his upbringing.

B A reader may make inferences about characters from a book review as well. In this passage, you can infer the differences between Dudley and Harry.

WHY IS HARRY TREATED POORLY BY HIS AUNT AND UNCLE?

Harry Potter and the Sorcerer's Stone is book one of a series of seven written by J.K. Rowling. <u>Orphaned as an infant</u>, Harry Potter lives with his nasty Aunt Petunia and Uncle Vernon, and their awful son, Dudley. <u>While Dudley</u>
(5) <u>has everything, including a spare bedroom for his toys, Harry is forced to live in a tiny space under the stairs</u>. On his eleventh birthday, however, Harry learns he is a wizard. He enters Hogwarts School for Witchcraft and Wizardry. There, Harry learns about love, bravery, and how he and
(10) the lightening bolt shaped scar on his forehead are rather famous in the wizarding world.

USING LOGIC

You can logically make an inference by examining the supporting details within a text. In this review, the main idea about Harry's living situation can help you understand the author's intent.

1 What can you infer about Aunt Petunia and Uncle Vernon? Aunt Petunia and Uncle Vernon
   A don't mind raising Harry.
   B treat Harry better than their own son.
   C like the idea that their nephew is a wizard.
   D do not give Harry enough love and support.

③ Apply the Skill

Directions: Questions 2 through 4 are based on the excerpt below.

WHAT IS THE AUTHOR IMPLYING THROUGH HER HUMOR?

Someone has to speak for them, because they have, to a person, lost the power to speak for themselves. I am referring to that great mass of Americans who were once known
(5) as the "salt of the earth," then as "the silent majority," more recently as the "viewing public," and now, alas, as "couch potatoes." What drives them—or rather, leaves them sapped and spineless on their reclining chairs? What
(10) are they seeking—beyond such obvious goals as a tastefully colorized version of *The Maltese Falcon*?

My husband was the first in the family to "spud out," as the expression now goes. Soon
(15) everyone wanted one of those zip-up "Couch Potato Bags," to keep warm in during David Letterman. The youngest, and most thoroughly immobilized, member of the family relies on a remote that controls his TV, stereo, and
(20) VCR, and can also shut down the neighbor's pacemaker...

But we never see the neighbors anymore, nor they us. This saddens me, because Americans used to be a great and restless
(25) people, fond of the outdoors in all of its manifestations, from Disney World to miniature golf. Some experts say there are virtues in mass agoraphobia, that it strengthens the family and reduces highway deaths. But I
(30) would point out that there are still a few things that cannot be done in the den, especially by someone zipped into a body bag. These include racquetball, voting, and meeting strange people in bars.

From Barbara Ehrenreich's SPUDDING OUT, © 1990

2 Based on the information from the excerpt, what can you infer about *The Maltese Falcon* (lines 11–12)? *The Maltese Falcon*
- **A** is a type of bird people could see if they went outside more.
- **B** is a black-and-white movie.
- **C** is an agoraphobe.
- **D** is a painting that might hang in a person's living room.

3 What is the topic of this excerpt?
- **A** peoples' love of television
- **B** peoples' love of outdoor activities
- **C** television shows
- **D** peoples' hatred of spending time with family

4 What inference can be made from the third paragraph?
- **A** Due to too much television, people do not go out of their homes as much as in the past.
- **B** Due to television, families spend more quality time together.
- **C** Due to television, people stay home more and thus there are less car accidents.
- **D** Due to television, strangers have topics to discuss when meeting for the first time.

Directions: Questions 5 through 7 are based on the excerpt below.

WHY IS THOREAU COMPARING HIS LIFE TO HIS PREDECESSORS?

When I walk in the fields of Concord and meditate on the destiny of this prosperous slip of the Saxon *family*—the unexhausted energies of this new country—I forget that this
(5) which is now Concord was once Musketaquid and that the *American race* has had its destiny also. Everywhere in the fields—in the corn and grain land—the earth is strewn with the relics of a race which has vanished as completely as
(10) if trodden in with the earth.

I find it good to remember the eternity behind me as well as the eternity before. Where ever I go I tread in the tracks of the Indian—I pick up the bolt which has but just
(15) dropped at my feet. And if I consider destiny I am on his trail. I scatter his hearth stones with my feet, and pick out of the embers of his fire the simple but enduring implements of the wigwam and the chase—In planting my corn in
(20) the same furrow which yielded its increase to support so long—I displace some memorial of him....

Nature has her russet [reddish-brown] hues as well as green—Indeed our eye splits
(25) on every object, and we can as well take one path as the other—If I consider its history it is old—if its destiny it is new—I may see a part of an object or the whole—I will not be imposed on and think nature is old, because
(30) the season is advanced. I will study the botany of the mosses and fungi on the decayed—and remember that decayed wood is not old, but has just begun to be what it is. I need not think of the pine almond or the acorn and sapling
(35) when I meet the fallen pine or oak—more than of the generations of pines and oaks which have fed the young tree."

From Henry David Thoreau's JOURNALS, © 1842

5. **Based on the first paragraph, of whom is the author speaking in the line "relics of a race which has vanished" (line 9)?**
   A the Americans who settled the land before him
   B the animals that lived on the land first
   C neighbors who have moved far away from his cabin
   D the Native Americans who lived on the land before other people

6. **What is the author implying when he says "In planting my corn in the same furrow which yielded its increase to support so long—I displace some memorial of him" (lines 19–22)?**
   A He has planted corn in the same place as his ancestors.
   B As he plants his own corn, he is taking away any traces of Native Americans.
   C He is acknowledging the fact that others have planted in this spot before him.
   D He is claiming the land as his own through his planting ritual.

7. **Based on the excerpt, which activity might the author most enjoy doing as a hobby?**
   A gardening
   B painting
   C hunting
   D racing cars

Unit 1 | Non-Fiction

Directions: Questions 8 through 10 are based on the excerpt below.

WHAT WAS THE AUTHOR'S QUEST?

Sometimes, without warning, the future knocks on our door with a precious and painful vision of what might be. One hundred and nineteen years ago, a wealthy inventor
(5) read his own obituary, mistakenly published years before his death. Wrongly believing the inventor had just died, a newspaper printed a harsh judgment of his life's work, unfairly labeling him "The Merchant of Death" because
(10) of his invention—dynamite. Shaken by this condemnation, the inventor made a fateful choice to serve the cause of peace. Seven years later, Alfred Nobel created this prize and the others that bear his name.
(15) Seven years ago tomorrow, I read my own political obituary in a judgment that seemed to me harsh and mistaken—if not premature. But that unwelcome verdict also brought a precious, if painful, gift: an opportunity to search for fresh
(20) new ways to serve my purpose. Unexpectedly, that quest has brought me here. Even though I fear my words cannot match this moment, I pray what I am feeling in my heart will be communicated clearly enough that those who
(25) hear me will say, "We must act...."

We, the human species, are confronting a planetary emergency—a threat to the survival of our civilization that is gathering ominous and destructive potential even as we gather here.
(30) But there is hopeful news as well: we have the ability to solve this crisis and avoid the worst—though not all—of its consequences, if we act boldly, decisively, and quickly. ...

So today, we dumped another 70 million
(35) tons of global-warming pollution into the thin shell of atmosphere surrounding our planet, as if it were an open sewer. And tomorrow, we will dump a slightly larger amount, with the cumulative concentrations now trapping more
(40) and more heat from the sun.

As a result, the earth has a fever. And the fever is rising. The experts have told us it is not a passing affliction that will heal by itself. We asked for a second opinion. And a third. And a
(45) fourth. And the consistent conclusion, restated with increasing distress, is that something basic is wrong. We are what is wrong, and we must make it right.

From Al Gore's NOBEL PEACE PRIZE LECTURE, © 2007

8 From the first paragraph, what can be inferred about why a prize was created which bears Alfred Nobel's name?
   A to credit his accomplishments as an inventor
   B after his death by people who appreciated his life's work
   C in order to continue his legacy and encourage others to pursue peace
   D to serve the cause of peace after creating a destructive weapon

9 To what event is the speaker most likely referring in lines 15 through 17?
   A an event that occurred during his time as Vice-President
   B his loss in the 2000 Presidential election
   C the death of a friend who was involved in politics
   D a reporter wrote that he had died

10 What is the author implying when he says, "we ... are confronting a planetary emergency" (lines 26–27)?
   A All of Earth's citizens are already facing an environmental problem.
   B The human species is not concerned about a planetary emergency.
   C The human species is facing a global political problem.
   D The human species is removed from any planetary emergencies.

Directions: Questions 11 through 13 are based on the speech below.

HOW DID THE AUTHOR FEEL ABOUT WRITERS OF THE TIME?

Our tragedy today is a general and universal physical fear so long sustained by now that we can even bear it. There are no longer problems of the spirit. There is only the
(5) question: When will I be blown up? Because of this, the young man or woman writing today has forgotten the problems of the human heart in conflict with itself which alone can make good writing because only that is worth writing
(10) about, worth the agony and the sweat.

He must learn them again. He must teach himself that the basest of all things is to be afraid; and, teaching himself that, forget it forever, leaving no room in his workshop
(15) for anything but the old verities and truths of the heart, the old universal truths lacking which any story is ephemeral [short-lived] and doomed—love and honor and pity and pride and compassion and sacrifice. Until he
(20) does so, he labors under a curse. He writes not of love but of lust, of defeats in which nobody loses anything of value, of victories without hope and, worst of all, without pity or compassion. His griefs grieve on no universal
(25) bones, leaving no scars. He writes not of the heart but of the glands.

Until he relearns these things, he will write as though he stood among and watched the end of man. I decline to accept the end of man.
(30) It is easy enough to say that man is immortal simply because he will endure: that when the last ding-dong of doom has clanged and faded from the last worthless rock hanging tideless in the last red and dying evening, that even
(35) then there will still be one more sound: that of his puny inexhaustible voice, still talking. I refuse to accept this. I believe that man will not merely endure: he will prevail. He is immortal, not because he alone among creatures has an
(40) inexhaustible voice, but because he has a soul, a spirit capable of compassion and sacrifice and endurance.

The poet's, the writer's, duty is to write about these things. It is his privilege to help
(45) man endure by lifting his heart, by reminding him of the courage and honor and hope and pride and compassion and pity and sacrifice which have been the glory of his past. The poet's voice need not merely be the record of
(50) man, it can be one of the props, the pillars to help him endure and prevail.

From William Faulkner's SPEECH ACCEPTING THE NOBEL PRIZE IN LITERATURE, © 1950

11 Based on the excerpt, what does the author think young writers are missing in their work?
  A lust
  B fearlessness
  C endurance
  D devastation

12 What is the author implying about man in the third paragraph?
  A Man has the ability to transcend due to his spirit.
  B Man will surely die.
  C New writers will perish just as a man perishes.
  D Man has no spirit or soul.

13 How does the author view the poet and writer in the last paragraph?
  A as messengers to carry on the emotions of humankind
  B as duty bound to report the evil truths to society
  C as those who merely provide information
  D as pillars with the gifts to prove mankind can prevail

LESSON 9

Draw Conclusions

① Learn the Skill

Drawing conclusions is similar to making inferences. As you know, an inference is an educated guess based on facts or evidence. By combining several inferences together to make a judgment, you can **draw conclusions**. Determining a cause and its effect can help you draw conclusions.

② Practice the Skill

By mastering the skill of drawing conclusions, you will improve your study and test-taking skills, especially as they relate to high school equivalency language arts/reading tests. Read the excerpt and strategies below.

A The first and second sentences present facts about gas prices. You can conclude that gas in Venezuela is cheaper than gas in the United States.

B This sentence gives you a cause and effect. One conclusion you might draw is that Venezuela has lower gas taxes than the United States.

WHY DO SOME COUNTRIES PAY MORE FOR GAS?

A Gasoline in the United States is cheap. Not as cheap as American drivers would like, of course. And not as cheap as it is in Venezuela and other major oil-producing countries, where it is heavily
(5) subsidized. Compared to prices in most other industrialized nations, however, the American national average of $4 a gallon is a bargain.
B The chief reason for the disparity with the high-priced nations is taxation. Take away the taxes, and the remaining
(10) gas price is similar from place to place.

From Bill Marsh's SAVORING BARGAINS AT THE AMERICAN PUMP, © 2008

MAKING ASSUMPTIONS

Drawing conclusions and making inferences both rely on making assumptions or educated guesses about a topic. If the topic or the author's purpose is not clear, carefully read the text and make assumptions that can lead to inferences or conclusions.

1 What can you conclude based on this excerpt?
  A Gasoline in the United States is less than gasoline in Venezuela.
  B The United States has the highest prices for gasoline in the world.
  C Gasoline in the United States is as cheap as it is in those countries where it is highly subsidized.
  D The United States pays higher prices for gasoline than some countries, but pays significantly less per gallon than others.

Apply the Skill

Directions: Questions 2 through 4 are based on the excerpt below.

WHAT ARE THE AUTHOR'S VIEWS ABOUT SEPARATE CLASSROOMS FOR BOYS AND GIRLS?

If schools shortchange girls, why is it surprising when the tests show that they're doing less well? It isn't just the P.S.A.T.'s, where 18,000 boys generally reach the top
(5) categories and only 8,000 girls do. While the gap has narrowed, boys also outscore girls on 11 of the 14 College Board Achievement tests, and on the A.C.T. exams and on the S.A.T.'s. It is possible to jimmy selection standards
(10) to make sure girls win more scholarships, but equal results don't count for much if those results are forced. Instead of declaring equality, society should be advancing it. The challenge isn't to get more scholarships for
(15) baton twirlers but to get more baton twirlers to take up advanced mathematics.

One place that happens is in girls' schools and women's colleges. Sometimes separate isn't equal; it's better. Changing the way
(20) teachers teach in coed schools, changing the textbooks to make sure they talk about women as well as men, educating parents about raising daughters—all of these things make sense, since most girls will be educated in
(25) coed classrooms. But we've been talking about them for a decade, and the problems of gender bias stubbornly persist. In the meantime, for many girls, single-sex education is working….

The evidence, though scant, is promising.
(30) In Ventura, Calif., the public high school has begun offering an all-girls Algebra II course. The girls, one teacher says, think so little of their ability that the teacher spends her time not only teaching math but also building self-
(35) confidence, repeatedly telling the girls that they're smart and that they can do it.

_{From Susan Estrich's FOR GIRLS' SCHOOLS AND WOMEN'S COLLEGES, SEPARATE IS BETTER, © 1994}

2 Based on the excerpt, which of the following conclusions might best reflect the author's viewpoint?
- **A** Math and science are as important for girls as they are for boys.
- **B** Girls may do better in math and science if they learn in all-girl classrooms.
- **C** Girls will do better in math and science if they are taught in coed classrooms.
- **D** Girls deserve to win more scholarships based on standardized tests.

3 Which conclusion can be drawn from the third paragraph?
- **A** Separate classrooms have no impact on education.
- **B** Teachers spend too much time enhancing girls' self-esteem.
- **C** The reactions of girls taking all-girls' math and science classes are poorer.
- **D** The evidence shown from the few schools that have offered all-girls' classes is promising.

4 What evidence from the excerpt supports the conclusion that separate is better?
- **A** "...for many girls, single-sex education is working..."
- **B** "...the teacher spends her time not only teaching math but also building self-confidence..."
- **C** "...the problems of gender bias stubbornly persist."
- **D** "...equal rights don't count for much if those results are forced."

Directions: Questions 5 through 8 are based on the excerpt below.

WORKING VIRTUALLY

Yes, working virtually has revolutionized the workplace, unshackling workers from nasty office vibes, bad feng shui, and the soul-crushing power of the cubicle. The butt-in-chair mandates of
(5) yore are ridiculous at a time when we collaborate across continents and carry around our office in our palms. ... That's why companies like Best Buy, Microsoft, and IBM have long encouraged employees to work wherever and whenever they
(10) want. It's the future. And it's great. ...

Though the vast majority of employees adore the *nouveau* flex, there are those who are simply not wired that way. They feel socially unemployed. One executive
(15) headhunter in New Jersey missed office life so much—and got so depressed from working in his ratty sweats with unbrushed teeth—that he started putting on a suit and tie every day before traipsing across his bedroom to his
(20) desk. "Some people don't work well alone," says IBM's director of global diversity, Ron Glover. "They need to be engaged with others and close together so they can be supported and developed and performance managed."...

(25) A recent study by Rensselaer Polytechnic Management Professor Tim Golden found that the greater the prevalence of teleworkers in an office, the less others in the office are apt to be satisfied with their jobs. The non-teleworkers
(30) tend to find the workplace less enjoyable, have fewer and weaker emotional ties to co-workers, and generally feel less obligated to the organization, Golden found.

Such research is spurring managers to
(35) realize how vital it is to mitigate some of the adverse impacts of working remotely. According to Wright State University management professor Todd Dewett, there are four reasons remote work arrangements flop: choosing the
(40) wrong people, improper communication, setting weak or unclear goals, and unproductive home and work environments (think babies and dogs). That's why Hewlett Packard now offers employees self-assessments they can take to
(45) see if they are cut out for the world of virtual work. Managers are also receiving coaching on how to deal with a largely invisible workforce.

From the businessweek.com article WORKING REMOTELY...OR REMOTELY WORKING? by Michelle Conlin, © 2008 accessed 2013

5 Which statement best explains the author's conclusion about why telecommuting is not for everyone?
  A Telecommuting has revolutionized the workplace.
  B Some people are become depressed when working alone.
  C New technologies make telecommuting easier.
  D Some employees now take self-assessments.

6 From the information in paragraph 3, what is the best conclusion to draw about why non-telecommuters are less satisfied when many of their co-workers telecommute?
  A They lack the self-discipline to work from home.
  B They don't like working for large companies with offices around the world.
  C They develop stronger ties when co-workers are physically present in the office.
  D They don't understand the technology that makes communication effective.

7 Which statement best supports the conclusion about why the majority of employees like telecommuting?
  A People have co-workers around the world, so being required to go to an office does not make sense.
  B It is difficult to manage employees when they are not in the office.
  C Employees who telecommute are less obligated to their companies.
  D They can dress for work before going to their desk at home.

8 The most logical conclusion to draw from this passage is that
  A Companies like telecommuting because it saves them money on office space.
  B Employees like telecommuting because it gives them more free time.
  C More studies are needed to determine whether most people like to telecommute.
  D There are reasons to encourage telecommuting and reasons to restrict it.

Directions: Questions 9 through 11 are based on the excerpt below.

WHAT DOES THE AUTHOR WANT WOMEN TO ACHIEVE?

Twenty years ago, when I attended Wellesley College, an all-women's college, coeducation fever was gripping America. Yale and Princeton had just "gone"; Dartmouth
(5) "went" next. My freshman year, we were polled on whether we thought Wellesley should join the stampede. What did I know? I said yes. But now I know I was wrong, and I'm glad my vote didn't change anything.
(10) This year, 60 percent of the National Merit Scholarship finalists are boys, because boys outscored girls on the Preliminary Scholastic Assessment Test (P.S.A.T.), which determines eligibility for the scholarships. The test doesn't
(15) ask about sports; it does ask about math and science, though, and that's where the differences between boys and girls are most pronounced. The American Civil Liberties Union and the National Center for Fair and
(20) Open Testing filed a Federal civil rights suit in February charging that the test discriminates against women. The plaintiffs want more girls to get National Merit Scholarships. So do I. But I want to see girls earn them, in schools that
(25) give them a fair chance.
I didn't win a Merit Scholarship either, although if the Fair Test people had their way, I might have. My grades were near perfect. But I didn't take the tough math and science
(30) courses. I had different priorities. I started junior high as the only girl on the math team. By high school, I'd long since quit. Instead, I learned to twirl a baton, toss it in the air and catch it while doing a split in the mud or the
(35) ice. The problem wasn't the P.S.A.T., but me, and my school.
Things have changed since then, but not as much as one would hope. The American Association of University Women did a major
(40) study in 1992 about how schools shortchange girls and concluded that even though girls get better grades (except in math), they get less from school.

From Susan Estrich's FOR GIRLS' SCHOOLS AND WOMEN'S COLLEGES, SEPARATE IS BETTER, © 1994

9 Based on the excerpt, why is the author glad her vote did not change anything regarding the structure at Wellesley College (lines 8–9)?
 A because was young and thoughtless
 B because does not believe in coeducation
 C because believes that women thrive better educationally in a single sex setting
 D because did not know the reasons behind coeducation schooling

10 From the second paragraph, what can be concluded about why boys do better on the P.S.A.T.'s than girls? Boys do better on the P.S.A.T.'s because
 A boys excel at standardized tests.
 B the tests are designed toward boys' interests.
 C boys excel over girls in school courses and thus test better.
 D the test is heavily math based.

11 What is the author's overall purpose in this excerpt?
 A Girls should get the same attention from their schools as boys so they may achieve higher test scores.
 B Girls excel more at school academics than on tests and this should change.
 C Boys get less attention in school than girls.
 D Boys take standardized tests better because of their content.

Directions: Questions 12 through 15 are based on the excerpt below.

HOW WAS THE AUTHOR RECEIVED BY PEOPLE AFTER HIS SPEECH?

When I arose to speak, there was considerable cheering, especially from the coloured people. As I remember it now, the thing that was uppermost in my mind was the
(5) desire to say something that would cement the friendship of the races and bring about hearty cooperation between them. So far as my outward surroundings were concerned, the only thing that I recall distinctly now is that
(10) when I got up, I saw thousands of eyes looking intently into my face. …

The first thing that I remember, after I had finished speaking, was that Governor Bullock rushed across the platform and took me by the
(15) hand, and that others did the same. I received so many and such hearty congratulations that I found it difficult to get out of the building. I did not appreciate to any degree, however, the impression which my address seemed to
(20) have made, until the next morning, when I went into the business part of the city. As soon as I was recognized, I was surprised to find myself pointed out and surrounded by a crowd of men who wished to shake hands with me. This was
(25) kept up on every street on to which I went, to an extent which embarrassed me so much that I went back to my boarding-place. The next morning I returned to Tuskegee. At the station in Atlanta, and at almost all of the stations at
(30) which the train stopped between the city and Tuskegee, I found a crowd of people anxious to shake hands with me. …

I very soon began receiving all kinds of propositions from lecture bureaus, and editors
(35) of magazines and papers, to take the lecture platform, and to write articles.

From Booker T. Washington's UP FROM SLAVERY, © 1901

12 Given the content of the first paragraph, why would the author want to "cement the friendship of the races" (lines 5–6)?
  A to continue the existing friendship between the races
  B to extend the invitation of friendship from one race to another
  C to cement the differences between the races while remaining friends
  D to bridge the gap between the races to create a friendship

13 Why did the author receive invitations from "lecture bureaus, and editors of magazines and papers" (lines 34–35)?
  A because his speech was very successful
  B because his speech enraged so many
  C because his speech caused great debate
  D because his speech created a gap between races

14 Based on what was learned about the author in this excerpt, how would you describe his personality?
  A playful
  B joyful
  C pessimistic
  D humble

15 Based on this excerpt, to what could you compare the author's experiences?
  A people protesting a campaign
  B people jeering a performer off stage
  C people accepting a speech quietly
  D people welcoming war heroes home

LESSON 10
Determine Author's Purpose

1 Learn the Skill

Authors write for different **purposes**, or reasons: to describe, inform, persuade, entertain, or tell a story. In fact, authors often write for more than one purpose. For example, in a persuasive article encouraging regular exercise, an author may tell a funny story about trying to keep up in an aerobics class. The main purpose of this article may be to persuade, but the author does so by entertaining. Sometimes authors directly state their purpose. Other times they have implicit, or unstated, purposes.

Authors keep their readers, or **audience**, in mind. Audiences may be general—anyone who chooses to read the work. Or they may be specific according to age, political view, income, education, technical background, interest, or profession. Authors try to appeal to their audiences and use appropriate language.

2 Practice the Skill

By practicing the skills of determining author's purpose and identifying audience, you will improve your study and test-taking abilities, especially as they relate to the reading tests for high school equivalency. Read the excerpt and strategies below.

A The author's stated purpose often appears early in a passage. The authors of this passage want to persuade readers to get a flu shot. This sentence makes the claim that the flu shot is "worth getting."

B The CDC is a government agency that studies and advises about health issues. Authors refer to reliable sources to make their arguments more persuasive.

GETTING A FLU SHOT

Getting a flu shot often protects you from coming down with the flu. And although the flu shot doesn't always provide total protection, it's worth getting.

This year's annual flu shot will offer protection against (5) H1N1 flu (swine flu) virus, in addition to two other influenza viruses that are expected to be in circulation this fall and winter.

Influenza is a respiratory infection that can cause serious complications, particularly to young children and to older adults. Flu shots are the most effective way to prevent (10) influenza and its complications. The Centers for Disease Control and Prevention (CDC) now recommends that everyone 6 months of age or older be vaccinated annually against influenza.

From the MayoClinic.com article FLU SHOT: YOUR BEST BET FOR AVOIDING INFLUENZA, accessed 2013

Making Assumptions

Knowing an author's reputation may give you information about the purpose of the passage. The Mayo Clinic is a respected medical facility. You can assume that staff members are reliable sources of medical information.

1 Which statement best supports the purpose of persuading readers to get a flu shot?
   A The flu shot does not always provide total protection.
   B The flu shot will offer protection against H1N1 flu (swine flu) virus.
   C Influenza is a respiratory infection.
   D Flu shots are the most effective way to prevent influenza.

Apply the Skill

Directions: Questions 2 through 5 are based on the passage below.

THE IMPACT OF EDUCATION ON POVERTY

For decades, America has wrestled with poverty but with little success. In 1964, President Lyndon Johnson famously declared "war on poverty." A 2012 study by the Cato
(5) Institute estimates that the United States has spent roughly $15 trillion since then, and yet the poverty rate is close to where it was more than 40 years ago. Cato reports that the United States spends nearly $1 trillion a year between
(10) federal and state programs to fight poverty.

That amounts to more than $20,000 per poor person and more than $60,000 for a family of three. And yet, the problem has not improved.

Both liberals and conservatives recognize
(15) this reality. However . . . some on the left think the problem is that the government has not gone far enough. They call for more government intervention, like living wages and expanded social services. Granted, the government has a
(20) role in aiding the poor, particularly the disabled, handicapped and those who are poor largely at no fault of their own.

But if history is any indicator, government transactions and services don't seem to be
(25) the key drivers of upward mobility. In fact, they can have the opposite effect and insulate lower classes from upward mobility.

Instead, conservatives would argue that education, earned success and the all-
(30) important mediating institutions—families, churches, communities, private and philanthropic enterprises, associations of coaches, teachers, parents, doctors, civil servants and religious and non-religious
(35) volunteers . . . are the pillars of upward mobility.

The evidence seems to support that. In a landmark study, the Brookings Institution found that young adults who finish high school, get a full-time job and wait until age 21 to
(40) get married and have children have just a 2% chance of falling into poverty and a 74% chance of ending up in the middle class.

From the cnn.com article REDUCE POVERTY BY PROMOTING SCHOOLS, FAMILIES by William J. Bennett, © 2013

2. What is the author's main purpose in writing this passage?
   A to persuade readers to support expanded social services
   B to inform readers about how much the U.S. government spends to fight poverty
   C to inform readers about high-school graduation rates
   D to persuade readers that education is a key factor in overcoming poverty

3. Which statement best explains the author's view about social services and other government programs that aid the poor?
   A Government programs are not the solution to fighting poverty.
   B Government programs should be expanded until poverty is largely eliminated.
   C Graduation rates improve when social services are available.
   D The government should not spend any more money on social services.

4. The author assumes that his audience will include liberals as well as conservatives. Which statement best supports this assumption?
   A He says that both liberals and conservatives agree about reality.
   B He provides facts about the amounts of money spent on fighting poverty.
   C He presents the liberal viewpoint and counters it with the conservative one.
   D He mentions historical viewpoints other than those of liberals and conservatives.

5. How does paragraph 6 relate to the author's purpose?
   A It explains the details of the Brookings Institution study.
   B It supports the author's viewpoint stated in paragraph 5.
   C It confirms the findings of the Cato Institute study mentioned in paragraph 1.
   D It contradicts the figures the author presents in paragraph 2.

Directions: Questions 6 and 7 are based on the passage below.

STRATEGIC PLANS FOR ATLANTA

GENERAL [J.B. Hood, commanding Army of Tennessee, Confederate Army]: I have the honor to acknowledge the receipt of your letter of this date . . . consenting to the arrangements
(5) I had proposed to facilitate the removal south of the people of Atlanta, who prefer to go in that direction. I [e]nclose . . . a copy of my orders, which will, I am satisfied, accomplish my purpose perfectly.
(10) You style the measures proposed "unprecedented," and appeal to the dark history of war for a parallel, as an act of "studied and ingenious cruelty." It is not unprecedented; for General Johnson himself
(15) very wisely and properly removed families all the way from Dalton down, and I see no reason why Atlanta should be excepted. Nor is it necessary to appeal to the dark history of war, when recent and modern examples are so
(20) handy. You yourself burned dwelling-houses along your parapet, and I have seen to-day fifty houses that you have rendered uninhabitable because they stood in the way of your forts and men. You defended Atlanta on a line so close
(25) to town that every cannon-shot and many musket-shots for our line of investment, that overshot their mark, went into the habitations of women and children. General Hardee did the same at Jonesboro', and General
(30) Johnston did the same, last summer, at Jackson, Mississippi. I have not accused you of heartless cruelty, but merely instance these cases of very recent occurrence, and could go on and enumerate hundreds of others, and
(35) challenge any fair man to judge which of us has the heart of pity for the families of a "brave people.". . .
If we must be enemies, let us be men, and fight it out as we propose to do, and not
(40) deal in such hypocritical appeals to God and humanity. God will judge us in due time, and he will pronounce whether it be more humane to fight with a town full of women and the families of a brave people at our back or to remove
(45) them in time to places of safety among their own friends and people. I am, very respectfully, your obedient servant,
    W.T. Sherman, Major-General commanding [Union Army]

From HEADQUARTERS MILITARY DIVISION OF THE MISSISSIPPI, IN THE FIELD, ATLANTA, GEORGIA by General William T. Sherman, © 1864

6 What does the author state as his explicit purpose in writing the letter?
  A to confirm the plans for evacuating Atlanta
  B to use the army for unprecedented actions
  C to defend Atlanta from cannon and musket shots
  D to accuse General Hood of cruel actions

7 What is the author's implicit purpose in writing the letter?
  A to show that he outranked General Hood
  B to reveal that he had been thoughtful in his decision
  C to justify his invasion of Atlanta because such destruction had recent precedents
  D to demonstrate that he and General Hood are enemies on opposing sides

Directions: Questions 8 through 11 are based on the passage below.

THE AMERICAN NEED FOR MORE

Many of us find that we seem to require more necessities than we can get the money to pay for. Our friends with more money are constantly showing how indispensably
(5) convenient these necessities are, and we keep buying them until we either outspend our incomes or miss the higher concerns of life. The saddest part of all is that it is in great measure an American development, and we
(10) Americans keep inventing new necessities. Of course it all belongs to "progress," and no one is quite willing to have it stop.

Take houses, for example. An ideal of earthly comfort is to get a house so big that
(15) it is burdensome to maintain and fill it up so full of extras that it is a constant occupation to keep it in order. However, when nature provides a house, that house fits the occupant. Animals, which build by instinct, build only
(20) what they need. But man's building instinct is boundless. Nature never tells him when he has finished. And perhaps it should not surprise us that in so many cases he doesn't know. He just goes ahead as long as the materials last.

(25) If another man tries to oppress him, he understands this kind of tyranny. . . . He is ready to fight and sacrifice all he has, rather than submit to it. But the tyranny of things is so subtle, so gradual in its approach, and comes
(30) so masked with seeming benefits, that it has him hopelessly bound before he suspects. He says, "I will add thus to my house," "I will have one or two more horses," "I will make a little greenhouse in my garden," and so he goes on
(35) having things and imagining that he is richer for owning them. It is only over time that he begins to realize that it is the things that own him.

Adapted from THE TYRANNY OF THINGS by Edward Sanford Martin, © 1893

8 What is the author's main purpose?
   A to tell a story about expanding a house
   B to inform readers about animals' instincts
   C to persuade readers to think about their real needs
   D to describe the newest conveniences for the home

9 How does contrasting the tyranny of things with oppression by another person (paragraph 3) advance the author's purpose? The contrast shows that
   A people are unaware of the way things come to rule them.
   B people confuse what they want with what they need.
   C oppression by a ruler is much more common.
   D humans often destroy themselves needlessly or unknowingly.

10 How might a reader respond if he or she finds the author's argument convincing?
   A The reader might try to live without material possessions.
   B The reader might seek to overthrow the government.
   C The reader might buy fewer luxury or convenience items.
   D The reader might try to study and learn from nature.

11 How does the structure of the last two sentences emphasize a key idea of the passage?
   A The last sentence summarizes the quotations in the sentence before to emphasize that people do not have good instincts.
   B The last sentence reverses the wording of the sentence before to emphasize that possessions can limit a person's freedom.
   C The last sentence paraphrases the sentence before to emphasize that people are quick to respond to tyranny.
   D The last sentence adds details to the sentence before to emphasize that people want to live lifestyles they cannot afford.

Directions: Questions 12 through 16 are based on the passage below.

THE HOME OFFICE TAX DEDUCTION

As part of ongoing efforts by the Administration to reduce paperwork burdens, the Internal Revenue Service (IRS) announced today that it is providing a new, simpler
(5) option for calculating the home office tax deduction, allowing small business owners and employees who work from home and who maintain a qualifying home office to deduct up to $1,500 per year.
(10) The IRS also expects taxpayers to save more than 1.6 million hours per year in tax preparation time from this simpler calculation method.
The new option allows qualified taxpayers
(15) to deduct annually $5 per square foot of home office space on up to 300 square feet, for as much as $1,500 in deductions. To take advantage of the new option, taxpayers will complete a much simpler version of the current
(20) 43-line form.
The announcement builds on the President's commitment to streamline and simplify the tax code for small businesses and to reduce the burden for tax compliance. It
(25) is part of broader efforts to make interacting with the federal government easier and more efficient for businesses of all sizes.
These new rules help our tax code better reflect the needs of America's 21st Century
(30) workforce and especially small businesses, which play a vital role in our economy. Today, more than half of all working Americans own or work for a small business. An estimated 52 percent of small businesses are home-
(35) based, and many of these small businesses have home office space that would qualify for the deduction. And as technology improves, more businesses—large and small—are going virtual and recruiting employees from across
(40) the country, many of whom work from home offices.

From the treasury.gov article THE HOME OFFICE TAX DEDUCTION: SIMPLIFYING RULES AND HELPING SMALL BUSINESS OWNERS SUCCEED by Neal S. Wolin and Karen G. Mills, accessed 2013

12 What is the explicit purpose of the IRS announcement?
  A to inform readers about the new home office tax deduction
  B to persuade taxpayers to take the home office deduction
  C to describe the size and layout of a home office
  D to persuade taxpayers to work from home

13 What is the implicit purpose of the passage?
  A to inform readers about which tax forms to file
  B to persuade readers to support the current administration
  C to explain proposed changes to the tax code
  D to tell a story about a successful home-based business

14 Which piece of evidence best supports the claim that small businesses "play a vital role in our economy"?
  A The government is trying to to simplify the tax code for small businesses.
  B Owners of small businesses could deduct up to $1,500 per year.
  C More than half of all working Americans own or work for a small business.
  D An estimated 52 percent of small businesses are home-based.

15 If the audience were limited only to owners of home businesses, what additional details or information might the passage include?
  A an explanation of how the IRS determined the new calculation method
  B an estimate of how many people failed to claim the old deduction
  C a tax form showing a sample calculation of the deduction
  D an address to which taxpayers can send comments about the tax code

16 In paragraph 5, the authors address their audience, which is "the 21st-century workforce." Which word best describes this group?
  A flexible
  B traditional
  C organized
  D loyal

LESSON 11
Analyze Elements of Persuasion

1 Learn the Skill

When an author writes to **persuade**, he or she tries to convince readers to agree with his or her point of view or to do something. **Argument** is a type of persuasion that uses logic and evidence to persuade. Persuasive writing usually starts with a **claim**, or a statement about an issue or a problem. The claim reflects the author's **position**, or point of view. Often, arguments present a **counterclaim**, or response to an opposing view. Counterclaims show that the author has considered both sides of an argument.

Authors use **evidence** to support their claims. Evidence may be facts, examples, or other reliable information. Authors also try to persuade by appealing to an audience's emotions, such as fear or anger. The writing ends with a **conclusion** that asks readers to do something or think in a particular way.

2 Practice the Skill

By practicing the skill of analyzing elements of persuasion and argument, you will improve your study and test-taking abilities. Read the passage below.

A The terms **public transportation** and **mass transit** refer to buses, trains, subways, and other means of transportation operated for the benefit of the public.

B Here, the author responds to the **opposing viewpoint** that investment in mass transit is not affordable.

SUPPORTING INVESTMENT IN PUBLIC TRANSPORTATION

Investment in public transportation generates jobs and boosts the economy. Thousands of workers are engaged in building buses, repairing, and maintaining rail lines. These jobs are located in the areas served by mass transit and in
(5) regions throughout the country. In Michigan, for example, workers build buses that are used across the United States.
Also, transportation workers and riders spend money throughout a mass transit network, enabling businesses to expand and hire. Although some think we cannot afford
(10) public investment in mass transit, the American Public Transportation Association estimates that for every dollar spent in such investment, approximately six dollars are generated in jobs and public benefits. Support legislation to develop mass transit, and help yourself to a better future.

TEST-TAKING TIPS

Take enough time to read the question and all the answer choices very carefully. Even wrong answers can relate to information in the passage or can include language from the passage.

1. Which sentence best states the call to action?
   A Take public transportation whenever you can.
   B Encourage investment in public transportation.
   C Get a job in mass transit in order to have a secure future.
   D Invest in mass transit only if you will benefit directly.

Apply the Skill

Directions: Questions 2 through 5 are based on the excerpt below.

FOSTER YOUTH AND HEALTH CARE

What I hope would be neither partisan nor divisive is one small but important provision [of the Patient Protection and Affordable Care Act]: because of the Act, former foster youth
(5) may continue to have Medicaid coverage until they turn 26.

Why does this matter?

These are young people for whom we—and by this I mean all of civil society—have
(10) taken responsibility. They have been removed from their homes primarily because they could no longer live there safely. Some are fortunate enough to find a permanent, loving home where they can thrive. But others are not: they
(15) grow up in foster care or group homes.

Every year, some 26,000 young people who live in foster homes or group homes turn 18 (or in some states, 21) and "age out" of the system. Overnight, crucial support vanishes.
(20) Gone is the financial support paid to their foster parents or group homes on their behalf. Gone is any consistent, responsible adult presence or guidance. Gone is their health care coverage.

(25) These youth face incredibly long odds if they have to try [to] succeed on their own during their late teens and early 20s. The label "former foster youth" makes it hard for them to get jobs or rent apartments. For them, there is
(30) a high risk of becoming homeless. We know these young people have a low rate of college entry, and even if they are admitted to college, many do not complete a degree.

It is both compassionate and less
(35) expensive for taxpayers to ensure that young adults who grew up in foster care have some basic support during this crucial formative period. One key to this support is health care coverage.

From "The Affordable Care Act: Good News for Former Foster Youth" by Michael S. Piraino, CEO, National Court Appointed Special Advocate Association (CASA for Children)

2 Why does the author pose the question "Why does this matter?"
- **A** to introduce supporting evidence and reasons
- **B** to express frustration with opposing viewpoints
- **C** to invite readers to draw their own conclusions
- **D** to create a sense of tension in the passage

3 Which statement best expresses the author's main claim?
- **A** Society is responsible for supporting former foster youth.
- **B** Foster youth face problems when trying to rent apartments.
- **C** Extending Medicaid is an important way of helping former foster youth.
- **D** Providing employment is the best solution to the problem of homelessness.

4 In paragraph 5, the author explains the challenges former foster youth face. How does this paragraph support the author's claim?
- **A** It contrasts the lives of former foster youth with the lives of those in permanent homes.
- **B** It explains why former foster youth are more likely to need health care services.
- **C** It shows how not having health insurance affects former foster youth.
- **D** It emphasizes that extending Medicaid is one way to help former foster youth.

5 The author assumes that readers will feel sympathy and compassion for former foster youth. The author appeals to these feelings by
- **A** scolding readers for not doing more to help former foster youth.
- **B** detailing the overwhelming lack of support former foster youth face.
- **C** providing facts about the expenses of taking care of former foster youth.
- **D** calculating the costs of providing Medicaid to former foster youth.

Directions: Questions 6 through 8 are based on the passage below.

WE ARE NOT YET FREE

It ought to be possible, in short, for every American to enjoy the privileges of being American without regard to his race or his color. In short, every American ought to have
(5) the right to be treated as he would wish to be treated, as one would wish his children to be treated. But this is not the case.

The Negro baby born in America today, regardless of the section of the Nation in which
(10) he is born, has about one-half as much chance of completing high school as a white baby born in the same place on the same day, one-third as much chance of completing college, one-third as much chance of becoming a
(15) professional man, twice as much chance of becoming unemployed, about one-seventh as much chance of earning $10,000 a year, a life expectancy which is 7 years shorter, and the prospects of earning only half as much.

(20) This is not a sectional issue. Difficulties over segregation and discrimination exist in every city, in every State of the Union, producing in many cities a rising tide of discontent that threatens the public safety. Nor
(25) is this a partisan issue. In a time of domestic crisis men of good will and generosity should be able to unite regardless of party or politics. This is not even a legal or legislative issue alone. It is better to settle these matters in the
(30) courts than on the streets, and new laws are needed at every level, but law alone cannot make men see right. ...

One hundred years of delay have passed since President Lincoln freed the slaves, yet
(35) their heirs, their grandsons, are not fully free. They are not yet freed from the bonds of injustice. They are not yet freed from social and economic oppression. And this Nation, for all its hopes and all its boasts, will not be fully
(40) free until all its citizens are free.

From ADDRESS ON CIVIL RIGHTS by John F. Kennedy, 1963

6 Which statement in the passage is a claim in the argument?

A "It ought to be possible, in short, for every American to enjoy the privileges of being American without regard to his race or his color."

B "The Negro baby born in America today . . . has about one-half as much chance of completing high school as a white baby . . . ."

C "The Negro baby born in America today . . . [has] twice as much chance of becoming unemployed . . . ."

D "One hundred years of delay have passed since President Lincoln freed the slaves, yet their heirs, their grandsons, are not fully free."

7 Which statement in the passage is evidence in the argument?

A "It ought to be possible, in short, for every American to enjoy the privileges of being American without regard to his race or his color."

B "Difficulties over segregation and discrimination exist in every city, in every State of the Union."

C "In a time of domestic crisis men of good will and generosity should be able to unite regardless of party or politics."

D "And this Nation, for all its hopes and all its boasts, will not be fully free until all its citizens are free."

8 Which statement in the passage is a conclusion in the argument?

A "It ought to be possible, in short, for every American to enjoy the privileges of being American without regard to his race or his color."

B "The Negro baby born in America today . . . has about one-half as much chance of completing high school as a white baby. ..."

C "It is better to settle these matters in the courts than on the streets, and new laws are needed at every level. ..."

D "One hundred years of delay have passed since President Lincoln freed the slaves, yet their heirs, their grandsons, are not fully free."

Directions: Questions 9 through 12 are based on the excerpt below.

VIOLENCE ON TV AND IN VIDEO GAMES

It has long been asserted that watching crime on television or playing violent video games contributes to violent behavior. In other words, it is what a person watches
(5) that allegedly influences and desensitizes him. Thus he becomes violent. Consider the absurdity of such a thesis!

1. People who are fascinated and excited by violence and other crimes gravitate to
(10) particular types of programs and games and immerse themselves in them, some for hours each day. Their absorption with violence reflects their personality.

2. Millions of people view violence in
(15) television programming. ... It is entertainment or news. That's it! The viewers do not consider for a moment enacting what they see. The same is true with playing video games. They are solely for recreation.

(20) 3. There is such a thing as a "copycat" crime. A person watches a crime enacted in detail on television and then does the same thing. His decision to do so reflects a mind that has long been fascinated and excited by crime
(25) and violence. For every person who might fantasize about, then replicate, the crime, millions of people who saw the very same thing reject it, are repulsed by it, and never would be tempted to enact what they watched.

(30) Critical is not what is on the screen or in the game but what already resides in the mind of the viewer, reader, game player, or listener. A "not guilty by reason of television" defense failed many years ago in a Florida
(35) courtroom. Violent tendencies reside within the personality, whether or not the person watches programming depicting violence.

From INSIDE THE CRIMINAL MIND by Stanton E. Samenow, © 2004

9 Which statement best describes the overall structure of the passage?
- A A series of true stories supports the claim that violence in the media leads to violent behavior.
- B The author provides a series of steps that he believes can reduce violence in the media.
- C Evidence builds to the conclusion that violent personalities are not caused by violent media.
- D The author compares and contrasts different arguments about violence in the media.

10 How does the author counter the claim that a violent person may play violent video games for hours at a time? The author believes that
- A the violence in video games appeals to the person.
- B video games have caused the person to be violent.
- C video games and a violent personality are not connected.
- D playing violent video games keeps the person from acting violently.

11 How does the author counter the claim that some people copy crimes that they see on television?
- A He argues that some crimes are too violent to show on television.
- B He presents statistics to show that such copycat crimes are few.
- C He suggests that people who copy crimes were likely themselves victims of crimes.
- D He states that people who copy the crimes are already violent.

12 What assumption does the author make in presenting evidence to support his main claim?
- A Readers will have little experience of violent media themselves.
- B Readers will be in favor of reducing the amount of violence in media.
- C Readers will disagree with the verdict in the Florida criminal case.
- D Readers will consider his background as part of the supporting evidence.

Directions: Questions 13 through 16 are based on the passage below.

THE SUPREME COURT RULES ON THE AFFORDABLE CARE ACT

In 2012, the United States Supreme Court issued a ruling on the Patient Protection and Affordable Care Act. After the passage of the Affordable Care Act, as it is commonly called, (5) several states sued the federal government. They argued that the individual mandate was beyond the scope of Congress's power. The "individual mandate," or the requirement that most Americans buy health insurance or pay a (10) fine if they do not, is an important part of the act. The government argued that Congress passed the act under the powers granted to it by the Commerce Clause of the U.S. Constitution. This part of the Constitution states that Congress has (15) the power to regulate interstate commerce, or business that crosses state boundaries.

Although the court finally upheld the individual mandate, Chief Justice John Roberts did find that passage of the individual mandate (20) was unconstitutional. In the majority opinion [the document stating the court's ruling], Justice Roberts argued that Congress acted beyond the powers granted to it by the Commerce Clause.

In evaluating whether the individual mandate (25) is constitutional, Justice Roberts found that the individual mandate does not regulate commerce that already exists. Instead, it compels, or forces, people into commerce by making them buy a product. Roberts noted that no historical (30) precedents, or examples, exist of Congress's acting to compel people into commerce. He also noted that the language of the Constitution, which states that Congress may "regulate Commerce," assumes that the commerce (35) already exists. The individual mandate would bring new people into the market; consequently, it would not be regulating commerce that already exists, but creating commerce.

Therefore, Roberts determined that the act (40) reached beyond the scope of the power described in the Constitution. He wrote that understanding the Commerce Clause "to permit Congress to regulate individuals precisely because they are doing nothing would open a new and potentially (45) vast domain to congressional authority."

<small>Adapted from the United States Supreme Court's ruling on the AFFORDABLE CARE ACT, 2012</small>

13 How does paragraph 1 relate to the rest of the passage?
  A It explains the government's claim, which is supported by the rest of the passage.
  B It provides background information to help readers understand Roberts's argument.
  C It gives evidence to support Roberts's claim at the end of the passage.
  D It states the viewpoint of those opposed to the act, which the rest of the passage counters.

14 Which transition word in paragraph 3 indicates a result?
  A whether   C also
  B instead   D consequently

15 How does the word *therefore* in paragraph 4 emphasize Roberts's purpose?
  A It connects Roberts's understanding of the Commerce Clause to his decision.
  B It indicates why the government believed the act was constitutional under the Commerce Clause.
  C It indicates how the individual mandate results in business that crosses state boundaries.
  D It connects states' reasons for suing with the requirements of the individual mandate.

16 Which statement best summarizes the steps in Roberts's argument?
  A The Commerce Clause grants Congress certain powers. Congress passed the act under the Commerce Clause. The act is constitutional.
  B The Supreme Court decides whether acts are constitutional. The individual mandate is part of an act. The Supreme Court can decide whether it is constitutional.
  C The individual mandate creates commerce. The Commerce Clause allows Congress to regulate only existing commerce. The individual mandate is unconstitutional.
  D Congress cannot pass acts that affect only one state. The Affordable Care Act crosses state boundaries. Congress can pass the act.

LESSON 12

Identify Evidence

1 Learn the Skill

Claims are supported by **evidence**—reasons and information that show why readers should believe or agree with the claim. Claims are usually **opinions**, or judgments. Opinions cannot be proven, but they can be supported by strong, convincing evidence. **Facts**, on the other hand, can be proven true or untrue. Authors often use facts, as well as other evidence, to support their claims.

Writers may use appeals to **logic** (reason), appeals to **emotion** (feelings), and appeals to **ethics** (credibilty) to persuade readers.

2 Practice the Skill

By refining the skill of identifying evidence, you will improve your study and test-taking abilities, especially as they relate to the reading tests for high school equivalency. Read the passage and strategies below.

PROTECTING BUTTERFLY HABITATS

A The first paragraph contains facts. Details about how many butterflies travel and how many miles can all be proved correct or incorrect.

B The author uses strong words like **imperil** and describes the migration as **phenomenal**. These words appeal to readers' emotions.

Every fall, tens of millions of monarch butterflies ... travel up to 3,000 miles in their migration—monarchs east of the Rocky Mountains make their way to central Mexico and those west of the Rockies fly to the California coast. ...

(5) Monarchs must reach their destination before it gets too cold or else they risk death. But cold weather is far from their greatest threat. Habitat destruction and harm to their food sources imperil this phenomenal migration.

Much of their spring and summer habitat in the U.S. has been
(10) ruined by new roads, housing developments, and expanding agriculture. Monarch larvae's only food source—milkweed—has been destroyed by people who consider it a harmful weed. Pesticides and herbicides threaten milkweed, nectaring plants on which the adults feed, and the monarchs themselves.

From the nationalzoo.si.edu article MONARCH BUTTERFLY MIGRATION UNDERWAY, accessed 2013

USING LOGIC

Appeals to emotion can be an important part of persuasion. However, if an author uses only emotional appeals and no facts to support a claim, think carefully about whether the claim is valid or well supported.

1 In stating the claim, the author uses words such as *greatest threat* and *imperil* to
   A show readers that he or she is a credible source.
   B mislead readers about the challenges butterflies face.
   C emphasize how far butterflies travel on their migrations.
   D make the dangers butterflies face seem real and urgent.

Unit 1 | Non-Fiction

57

Apply the Skill

Directions: Questions 2 through 5 are based on the passage below.

In 1946, J. A. Krug, Secretary of the Interior, wrote a letter to the Speaker of the House of Representatives asking him to support legislation that would make it easier for Japanese Americans to receive payment for losses they suffered as a result of movement, or "evacuation," to camps during World War II. Part of this letter is paraphrased below.

COMPENSATING JAPANESE AMERICAN EVACUEES

In 1942, the War Department ordered that all Japanese Americans be removed from the Pacific Coast of the United States. For approximately two and a half years, more than
(5) 100,000 of these American citizens and their alien parents could not return to their homes. In January of 1945, they were allowed to return to their homes to try to resume their lives. It is too early to establish the total financial and
(10) property losses the Japanese Americans experienced, but the losses are undoubtedly heavy. Some lost everything they had. Many lost most of what they had.

None of these Japanese American
(15) evacuees was charged with any crime. Experience has shown that most of them were and are good Americans. The 23,000 Japanese Americans who served in the armed forces in both Europe and the Pacific have an
(20) outstanding record. The intelligence agencies have uncovered no instances of sabotage or espionage by Americans of Japanese ancestry during the war.

The evacuation orders left people with very
(25) little time to get their affairs in order. Merchants had to sell their stocks and businesses at sacrifice prices. Many evacuees sold personal possessions for a fraction of their value. A large number of people had to accept
(30) inadequate arrangements for the protection of their property. Some property was abandoned.

These losses are the direct result of the evacuation. Now, for the first time in the history of our nation, Japanese Americans are asking
(35) for public assistance in substantial numbers. The least that this country can do, in simple justice, is offer some degree of compensation for the incredible losses the evacuees have suffered.

2 Which fact supports the author's claim that Japanese Americans were evacuated without cause?
  A More than 100,000 Japanese Americans were not allowed to return to their homes.
  B The intelligence agencies uncovered no espionage by Japanese Americans.
  C Merchants had to sell their stocks and businesses at sacrifice prices.
  D Japanese Americans are asking for public assistance in substantial numbers.

3 In paragraph 2, why does the author discuss the service record of Japanese Americans during the war?
  A to suggest that evacuees made greater sacrifices than other Americans
  B to express appreciation for what members of the Armed Forces had done
  C to explain why so few men were among the evacuees
  D to show that Japanese Americans were patriotic and brave

4 Which statement best summarizes the evidence presented in paragraph 3?
  A The haste of the evacuation resulted in financial losses for Japanese Americans.
  B More planning could have helped the evacuation run more smoothly.
  C Japanese Americans had to leave their property with people they did not trust.
  D Japanese Americans had trouble determining the value of their possessions.

5 Which statement best explains the way in which the author uses evidence in this passage?
  A He relies on his position as Secretary of the Interior to persuade readers.
  B He states a claim and uses statistics and personal stories to show that it is valid.
  C He builds to a claim by presenting facts as logical evidence.
  D He uses emotional language to make readers feel sympathy for Japanese Americans.

Directions: Questions 6 through 8 are based on the excerpt below.

ABOLISHING THE ELECTORAL COLLEGE

I am pleased to be here today to express the League's [League of Women Voters] support for a constitutional amendment to abolish the electoral college. ...
(5) The electoral college system is fundamentally unfair to voters. In a nation where voting rights are grounded in the one person, one vote principle, the electoral college is a hopeless anachronism.
(10) The current system is unfair for two reasons.
First, a citizen's individual vote has more weight if he or she lives in a state with a small population than if that citizen lives in a state
(15) with a large population.
For example, each electoral vote in Alaska is equivalent to approximately 112,000 people. Each electoral vote in New York is equivalent to approximately 404,000 eligible people
(20) (based on 1990 census data). And that's if everyone votes!
The system is also unfair because a citizen's individual vote has more weight if the percentage of voter participation in the state
(25) is low. For example, if only half of all people in Alaska vote, then each electoral vote is equivalent to roughly 56,000 people.
Moreover, the electoral vote does not reflect the volume of voter participation within a
(30) state. If only a few voters go to the polls, all the electoral votes of the state are still cast.
Finally, the electoral college system is flawed because the constitution does not bind presidential electors to vote for the candidates
(35) to whom they have been pledged. For example, in 1948, 1960 and 1976, individual electors pledged to the top two vote getters cast their votes for third place finishers and also-rans. Defecting electors in a close race
(40) could cause a crisis of confidence in our electoral system.

From TESTIMONY BEFORE THE U.S. HOUSE SUBCOMMITTEE ON THE CONSTITUTION: PROPOSALS FOR ELECTORAL COLLEGE REFORM by Becky Cain, 1997

6. Which of these excerpts from the passage presents details that the speaker used to appeal to logic?
   A "I am pleased to be here today to express the League's [League of Women Voters] support for a constitutional amendment to abolish the electoral college."
   B "In a nation where voting rights are grounded in the one person, one vote principle, the electoral college is a hopeless anachronism [something outdated]."
   C "Each electoral vote in Alaska is equivalent to approximately 112,000 people. Each electoral vote in New York is equivalent to approximately 404,000 eligible people."
   D "Defecting electors in a close race could cause a crisis of confidence in our electoral system."

7. Which of these is a detail that the speaker used to appeal to emotion?
   A "First, a citizen's individual vote has more weight if he or she lives in a state with a small population than if that citizen lives in a state with a large population."
   B "For example, if only half of all people in Alaska vote, then each electoral vote is equivalent to roughly 56,000 people."
   C "Moreover, the electoral vote does not reflect the volume of voter participation within a state. If only a few voters go to the polls, all the electoral votes of the state are still cast."
   D "Defecting electors in a close race could cause a crisis of confidence in our electoral system."

8. Which of these details appeals to ethics?
   A "I am pleased to be here today to express the League's [League of Women Voters] support for a constitutional amendment to abolish the electoral college."
   B "For example, if only half of all people in Alaska vote, then each electoral vote is equivalent to roughly 56,000 people."
   C "For example, in 1948, 1960 and 1976, individual electors pledged to the top two vote getters cast their votes for third place finishers and also-rans."
   D "Finally, the electoral college system is flawed because the constitution does not bind presidential electors to vote for the candidates to whom they have been pledged."

Directions: Questions 9 through 12 are based on the passage below.

THE MOON IS AN INSPIRING GOAL

The inspiration provided by the goal of sending humans to the moon is credited for laying the groundwork for, and making widely available, a host of technologies that society
(5) depends on today.

As an example, [Steven Dick, NASA's chief historian] points to the integrated circuit, commonly referred to as a computer chip. The Apollo Guidance Computer, used for the Apollo
(10) program, was the largest single consumer of integrated circuits between 1961 and 1965.

"NASA did not invent the integrated circuit, but a good case could be made that it played a major role in making the integrated circuit
(15) commercially viable," he said.

In addition to encouraging the push toward the development of the personal computer, [Jeffrey Bennett, a noted astronomy teacher and writer] also credits the Apollo program for
(20) sowing the seeds of the Internet.

"I wouldn't attribute the technological advances solely to Apollo, but I do think that the inspiration of 'we're going to the moon' made things happen much more quickly than they
(25) would have happened otherwise," Bennett said.

Once on the moon, [astronauts Neil Armstrong and Edwin "Buzz" Aldrin] spent about two and a half hours exploring the surface. They collected 47 pounds (21
(30) kilograms) of surface material to be returned to Earth for analysis.

Over the next several years, space scientists continued to visit and study the moon, learning about its composition, age, and rocks
(35) and about the similarities between the moon and Earth. Extensive testing found no evidence for life, past or present, on the moon. …

"The moon program was a race, and when we won that race, interest dwindled from the
(40) political point of view," Dick said. "But not from the scientific point of view. Scientists remained eager to learn even more."

From nationalgeographic.com article APOLLO ANNIVERSARY: MOON LANDING "INSPIRED WORLD," by John Roach, © 2004 accessed 2013

9 How does the author appeal to ethics to support the claim that the goal of sending people to the moon inspired new technology?
   A He quotes people with in-depth knowledge about the space program.
   B He describes inventions that came about because of the space program.
   C He provides a detailed account of astronauts' activities during the moon landing.
   D He uses strong language to emphasize the importance of the moon landing.

10 How is the example in paragraph 2 related to the claim made in paragraph 1?
   A It restates the claim.
   B It supports the claim.
   C It counters the claim.
   D It broadens the claim.

11 Which statement from the passage is an opinion?
   A "The Apollo Guidance Computer, used for the Apollo program, was the largest single consumer of integrated circuits between 1961 and 1965."
   B "I wouldn't attribute the technological advances solely to Apollo …"
   C "They collected 47 pounds (21 kilograms) of surface material to be returned to Earth for analysis."
   D "Over the next several years, space scientists continued to visit and study the moon …"

12 Which implicit claim does the evidence in this passage support?
   A Politicians can get in the way of technological advancements and scientific discovery.
   B Without an inspiring goal, the United States will lose the technology race.
   C The government should offer greater financial support to the space program.
   D Investment in scientific projects can bring unexpected and far-reaching benefits.

Directions: Questions 13 through 16 are based on the passage below.

PRESERVING OUR PRAIRIES

Native prairie once stretched for hundreds of miles across the middle section of our country, covering nearly a quarter of the lower 48 states. Prairie supported an enormous variety of plant
(5) and animal life, including large herds of bison, pronghorn, elk, plains grizzlies, and wolves. The wild prairie inhabitants thrived with wildfires, grazing, drought, heat and cold. …

Prairie is now considered one of our most
(10) imperiled habitats worldwide. In North Dakota, approximately 80% of our prairie is gone, with most remaining areas found in the arid west. In the Red River Valley, over 95% of our prairie is gone. With this loss, prairie plant and animal
(15) populations have also declined, with some species now becoming rare.

Many prairie birds currently show population declines; the western prairie fringed orchid is now a rare flower of the tallgrass
(20) prairie; and the Dakota skipper butterfly is another prairie inhabitant whose numbers are decreasing. Each of these declines is believed to be directly related to the loss of prairie.

Prairie provides important values to
(25) people. It contains dozens of animals, hundreds of different plants, and thousands of insects. These species provide genetic diversity important to agriculture and medicine. Planted grasslands do not begin to match the
(30) diversity found in native prairie.

In addition to its importance to wildlife, prairie is also crucial for soil and water conservation. Prairie provides a reminder of our rural and pioneer heritage; it provides
(35) recreational activities such as hunting, hiking, and birdwatching; and it offers living laboratories for scientific research. Prairie also provides economic benefits through cattle grazing, haying, and native seed harvesting.
(40) When we lose prairie, we lose part of our natural heritage, and we lose a valuable resource.

From the npwrc.usgs.gov article NORTH DAKOTA PRAIRIE: OUR NATURAL HERITAGE, accessed 2013

---

13 Which implicit claim does the evidence in this passage support?
- A Park rangers should use controlled fires to keep prairie habitats healthy.
- B Prairie is one of the most endangered habitats in the world.
- C Certain animal species are declining because of lost prairie habitats.
- D Prairies are important habitats that people should conserve.

14 What evidence best supports the opinion that prairie provides important values to people?
- A The prairie is a site for recreation and offers scientists living laboratories.
- B Prairie once supported an enormous variety of plant and animal life.
- C Most remaining prairie is found in North Dakota's arid west.
- D The western prairie fringed orchid and Dakota skipper butterfly are prairie inhabitants.

15 In paragraph 2, the author states that 80% of North Dakota's prairie is gone, and 90% of the prairie is gone in the Red River Valley. Which statement best describes this type of evidence?
- A an appeal to reason by providing data
- B an appeal to the emotion of patriotism
- C a strong opinion supported by facts
- D an appeal to ethics by naming the source of the data

16 Which claim lacks supporting evidence in the passage?
- A There are environmental, scientific, and economic reasons to protect the prairie.
- B Planted grasslands cannot replace prairies as habitats for prairie plant and animals species.
- C Efforts to conserve prairies are expensive and may not be successful.
- D Americans did not take appropriate steps to protect prairies in the past.

LESSON 13

Determine Point of View

1 Learn the Skill

Non-fiction texts are written with different **points of view**—the perspectives and purposes with which the author writes the piece. A reader can determine an author's point of view based on clues from the text, such as details that point out what the author likes or dislikes, the vocabulary and adjectives used to describe certain situations, even the author's interests or background.

2 Practice the Skill

By mastering how to determine an author's point of view, you will improve your study and test-taking skills, especially as they relate to high school equivalency language arts/reading tests. Read the excerpt and strategies below.

A The byline tells you that this piece comes from a newspaper editorial. This tells us that the author is basing this piece on his or her own point of view.

B Words that have positive or negative descriptions may help indicate the author's point of view.

WHAT PROBLEM IS THE AUTHOR ADDRESSING?

The need for a criminal inquiry into the Crandall Canyon mine disaster is shockingly clear now that investigators have detailed how greedy mine operators **B** concealed danger warnings and literally chiseled
(5) underground pillar supports to the breaking point. The roof of the Utah mine collapsed last summer, killing six miners and leading three would-be rescuers to their deaths.

A From New York Times' editorial GREED ABOVE, DEATH BELOW, © 2008

✓ TEST-TAKING TIPS

Some questions might ask you to consider an author's purpose in writing. The author's point of view is often related to his or her purpose for writing. For instance, an editorial piece is usually written because the author sees some sort of problem and wants to address it.

1. Which of the following best describes the author's point of view?
   A the dead miners should have been more careful
   B mine operators are not to be trusted
   C people should not work in mines
   D the practices of mine operators need to be changed

Apply the Skill

Directions: Questions 2 through 4 are based on the excerpt below.

WHY DOES THE AUTHOR THINK THAT PARKS NEED HELP?

One piece of legislation that deserves a serious push is the National Park Service Centennial Initiative. A brainchild of Dirk Kempthorne, the Interior secretary, the
(5) initiative would use the years leading up to the park system's 100th birthday in 2016 to raise $1 billion in private money and match that with $1 billion in federal money—above and beyond normal appropriations—to rejuvenate
(10) the national parks.

As recent visitors can attest, the parks need all the help they can get. Stingy budget appropriations and decades of deferred maintenance have taken a toll on everything
(15) from park roads to day-to-day operations. In his brief tenure, Mr. Kempthorne has done several good things for the parks—including killing a potentially harmful rewrite of the service's management policies that would
(20) have promoted inappropriate commercial and recreational activities at the expense of conservation. He wants now to provide a special revenue stream by using the promise of a federal match to entice private donors to help
(25) underwrite vital projects.

The idea was so appealing that the House Natural Resources Committee approved it by a voice vote. It has languished ever since, …

The solution seems ridiculously obvious.
(30) The budget office should find the offsets (an increase in park concession fees would do the trick), and the Democratic leadership should schedule a vote. We predict that the verdict would be overwhelmingly positive, and the
(35) Senate would follow suit. The parks and their millions of visitors would be the winners, and Congress could show that it can get things done—even in an election year.

From New York Times' editorial HELP THE PARKS, © 2008

2 Based on the excerpt, which of the following best describes how the author feels the legislature should proceed? The author feels the legislature should
   A continue focusing on the election year.
   B withhold voting on the park initiative until after the election.
   C find the money to back the National Park Service Centennial Initiative.
   D hold another committee meeting and vote again on the issue.

3 Which of the following expresses the author's overall point of view?
   A Representatives are doing all they can to help the National Park Service.
   B The National Park Service Centennial Initiative deserves positive attention.
   C The National Park Service needs to rewrite management policies.
   D The National Park Service has an above average budget that should be maintained.

4 Based on the excerpt, with which of the following statements would the author most likely agree?
   A The National Parks Service needs more support from the federal government.
   B The federal government works quickly to help the programs it oversees.
   C The Democratic leadership should not vote on the proposed bill.
   D National parks should rely on visitors to get the funding for their upkeep.

Directions: Questions 5 and 6 are based on the following passage.

WHAT IS THE AUTHOR'S PURPOSE IN WRITING THIS PIECE?

The pace of recovery is slowing in New Orleans as the city approaches the third anniversary of Hurricane Katrina late this month. The next president and Congress will
(5) need to expedite assistance before the city's mood turns from guarded optimism back to despair.

With a mélange [mixture] of federal, state, city and private recovery efforts under way, it is
(10) difficult to grasp what is really happening in the stricken city. Fortunately, two reports on New Orleans's condition have just been issued by authoritative outside organizations.

The Henry J. Kaiser Family Foundation
(15) released its second survey of the attitudes and experiences of the city's residents. The good news is that 6 in 10 Katrina survivors say that their lives are almost or largely back to normal, and most see recovery moving
(20) in the right direction. The bad news is that 4 in 10 respondents say their lives are still disrupted, and more than 7 in 10 see little or no progress in making housing affordable or in controlling crime, which they view as the city's
(25) top problem. Smaller majorities see little or no progress in making medical services available, strengthening public schools, attracting jobs or rebuilding neighborhoods.

These perceptions are largely consistent
(30) with an index of progress compiled by the Brookings Institution and the Greater New Orleans Community Data Center. Their third-year report finds that the greater New Orleans area has recovered the vast majority of its pre-
(35) Katrina population and jobs but that recovery trends have slowed in the past year. Tens of thousands of blighted properties, a lack of affordable housing and thin public services continue to plague the city. Rents are 46
(40) percent higher than before the storm.

New Orleans residents expressed mixed attitudes about their prospects. Three-fourths told Kaiser that they remained optimistic about the future even though most felt that both
(45) Washington and the American public have largely forgotten them. What is worrisome is that half of the residents are dissatisfied with or angry about the lack of progress, most think it is a bad time for children to grow up in New
(50) Orleans and 22 percent (predominantly young) are seriously considering moving away.

Unless government agencies and private organizations pick up the pace of recovery efforts, New Orleans may see its future pack
(55) up and go with them.

From the New York Times' editorial THREE YEARS AFTER KATRINA, © 2008

5 What is the general point of view of New Orleans' residents regarding the city's recovery after Katrina?
  A Recovery is moving in the proper direction.
  B The city has completely recovered.
  C Recovery has not began at all.
  D Recovery is moving in the right direction at an increasing rate.

6 What is the point of view of smaller majorities in New Orleans (line 25–29)? Smaller majorities feel
  A a great deal of progress has been made throughout the entire city.
  B progress has been made, but there is use for more.
  C little to no progress has been made, especially when looking at medical services and rebuilding neighborhoods.
  D mediocre progress has been made, but things are going in the right direction.

Directions: Questions 7 through 9 are based on the following passage.

WHY DOES THE AUTHOR FOCUS ON A PROPOSAL FROM THE BOARD OF REGENTS?

Thousands of students rejected by American medical schools are attending second-rate schools abroad and then returning for further clinical training and eventually a
(5) license to practice medicine in the United States. The situation has stirred bitter controversy. Parents of the overseas students are pressing to facilitate their return while American medical schools are resisting.
(10) Now the battle is joined in New York State. The Board of Regents recently proposed to rate some of the foreign schools and to admit some of their students for clinical training (the third and fourth years of medical school) in
(15) New York teaching hospitals. The Association of American Medical Colleges protests that this would produce inferior physicians. So far, neither side has a fully persuasive case.

Medical educators make some telling
(20) points against the Regents' plan. The foreign schools probably cannot be rated reliably by questionnaire, as is planned in most cases. And a flood of students with mediocre preparation could well lower the quality of care
(25) given patients in teaching hospitals. Moreover, since slots for students in the best hospitals are oversubscribed, the returning students would be apt to wind up in hospitals with weak teaching programs and supervision.
(30) Worse yet, once New York welcomes back these students, it would only encourage more aspiring physicians to enroll for questionable two-year training periods abroad. Some 10,000 to 11,000 American students already attend
(35) foreign medical schools, mostly in Mexico, the Caribbean and Europe. Now that American medical schools and Federal authorities feel that the country is already producing enough doctors, why should the applicants that those
(40) schools rejected be encouraged to enter the profession by the back door?

From the New York Times' editorial BACK DOOR PHYSICIANS, © 1981

7 In the first paragraph, what is the author's point of view about overseas medical schools? The author thinks overseas medical schools
  A are not as qualified as medical schools in the United States.
  B train their students as well as medical schools in the United States.
  C have an edge over medical schools in the United States.
  D are just slightly below the training received at medical schools in the United States.

8 Which best describes the author's viewpoint regarding the Board of Regents proposal?
  A The proposal is solid.
  B The proposal will benefit students receiving overseas medical education.
  C The proposal offers a good compromise.
  D The proposal has several flaws, as pointed out by the Association of Medical Colleges.

9 The editorial suggests the Regents proposal would only encourage aspiring physicians to enroll in "questionable" two-year programs (lines 32–33). What might the author say these physicians would be most like?
  A law students seeking their degrees from Ivy League schools
  B pilots being trained by the Air Force
  C chefs being taught by amateur cooks
  D writers publishing books with good editors

Directions: Questions 10 through 12 are based on the following passage.

HOW DOES THE AUTHOR USE INFORMATION TO INDICATE HIS OR HER POINT OF VIEW?

A federal judge in Missoula, Mont., has given Rocky Mountain gray wolves a well-deserved reprieve. In February, the federal Fish and Wildlife Service had effectively
(5) sentenced hundreds of wolves to death by lifting the protections provided by the Endangered Species Act. Since then, because of far weaker state protections in Wyoming, Montana and Idaho, more than 100 wolves out
(10) of a total population of 1,500 have been killed. As many as 500 more were doomed to die in state-authorized hunts this fall.

Judge Donald Molloy issued a preliminary injunction last week restoring federal
(15) protections. That ends the slaughter, at least for now. And while the case is far from settled, the dozen conservation groups that brought the suit are hopeful that his injunction will survive further court tests and that the Fish
(20) and Wildlife Service will be forced to provide a better plan to protect the wolves.

The centerpiece of Judge Molloy's decision was his finding that the Fish and Wildlife Service had failed to meet its own criteria
(25) for removing the wolf from the endangered species list. Before stripping the wolves of federal protection, the agency was required to show that wolf subpopulations across the area were interbreeding—a genetic necessity for
(30) healthy, sustainable numbers. The judge found that the agency had offered no such evidence.

Judge Molloy also found that this fall's hunts could irreparably damage the species. He seemed particularly annoyed at the
(35) agency's failure to explain why it had "flip-flopped" on Wyoming's plan, which allows unregulated hunting on most state lands. The agency had previously rejected it as insufficiently protective....

(40) This deep-set hostility has only a little to do with ranching. It is really driven by the competition between human hunters and wolves for the same game animals: elk and deer. And underneath it all is a false myth—
(45) the wolf as a kind of ferocious coward and an indiscriminate killer—that says less about the true nature of wolves than it does about human fear.

From the New York Times' editorial A STAY OF EXECUTION FOR THE WOLVES, © 2008

10 What does the author imply in the first three paragraphs? The author implies he or she
  A has not done a lot of research on the topic.
  B does not favor the judge's opinions.
  C has researched the topic and is trying to present information mixed with opinion.
  D has a bias toward human hunters.

11 In paragraph four, the author alludes to the judge's point of view. How does the author describe the judge's point of view?
  A pleased with the Fish and Wildlife service
  B irritated with the Fish and Wildlife service
  C indifferent toward the entire case
  D bored with the entire case

12 How is the author's point of view on the topic best described?
  A The author is writing on the topic to provide information only.
  B The author is not in favor of postponing the wolf hunts.
  C The author agrees with the states of Wyoming, Montana, and Idaho regarding the disposal of wolves.
  D The author disagrees with the states about wolf hunting and believes the animals should be left alone.

LESSON 14
Style and Tone

① Learn the Skill

Authors have specific writing **styles**, made up of the ways in which they use words to communicate thoughts or ideas. A style is sometimes determined by the type of writing. For example, a non-fiction style would be very different from a fiction or poetry style. Style can also affect an author's **tone**, which shows how the author feels about the topic. Tone is revealed through the author's choice of words.

② Practice the Skill

By mastering how to identify style and tone, you will improve your study and test-taking skills, especially as they relate to high school equivalency language arts/reading tests. Read the excerpt and strategies below.

A This author uses repetition as a style to emphasize the points that follow the repeated words.

B The author's tone describes the Democratic Party as one to which people can turn for change.

HOW DOES THE AUTHOR FEEL ABOUT THE DEMOCRATIC PARTY?

Throughout–Throughout our history, when people have looked for new ways to solve their problems and to uphold the principles of this nation, many times they have turned to political parties. They have often turned
(5) to the Democratic Party. What is it? What is it about the Democratic Party that makes it the instrument the people use when they search for ways to shape their future? Well I believe the answer to that question lies in our concept of governing. Our concept of governing is derived from our
(10) view of people. It is a concept deeply rooted in a set of beliefs firmly etched in the national conscience of all of us.

From Barbara Jordan's 1976 DEMOCRATIC NATIONAL CONVENTION KEYNOTE ADDRESS, © 1976

USING LOGIC

When you read an excerpt, identify the emotions that the words might evoke. In doing so, you can often determine the tone of the piece: happy, pessimistic, sorrowful, etc. This will help you determine the author's message.

1 Which of the following best describes the tone of this excerpt?
   A depressed
   B encouraging
   C sarcastic
   D condescending

③ Apply the Skill

Directions: Questions 2 through 5 are based on the speech below.

WHAT MESSAGE IS THE SPEAKER CONVEYING?

But I have an uncomfortable feeling that this prosperity isn't something on which we can base our hopes for the future. No nation in history has ever survived a tax burden that
(5) reached a third of its national income. Today, 37 cents out of every dollar earned in this country is the tax collector's share, and yet our government continues to spend 17 million dollars a day more than the government takes
(10) in. We haven't balanced our budget 28 out of the last 34 years. We've raised our debt limit three times in the last twelve months, and now our national debt is one and a half times bigger than all the combined debts of all the nations of
(15) the world. We have 15 billion dollars in gold in our treasury; we don't own an ounce. Foreign dollar claims are 27.3 billion dollars. And we've just had announced that the dollar of 1939 will now purchase 45 cents in its total value.
(20) As for the peace that we would preserve, I wonder who among us would like to approach the wife or mother whose husband or son has died in South Vietnam and ask them if they think this is a peace that should be maintained
(25) indefinitely. Do they mean peace, or do they mean we just want to be left in peace? There can be no real peace while one American is dying some place in the world for the rest of us. We're at war with the most dangerous
(30) enemy that has ever faced mankind in his long climb from the swamp to the stars, and it's been said if we lose that war, and in so doing lose this way of freedom of ours, history will record with the greatest astonishment that
(35) those who had the most to lose did the least to prevent its happening. Well I think it's time we ask ourselves if we still know the freedoms that were intended for us by the Founding Fathers.

From Ronald Reagan's A TIME FOR CHOOSING, © 1964

2 What word best describes the tone of the first paragraph?
  A flamboyant
  B matter-of-fact
  C sad
  D opinionated

3 What might be the author's intention in writing the first paragraph?
  A to congratulate the government on its budget
  B to ask people for money
  C to explain his uncomfortable feeling
  D to point out the budgetary problems

4 Which line best indicates that the tone of the second paragraph is one of action?
  A "There can be no real peace while one American is dying some place in the world for the rest of us." (lines 26–29)
  B "I wonder who among us would like to approach the wife or mother whose husband or son has died in South Vietnam." (lines 20–23)
  C "Well I think it's time we ask ourselves if we still know the freedoms that were intended for us by our Founding Fathers." (lines 36–38)
  D "Do they mean peace, or do they mean we just want to be left in peace?" (lines 25–26)

5 Which of the following best describes the author's style?
  A informative
  B ambiguous
  C peaceful
  D unpatriotic

Directions: Questions 6 through 9 are based on the excerpt below.

WHAT DOES THE AUTHOR BELIEVE IS THE PURPOSE OF THE AWARD?

No human being could fail to be deeply moved by such a tribute as this [Thayer Award]. Coming from a profession I have served so long, and a people I have loved
(5) so well, it fills me with an emotion I cannot express. But this award is not intended primarily to honor a personality, but to symbolize a great moral code—the code of conduct and chivalry of those who guard this
(10) beloved land of culture and ancient descent. That is the animation of this medallion. For all eyes and for all time, it is an expression of the ethics of the American soldier. That I should be integrated in this way with so noble an ideal
(15) arouses a sense of pride and yet of humility which will be with me always.

Duty, Honor, Country: Those three hallowed words reverently dictate what you ought to be, what you can be, what you will be.
(20) They are your rallying points: to build courage when courage seems to fail; to regain faith when there seems to be little cause for faith; to create hope when hope becomes forlorn.

Unhappily, I possess neither that
(25) eloquence of diction, that poetry of imagination, nor that brilliance of metaphor to tell you all that they mean....

But these are some of the things they do. They build your basic character. They mold
(30) you for your future roles as the custodians of the nation's defense. They make you strong enough to know when you are weak, and brave enough to face yourself when you are afraid.... They create in your heart the sense of wonder,
(35) the unfailing hope of what next, and the joy and inspiration of life. They teach you in this way to be an officer and a gentleman.

From Douglas MacArthur's DUTY, HONOR, COUNTRY, © 1962

6 How does the author regard his country?
- A in a professional manner
- B with love and respect
- C with hostility
- D without courtesy

7 How might the style of the second paragraph be described?
- A complex
- B technical
- C repetitive
- D simple

8 The author says he does not "possess... that brilliance of metaphor to tell you all that they mean" (line 24–27) when discussing the ideals behind the words *duty, honor,* and *country*. How does he describe the ideals? He describes them by speaking
- A about how they build a person's character.
- B in a reserved manner.
- C of them as though in a fantasy.
- D of them in a bold and disrespectful manner.

9 How might the tone of the passage be described?
- A grateful
- B weak
- C emotionless
- D awkward

Directions: Questions 10 and 11 are based on the following letter.

WHAT IS THE TONE OF THIS LETTER?

Harmon Lamar, President
President, Kids' Eats, Inc.
4501 N. Burnet Road
Arlen, Texas 75709

(5) Julie Harrison, Chair
Rosedale Neighborhood Association
4949 W. Sinclair

Dear Ms. Harrison,

I am writing to follow up on the surveys that you distributed through your neighborhood association
(10) regarding our new restaurant. As you know, Kids' Eats is very sensitive about renovating the beloved Garcia's Hamburgers site and wants our changes to reflect the needs and considerations of the community.

The feedback we received from the surveys has helped us reach the following decisions:

- We will make as few cosmetic changes as possible. Although we will be upgrading the building's
(15) structure to make it more energy efficient, the twirly barstools, bouncy-horse seating, and period neon signs will all remain.

- Your surveys request meals that are both healthy and kid-friendly. In response, we are developing salads and fresh vegetable combos that are appealing to both kids and adults.

- Many of your surveys requested the addition of playscape facilities. You will be pleased to know
(20) that we will develop an outdoor dining area that will be built around a playscape.

Please tell your neighborhood association members how much we appreciate their feedback, and encourage them to contact us with additional concerns or suggestions. Kids' Eats is honored to be part of the Rosedale neighborhood and its special history.

Sincerely,

(25) Harmon Lamar

---

10 Which word best describes the tone of this letter?
- A disdainful
- B respectful
- C curious
- D encouraging

11 Based on the responses from the neighborhood survey, what type of grocery store might be popular in the Rosedale area? A popular food store might be one with
- A free samples of children's snacks.
- B tables set with matching china.
- C a large section of bulk coffee and tea.
- D stations that offer sodas and salty snacks.

Directions: Questions 12 through 14 are based on the excerpt below.

WHO IS THE SPEAKER TRYING TO INSPIRE?

In this vote-harvesting time, they use terms like the "Great Society," or as we were told a few days ago by the President, we must accept a greater government activity in the affairs
(5) of the people. But they've been a little more explicit in the past and among themselves; and all of the things I now will quote have appeared in print. These are not Republican accusations. For example, they have voices
(10) that say, "The cold war will end through our acceptance of a not undemocratic socialism." Another voice says, "The profit motive has become outmoded. It must be replaced by the incentives of the welfare state." Or, "Our
(15) traditional system of individual freedom is incapable of solving the complex problems of the 20th century. Senator Fulbright has said at Stanford University that the Constitution is outmoded. He referred to the President as "our
(20) moral teacher and our leader,"; and he says he is "hobbled in his task by the restrictions of power imposed on him by this antiquated document." He must "be freed," so that he "can do for us" what he knows 'is best.' And Senator
(25) Clark of Pennsylvania, another articulate spokesman, defines liberalism as "meeting the material needs of the masses through the full power of centralized government."

Well, I, for one, resent it when a
(30) representative of the people refers to you and me, the free men and women of this country, as "the masses." This is a term we haven't applied to ourselves in America. But beyond that, "the full power of centralized
(35) government" —this was the very thing the Founding Fathers sought to minimize. They knew that governments don't control things. A government can't control the economy without controlling people. And they know when a
(40) government sets out to do that, it must use force and coercion to achieve its purpose. They also knew, those Founding Fathers, that outside of its legitimate functions, government does nothing as well or as economically as the
(45) private sector of the economy.

Now, we have no better example of this than government's involvement in the farm economy over the last 30 years. Since 1955, the cost of this program has nearly
(50) doubled. One-fourth of farming in America is responsible for 85% of the farm surplus. Three-fourths of farming is out on the free market and has known a 21% increase in the per capita consumption of all its produce. You see, that
(55) one-fourth of farming—that's regulated and controlled by the federal government.

From Ronald Reagan's A TIME FOR CHOOSING, © 1965

12 When the speaker uses the word "resent" (line 30), which feeling is he trying to evoke in his audience?
  A sadness
  B excitement
  C offense
  D thrill

13 What does the speaker hope to accomplish by referencing the "Founding Fathers" twice in the second paragraph (lines 37 and 43)?
  A to bring a spirit of history to his speech
  B to quote their words
  C to emulate their actions
  D to sway his audience

14 The speaker switches to a different topic in the third paragraph. What style does he use when discussing the farmers?
  A factual
  B urgent
  C demanding
  D conversational

LESSON 15

Generalize

① Learn the Skill

A **generalization** is a broad statement that applies to a group of people, places, and events. Authors use generalizations as a kind of style, or to make a point about a group. As a reader, understanding generalizations can help you determine an author's purpose in writing.

② Practice the Skill

By understanding generalizations, you will improve your study and test-taking skills, especially as they relate to high school equivalency language arts/reading tests. Read the excerpt and strategies below.

> **A** Generalizations sometimes contain words such as *all, everyone, few, some,* or *usually,* such as the statement about German shepherds.
>
> **B** It is important to understand a generalization that seems valid may not be so. The generalization about pit bulls is contradicted in the last sentence.

FOR WHAT REASONS ARE PIT BULLS SEEN AS DANGEROUS?

Pit bulls, descendants of the bulldogs used in the nineteenth century for bull baiting and dogfighting, have been bred for "gameness", and thus a lowered inhibition to aggression. … A pit bull is willing to fight with little or
(5) no provocation. Pit bulls seem to have a high tolerance for pain, making it possible for them to fight to the point of exhaustion. Whereas guard dogs like **A** German shepherds usually attempt to restrain those they perceive to be threats by biting and holding, pit bulls try to inflict the maximum
(10) amount of damage on an opponent. They bite, hold, shake, and tear. They don't growl or assume an aggressive facial expression as warning. They just attack. …
B Of course, not all pit bulls are dangerous. Most don't bite anyone.

From Malcolm Gladwell's ANNALS OF PUBLIC POLICY: TROUBLEMAKERS, © 2006

MAKING ASSUMPTIONS

Understanding style and tone can help you determine if generalizations are valid. A factual style will likely indicate a valid generalization, while a tone based on the author's emotions will likely indicate invalid generalizations.

1 Which generalization might be the main idea of the first paragraph?
  A All German shepherds attempt to restrain those they perceive as threats.
  B Both pit bulls and German shepherds demonstrate a great amount of aggressiveness.
  C All pit bulls are vicious fighters.
  D All pit bulls show little to no aggression.

Apply the Skill

Directions: Questions 2 through 4 are based on the pamphlet below.

WHAT SERVICES DOES THIS COMPANY OFFER?

Deep Shade Tree Company: We're there for the life of your trees.

A healthy tree is like a member of the family. They give your home personality, character, and—most important in this hot climate—they provide you with cool, money-saving shade.

(5) Deep Shade has been caring for trees for 25 years, working not only to increase their leafy beauty, but also lengthen the trees' lifespan. A certified arborist is on staff for consultations and diagnosis of tree diseases.

The services we offer include:
- Pruning. Limbs on the roofs of property damage siding and shingles. In addition, they allow entry to insects and rodents. Our pruning service can save you thousands of dollars in construction repairs
(10) by removing small problem areas before they become bigger ones.
- Removal of dead or dangerous trees. Our experienced staff can evaluate the trees to see if they pose a risk of falling.
- Tree maintenance. We offer deep fertilization, ball moss removal, and web-worm treatments. Our policy is to provide your trees with the nutrients they need to be healthy, not to provide chemical
(15) treatments that could be harmful to children or pets.

Let us keep you in the shade. Contact us for an estimate. http://www.deepshadetrees.com

---

2 What fact does the pamphlet disclose about Deep Shade Tree Company? The company
   A has been in business for 25 years.
   B refers clients to an arborist.
   C maintains trees with chemical applications.
   D repairs roof damage caused by limbs.

3 How can the company's attitude about trees be best described? Trees are
   A liable to be stricken with numerous diseases.
   B sources of beauty and comfort.
   C capable of causing extensive damage.
   D dangerous when untended.

4 The company suggests that limbs be removed from building roofs. Which policy does this suggestion most resemble?
   A treating a cold with bed rest and fluids
   B visiting the emergency room with a broken bone
   C taking a flu vaccination each winter
   D using physical therapy to strengthen a strained back

Unit 1 | Non-Fiction

Directions: Questions 5 through 7 are based on the excerpt below.

WHY ARE MINORITY CHILDREN MORE LIKELY TO BE PUT INTO FOSTER CARE?

The white social worker looked at the dark spots on the black child's body and assumed the youngster had been beaten. The family denied it, but the social worker insisted.

(5) It turned out the child had "Mongolian spots"—harmless skin blotches common among black children. The social worker's mistake was discovered before the parents got into trouble.

(10) But researchers and policymakers say such episodes help explain why black, Hispanic and other minority children in the United States are far more likely than white youngsters to be taken from their homes and
(15) placed in foster care.

Racial or ethnic prejudices—conscious or unconscious—can lead social workers to see abuse or neglect where none exists, these experts say.

(20) The experts caution that stereotyping on the part of social workers is just one factor in the racial gap, and probably a small one at that. Other factors—higher rates of poverty, inadequate housing and child
(25) care, for example—are believed to be major contributors to abuse and neglect among minorities.

Nevertheless, stereotyping is enough of a concern that cultural-awareness training
(30) for social workers has been instituted in 45 states, many of them in just the past few years, according to a recent report by the Government Accountability Office, the investigative arm of Congress.

From the Associated Press's RACIAL BIAS TO BLAME FOR FOSTER CARE DISPARITY?, © 2007

5 Which generalization did the social worker in the first paragraph make?
   A The boy was being abused by his family.
   B The boy was getting into fights at school.
   C The boy had Mongolian spots.
   D The boy bruised easily.

6 Based on the excerpt, what can be concluded about children in foster care? One can conclude that
   A white children are more likely than minority children to be put into foster care.
   B white children are as likely as minority children to be put into foster care.
   C white children are never placed into foster care.
   D minority children are more likely than white children to be placed into foster care.

7 Given the information in the excerpt, which generalization can be made about why social workers are undergoing cultural-awareness training (lines 29–30)?
   A to further their careers
   B to prevent stereotyping
   C to learn about their own cultures
   D to differentiate physical abuse from neglect

Directions: Questions 8 through 11 are based on the excerpt below.

WHAT DOES THE AUTHOR BELIEVE THE LEGAL SYSTEM THINKS ABOUT MEN?

Every few years, some father who believes he's been wronged by the family court system grabs headlines and draws attention to the flawed ways in which we split up families.
(5) Custody proceedings are often brutal and adversarial. Otherwise fit parents can be drawn into a bare-knuckle fight over who poses a greater danger to the children. ...

Despite the fact that divorce is rarely
(10) triggered by violence or abuse, the incentives to allege that a man is abusive and out of control are undeniable. They tap into age-old stereotypes about men and ensure that Mom becomes the primary custodian. Even without
(15) abuse allegations, simple rules of physics (one child cannot be split into two and two cannot be split into four) make it likely that many good fathers will be downgraded from full-time dads to alternating-weekend carpool dads. They will
(20) be asked to pay at least a third of their salaries in child support for that privilege. Simple rules of modern life make it likely that an ex-wife will someday decide that a job or new husband demands a move to a faraway state. At which
(25) point the alternating-weekend-carpool dad is again demoted, to a Thanksgivings-if-you're-lucky dad.

I recognize the allure for some men of the man-pushed-until-he-snaps narrative. My
(30) husband rents those movies, too. But ... there are dozens of nonviolent fathers who believe that the mere fact of their divorce should not result in an arrangement in which they pay for the right to see their kids on alternating
(35) Sundays. If the family-court system is ever going to improve, we need to hear their stories, not tales of kidnappings and murder. Much of what's wrong with family law today lies in warmed-over stereotypes of men as
(40) fundamentally unsuited to caring for children.

From Dahlia Lithwick's RETHINKING FATHERS' RIGHTS, © 2008

8 What generalization is made about which parent gets custody of the children after a divorce?
  A Fathers always get full custody.
  B Mothers always get full custody.
  C Mothers and fathers always split custody equally.
  D Fathers always get zero custody.

9 According to the excerpt, which stereotype is associated with men after a divorce?
  A less likely to want custody of their children
  B more interested in their careers than their families
  C rarely fight for legal custody
  D assumed to be abusive because they are male

10 The excerpt discusses the allure of violent movies (line 29–30). In a similar scenario, how might one generalize a woman? Given the example, one might generalize women as liking movies about
  A romance.
  B murder.
  C kidnapping.
  D carpooling.

11 Based on the excerpt, how might the author describe today's legal system?
  A It is based on old stereotypes in which men cannot be proper caregivers to children.
  B It is working well, splitting the time children spend with both parents
  C It is not at all out of date.
  D It has moved forward to accept men as equally good care givers as women.

Directions: Questions 12 and 13 are based on the following memo.

WHAT HAS HAPPENED TO QUARTERLY SALES?

To: Fresh Foods Grocery Employees

Second quarter sales figures for Fresh Foods were $770,000, up 5 percent from the previous year's quarterly totals. Much of this increase can be traced to the success of our new Farmers' Market Days and the increased traffic generated by those weekend events.

(5) The national economic downturn generally has kept retail grocery store sales static throughout the country. However, Fresh Foods has shown increased sales in a number of areas, particularly organic dairy and produce selections. This trends with the figures from the Organic Foods Trade Group, which shows organic food sales growing between 17 and 21 percent annually since 1997. In general, the strength of organic food sales reflects shoppers' confidence in the safety and purity of organically
(10) grown produce and dairy selections.

Highlights of Fresh Foods' quarterly sales include:
- a 47 percent decrease in sales of luxury foods, such as prepared deli items and higher-priced wines.
- a 50 percent increase in the sales of competitively priced store-brand items
(15) - a 30 percent increase in locally grown and organic produce sales.

Based on the information provided by department managers this quarter, we will be initiating the following general changes:
- improving and increasing the variety of Fresh Foods store brand products in our grocery aisle
- advertise the Fresh Foods brand prominently in newspapers
(20) - decrease the selection of higher-priced prepared deli items, while offering more "make-it-at-home" packages
- continue to promote our local farmers and dairy suppliers
- highlight opportunities to showcase cost-saving and bargain opportunities for customers

---

12 Which generalization does the memo make in the first paragraph?
- A A 5 percent increase is satisfactory.
- B Attendance at Farmers' Market Days brought up the quarterly sales.
- C Farmers' Market Days have not met expectations.
- D Fresh Foods Grocery expected only a 2 percent increase.

13 The memo uses sales figures to plan for future changes for Fresh Foods. Based on the excerpt, what can be concluded about Fresh Foods' plans to increase sales?
- A to appeal to shoppers who need to spend less money
- B to continue to offer the highest quality groceries and produce
- C to improve its service by adding more employees
- D to expand its deli department with more prepared foods

Unit 1 Review

The Unit Review is structured to resemble high school equivalency language arts/reading tests. Be sure to read each question and all possible answers carefully before choosing your answer. To record your answers, fill in the circle with the letter that corresponds to the answer you select for each question in the Unit Review.

Do not rest your pencil on the answer area while considering your answer. Make no stray or unnecessary marks. If you change an answer, erase your first mark completely. Mark only one answer space for each question; multiple answers will be scored as incorrect.

Sample Question
What does the excerpt tell you about the author?
- A The author probably uses the public library's resources to hunt for jobs.
- B The author probably tutors adult learners at the public library.
- C The author probably uses the public library's resources a lot.
- D The author probably is a children's librarian.

Directions: Questions 1 through 5 are based on the following letter to a newspaper.

PUBLIC LIBRARY IS A VALUABLE RESOURCE

Dear Editor:

The proposed budget for next year has large cuts to the town's public library. I urge everyone to reconsider this severe reduction
(5) because the magnitude of these cuts would have a negative effect on most residents. For example, in the proposed budget, librarians for the children's department would have to be let go. Also, free access to computers
(10) would have to be reduced, and free computer training would be eliminated. Furthermore, the number of hours for adult learning would be reduced. Additionally, the library would be closed in the evenings and on weekends.
(15) Children to teenagers to the elderly would have no place to turn if they are busy during the day and usually visit the library in the evenings or on weekends.

As a result of these changes, people
(20) who use the library for learning, homework, reading newspapers and magazines, research, and job hunting would lose a valuable resource. Many cannot afford to buy books, audiotapes, CDs, and movies,
(25) and rely on the public library to be open during convenient hours to check out these resources. In addition, many members of the community benefit from the library's book group, robotics club, live demonstrations,
(30) author readings, and educational children's activities. Many adults come to the library after work for free tutoring to help them prepare for high-school equivalency tests and citizenship tests. The adult learning program
(35) also provides free tutoring for those who have dyslexia. There is even a free program for learning English fluently. These offerings would be reduced or abolished altogether.

The positive impact of this excellent
(40) library and staff is central to our town's being a great community. More than a thousand people have already signed a protest sheet against firing more librarians, especially for the children. Please contact members of
(45) the city council and let them know that you are against these radical cuts to our public library's budget. Their vote on the budget is next Tuesday at 7 p.m. in City Hall. Let them hear your voice before they vote!

(50)   Sincerely,

A Concerned Citizen

1. **For what reason did the author write this letter?**
   A. to persuade readers to protest cuts to the library's budget
   B. to inform readers about the free programs at the library
   C. to entertain readers with books, CDs, audiotapes, and activities
   D. to inform and entertain readers with all the free resources at the library

   Ⓐ Ⓑ Ⓒ Ⓓ

2. **According to the letter, what might be an effect of reducing the public library's budget?**
   A. increased workload for the librarians, who would have to do more work with fewer resources
   B. fewer books, magazines, newspapers, CDs, audiotapes, and DVDs for people to check out
   C. fewer resources available and less convenient hours
   D. more costs for people who want to join a book group, robotics club, or educational activities

   Ⓐ Ⓑ Ⓒ Ⓓ

3. **Based on the letter, what can you generalize about the residents' use of the public library?**
   A. more retirees use the library's services than children
   B. people of all ages use the library's services and resources
   C. more families use the library's resources than single people
   D. more people use the library for free access to computers than to check out books

   Ⓐ Ⓑ Ⓒ Ⓓ

4. **Which line best represents an opinion from the letter?**
   A. "Additionally, the library would be closed in the evenings and on weekends."
   B. "As a result of these changes, people who use the library … would lose a valuable resource."
   C. "More than a thousand people have already signed a protest sheet against firing more librarians, especially for the children."
   D. "Their vote on the budget is next Tuesday at 7 p.m. in City Hall."

   Ⓐ Ⓑ Ⓒ Ⓓ

5. **In the last paragraph, the author writes, "Please contact members of the city council and let them know that you are against these radical cuts to our public library's budget." What is the author most likely implying?**
   A. City council members do not know about all the services and resources the public library has to offer its patrons.
   B. Most members of the city council do not use the public library, so they don't know how important it is to residents.
   C. People who do not use the public library don't care about people who have to rely on the library's services and resources.
   D. Readers can have an influence on how the city council votes on the budget if they are willing to voice their concerns.

   Ⓐ Ⓑ Ⓒ Ⓓ

Directions: Questions 6 through 10 are based on the following business letter.

WHAT IS THE PURPOSE OF THIS LETTER?

The Maple Hotel
226 Maple Street
Louisville, KY 40201

Mr. Frank Thomas, CEO
(5) Thomas Building Supplies
864 Fellows Street
Cincinnati, OH 45201

Dear Mr. Thomas,

(10) I am writing to introduce myself to you and your associates. My name is Miranda Snyder and I am the new Sales Account Manager at The Maple Hotel.

I have learned from Pat Higgins, The Maple Hotel's former Sales Account Manager and new Director of Sales, that your company often does business in the Louisville area and frequents our hotel on a regular basis. We thank you so much for your business. I will now be Thomas Building Supplies' main sales correspondent from this point forward, and
(15) am looking forward to working with you and your staff for any of your upcoming business trips, conventions, and catering events.

Your Administrative Assistant, Angela, has scheduled a block of rooms for you and your Board of Directors for the week of September 18th. We have you booked in our newly renovated Maple Suite. Additionally, we will have a board room available for your use each
(20) day from 8:00 am until 2:00 pm with access to wireless Internet and conference calling. Each day our banquet staff will provide you with a mid-morning break of coffee, teas, and pastries, as well as lunch services.

Furthermore, as part of my introduction to The Maple Hotel's preferred guests, I would like to offer you 500 extra Maple Points that will be added to your account renewable upon
(25) your next stay with us. As you may know, Maple Points can be used toward complimentary rooms, dining services in our restaurant, and discounts on catering services for any events Thomas Building Supplies may hold in the future.

I look forward to meeting you in person and working with you and your staff during your stay with us in September, as well as any upcoming events you may be planning.
(30) If I can be of assistance in any way, please do not hesitate to call; I have included my business card for your convenience. Thank you again for your continued business.

At your service,

Miranda Snyder, Sales Account Manager

6. **Why is the author writing this letter?**
   A to apply for a job with Thomas Building Supplies
   B to arrange a face-to-face meeting with Frank Thomas
   C to introduce herself as the new sales manager at the Maple Hotel
   D to determine how many Maple Points she has earned

   Ⓐ Ⓑ Ⓒ Ⓓ

7. **What is the author implying when she writes "as part of my introduction to The Maple Hotel's preferred guests" (line 23)?**
   A The author is only introducing herself to the hotel's new guests.
   B The author is writing letters to many people.
   C The author is planning on scheduling a face-to-face meeting.
   D The recipient of her letter is an important client of the Maple Hotel.

   Ⓐ Ⓑ Ⓒ Ⓓ

8. **Which fact does the reader learn about Mr. Thomas from the letter?**
   A Mr. Thomas has a total of 500 Maple Points.
   B Mr. Thomas is the CEO of a building supplies company.
   C Mr. Thomas visits Louisville weekly.
   D Mr. Thomas always reserves a board room when he visits the Maple Hotel.

   Ⓐ Ⓑ Ⓒ Ⓓ

9. **Which meaning is the author implying when she writes "If I can be of assistance in any way, please do not hesitate to call" (line 30)? The author means she will**
   A make sure she is available any time Mr. Thomas calls.
   B refer Mr. Thomas's business to another associate at the Maple Hotel.
   C only be of assistance to Mr. Thomas and his company.
   D help Mr. Thomas schedule and modify events at the Maple Hotel.

   Ⓐ Ⓑ Ⓒ Ⓓ

10. **Based on the character of the author as provided in this letter, how does she perform her job as a sales account manager?**
    A harshly
    B cautiously
    C caringly
    D indifferently

    Ⓐ Ⓑ Ⓒ Ⓓ

Unit 2

Unit Overview

Fiction is one of the more popular forms of writing. Each year, millions of people read novels, short stories, and even comic books by authors who use their imaginations to create tales of adventure, romance, and mystery. Similarly, fiction pieces appear on high school equivalency language arts/reading tests.

The selections that follow are similar to those you will see on high school equivalency language arts/reading tests. In Unit 2, the further use of skills such as identifying a cause and its effect, comparing and contrasting, and understanding point of view, as well as the introduction of ideas such as theme, setting, and tone, will help you prepare for high school equivalency language arts/reading tests.

Table of Contents

Lesson 1: Context Clues 83
Lesson 2: Cause and Effect 88
Lesson 3: Compare and Contrast 93
Lesson 4: Plot Elements 98
Lesson 5: Characters 103
Lesson 6: Motivation 108
Lesson 7: Point of View 113
Lesson 8: Theme 118
Lesson 9: Setting 123
Lesson 10: Tone 128
Lesson 11: Figurative Language 133
Lesson 12: Symbols and Imagery 138
Lesson 13: Make Inferences 143
Lesson 14: Draw Conclusions 148
Lesson 15: Apply Ideas 153
Unit 2 Review 158

Fiction

Glossary

Analogy: a type of figurative language, such as similes and metaphors, which compares two unlike things

Cause: an action that makes another event happen

Climax: the point in a piece of fiction at which the tension is greatest

Compare: look for similarities between two things

Complication: a difficulty or an obstacle that characters within a piece of fiction must overcome

Context clues: the details that surround an unknown word

Contrast: look for differences between two things

Effect: something that happens as the result of a cause

Exposition: the background and details of a piece of fiction

Fact: a piece of information that can be proven true

Fiction: writing that is created from the author's imagination, such as poems, novels, and plays

Hyperbole: exaggeration; a type of figurative language used to emphasize or provide humor

Imagery: a type of figurative language that appeals to the reader's senses of taste, smell, vision, hearing, or touch

Inference: an idea drawn by evaluating facts or circumstances

Metaphor: a type of figurative language that compares two unlike things

Mood: the emotional atmosphere of a story

Motivation: the reason for a character's behaving in a particular way

Nonfiction: writing that is presented as factual, including newspaper articles, editorials, textbooks, and legal documents

Omniscient: a narrator in a work of fiction who knows the thoughts and feelings of the other characters

Opinion: a person's view or judgment that cannot be proven true or untrue

Personification: a type of figurative language characterized by a writer's giving human qualities to animals or objects

Point of view: who tells the story; usually, a first-person narrator or an omniscient narrator who knows what every character is thinking and feeling

Protagonist: the main character in a piece of fiction

Resolution: the point in a work of fiction at which complications are resolved

Simile: a type of figurative language that compares two unlike things using the words *like* or *as*

Setting: where and when a story takes place

Symbol: a type of figurative language that uses people, places, or things to stand for a larger idea

Theme: the central or overall idea in a work of fiction

Tone: the expression of a writer's feelings about a subject

LESSON 1

Context Clues

① Learn the Skill

Context clues can help you figure out the meaning of a word or a passage of text. Context means the clues, details, or restatements that surround an unknown word. Understanding how to use context clues to determine a word's meaning will help you grasp the overall idea of a passage.

② Practice the Skill

By mastering the skill of understanding context clues, you will improve your study and test-taking skills, especially as they relate to high school equivalency language arts/reading tests. Read the excerpt and strategies below.

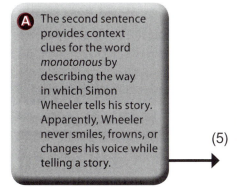

A The second sentence provides context clues for the word *monotonous* by describing the way in which Simon Wheeler tells his story. Apparently, Wheeler never smiles, frowns, or changes his voice while telling a story.

B The words "without ever smiling" in the paragraph emphasize that the speaker tells his story without emotion or emphasis.

WHAT PROBLEM DOES THE NARRATOR HAVE WITH SIMON WHEELER?

... Simon Wheeler backed me into a corner and blockaded me there with his chair, and then sat me down and reeled off the monotonous narrative which follows this paragraph. He never smiled, he never frowned, he never
(5) changed his voice from the gentle-flowing key to which he tuned the initial sentence, he never betrayed the slightest suspicion of enthusiasm; but all through the interminable narrative there ran a vein of impressive earnestness and sincerity, which showed me plainly that, so far from his
(10) imagining there was any thing ridiculous or funny about his story, he regarded it as a really important matter, and admired its two heroes as men of transcendent genius in finesse. To me the spectacle of a man drifting serenely along through such a queer yarn without ever smiling, was
(15) exquisitely absurd.

From Mark Twain's THE CELEBRATED JUMPING FROG OF CALAVERAS COUNTY, © 1867

✓ **TEST-TAKING TIPS**

Context clues may come from synonyms. Check for other words in the sentence or surrounding sentences that make comparisons with an unfamiliar word.

1 The narrator says that Simon Wheeler tells a "**monotonous narrative**." Which statement best describes a monotonous voice?
   A It is loud.
   B It is expressive.
   C It has a tone that stays the same.
   D It has a high pitch.

Unit 2 | Fiction

③ Apply the Skill

Directions: Questions 2 and 3 refer to the following excerpt.

WHY IS THE NARRATOR GETTING ON A TRAIN?

I held a florin tightly in my hand as I strode down Buckingham Street towards the station. The sight of the streets thronged with buyers and glaring with gas recalled to
(5) me the purpose of my journey. I took my seat in a third-class carriage of a deserted train. After an intolerable delay the train moved out of the station slowly. It crept onward among ruinous houses and over the twinkling river.
(10) At Westland Row Station a crowd of people pressed to the carriage doors; but the porters moved them back, saying that it was a special train for the bazaar. I remained alone in the bare carriage. In a few minutes the train drew
(15) up beside an improvised wooden platform. I passed out on to the road and saw by the lighted dial of a clock that it was ten minutes to ten. In front of me was a large building which displayed the magical name.
(20) I could not find any sixpenny entrance and, fearing that the bazaar would be closed, I passed in quickly through a turnstile, handing a shilling to a weary-looking man. I found myself in a big hall girdled at half its height by
(25) a gallery. Nearly all the stalls were closed and the greater part of the hall was in darkness. I recognized a silence like that which pervades a church after a service. I walked into the center of the bazaar timidly. A few people
(30) were gathered about the stalls which were still open. Before a curtain, over which the words *Café Chantant* were written in colored lamps, two men were counting money on a salver. I listened to the fall of the coins.

From James Joyce's ARABY, © 1914

2. The narrator rides in the carriage of a "deserted train" (line 6). Which of the following probably could be found in a "deserted" room?
   A a large party of people
   B a political meeting
   C no men, women, or children
   D a church service

3. The narrator of the story "passed quickly through a turnstile, handing a shilling to a weary looking man." What is a shilling?
   A a kind of entrance
   B another word for a turnstile
   C something at a bazaar
   D a type of money

Directions: Question 4 refers to the following excerpt.

WHAT IS THE NARRATOR DESCRIBING?

The hamlet of Barry's Ford is situated in a sort of high valley among the mountains. Below it the hills lie in moveless curves like a petrified ocean; above it they rise in green-
(5) cresting waves which never break. It is *Barry's* Ford because at one time the Barry family was the most important in the place; and *Ford* because just at the beginning of the hamlet the little turbulent Barry River is fordable. There is,
(10) however, now a rude bridge across the river.

From Mary E. Wilkins Freeman's OLD WOMAN MAGOUN, © 1891

4. Based on the information in the excerpt, what is a ford?
   A a place to cross a river
   B a type of bridge
   C a small village
   D a high valley

Directions: Questions 5 and 6 refer to the following excerpt.

WHAT DOES THE NARRATOR SAY A MAN MUST FORGET?

When a man journeys into a far country, he must be prepared to forget many of the things he has learned, and to acquire such customs as are inherent with the existence in
(5) the new land; he must abandon the old ideals and the old gods, and oftentimes he must reverse the very codes by which his conduct has hitherto been shaped … [To] those who happen to be hardened to the ruts in which
(10) they were created, the pressure of the altered environment is unbearable, and they chafe in body and in spirit under the new restrictions which they do not understand.

From Jack London's IN A FAR COUNTRY, © 1899

5. The narrator describes "such customs as are inherent with the existence in the new land" (lines 3–5). Something that is inherent is
   A similar to something else.
   B separate but equal.
   C part of something else.
   D removed from the whole.

6. What does the author mean by stating that travelers "must abandon the old ideals and the old gods" (lines 5–6)?
   A People must give up their previous habits when they go to another country.
   B Travelers often introduce new customs to faraway countries.
   C In foreign countries, people must remember the practices of their homeland.
   D Going to a foreign country is the best way to learn a new language.

Directions: Questions 7 and 8 refer to the following excerpt.

WHAT HAPPENED TO THE TOWN?

All demeanor of rural serenity had been wrenched violently from the little town by the guns and by the waves of men which had surged through it. … The artillery had not
(5) neglected the rows of gentle shade-trees, which had lined the streets. Branches and heavy trunks cluttered the mud in driftwood tangles, while a few shattered upright forms had contrived to remain dejectedly,
(10) mournfully upright.

From Stephen Crane's THE LITTLE REGIMENT, © 1896

7. In line 1, the author describes the "demeanor of rural serenity." What is the opposite of serenity?
   A peace
   B violence
   C joy
   D forgiveness

8. What is the meaning of the statement that a few trees "contrived to remain dejectedly, mournfully upright" (lines 9–10)?
   A The remaining trees looked broken and sad.
   B Townspeople grieved because the trees were damaged.
   C The soldiers mourned the destruction of the town.
   D The trees escaped the violence felt in the rest of the town.

Directions: Questions 9 through 13 refer to the following excerpt.

WHY DOES THE NARRATOR NOT WANT TO CALL HER HUSBAND?

She wondered restlessly if he wanted anything and if she could hear him if he called. His voice had grown very weak within the last months and it irritated him when she did not
(5) hear. This irritability, this increasing childish petulance seemed to give expression to their imperceptible estrangement. Like two faces looking at one another through a sheet of glass they were close together, almost touching,
(10) but they could not hear or feel each other: the conductivity was broken. She, at least, had this sense of separation, and she fancied sometimes that she saw it reflected in the look with which he supplemented his failing
(15) words. Doubtless the fault was hers. She was too impenetrably healthy to be touched by the irrelevancies of disease. Her self-reproachful tenderness was tinged with the sense of his irrationality: she had a vague feeling that there
(20) was a purpose in his helpless tyrannies.

From Edith Wharton's A JOURNEY, © 1899

9 Lines 14 and 15 refer to the man's "failing words." What might this imply about the man? This description is a clue that
  A his wife no longer listens to him.
  B he has a poor vocabulary.
  C his health is failing.
  D he enjoys talking with his wife.

10 Based on the excerpt, what qualities would you probably see in people who showed petulance?
  A They would be in ill health.
  B They would be friendly with one another.
  C They would be enjoyable company.
  D They would be hard to get along with.

11 Based on the narrator's description, what might an estrangement between people reveal?
  A They have traveled to be together.
  B They are no longer emotionally close.
  C They help one another in times of ill health.
  D They have excellent communication.

12 Based on the narrator's attitude, what do you think are her feelings toward her husband?
  A She has always resented her husband.
  B She has grown to love her husband despite his flaws.
  C She and her husband are best friends and soul mates.
  D She loves her husband but cannot cope with his illness.

13 The narrator says "the conductivity is broken" (line 11). Which of the following might also be conductive?
  A a train operator
  B a pencil eraser
  C a light bulb socket
  D an orchestra leader

Directions: Questions 14 through 17 refer to the following excerpt.

HOW DO PEOPLE DESCRIBE ZELIG?

Old Zelig was eyed askance by his brethren. No one deigned to call him "Reb" Zelig, nor to prefix to his name the American equivalent—"Mr." "The old one is a barrel
(5) with a stave missing," knowingly declared his neighbors. …

In the cloakshop where Zelig worked he stood daily, brandishing his heavy iron on the sizzling cloth, hardly ever glancing about him.
(10) The workmen despised him, for during a strike he returned to work after two days' absence. He could not be idle, and thought with dread of the Saturday that would bring him no pay envelope.

(15) His very appearance seemed alien to his brethren. His figure was tall, and of cast-iron mold. When he stared stupidly at something, he looked like a blind Samson. His gray hair was long, and it fell in disheveled curls on
(20) gigantic shoulders somewhat inclined to stoop. His shabby clothes hung loosely on him; and, both summer and winter, the same old cap covered his massive head.

From Benjamin Rosenblatt's ZELIG, © 1915

14 Zelig is described as "alien" in line 15. What can you conclude about a person who seems alien to others?
- A That person appears different.
- B That person is neighborly.
- C That person has many friends.
- D That person is neatly dressed.

15 The story states that neighbors never call the main character "Reb Zelig." What is implied about the term "Reb?" The story indicates that "Reb" is
- A an affectionate joke.
- B a religious name.
- C a courtesy title.
- D a slanderous term.

16 What do Zelig's neighbors mean when they say "the old one is a barrel with a stave missing" (lines 4–5)?
- A Zelig has broken items in his workplace.
- B Zelig is a person who loses property.
- C Zelig has physical problems.
- D Zelig is not mentally stable.

17 The state of Zelig's hair and clothing is described as "disheveled" (line 19). Describing Zelig as "disheveled" most likely means that
- A his co-workers tease him.
- B he needs to improve his grooming.
- C he is emotionally upset.
- D he is careful of his appearance.

LESSON 2

Cause and Effect

Fiction

1 Learn the Skill

As you learned in Unit 1, authors often use **cause and effect** to create the events of their stories. A **cause** is an element, such as an action, that makes something happen. An **effect** is what happens as a result of that cause. What one person does in one part of the story can affect another person in another part of the story. A cause can have more than one effect, and an effect may have more than one cause.

Effects can be both positive and negative. The outcome of stories often depends on whether causes lead to effects that are planned or unplanned.

2 Practice the Skill

By mastering the skill of identifying cause and effect, you will improve your study and test-taking skills, especially as they relate to high school equivalency language arts/reading tests. Read the excerpt and strategies below.

A Causes and effects have connections. "Some legal trouble" led to the house being empty for years.

B Signal words such as *because*, *so*, or *therefore* can signal a cause or effect. Here, the phrase "due to" signals a cause-and-effect relationship. The narrator's sensitivity is due to, or caused by, the nervous condition.

HOW DOES THE NARRATOR FEEL ABOUT THE HOUSE?

So I will let it alone and talk about the house. …

A There was some legal trouble, I believe, something about the heirs and co-heirs; anyhow, the place has been empty for years.

(5) That spoils my ghostliness, I am afraid, but I don't care—there is something strange about the house—I can feel it.

I even said so to John one moonlight evening, but he said what I felt was a draught, and shut the window.

(10) I get unreasonable angry with John sometimes. I'm sure I never used to be so sensitive. I think it is due to this nervous condition.

From Charlotte Perkins Gilman's THE YELLOW WALLPAPER, © 1892

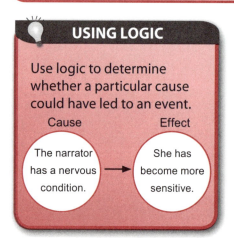

USING LOGIC

Use logic to determine whether a particular cause could have led to an event.

Cause → Effect

The narrator has a nervous condition. → She has become more sensitive.

1 What causes John to shut the window?
A The narrator says there is a draft.
B The narrator says the house is strange.
C The narrator is cold.
D John has a nervous condition.

Apply the Skill

Directions: Questions 2 through 5 refer to the following excerpt.

WHAT IS THE RELATIONSHIP OF THE CHARACTERS?

Dick had been under [Mrs. Jennett's] care for six years, during which time she had made her profit of the allowances supposed to be expended on his clothes, and, partly through
(5) thoughtlessness, partly through a natural desire to pain,—she was a widow of some years anxious to marry again,—had made his days burdensome on his young shoulders.
Where he had looked for love, she gave
(10) him first aversion and then hate.
Where he growing older had sought a little sympathy, she gave him ridicule. ...
Since she chose to regard him as a hopeless liar, but an economical and self-
(15) contained one, never throwing away the least unnecessary fib, and never hesitating at the blackest, were it only plausible, that might make his life a little easier. The treatment taught him at least the power of living alone,—
(20) a power that was of service to him when he went to a public school and the boys laughed at his clothes, which were poor in quality and much mended.

From Rudyard Kipling's THE LIGHT THAT FAILED, © 1890

2 What effect does Mrs. Jennett have on Dick when she considers him a liar?
  A   He tries to win her favor.
  B   He seeks the company of boys at school.
  C   He prefers to avoid people.
  D   He apologizes for lying.

3 What causes Mrs. Jennett to treat Dick poorly?
  A   Mrs. Jennett has had to take care of Dick for six years.
  B   Dick behaves badly toward Mrs. Jennett, so she laughs at him.
  C   Mrs. Jennett is unkind by nature and likes to cause pain.
  D   Dick needs to rely on himself before he goes to school.

4 Which of the following most likely makes Dick unhappy?
  A   Mrs. Jennett has been a widow for many years.
  B   Dick wants to start attending public school sooner.
  C   Dick knows Mrs. Jennett makes a profit on his allowances.
  D   Mrs. Jennett lacks sympathy for Dick, making his childhood miserable.

5 Why are Dick's clothes of such poor quality that they require a lot of mending?
  A   because Mrs. Jennett does not spend all of the money on his clothing that she is supposed to
  B   because Mrs. Jennett is a widow and is anxious to marry again
  C   because Dick wants love, but instead receives heartlessnes
  D   because Dick lies about everything in order to make his life easier

Directions: Questions 6 through 9 refer to the following excerpt.

HOW CAN THE NARRATOR'S FEELINGS BE BEST DESCRIBED?

I was on my way to Montreal to deliver a lecture. It was mid-winter and I had been warned that the temperature was ten degrees lower than in New York. Newspapers reported
(5) that trains had been stalled in the snow and fishing villages cut off, so that food and medical supplies had to be dropped to them by plane.

I prepared for the journey as though it
(10) were an expedition to the North Pole. I put on a heavy coat over two sweaters and packed warm underwear and a bottle of cognac in case the train should be halted somewhere in the fields. In my breast pocket I had the
(15) manuscript I intended to read—an optimistic report on the future of the Yiddish language.

In the beginning, everything went smoothly. As usual, I arrived at the station an hour before train departure and therefore could find no
(20) porter. The station teemed with travelers and I watched them, trying to guess who they were, where they were going, and why.

None of the men was dressed as heavily as I. Some even wore spring coats.

From Isaac Bashevis Singer's THE LECTURE, © 1968

6 The narrator arrives at the station early. Which of the following is an effect of this? Because of his early arrival, he
 A is late to Montreal.
 B cannot find an attendant.
 C misses his train.
 D goes over his lecture.

7 Which of the following is most like the situation reported in the newspapers?
 A There is a collection of deserted islands.
 B An army's supply lines are increasing.
 C A fishing boat is struggling in dangerous waters.
 D A small island town's bridge to the mainland is washed out.

8 What is the effect of the author's description of the narrator's preparation for his trip?
 A It emphasizes the seriousness of the weather.
 B It shows the foolishness of the narrator.
 C It illustrates the narrator's lack of resources.
 D It underscores the mild weather in Montreal.

9 Later in the story, the train becomes stuck near the Canadian border because of the snow. This reminds the narrator of his terrible experiences in a concentration camp during World War II. Which of the following is the most likely effect of this tragic memory on the narrator's initial optimism for going to Montreal?
 A The narrator would choose to stay in Montreal.
 B The narrator would not feel so optimistic about the future of the Yiddish language.
 C The narrator would leave the train and hitchhike back to New York.
 D The memories would have no effect on the narrator.

Directions: Questions 10 through 13 refer to the following excerpt.

WHAT DOES THE GUEST WANT SYLVIA TO TELL HIM?

"Sylvy, Sylvy!" called the busy old grandmother again and again, but nobody answered, and the small husk bed was empty and Sylvia had disappeared.

(5) The guest waked from a dream, and remembering his day's pleasure hurried to dress himself that it might sooner begin. He was sure from the way the shy little girl looked once or twice yesterday that she had at least (10) seen the white heron, and now she must really be made to tell. Here she comes now, paler than ever, and her worn old frock is torn and tattered, and smeared with pine pitch. The grandmother and the sportsman stand in (15) the door together and question her, and the splendid moment has come to speak of the dead hemlock-tree by the green marsh.

But Sylvia does not speak after all, though the old grandmother fretfully rebukes her, (20) and the young man's kind, appealing eyes are looking straight in her own. He can make them rich with money; he has promised it, and they are poor now. He is so well worth making happy, and he waits to hear the story she can (25) tell.

No, she must keep silence! What is it that suddenly forbids her and makes her dumb? Has she been nine years growing and now, when the great world for the first time puts out (30) a hand to her, must she thrust it aside for a bird's sake? ... Sylvia cannot speak; she cannot tell the heron's secret and give its life away.

From Sarah Orne Jewett's A WHITE HERON, © 1886

10 What happens when Sylvia does not tell her grandmother and the guest what they want to know?
  A The guest pays the grandmother for his lodging.
  B The heron flies away.
  C Sylvia's grandmother scolds her for her messy dress.
  D Sylvia's grandmother gets angry with her for not sharing the location of the white heron.

11 What is shown by the author's description of Sylvia's torn, dirty dress?
  A It makes Sylvia appear poor, but shows that she dresses well.
  B It shows that her grandmother takes good care of her.
  C It indicates that the stranger is critical to notice such details.
  D It proves that she is careless with her clothes.

12 What leads the guest to think Sylvia has seen a white heron?
  A her inability to speak
  B her torn dress
  C her knowledge of trees
  D the way she looks

13 Sylvia decides to keep her silence, even though the guest is willing to offer money to know the location of the white heron. What most likely happens because Sylvia keeps her secret?
  A Sylvia's grandmother becomes rich.
  B The guest finds the white heron.
  C The white heron escapes capture.
  D The guest thanks Sylvia for her help.

Directions: Questions 14 through 17 refer to the following excerpt.

HOW DOES THE WOMAN FEEL ABOUT FLYING?

A woman who had traveled a great deal in planes, and had never trusted them because she understood nothing about them, sat in the double front seat behind the magazine
(5) rack. This was the best seat, as she knew, because there was enough room to stretch your legs. Also you could see well from here, if you wanted to see. Now, for a moment she looked out the window and saw that the few
(10) palm trees at the far edge of the field were blowing out in heavy plumes against the sky. There was something so wrong about Miami that even a beautiful night, sharp with stars, only seemed a real-estate advertisement. The
(15) woman pulled off her earrings and put them carelessly in her coat pocket. She ran her hands through her very short dark upcurling hair, deliberately making herself untidy for the night ahead. She hunched her shoulders
(20) to ease the tired stiffness in her neck and slouched down in the chair. She had just leaned her head against the chair back and was thinking of nothing when the man's voice said, Is this place taken? No, she said without
(25) looking at him. She moved nearer to the window. Anyhow, she said to herself, only eight or ten hours or whatever it is to New York; even if he snores, he can't snore all the time.

From Martha Gellhorn's MIAMI-NEW YORK, © 1948

14 What is the effect of the woman's experience with traveling on planes?
   A She always arrives at the airport on time.
   B She selects the best seat.
   C She is not bothered by delays.
   D She refuses to sit near other passengers.

15 Later in the story, the man tries to talk to the woman after the plane lifts off. Based on the woman's behavior in this excerpt, what is the most likely effect the man's attempts at conversation might have on the woman?
   A They will have a long conversation.
   B She will begin to snore.
   C She will try to ignore the man.
   D She will ask the attendant to change her seat.

16 The woman speaks to the man and then moves nearer the window. Which of the following is the most probable reason for her change of position?
   A to better hear the man's conversation
   B to make sure the man will not rob her
   C to get the attention of the stewardess
   D to make room for the man

17 Why might travelers behave as the woman in the story does?
   A They want to meet other travelers.
   B They want to be left alone.
   C They want to enjoy the scenery.
   D They want to listen to other people's problems.

LESSON 3
Compare and Contrast

Fiction

① Learn the Skill

Authors use **comparisons** and **contrasts** to describe parts of their stories, such as people, places, or conflicts. When authors make comparisons, they show the similarities between two or more things. When they show contrast, they emphasize the differences. Comparing and contrasting can help you sort out and analyze information. You can group details, events, or people by their similarities and differences.

② Practice the Skill

By mastering the skills of comparing and contrasting, you will improve your study and test-taking skills, especially as they relate to high school equivalency language arts/reading tests. Read the excerpt and strategies below. Then answer the question that follows.

A Here, the author contrasts two sisters, Susan and Emily. The author describes Susan, and then says that Emily is not the same at all.

B The narrator continues to emphasize the differences between Susan and Emily, explaining that Susan is outgoing and amuses her audiences while Emily is quiet.

HOW ARE THE NARRATOR'S CHILDREN DESCRIBED?

Oh there are conflicts between the others too, each one human, needing, demanding, hurting, taking—but only between Emily and Susan, no, Emily toward Susan that corroding resentment. It seems so obvious on the surface, (5) yet it is not obvious. Susan, the second child, Susan, **A** golden-and curly-haired and chubby, quick and articulate and assured, everything in appearance and manner Emily was not; Susan, not able to resist Emily's precious things, losing or sometimes clumsily breaking them; Susan telling (10) jokes and riddles to company for applause while Emily sat **B** silent (to say to me later: that was my riddle, Mother, I told it to Susan). …

From Tillie Olsen's I STAND HERE IRONING, © 1961

✓ TEST-TAKING TIPS

A Venn diagram is a useful tool for organizing comparison and contrast. A Venn diagram of Emily and Susan might look like this:

Emily   Susan
    both

1. How would you compare Emily's personality traits with those of Susan's?
   A Emily is more outgoing than Susan.
   B Susan finds more riddles than Emily does.
   C Emily is the quick-witted sister.
   D Emily speaks less confidently in public than Susan.

③ Apply the Skill

Directions: Questions 2 through 5 refer to the following excerpt.

WHAT INFLUENCES THE NARRATOR'S MUSICAL TASTE?

No one will believe that I like country music. Even my wife scoffs when told such a possibility exists. "Go on!" Gloria tells me. "I can see blues, bebop, maybe even a little
(5) buckdancing. But not bluegrass." Gloria says, "Hillbilly stuff is not just music. It's like the New York Stock Exchange. The minute you see a sharp rise in it, you better watch out."

I tend to argue the point, but quietly, and
(10) mostly to myself. Gloria was born and raised in New York; she has come to believe in the stock exchange as the only index of economic health. My perceptions were shaped in South Carolina; and long ago I learned there, as a
(15) waiter in private clubs, to gauge economic flux by the tips people gave. We tend to agree on other matters too, but the thing that gives me most frustration is trying to make her understand why I like country music. Perhaps
(20) it is because she hates the South and has capitulated emotionally to the horror stories told by refugees from down home. Perhaps it is because Gloria is third generation Northern-born. I do not know. What I do know is that,
(25) while the two of us are black, the distance between us is sometimes as great as that between Ibo and Yoruba.

From James Alan McPherson's WHY I LIKE COUNTRY MUSIC, © 1972

2 How do the musical tastes of Gloria and her husband compare?
   A They enjoy the same types of music.
   B They both dislike bluegrass.
   C Only the husband likes hillbilly music.
   D Only Gloria enjoys bebop.

3 Gloria says that hillbilly music is "like the New York Stock Exchange" (lines 6–7). What is meant by this comparison?
   A to show similarities that are both negative
   B to give country music a positive association
   C to associate hillbilly music with prosperity
   D to imply that stock brokers enjoy country music

4 The narrator says that "Gloria is third generation Northern-born" (lines 23–24). Why might the author provide this information?
   A to show that she and her husband have a similar background
   B to contrast her background with her husband's
   C to imply that her husband is also from the North
   D to emphasize her preference for the South

5 Based on the information in the text, how might the author describe the Yoruba and Ibo tribes?
   A the beginning and the start
   B warm and hot
   C girls and women
   D night and day

Directions: Questions 6 through 9 refer to the following excerpt.

WHY MIGHT THE KELVEY GIRLS BE SHUNNED?

Playtime came and Isabel was surrounded. … She held quite a court under the huge pine trees at the side of the playground. Nudging, giggling together, the
(5) little girls pressed up close. And the only two who stayed outside the ring were the two who were always outside, the little Kelveys. They knew better than to come anywhere near the Burnells.
(10) For the fact was, the school the Burnell children went to was not at all the kind of place their parents would have chosen if there had been any choice. But there was none. It was the only school for miles. And
(15) the consequence was all the children in the neighborhood, the judge's little girls, the doctor's daughters, the store-keeper's children, the milkman's, were forced to mix together. … But the line had to be drawn somewhere. It
(20) was drawn at the Kelveys. Many of the children, including the Burnells, were not allowed even to speak to them. They walked past the Kelveys with their heads in the air, and as they set the fashion in all matters of behaviour, the
(25) Kelveys were shunned by everybody. Even the teacher had a special voice for them, and a special smile for the other children when Lil Kelvey came up to her desk with a bunch of dreadfully common-looking flowers.

From Katherine Mansfield's THE DOLL'S HOUSE, © 1922

6 What do the Kelveys and the Burnells have in common?
  A They attend the same school.
  B They play with the same girls.
  C They both like wildflowers.
  D They are both shunned by other children.

7 What does the narrator imply about the children who do not speak to the Kelveys?
  A Their families are poorer than the Kelveys.
  B Their families are better off than the Kelveys.
  C The Kelveys have more social status than the families of those children.
  D The Kelveys are more educated than the families of those children.

8 The passage states that the teacher has a "special voice" for the Kelvey children (lines 25–26). What does this tell readers about the teacher?
  A The teacher is equally fair to both types of children.
  B She gives more attention to poorer children.
  C The teacher is more fair than teachers who speak in the same voice.
  D The teacher is less fair to the poorer students.

9 The author contrasts the children who are inside Isabel's ring with those who are outside it (lines 5–6). What might be the author's purpose in doing so?
  A to show the difference in social status
  B to indicate a difference in ages
  C to emphasize a difference in size
  D to reveal that not all children like Isabel

Directions: Questions 10 through 13 refer to the following excerpt.

WHAT ARE SOME THINGS THE NARRATOR USES TO DESCRIBE HIS HERITAGE?

You would not know or remember, as I do, that in those days, in our area of the country, we enjoyed a pleasingly ironic mixture of Yankee and Confederate folkways.
(5) Our meals and manners, our speech, our attitudes towards certain ambiguous areas of history, even our acceptance of tragedy as a normal course of life—these things and more defined us as Southern. Yet the stern morality
(10) of our parents, their toughness and penny-pinching and attitudes toward work, their covert allegiance toward certain ideals, even the directions toward which they turned our faces, made us more Yankee than Cavalier.
(15) Moreover, some of our schools were named for Confederate men of distinction, but others were named for the stern-faced believers who had swept down from the North to save a people back, back long ago, in those long
(20) forgotten days of once upon a time. Still, our schoolbooks, our required classroom songs, our flags, our very relation to the statues and monuments in public parks, negated the story that these dreamers from the North had ever
(25) come.

From James Alan McPherson's WHY I LIKE COUNTRY MUSIC, © 1972

10 The narrator describes his upbringing as an "ironic mixture of Yankee and Confederate folkways" (lines 3–4). What does this description tell us? His description indicates that he
  A does not agree with Yankee or Confederate ideals.
  B identifies with Confederates more than Yankees.
  C holds to both Yankee and Confederate beliefs.
  D mostly rejects Yankee ideals.

11 How does the narrator contrast Yankees and Confederates?
  A Yankees accept tragedy quickly.
  B Confederates understand history very well.
  C Yankees spend a lot of money.
  D Yankees are very careful with their money.

12 The narrator describes Northern and Southern attitudes. For what reason might the author have chosen to describe these attitudes?
  A to prove the superiority of Northern folkways
  B to illustrate that most schools are named for Northern men
  C to indicate that Northern and Southern practices are very much alike
  D to show that the author absorbed two different types of attitudes

13 What does the narrator imply about the schoolbooks, songs, and flags of his area of the country?
  A They agree more with the North than the South.
  B They favor the South over the North.
  C They treat the North and South equally.
  D They show only the best qualities of the North.

Directions: Questions 14 through 17 refer to the following excerpt.

HOW DOES THE NARRATOR FEEL ABOUT HER OLDEST DAUGHTER?

I will never total it all. I will never come to say: She was a child seldom smiled at. Her father left me before she was a year old. I had to work her first six years when there was
(5) work, or I sent her home and to his relatives. There were years she had care she hated. She was dark and thin and foreign-looking in a world where the prestige went to blondness and curly hair and dimples, she was slow
(10) where glibness was prized. She was a child of anxious, not proud, love. We were poor and could not afford for her the soil of easy growth. I was a young mother, I was a distracted mother. There were the other children pushing
(15) up, demanding. Her younger sister seemed all that she was not. … My wisdom came too late. She has much to her and probably little will come of it. She is a child of her age, of depression, of war, of fear.

From Tillie Olsen's I STAND HERE IRONING, © 1961

14 How does the narrator contrast conditions during her daughter's early life and the later years?
  A The family had more money during that time than in the present.
  B Financial conditions were more difficult during that time.
  C Current times are less peaceful than earlier times.
  D She was a less distracted mother during her child's early life.

15 How does the author compare her children in the passage?
  A The younger children look more foreign than her oldest daughter.
  B Her oldest daughter has better verbal skills than her younger children.
  C Her younger children are less attractive than their older sister.
  D Her oldest daughter experiences more difficulties than her younger children do.

16 The narrator states that "my wisdom came too late" (lines 16–17). What does the narrator mean?
  A Younger parents are more patient with their children than older parents.
  B People cannot learn from their mistakes.
  C People gain insight into parenting as they grow older.
  D Age and experience can solve all problems.

17 The narrator contrasts the difference between "anxious" love and "proud" love (line 11). Why might the author have made this distinction?
  A to emphasize that worries affected her child
  B to argue that all parents should be proud of their children
  C to justify the way she raised her child
  D to apologize for her child's behavior

LESSON 4

Plot Elements

Fiction

1. Learn the Skill

The **plot** of the story is made up of the series of events that occur in a story. Authors use specific **plot elements** to tell the events of stories in a particular order. The author sets the scene at the beginning with **exposition**, the background and details of a story.

The story then introduces **complications**, or difficulties, that the people in the story must overcome. Complications are often the result of conflicts between two or more people, or within one person. The complications are most intense at the story's **climax**, which usually comes just before the end. Complications are resolved, happily or unhappily, in the **resolution** at the end of the story.

2. Practice the Skill

By mastering the skill of identifying plot elements, you will improve your study and test-taking skills, especially as they relate to high school equivalency language arts/reading tests. Read the excerpt and strategies below. Then answer the question that follows.

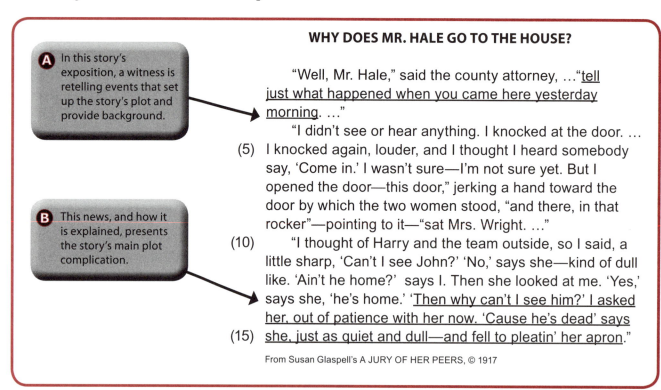

WHY DOES MR. HALE GO TO THE HOUSE?

A — In this story's exposition, a witness is retelling events that set up the story's plot and provide background.

"Well, Mr. Hale," said the county attorney, …"tell just what happened when you came here yesterday morning. …"

"I didn't see or hear anything. I knocked at the door. …
(5) I knocked again, louder, and I thought I heard somebody say, 'Come in.' I wasn't sure—I'm not sure yet. But I opened the door—this door," jerking a hand toward the door by which the two women stood, "and there, in that rocker"—pointing to it—"sat Mrs. Wright. …"

B — This news, and how it is explained, presents the story's main plot complication.

(10) "I thought of Harry and the team outside, so I said, a little sharp, 'Can't I see John?' 'No,' says she—kind of dull like. 'Ain't he home?' says I. Then she looked at me. 'Yes,' says she, 'he's home.' 'Then why can't I see him?' I asked her, out of patience with her now. 'Cause he's dead' says
(15) she, just as quiet and dull—and fell to pleatin' her apron."

From Susan Glaspell's A JURY OF HER PEERS, © 1917

TEST-TAKING TIPS

Think of complications as roadblocks that must be avoided or moved in order for the plot to continue.

1. What complication does the speaker discover at Mrs. Wright's house?
   A He finds that Mrs. Wright is ill.
   B He learns that John is dead.
   C No one can answer the door.
   D Mrs. Wright cannot speak.

Apply the Skill

Directions: Questions 2 through 5 refer to the following excerpt.

WHY IS GOODMAN PARKER OUTSIDE THE WIDOW'S HOUSE?

"What would you have, Goodman Parker?" cried the widow.

"Lack-a-day, is it you, Mistress Margaret?" replied the innkeeper. "I was afraid it might
(5) be your sister Mary; for I hate to see a young woman in trouble, when I haven't a word of comfort to whisper her."

"For Heaven's sake, what news do you bring?" screamed Margaret.

(10) "Why, there has been an express through the town within this half hour," said Goodman Parker, "traveling from the eastern jurisdiction with letters from the governor and council. He tarried at my house to refresh himself with
(15) a drop and a morsel, and I asked him what tidings on the frontiers. He tells me we had the better in the skirmish you wot of, and that thirteen men reported slain are well and sound, and your husband among them. … I judged
(20) you wouldn't mind being broke of your rest, and so I stept over to tell you. Good night."

From Nathaniel Hawthorn's THE WIVES OF THE DEAD, © 1832

2. Goodman Parker is pleased that Margaret answers him instead of Mary because he does not have "a word of comfort" for Mary (lines 6–7). What exposition does this statement give about Mary? From his statement we can infer that
   A Goodman Parker wants to see only Mary.
   B Mary and Margaret do not get along.
   C Goodman Parker has good news for Mary.
   D Mary is experiencing difficulty.

3. Goodman Parker's speech reveals what complication?
   A Margaret's husband was reported dead, but he is actually alive.
   B Mary's husband is dead.
   C Margaret's husband is dead.
   D Thirteen men have been killed.

4. Margaret screams at Goodman Parker to find out his news (lines 8–9). What might be the author's purpose in delaying Goodman Parker's information?
   A to show how Mary's problems are resolved
   B to provide additional exposition
   C to resolve the conflicts in the plot
   D to heighten the suspense of the plot

5. Based on the excerpt, what might be one possible conflict between Mary and Margaret?
   A Goodman Parker's news is revealed to be false.
   B Mary is pleased with Margaret's good news.
   C Margaret has received happy news, but Mary remains unhappy.
   D Both Margaret and Mary will receive happy news.

Directions: Questions 6 through 9 refer to the following excerpt.

WHAT ARE THE WOMEN TRYING TO HIDE?

The sheriff followed the county attorney into the other room. Again—for one final moment—the two women were alone in the kitchen.

(5) Martha Hale sprang up, her hands right together, looking at that other woman, with whom it rested. ... Slowly, unwillingly, Mrs. Peters turned her head until her eyes met the eyes of the other woman. There was
(10) a moment when they held each other in a steady, burning look in which there was no evasion nor flinching. Then Martha Hale's eyes pointed the way to the basket in which was hidden the thing that would make certain
(15) the conviction of the other woman—that woman who was not there and yet who had been there with them all through that hour.

For a moment Mrs. Peters did not move. And then she did it. With a rush forward,
(20) she threw back the quilt pieces, got the box, tried to put it in her hand-bag. It was too big. Desperately she opened it, started to take the bird out. But there she broke—she could not touch the bird. She stood there, helpless,
(25) foolish.

There was the sound of a knob turning in the inner door. Martha Hale snatched the box from the sheriff's wife, and got it in the pocket of her big coat just as the sheriff and the
(30) county attorney came back into the kitchen.

From Susan Glaspell's A JURY OF HER PEERS, © 1917

6 What is the climax of this excerpt?
  A The sheriff leaves the room.
  B Martha Hale snatches the box.
  C Mrs. Peters moves quilt pieces.
  D The women decide to act.

7 Based on the women's actions, what kind of complication might have arisen before the beginning of the excerpt?
  A The women stole a parakeet from a friend.
  B The sheriff arrested Mrs. Peters' husband.
  C The women found a dead canary in a box.
  D The sheriff and the county attorney questioned the women.

8 Martha Hale "snatched the box" from Mrs. Peters (line 27). What might this imply about the rest of the story? This action might imply that
  A the box was not important to the plot's resolution.
  B Mrs. Peters changed her mind about hiding the box.
  C Martha Hale revealed Mrs. Peters's actions.
  D Martha Hale resolved the conflict by hiding the box.

9 Based on the information about the women in this passage, how might they behave at a sporting event?
  A They would cheer for the same team.
  B They would sit on opposite sides of the field.
  C They would sit next to one another but not speak.
  D They would work in the concession stand.

Directions: Questions 10 through 13 refer to the following excerpt.

HOW MIGHT STEPHEN'S NEWS AFFECT MARY?

A young man in a sailor's dress, wet as if he had come out of the depths of the sea, stood alone under the window. Mary recognized him as one whose livelihood was
(5) gained by short voyages along the coast; nor did she forget, that, previous to her marriage, he had been an unsuccessful wooer of her own.

"What do you seek here, Stephen?" asked
(10) she.

"Cheer up, Mary, for I seek to comfort you," answered the rejected lover. "You must know I got home not ten minutes ago, and the first thing my good mother told me was the news
(15) about your husband. So without saying a word to the old woman, I clapt on my hat, and ran out of the house. I couldn't have slept a wink before speaking to you, Mary, for the sake of old times."

(20) "Stephen, I thought better of you!" exclaimed the widow. …

"But stop, and hear my story out," cried the young sailor. "I tell you we spoke a brig yesterday afternoon, bound in from Old
(25) England. And who do you think I saw standing on deck, well and hearty, only a bit thinner than he was five months ago?"

Mary leaned from the window, but could not speak.

(30) "Why, it was your husband himself," continued the generous seaman. "He and three others saved themselves on a spar when the Blessing turned bottom upwards."

From Nathaniel Hawthorne's THE WIVES OF THE DEAD, © 1832

10 The passage states that Stephen was Mary's "unsuccessful wooer" (line 7). What type of plot element is this information about Mary and Stephen's past?
   A exposition
   B complication
   C climax
   D conflict

11 Based on the details in the excerpt, what can we infer is the source of Mary's conflict?
   A her love of Stephen
   B her disappointment in Stephen
   C her broken friendship with Stephen's mother
   D her belief that her husband has died

12 Stephen's message to Mary is the climax of the excerpt. How might the story be resolved?
   A Stephen asks Mary to marry him.
   B Mary's husband comes home.
   C Mary leaves her husband.
   D Stephen rescues Mary's husband.

13 Mary doubts Stephen's reasons for visiting her, saying, "I thought better of you" (line 20). What is implied by this statement? Mary thinks that Stephen
   A is there to tell her good news of her husband's survival.
   B has never had good intentions.
   C is there to console her.
   D is going to ask her to marry him so soon after her husband's death.

Directions: Questions 14 through 18 refer to the following excerpt.

WHY IS MOTHER UPSET?

"Now father, look here"—Sarah Penn had not sat down; she stood before her husband in the humble fashion of a Scripture woman—"I'm going to talk real plain to you: I never have
(5) sence I married you, but I'm going' to now. I 'ain't never complained, an' I ain't goin' to complain now, but I'm goin' to talk plain. You see this room here, father, you look at it well. You see there ain't no carpet on the floor, an'
(10) you see the paper is all dirty, an' droppin' off the walls. We 'ain't had no new paper on it for ten year, an' then I put it on myself, an' it didn't cost you but nine-pence a roll. You see this room, father; it's all the one I've had to work
(15) in an' eat in an' sit in sence we was married. There ain't another woman in the whole town whose husband 'ain't got half the means you have but what's got better. It's all the room Nanny's got to have her company in, an' there
(20) ain't one of her mates but what's got better, an' their father's not so able as hers is. It's all the room she'll have to be married in. ...Father, 'ain't you got nothin' to say?" said Mrs. Penn.

"I've got to go off after that load of gravel.
(25) I can't stan' here talkin' all day."

From Mary E. Wilkins' THE REVOLT OF "MOTHER," © 1890

14 What is the conflict between Mrs. Penn and her husband?
   A She wants gravel for their driveway.
   B She does not like the wallpaper pattern.
   C He objects to her housekeeping.
   D She wants him to improve their house.

15 How might you describe the events of the story?
   A a newlyweds' minor quarrel
   B a couple's deep-seated disagreement
   C a light-hearted tiff
   D a family members' meeting about finances

16 Based on Sarah's personality as described in the excerpt, how will her conflict likely be resolved?
   A She will only put up new wallpaper.
   B She will divorce her husband.
   C She will make improvements to her house.
   D Mr. Penn will change her mind.

17 Sarah Penn says she is going to "talk real plain" to her husband for the first time in her married life (lines 4–7). Why might Sarah mention this?
   A to emphasize that the couple usually communicate very well
   B to indicate that they are tense and emotional
   C to depict Mr. Penn's sensitivity
   D to show that her patience has finally worn out

18 What can you infer is a reason that Sarah Penn is particularly anxious to improve the condition of her home?
   A She has never complained before.
   B Her daughter will be married in the home.
   C The room is cold without a carpet.
   D Other people might be jealous of their nice house.

LESSON 5

Characters

① Learn the Skill

Characters are the fictional people authors create in their stories. Authors bring characters to life by describing their appearances, their thoughts and actions, and other characters' responses to them. On high school equivalency language arts/reading tests, you will be asked to analyze the traits and actions of different characters.

② Practice the Skill

By mastering the skill of analyzing characters, you will improve your study and test-taking skills, especially as they relate to high school equivalency language arts/reading tests. Read the excerpt and strategies below. Then answer the question that follows.

Ⓐ Details in the excerpt indicate that Mrs. Whipple acts a particular way around her neighbors. Think about reasons why Mrs. Whipple might act this way.

Ⓑ Here, the author provides both direct and indirect examples of Mrs. Whipple's character traits.

WHAT IS REVEALED ABOUT MRS. WHIPPLE?

Life was very hard for the Whipples. It was hard to feed all the hungry mouths. It was hard to keep the children in flannels during the winter, short as it was: "God knows what would become of us if we lived north," they would
(5) say: keeping them decently clean was hard. "It looks like our luck won't never let up on us," said Mr. Whipple, but Mrs. Whipple was all for taking what was sent and calling
Ⓐ it good, <u>anyhow when the neighbors were in earshot</u>. "Don't ever let a soul hear us complain," she kept saying to
(10) her husband. <u>She couldn't stand to be pitied.</u> "No, not if it
Ⓑ <u>comes to it that we have to live in a wagon and pick cotton around the country," she said, "nobody's going to get a chance to look down on us.</u>"

From Katherine Anne Porter's HE, © 1930

✓ TEST-TAKING TIPS

Look at details that indicate how characters think, move, and respond. Characters may not always mean what they say; these details are the clues about a character's personality.

1. Based on this excerpt, which of the following best describes the character of Mrs. Whipple?
   A She gives up easily.
   B She is sympathetic to others.
   C She is pitiful.
   D She is proud.

Apply the Skill

Directions: Questions 2 through 5 refer to the following excerpt.

GOLD RUSH BUSINESSWOMAN

Of all the girls and boys who grew up together in Black Hawk, Tiny Soderball was to lead the most adventurous life and to achieve the most solid worldly success.

(5) … While she was running her lodging-house in Seattle, gold was discovered in Alaska. Miners and sailors came back from the North with wonderful stories and pouches of gold. … That daring, which nobody had (10) ever suspected in her, awoke. She sold her business and set out for Circle City. …

That winter Tiny kept in her hotel a Swede … [who] … deeded Tiny Soderball his claim on Hunker Creek. Tiny … went off into the (15) wilds and lived on the claim. She bought other claims from discouraged miners, traded or sold them on percentages.

After nearly ten years in the Klondike, Tiny returned, with a considerable fortune, to live (20) in San Francisco. I met her in Salt Lake City in 1908. … She told me about some of the desperate chances she had taken in the gold country, but the thrill of them was quite gone. She said frankly that nothing interested her (25) much now but making money.

… I was in San Francisco two summers ago when both Lena and Tiny Soderball were in town. … Tiny audits Lena's accounts occasionally, and invests her money for her; (30) and Lena, apparently, takes care that Tiny doesn't grow too miserly.

From MY ÁNTONIA by Willa Cather, © 1918

2 Which detail is an example of Tiny's "adventurous life"?
  A She runs a lodging home in Seattle.
  B She goes to the wilds of Alaska to make a fortune during the gold rush.
  C She returns to San Francisco after nearly ten years in Alaska.
  D She invests Lena's money for her.

3 How does Tiny's character change over the years?
  A Tiny becomes bolder than she was during her childhood.
  B Tiny takes more risks than she did when she was younger.
  C Tiny spends money more recklessly than she did earlier in her life.
  D Tiny becomes more interested in making money than in taking chances.

4 The narrator describes all of the following to reveal Tiny's character except
  A actions.
  B responses.
  C appearance.
  D statements.

5 What does the narrator's description of Tiny reveal about her?
  A The hope of becoming rich is her only motivation for going to Alaska.
  B She has been a bold and resourceful explorer since she was a child.
  C She is obsessed with making money because she gave up her business for the chance to find gold.
  D Her sense of adventure has given way to a need for security.

Directions: Questions 6 through 10 refer to the following excerpt.

CAREFUL PREPARATIONS

It is impossible to say how first the idea entered my brain; but once conceived, it haunted me day and night. Object there was none. Passion there was none. I loved the old
(5) man. He had never wronged me. He had never given me insult. For his gold I had no desire. I think it was his eye! yes, it was this! He had the eye of a vulture—a pale blue eye, with a film over it. Whenever it fell upon me, my blood ran
(10) cold; and so by degrees—very gradually—I made up my mind to take the life of the old man, and thus rid myself of the eye forever.

Now this is the point. You fancy me mad. Madmen know nothing. But you should have
(15) seen me. You should have seen how wisely I proceeded—with what caution—with what foresight—with what dissimulation I went to work! I was never kinder to the old man than during the whole week before I killed him. And
(20) every night, about midnight, I turned the latch of his door and opened it—oh so gently! And then, when I had made an opening sufficient for my head, I first put in a dark lantern, all closed, closed, so that no light shone out, and
(25) then I thrust in my head. Oh, you would have laughed to see how cunningly I thrust it in! I moved it slowly—very, very slowly, so that I might not disturb the old man's sleep. It took me an hour to place my whole head within the
(30) opening so far that I could see the old man as he lay upon his bed. Ha!—would a madman have been so wise as this? And then, when my head was well within the room, I undid the lantern cautiously—oh, so cautiously (for the
(35) hinges creaked)—I undid it just so much that a single thin ray fell upon the vulture eye. And this I did for seven long nights—and every night just at midnight—but I found the eye always closed; and so it was impossible to do
(40) the work; for it was not the old man who vexed me, but his Evil Eye. And every morning, when the day broke, I went boldly into his chamber, and spoke courageously to him, calling him by name in a hearty tone, and inquiring how he
(45) had passed the night. So you see he would have been a very profound old man, indeed, to suspect that every night, just at twelve, I looked in upon him while he slept.

From THE TELL-TALE HEART by Edgar Allan Poe, © 1843

6 On the basis of the details in the passage, what relationship does the narrator most likely have with the old man?
 A The old man is the narrator's father.
 B The narrator takes care of the old man.
 C The narrator is the old man's employer.
 D The narrator and the old man are longtime enemies.

7 What is the narrator's motivation for planning to kill the old man?
 A He resents the old man's wealth.
 B He seeks revenge for the old man's cruelty toward him.
 C He is frightened by the old man's pale blue eye.
 D He wants to end the old man's suffering.

8 The narrator uses words such as *wisely* and *cunningly* to convince readers that he is
 A rational.
 B educated.
 C blameless.
 D organized.

9 The narrator says that moving his head through the doorway to look into the old man's bedroom took an hour. What does this statement reveal about the narrator?
 A He is sensibly cautious and methodical.
 B He respects the old man's need for rest.
 C His descriptions of his own actions are exaggerated.
 D His actions are not reasonable.

10 Which words best describe the narrator?
 A dependable and helpful
 B innocent and trusting
 C fearless and arrogant
 D irrational and obsessed

Directions: Questions 11 through 15 refer to the following excerpt.

HOW IS NICK DESCRIBED IN THIS EXCERPT?

It is difficult to convey in words the charm that Nick possessed. Seeing him, you beheld merely a medium-sized young mechanic in reasonably grimed garage clothes when
(5) working; and in tight pants, tight coat, silk shirt, long-visored green cap when at leisure. A rather pallid skin due to the nature of his work. Large deft hands, a good deal like the hands of a surgeon, square, blunt-fingered, spatulate.
(10) Indeed, as you saw him at work, a wire-netted electric bulb held in one hand, the other plunged deep into the vitals of the car on which he was engaged, you thought of a surgeon performing a major operation. …
(15) All this, of course, could not serve to endear him to the girls. On the contrary, you would have thought that his hands alone, from which he could never quite free the grease and grit, would have caused some feeling
(20) of repugnance among the lily-fingered. But they, somehow, seemed always to be finding an excuse to touch him: his tie, his hair, his coat sleeve. They seemed even to derive a vicarious thrill from holding his hat or cap when
(25) on an outing. They brushed imaginary bits of lint from his coat lapel. …

No; it can't be classified, this powerful draw he had for them.

From Edna Ferber's THE AFTERNOON OF A FAUN, © 1921

11 From the description in the excerpt, which is true about Nick?
  A He cannot fix cars.
  B He is attractive to women.
  C He takes good care of his hands.
  D He has one special girlfriend.

12 Nick's hands are "like the hands of a surgeon" (lines 8–9). What does this description tell us about Nick? This comparison implies that Nick
  A wants to buy his own car.
  B is vain about his looks.
  C often repairs the cars of doctors.
  D is a good mechanic.

13 Which of the following is a general description of Nick's effect on women?
  A Women are intrigued by sophisticated men.
  B Working-class men appeal to many women.
  C Women are charmed by nice guys.
  D Women are put off by sloppy dressers.

14 The narrator says that Nick's charm "can't be classified" (line 27). What does the passage reveal about the narrator's attitude toward Nick?
  A intense jealousy
  B affectionate disbelief
  C deep distrust
  D true dislike

15 What can readers conclude about the women surrounding Nick, based on their behavior?
  A They have crushes on Nick.
  B They are all old friends.
  C They share similar hobbies.
  D Nick has fixed their automobiles.

Directions: Questions 16 through 19 refer to the following excerpt.

WHY IS MRS. WHIPPLE CONCERNED ABOUT MR. WHIPPLE GOING OUTDOORS?

It was a hard winter. It seemed to Mrs. Whipple that they hadn't ever known anything but hard times, and now to cap it all a winter like this. The crops were about half of what
(5) they had a right to expect; after the cotton was in it didn't do much more than cover the grocery bill. They swapped off one of the plow horses, and got cheated, for the new one died of the heaves. Mrs. Whipple kept thinking
(10) all the time it was terrible to have a man you couldn't depend on not to get cheated. They cut down on everything, but Mrs. Whipple kept saying there are things you can't cut down on, and they cost money. It took a lot of
(15) warm clothes for Adna and Emly, who walked four miles to school during the three-months session. "He sets around the fire a lot, He won't need so much," said Mr. Whipple. "That's so," said Mrs. Whipple, "and when He does the
(20) outdoor chores He can wear your tarpaullion coat. I can't do no better, that's all."

In February, He was taken sick, and lay curled up under His blanket looking very blue in the face and acting as if He would choke. Mr.
(25) and Mrs. Whipple did everything they could for Him for two days, and then they were scared and sent for the doctor. The doctor told them they must keep Him warm and give Him plenty of milk and eggs. "He isn't as stout as He
(30) looks, I'm afraid," said the doctor. "You've got to watch them when they're like that. You must put more cover onto Him, too."

"I just took off His big blanket to wash," said Mrs. Whipple, ashamed. "I can't stand
(35) dirt."

"Well, you'd better put it back on the minute it's dry," said the doctor, "or He'll have pneumonia."

Mr. and Mrs. Whipple took a blanket off
(40) their own bed and put his cot in by the fire.

From Katherine Anne Porter's HE, © 1930

16 Mrs. Whipple's thinks that "it was terrible to have a man you couldn't depend on not to get cheated" (lines 10–11). What can readers infer from her statement?
 A She believes she was charged too much for groceries.
 B She resents her neighbor's unfairness.
 C She resents her husband's incompetence.
 D She does not trust the doctor.

17 Which of the following describes Mrs. Whipple?
 A determined
 B tender
 C compassionate
 D bitter

18 What is Mrs. Whipple's first response to the shortages her family faces?
 A She takes away from Adna and Emly.
 B She gives less to Him.
 C She does with less herself.
 D She asks neighbors for help.

19 Mrs. Whipple tells the doctor that she "took off His big blanket to wash" (line 33), although she later takes a blanket from her own bed. What is revealed about Mrs. Whipple's personality? Mrs. Whipple is
 A tidy.
 B unselfish.
 C dishonest.
 D forthright.

LESSON 6

Motivation

Fiction

① Learn the Skill

Motivation is the reason that characters act in a particular way or make certain choices. Characters may be motivated by fear, greed, embarrassment, or love of another character. By looking at what characters say, how they act, and how other characters respond, readers can determine why characters make certain decisions. Being able to identify characters' motivations will help you answer questions about why characters behave in a certain way.

② Practice the Skill

By mastering the skill of analyzing character motivation, you will improve your study and test-taking skills, especially as they relate to high school equivalency language arts/reading tests. Read the excerpt and strategies below. Then answer the question that follows.

A Perry Jr.'s mother made a business decision that he obviously does not agree with. Her presentation of the documents to her children shows that she is pleased with the decision she made.

B The daughter, Martha, calls her mother's action a "vengeful triumph." Based on this, we can tell that the mother had performed an act that she knows will displease her children.

WHY DOES THE MOTHER SELL THE HOUSE?

Some papers their mother had in her purse, that was the occasion. Notarized contracts. ... She'd sold Marlcrest ... to a developer who planned to bulldoze the house, clear the land, build a subdivision there. Plantation Oaks, he'd call it. "Here is a copy of the title deed," she (5) said, passing it to Perry Jr. "And you will see, it is properly signed and notarized." He turned it over, held it up to the light, looking for the error that would void the contract. As for the family records and belongings—the *contents* of the house, she said, leaning toward them from her wheelchair (10) with her hands folded in her lap and high color in her cheeks, savoring (Martha saw) the vengeful triumph of this theft—she'd sold them all to a young man from a southern history museum in Atlanta.

From Pam Durban's SOON, © 1996

✓ TEST-TAKING TIPS

In reading for motivation, look at how other characters respond to an action. These responses can help you figure out the reasons characters acted in a particular way.

1 Based on the excerpt, what is most likely the mother's motivation for selling her family's property?
  A to get money for her children
  B to preserve her history
  C to hurt her children's feelings
  D to pay off debts

Apply the Skill

Directions: Questions 2 through 5 refer to the following excerpt.

WHY ARE THE MEN ARGUING?

In the front Shirley was talking to Siggie, the cheese man. Seeing him up there, leaning casually on the counter, Greenspahn felt a quick anger. He walked up the aisle toward
(5) him.

Siggie saw him coming. "*Shalom*, Jake," he called.

"I want to talk to you."

"Is it important, Jake, because I'm in some
(10) terrific hurry. I still got deliveries."

"What did you leave me?"

"The same, Jake. The same. A couple pounds blue. Some Swiss. Delicious," he said, smacking his lips.

(15) "I been getting complaints, Siggie."

"From the Americans, right? Your average American don't know from cheese. It don't mean nothing." He turned to go.

"Siggie, where you running?"

(20) "Jake, I'll be back tomorrow. You can talk to me about it."

"Now."

He turned reluctantly. "What's the matter?"

"You're leaving old stuff. Who's your
(25) wholesaler?"

"Jake, Jake," he said. "We already been over this. I pick up the returns, don't I?"

"That's not the point."

"Have you ever lost a penny account of
(30) me?"

"Siggie, who's your wholesaler? Where do you get the stuff?"

"I'm cheaper than the dairy, right? Ain't I cheaper than the dairy? Come on, Jake. What
(35) do you want?"

"Siggie, don't be a jerk. Who are you talking to? Don't be a jerk. You leave me cheap, crummy cheese, the dairies are ready to throw it away. I get everybody else's returns.
(40) It's old when I get it. Do you think a customer wants a cheese it goes off like a bomb two days after she gets it home? And what about the customers who don't return it? They think I'm gypping them and they don't come back. I
(45) don't want the *schlak* stuff. Give me fresh or I'll take from somebody else."

_{From Stanley Elkin's CRIERS AND KIBITZERS, KIBITZERS AND CRIERS, © 1965}

2 Why does Greenspahn want to talk to Siggie?
  A He wants to offer Siggie cheese.
  B He wants to sell Siggie cheese.
  C Greenspahn thinks Siggie is cheating him.
  D Greenspahn intends to complement Siggie.

3 Why would a wholesaler be motivated to sell products that are outdated or inferior?
  A to maintain a good reputation
  B to increase profit
  C to please customers
  D to expand a base of operations

4 Siggie states that he cannot talk because he is in "some terrific hurry" (lines 9–10). Why do you think Siggie says he's in a hurry?
  A He does not want to talk to Greenspahn.
  B He is a very good worker.
  C He hates to be late.
  D He is helping Shirley.

5 What is the most likely reason that Greenspahn is confronting Siggie?
  A He is satisfied with Siggie's service.
  B His customers have complimented the cheese.
  C His sales have increased.
  D His customers have complained.

Directions: Questions 6 through 9 refer to the following excerpt.

WHAT IS THE SPEAKER TRYING TO DO?

Now this is the point. You fancy me mad. Madmen know nothing. But you should have seen *me*. You should have seen how wisely I proceeded—with what caution—with what
(5) foresight—with what dissimulation I went to work! I was never kinder to the old man than during the whole week before I killed him. And every night, about midnight, I turned the latch of his door and opened it—oh so gently! And
(10) then, when I had made an opening sufficient for my head, I first put in a dark lantern, all closed, closed, so that no light shone out, and then I thrust in my head. Oh, you would have laughed to see how cunningly I thrust it in! I
(15) moved it slowly—very, very slowly, so that I might not disturb the old man's sleep. It took me an hour to place my whole head within the opening so far that I could see the old man as he lay upon his bed. Ha!—would a madman
(20) have been so wise as this? And then, when my head was well within the room, I undid the lantern cautiously—oh, so cautiously (for the hinges creaked)—I undid it just so much that a single thin ray fell upon the vulture eye. And
(25) this I did for seven long nights—every night just at midnight—but I found the eye always closed; and so it was impossible to do the work; for it was not the old man who vexed me, but his Evil Eye. And every morning, when
(30) the day broke, I went boldly into his chamber, and spoke courageously to him, calling him by name in a hearty tone, and inquiring how he had passed the night.

From Edgar Allan Poe's THE TELL-TALE HEART, © 1843

6. The speaker states "You fancy me mad" (line 1). For what reason might the speaker say that readers will think he is mad? His audience
   A has seen him interact with the old man.
   B knows what he planned to do to the old man.
   C thinks he is in a mental institution.
   D is on the old man's side.

7. Which of the following was most likely the speaker's motivation for opening the door slowly?
   A The old man had booby-trapped the door.
   B The door was too small for him to fit through.
   C He wanted to have a chat with the old man, but did not want to scare him.
   D He did not want to wake the old man.

8. What effect did the closed "Evil Eye" (line 29) have on the speaker?
   A The speaker did not follow through on his plans to destroy the eye.
   B The speaker's plans were not changed at all by the closed eye.
   C The speaker was upset, because he was curious about the eye.
   D The closed eye had no effect on the speaker.

9. How would the speaker most likely open a gift?
   A carelessly
   B quickly
   C angrily
   D meticulously

Directions: Questions 10 through 13 refer to the following excerpt.

WHY DO MARTHA AND PERRY JR. LIE ABOUT ROWDY?

Even after she'd sold Marlcrest out from under them and momentarily righted the wrong of her life by taking from someone else what she felt had been taken from her, she hadn't
(5) been satisfied. Instead, she'd begun to pine and grieve over her old poodle.

Rowdy was his name, Martha's only inheritance. She'd taken him to her house when she and Perry Jr. had put their mother
(10) in a nursing home. He was thirteen years old then, morose and incontinent, a trembler, a fear-biter. …On a Saturday morning soon after he came to live with her, he turned over her garbage while she was at the grocery store
(15) and ate rancid bacon drippings out of a small Crisco can. She found him on her kitchen floor, greasy and struggling to breathe, and rushed him to the vet's, where he died two hours later, his blood so clogged with fat his old heart just
(20) choked on it.

Until her dying day their mother had been greedy for news of Rowdy, details of his diet, the consistency of his stools, and Martha and Perry Jr. had given them to her. They even
(25) pretended to be passing Rowdy back and forth between them, sharing the wealth…Toward the end, when she smiled at them, it was her skull that smiled; then the weeping would begin, the longing, the sorrow. "Why don't you bring my
(30) little dog to see me?" she would sob. "Soon, Mother," they would promise, patting her hand.

From Pam Durban's SOON, © 1996

10 What is the mother's motivation for selling Marlcrest?
   A She leaves the money to Rowdy.
   B She wants to take her poodle from the country.
   C She hopes to win her children's affection.
   D She wants to hurt other people as she has been hurt herself.

11 If Martha were a nurse, with which of the statements would she probably agree?
   A The children of aged parents needlessly make elderly people cry.
   B Animals are rarely a comfort to patients.
   C Patients should always know the truth.
   D Avoid giving patients bad news when possible.

12 In the excerpt the mother pines and grieves over her dog. What does this reveal about the mother's personality? We can infer that the mother
   A forgets her dog when she is in the nursing home.
   B treats her dog and her children with equal kindness.
   C treats her children better than she treats her dog.
   D treats her dog more kindly than she treats her children.

13 Rowdy dies while living with Martha. Why do Perry Jr. and Martha hide the truth from their mother?
   A because they are cruel
   B because they want to spare her feelings
   C because they are dishonest
   D because they want attention

Directions: Questions 14 through 17 refer to the following excerpt.

WHY DOES GREENSPAHN FIRE FRANK?

"Look, I caught her with the salmon. Would you want me to call the cops for a can of salmon? She's got a kid."

"Yeah, you got a big heart, Frank."

(5) "I would have let you handle it if I'd seen you. I looked for you, Jake."

"You shook her down. I told you before about that."

"Jake, it's ten bucks for the store. I get so…
(10) mad when somebody like that tries to get away with something."

"*Podler*," Greenspahn shouted. "You're through here. … Please, Frank. Get out of here," Greenspahn said.

(15) "Sure," Frank screamed. "Sure, sure," he shouted. Greenspahn, startled, looked at him. He seemed angrier than even himself. Greenspahn thought of the customers. They would hear him. What kind of a place, he
(20) thought. What kind of a place? "Sure," Frank yelled, "fire me, go ahead. A regular holy man. A saint! What are you, God? He smells everybody's rottenness but his own. Only when your own son—may he rest—when your own
(25) son slips five bucks out of the cash drawer, that you don't see."

Greenspahn could have killed him. "Who says that?"

From Stanley Elkin's CRIERS AND KIBITZERS, KIBITZERS AND CRIERS, © 1965

14 What might have been Frank's motivation for taking ten dollars from the woman in the store?
  A charity
  B greed
  C humor
  D fairness

15 If Greenspahn were a judge, with which of the following statements would he probably agree?
  A A hungry person who steals is worse than an honest person who overcharges him or her.
  B Shop owners should give their food away.
  C Shoplifting is always wrong.
  D A person who overcharges a hungry person is worse than a shoplifter.

16 Frank tells Greenspahn that his son took cash from the cash drawer. Why might Frank have told Greenspahn this? Frank is most likely motivated by
  A compassion.
  B jealousy.
  C anger.
  D grief.

17 Frank indicates that Greenspahn's son is dead when he says "your own son—may he rest" (line 24). Why might he have mentioned Greenspahn's son? His motivation is to
  A honor a dead boy.
  B hurt a grieving father.
  C share a happy memory.
  D praise a co-worker.

LESSON 7
Point of View

1 Learn the Skill

A story is told from a particular **point of view**. It may be told by an **omniscient**, or all-knowing, narrator who knows the thoughts and feelings of all the characters. Or it may be told through a **first-person** narrative. Both of these kinds of writing can affect how a reader receives information about a story. An omniscient point of view lets the reader know what multiple characters are thinking or feeling, while a first-person narrative requires the reader to rely on a single character's perception of events and other characters.

2 Practice the Skill

By mastering the skill of determining point of view, you will improve your study and test-taking skills, especially as they relate to high school equivalency language arts/reading tests. Read the excerpt and strategies below. Then answer the question that follows.

A The pronoun *her* indicates that this story is told from an omniscient point of view. This narrator informs readers about Connie's thoughts and feelings.

B The omniscient narrator also has access to the thoughts and feelings of Connie's mother, who "noticed everything."

WHAT DOES THIS PASSAGE REVEAL ABOUT CONNIE?

Her name was Connie. She was fifteen and she had a quick nervous giggling habit of craning her neck to glance into mirrors, or **A** checking other people's faces to make sure her own was all right. Her mother, who noticed everything
(5) and knew everything and who hadn't much reason any **B** longer to look at her own face, always scolded Connie about it. "Stop gawking at yourself, who are you? You think you're so pretty?" she would say. Connie would raise her eyebrows at those familiar complaints and look right
(10) through her mother, into a shadowy vision of herself as she was right at that moment: she knew she was pretty and that was everything.

From Joyce Carol Oates' WHERE ARE YOU GOING, WHERE HAVE YOU BEEN?, © 1967

TEST-TAKING TIPS

When analyzing point of view, look closely at which pronouns are used. The pronouns *I* and *we* indicate a first-person point of view, while *he* and *she* show that an omniscient narrator is telling the story.

1 The narrator of the passage depicts an exchange between a mother and daughter. How is this exchange described? In this excerpt, the narrator
   A depicts only the mother's thoughts.
   B describes the daughter's actions, but not her thoughts.
   C reveals the thoughts and actions of both characters.
   D does not explain the mother's feelings.

Unit 2 | Fiction

Apply the Skill

Directions: Questions 2 through 5 refer to the following excerpt.

WHAT DO WE LEARN ABOUT THE CHARACTERS IN THIS EXCERPT?

During my holidays from school, I was allowed to stay in bed until long after my father had gone to work. He left our house every weekday at the stroke of seven by the Anglican
(5) church bell. I would lie in bed awake, and I could hear all the sounds my parents made as they prepared for the day ahead. As my mother made my father his breakfast, my father would shave, using his shaving brush that had an
(10) ivory handle and a razor that matched; then he would step outside to the little shed he had built for us as a bathroom, to quickly bathe in water that he had instructed my mother to leave outside overnight in the dew. That way,
(15) the water would be very cold, and he believed that cold water strengthened his back. If I had been a boy, I would have gotten the same treatment, but since I was a girl, and on top of that went to school only with other girls, my
(20) mother would always add some hot water to my bathwater to take off the chill. On Sunday afternoons, while I was in Sunday school, my father took a hot bath; the tub was half filled with plain water, and then my mother would
(25) add a large caldronful of water in which she had just boiled some bark and leaves from a bay-leaf tree. The bark and leaves were there for no reason other than that he liked the smell. He would then spend hours lying in this
(30) bath, studying his pool coupons or drawing examples of pieces of furniture he planned to make. When I came home from Sunday school, we would sit down to our Sunday dinner.

From Jamaica Kincaid's THE CIRCLING HAND, © 1985

2. From whose point of view is the passage told?
   A the mother and father's
   B the father's
   C the mother's
   D the girl's

3. The girl in the excerpt says that "I would lie in bed awake, and I could hear all the sounds my parents made as they prepared for the day ahead" (lines 5–7). What does the pronoun "I" indicate?
   A The story is a first-person account.
   B An omniscient narrator will tell the story.
   C All the mother's thoughts will be revealed.
   D The story will be told from the parents' point of view.

4. What might be the author's purpose in presenting this point of view?
   A to provide insight into a family's feelings
   B to analyze a father's bathing habits
   C to reveal a mother's hidden resentment
   D to present the thoughts and feelings of one young girl

5. What does the daughter's account of her parents most resemble?
   A a journalist's objective account of an event
   B a diary writer explaining daily events
   C a person writing a poem to express feelings
   D a movie reviewer analyzing a film

Directions: Questions 6 through 9 refer to the following excerpt.

WHAT DO READERS LEARN ABOUT THE MARCH GIRLS?

Jo was the first to wake in the gray dawn of Christmas morning. No stockings hung at the fireplace, and for a moment she felt as much disappointed as she did long ago, when her
(5) little sock fell down because it was crammed so full of goodies. Then she remembered her mother's promise and, slipping her hand under her pillow, drew out a little crimson-covered book. She knew it very well, for it was that
(10) beautiful old story of the best life ever lived, and Jo felt that it was a true guidebook for any pilgrim going on a long journey. She woke Meg with a "Merry Christmas," and bade her see what was under her pillow. A green-covered
(15) book appeared, with the same picture inside, and a few words written by their mother, which made their one present very precious in their eyes. Presently Beth and Amy woke to rummage and find their little books also,
(20) one dove-colored, the other blue, and all sat looking at and talking about them, while the east grew rosy with the coming day.

In spite of her small vanities, Margaret had a sweet and pious nature, which unconsciously
(25) influenced her sisters, especially Jo, who loved her very tenderly, and obeyed her because her advice was so gently given.

"Girls," said Meg seriously, looking from the tumbled head beside her to the two little
(30) night-capped ones in the room beyond, "Mother wants us to read and love and mind these books, and we must begin at once. We must be faithful about it, but since Father went away and all this war trouble unsettled us, we
(35) have neglected many things. You can do as you please, but I shall keep my book on the table here and read a little every morning as soon as I wake, for I know it will do me good and help me through the day."

From Louisa May Alcott's LITTLE WOMEN, © 1868

6. The narrator in the passage knows that Jo is disappointed about the lack of presents, and that Meg (Margaret) has "a sweet and pious nature" (line 25). How might the narrator be described?
   A Jo
   B Meg
   C omniscient
   D first-person

7. In the excerpt, Meg says that "Mother wants us to read and love and mind these books" (lines 33–34). What does this information reveal?
   A The girls' mother has spent a lot of money to buy these books.
   B The mother believes that the girls should cherish and learn from the things they are given.
   C The mother thinks the girls are ungrateful.
   D Books are easy to come by in spite of the war.

8. What is the author's purpose in using this kind of point of view?
   A to provide insight into the reading habits of girls in the 1800s
   B to analyze the girls' reactions to their Christmas gifts
   C to reveal Jo's despair at the family's lack of money
   D to present the thoughts of all the characters

9. Based on this excerpt, which of the following jobs might Meg most enjoy?
   A teacher
   B office clerk
   C magazine writer
   D make-up consultant

Unit 2 | Fiction

Directions: Questions 10 through 13 refer to the following excerpt.

WHAT ARE THE LITTLE GIRL AND HER NURSE DOING IN THE EXCERPT?

The little girl who had done this was eleven—beautifully ugly, as little girls are apt to be who are destined after a few years to be inexpressibly lovely and bring no end of
(5) misery to a great number of men. The spark, however, was perceptible. There was a general ungodliness in the way her lips twisted down at the corners when she smiled, and in the— Heaven help us!—in the almost passionate
(10) quality of her eyes. Vitality is born early in such women. It was utterly in evidence now, shining through her thin frame in a sort of glow.

She had come eagerly out onto the course at nine o'clock with a white linen nurse and
(15) five small new golf clubs in a white canvas bag which the nurse was carrying. When Dexter first saw her she was standing by the caddie house, rather ill at ease and trying to conceal the fact by engaging her nurse in an obviously
(20) unnatural conversation graced by startling and irrelevant grimaces from herself. …

The smile again—radiant, blatantly artificial—convincing.

"I don't know what we're supposed to
(25) do now," said the nurse, looking nowhere in particular.

"Oh, that's all right. I'll fix it up."

Dexter stood perfectly still, his mouth slightly ajar. He knew that if he moved
(30) forward a step his stare would be in her line of vision—if he moved backward he would lose his full view of her face. For a moment he had not realized how young she was. Now he remembered having seen her several times the
(35) year before—in bloomers.

From F. Scott Fitzgerald's WINTER DREAMS, © 1922

10 How might the author's language be described?
A nervous and edgy
B sad and wistful
C brooding and angry
D confident and all-knowing

11 In the excerpt, the little girl's smile is "radiant, blatantly artificial—convincing" (lines 22–23). What does this tell us about the narrative point of view? The narrator
A knows only the thoughts of the nurse.
B knows the girl's thoughts.
C can describe the girl's actions, not her feelings.
D will not understand Dexter's attraction to her.

12 From the evidence in the excerpt, what information might you expect to find in the rest of the story?
A descriptions of characters' motives, but not their emotions
B unreliable information about the little girl
C limited access to Dexter's thoughts
D the thoughts and feelings of all characters

13 The passage describes "a general ungodliness in the way her lips twisted down at the corners" (lines 6–8). To what might this sort of description be compared?
A a job memorandum
B a diary entry
C a psychological profile
D a love letter

Directions: Questions 14 through 18 refer to the following excerpt.

WHAT IS THE NARRATOR DOING IN THE EXCERPT?

I was in those days a poor student and would brashly attempt to teach anybody anything for a buck an hour, although I have since learned better. Mostly I gave English
(5) lessons to recently arrived refugees. The college sent me; I had acquired a little experience. Already a few of my students were trying their broken English, theirs and mine, in the American marketplace. I was then
(10) just twenty, on my way into my senior year in college, a skinny, life-hungry kid, eating himself waiting for the next world war to start. It was a…cheat. Here I was palpitating to get going, and across the ocean Adolf Hitler,
(15) in black boots and a square mustache, was tearing up all the flowers. Will I ever forget what went on with Danzing that summer?

Times were still hard from the depression but anyway I made a little living from the poor
(20) refugees. They were all over uptown Broadway in 1939. I had four I tutored—Karl Otto Alp, the former film star; Wolfgang Novak, once a brilliant economist; Friedrich Wilhelm Wolff, who had taught medieval history at Heidelberg;
(25) and, after that night I met him in his disordered cheap hotel room, Oskar Gassner, the Berlin critic and journalist, at one time on the *Acht Uhr Abendblatt*. They were accomplished men. I had my nerve associating with them, but
(30) that's what a world crisis does for people— they get educated.

From Bernard Malamud's THE GERMAN REFUGEE, © 1963

14 Who is the narrator of the story?
  A Oskar Gassner
  B Friedrich Wilhelm Wolff
  C a college student
  D an omniscient narrator

15 Judging by the narrator's point of view, what information can readers expect will be available in the story?
  A the thoughts and feelings of students learning English
  B the thoughts and feelings of all German refugees
  C anything seen or thought by the college student
  D the thoughts and feelings of all characters

16 The narrator describes the "four I tutored" (line 21). To what might this description be compared? His presentation of this information is similar to a
  A professor giving a lecture.
  B host introducing guest speakers.
  C politician delivering a speech.
  D teacher assigning a lesson.

17 The point of view emphasizes which of the narrator's qualities?
  A youth
  B experience
  C cynicism
  D worldliness

18 Based on the information from the excerpt, why do you think the refugees were tutored by the narrator?
  A They needed to learn math.
  B They had nothing else to do.
  C They only knew German.
  D They wanted to learn to write.

LESSON 8

Theme

Fiction

1 Learn the Skill

A story's **theme** is the insight or general idea that the author shares with readers. A theme doe not sum up a story's plot. Instead, it gives a lesson or a moral about human nature. For example, the plot of the fairy tale *Cinderella* is about a poor girl who marries a prince. Its theme, however, might be stated as "keep hoping for better days." Themes are not often stated directly, so readers must use clues from the text to discover the implied message.

2 Practice the Skill

By mastering the skill of identifying a story's theme, you will improve your study and test-taking skills, especially as they relate to high school equivalency language arts/reading tests. Read the excerpt and strategies below. Then answer the question that follows.

A At the beginning of the excerpt, the author describes the scene. The descriptions give readers a better sense of how the children live.

B The author describes the children's activities and the different ways that the children play together, despite the cold weather.

WHAT IS THE SPEAKER DESCRIBING?

When the short days of winter came dusk fell before we had well eaten our dinners. **A** When we met in the street the houses had grown sombre. The space of sky above us was the colour of ever-changing violet and towards it the lamps of (5) the street lifted their feeble lanterns. The cold air stung us and we played till our bodies glowed. Our shouts echoed in the silent street. The career of our play brought us through the dark muddy lanes behind the houses where we ran the gauntlet of the rough tribes from the cottages, to the back doors of the (10) dark dripping gardens where odours arose from the ashpits, **B** to the dark odorous stables where a coachman smoothed and combed the horse or shook music from the buckled harness. When we returned to the street light from the kitchen windows had filled the areas. If my uncle was seen turning the corner we (15) hid in the shadow until we had seen him safely housed.

From James Joyce's ARABY, © 1914

🧩 MAKING ASSUMPTIONS

Based on the last part of the excerpt, you can assume that the speaker does not want to be caught playing outside. Think about ways in which this sort of conflict might affect the rest of the story.

1 Which of the following best describes the theme of the excerpt?
   A Children are able to find ways to have fun in different situations.
   B Cold air is bad for gardens.
   C Children should not hide from their relatives.
   D It is a description of a scene.

Apply the Skill

Directions: Questions 2 through 6 refer to the following excerpt.

WHY IS DONALD UPSET?

In a way, Donald's absences are a fine arrangement, even considerate. He is sparing them his darkest moods, when he can't cope with his memories of Vietnam. Vietnam had
(5) never seemed such a meaningful fact until a couple of years ago, when he grew depressed and moody. … He isn't really working regularly at the strip mines. He is mostly just hanging around there, watching the land being
(10) scraped away, trees coming down, bushes flung in the air. Sometimes he operates a steam shovel, and when he comes home his clothes are filled with the clay and it is caked on his shoes. The clay is the color of butterscotch
(15) pudding.

At first, he tried to explain to Jeannette. He said, "If we could have had tanks over there as big as Big Bertha, we wouldn't have lost the war. Strip mining is just like what we were
(20) doing over there. We were stripping off the top. The topsoil is like the culture and the people, the best part of the land and the country. America was just stripping off the top, the best. We ruined it. Here, at least the coal companies
(25) have to plant vetch and loblolly pines and all kinds of trees and bushes. If we'd done that in Vietnam, maybe we'd have left that country in better shape."

From Bobbie Ann Mason's BIG BERTHA STORIES, © 1988

2. **Which of the following best states the theme of this excerpt?**
   A Many men fought in the Vietnam War.
   B The wounds of war always heal.
   C War disrupts people deeply.
   D Jeannette does not understand war.

3. **Why is Donald depressed and moody?**
   A He does not like working at the strip mines.
   B His experience in Vietnam still haunts him.
   C He does not like living with his family.
   D His job is unsatisfying.

4. **Donald says that "We were stripping off the top. The topsoil is like the culture and the people…" (lines 19–20). What might this indicate?**
   A Both activities are destructive.
   B Both activities are productive.
   C Only strip mining damages a culture.
   D Neither strip mining nor war damage a culture.

5. **Which word best describes the way Donald feels in this excerpt?**
   A sensitive
   B compassionate
   C perplexed
   D haunted

6. **With which of the following statements would Donald probably agree?**
   A War is beneficial to society.
   B Big industry is vital to America's economy.
   C Families always understand soldiers' experiences.
   D If you break something, you should fix it.

Directions: Questions 7 through 10 refer to the following excerpt.

WHAT DOES RAY THINK IS UNFAIR?

The beauty of the country about Winesburg was too much for Ray on that fall evening. That is all there was to it. He could not stand it. All of a sudden he forgot all about
(5) being a quiet old farmhand and throwing off the torn overcoat began to run across the field. As he ran he shouted a protest against his life, against all life, against everything that makes life ugly. "There was no promise made,"
(10) he cried into the empty spaces that lay about him. "I didn't promise my Minnie anything and Hal hasn't made any promise to Nell. I know he hasn't. She went into the woods with him because she wanted to go. What he wanted
(15) she wanted. Why should I pay? Why should Hal pay? Why should anyone pay? I don't want Hal to become old and worn out. I'll tell him. I won't let it go on. I'll catch Hal before he gets to town and I'll tell him. ..."
(20)   Then as he ran he remembered his children and in fancy felt their hands clutching at him. All of his thoughts of himself were involved with the thoughts of Hal and he thought the children were clutching at the
(25) younger man also. "They are the accidents of life, Hal," he cried. "They are not mine or yours. I had nothing to do with them."

From Sherwood Anderson's THE UNTOLD LIE, © 1947

7 Ray asks "why should I pay?" (line 15). Based on the evidence in the passage, what is Ray protesting against? Ray is protesting against
   A his responsibilities.
   B his job.
   C where he lives in Winesburg.
   D the state of his overcoat.

8 What is the author's purpose in describing Ray's protest "against everything that makes life ugly" (line 8–9)?
   A to illustrate Ray's impact on the community
   B to show that Ray feels unfulfilled by his life
   C to illustrate the pettiness of Ray's feelings
   D to demonstrate Ray's job satisfaction

9 Which of the following best states the theme of this excerpt?
   A Farmhands are treated unfairly.
   B Marriage often leads to tragedy.
   C Disappointed people want to stop others from making their mistakes.
   D Good friends help one another avoid problems.

10 Which detail about Ray best supports the theme?
   A He throws off his torn overcoat.
   B He remembers when his children were younger.
   C He enjoys living in a beautiful place like Winesburg.
   D He is running to catch Hal before he does something Ray disagrees with.

Directions: Questions 11 through 14 refer to the following excerpt.

WHAT IS THE STRANGER'S DECISION?

It was many years ago. Hadleyburg was the most honest and upright town in all the region round about. It had kept that reputation unsmirched during three generations, and
(5) was prouder of it than of any other of its possessions. It was so proud of it, and so anxious to insure its perpetuation, that it began to teach the principles of honest dealing to its babies in the cradle, and made
(10) the like teachings the staple of their culture thenceforward through all the years devoted to their education. ...The neighbouring towns were jealous of this honourable supremacy, and affected to sneer at Hadleyburg's pride in
(15) it and call it vanity; but all the same they were obliged to acknowledge that Hadleyburg was in reality an incorruptible town...

But at last, in the drift of time, Hadleyburg had the ill luck to offend a passing stranger—
(20) possibly without knowing it, certainly without caring, for Hadleyburg was sufficient unto itself, and cared not a rap for strangers or their opinions. Still, it would have been well to make an exception in this one's case, for he
(25) was a bitter man, and revengeful. All through his wanderings during a whole year he kept his injury in mind, and gave all his leisure moments to trying to invent a compensating satisfaction for it. ...At last he had a fortunate
(30) idea, and when it fell into his brain it lit up his whole head with an evil joy. He began to form a plan at once, saying to himself "That is the thing to do—I will corrupt the town."

From Mark Twain's THE MAN THAT CORRUPTED HADLEYBURG, © 1899

11 What is the main idea of this excerpt?
  A Corruption brings down a town government.
  B Citizens do all they can to protect a town's reputation.
  C A town raises its children to be morally upright.
  D A stranger decides to trick a town known for its honesty.

12 The narrator states that the citizens of Hadleyburg had "the ill luck to offend a passing stranger" (line 19). What does this statement imply?
  A A traveler complained of service received at a town business.
  B Citizens pride themselves on hospitality.
  C A visitor was treated poorly while in Hadleyburg.
  D All visitors are shunned in Hadleyburg.

13 The stranger says that he will "corrupt the town" (line 33). Which of the following is the best illustration of his idea? His idea is most like
  A showing the hidden costs in a "bargain" item.
  B exposing the greed in a company known for its charity.
  C revealing that an expensive car does not work.
  D finding out that a man thought to be a miser is really a generous donor.

14 Which of the following best states the theme of this excerpt?
  A Hospitality is not important to having good relationships.
  B Honest people are known by their reputations
  C Honesty must be able to withstand challenges.
  D Bitter people are tricky and dangerous.

Directions: Questions 15 through 18 refer to the following excerpt.

WHAT UPSETS DONALD?

[T]hen he abruptly returns to tanks and helicopters.

"A Bell Huey Cobra—my God what a beautiful machine. So efficient!" Donald takes (5) the food processor blade from the drawer where Jeannette keeps it. He says, "A rotor blade from a chopper could just slice anything to bits."

"Don't do that," Jeannette says.

(10) He is trying to spin the blade on the counter, like a top. "Here's what would happen when a chopper blade hits a power line—not many of those over there!—or a tree. Not many trees, either, come to think of it, after all (15) the Agent Orange." He drops the blade and it glances off the open drawer and falls to the floor, spiking the vinyl.

At first, Jeannette thinks the screams are hers, but they are his. She watches him cry. (20) She has never seen anyone cry so hard, like an intense summer thundershower. All she knows to do is shove Kleenex at him. Finally, he is able to say, "You thought I was going to hurt you. That's why I'm crying."

(25) "Go ahead and cry," Jeannette says, holding him close.

"Don't go away."

"I'm right here. I'm not going anywhere."

From Bobbie Ann Mason's BIG BERTHA STORIES, © 1988

15 Of what does the food processor blade remind Donald?
  A a helicopter's rotor blade
  B his wife
  C a power line
  D a tree

16 Which of the following is most like Donald's situation?
  A a bicyclist returning from a long ride
  B a marathon runner who is hungry
  C a shark-attack survivor who has nightmares about sharks
  D a soldier returning home after an uneventful tour of duty

17 Which of the following best describes the theme of this passage?
  A People should forget the past and live for the future.
  B Unresolved past problems remain in the present.
  C Men should not cry in front of their wives.
  D Husbands and wives always share and understand each other's feelings.

18 Donald cries when he thinks Jeannette imagines that he will hurt her. What is the author's purpose in showing readers Donald's emotional response? The author's purpose is to
  A reveal Donald's capacity for violence.
  B show Donald's sensitivity and fragile emotional state.
  C indicate that Donald had resolved his problems.
  D illustrate that Jeannette knows how to comfort Donald.

LESSON 9

Setting

Fiction

① Learn the Skill

A story's **setting** is the time when and place where events happen. Authors develop a setting through details such as describing scenery, the items found in a room, or characters' clothing and accents. The setting adds depth and complexity to a tale. A story that takes place in the middle of the night, for example, is likely to have a different feel to it than a story set in a high school cafeteria.

② Practice the Skill

By mastering the skill of understanding setting, you will improve your study and test-taking skills, especially as they relate to high school equivalency language arts/reading tests. Read the excerpt and strategies below. Then answer the question that follows.

A The author provides many setting details for the reader, such as the gray color and rocky shape of the waves.

B The details in the setting can affect the feeling of a story. Here, the waves are described as wrong; barbarous, or cruel; sudden; and tall. The setting helps create a feeling of danger in the story.

WHAT DOES THE WATER LOOK LIKE?

A None of them knew the colour of the sky. Their eyes glanced level, and were fastened upon the waves that swept toward them. <u>These waves were of the hue of slate, save for the tops, which were of foaming white</u>, and
(5) all of the men knew the colours of the sea. The horizon narrowed and widened, and dipped and rose, and at all times <u>its edge was jagged with waves that seemed thrust up in points like rocks</u>.

Many a man ought to have a bath-tub larger than the
(10) boat which here rode upon the sea. <u>These waves were most wrongfully and barbarously abrupt and tall</u>, and each
B froth-top was a problem in small boat navigation.

From Stephen Crane THE OPEN BOAT © 1897

✓ TEST-TAKING TIPS

You may want to create a chart to organize categories of setting details.

Place	in a small boat on the sea
Time Period	during a storm
Important Details	gray, foaming waves that rise suddenly toward a small boat like tall, hard rocks

1. Based on the details provided, what can you conclude about the setting?
   A The men are sailing on a small but choppy lake.
   B The men are enjoying a calm boat ride on a river.
   C The men are in a small boat during a storm at sea.
   D The men are in a seaworthy boat during bad weather.

Apply the Skill

Directions: Questions 2 through 5 refer to the following excerpt.

HOW DOES THE SETTING AFFECT THE HAWK?

Hook, the Hawks' child, was hatched in a dry spring among the oaks beside the seasonal river, and was struck from the nest early. In the drought his single-willed parents
(5) had to extend their hunting ground by more than twice. The range became too great for them to wish to return and feed Hook, and when they had lost interest in each other they drove Hook down into the sand and brush
(10) and went back to solitary courses over the bleaching hills.

Unable to fly yet, Hook crept over the ground, challenging all large movements with recoiled head, erected rudimentary wings,
(15) and the small rasp of his clattering beak. It was during this time of abysmal ignorance and continual fear that his eyes took on the first quality of hawk, that of being wide, alert and challenging. He dwelt, because of his
(20) helplessness, among the rattling brush which grew between the oaks and the river.

Two spacious sounds environed Hook at this time. One was the great rustle of the slopes of yellowed wild wheat, with over it the
(25) chattering rustle of the leaves of the California oaks. The other was the distant whisper of the foaming edge of the Pacific, punctuated by the hollow shoring of the waves.

From Walter Van Tilburg Clark's HOOK, © 1940

2. **According to the details in the excerpt, where does the hawk live?**
   A   in the high prairie
   B   on an island
   C   in a mountain range
   D   near the Pacific Ocean

3. **In the passage, Hook's parents have to "extend their hunting ground" because of a drought (line 5). How might human parents deal with this difficulty?**
   A   buy food at discount stores
   B   accept help from a food bank
   C   move to a new town to find work
   D   enroll a child in a different school

4. **Hook lives "among the rattling brush" (line 20). What is the author's purpose in describing where the hawk lives?**
   A   to show the beauty of the landscape
   B   to emphasize the difficulty of the hawk's existence
   C   to illustrate humans' impact on the countryside
   D   to depict the ideal environment for hawks

5. **Because of a drought, Hook's parents move him from the nest early, driving him "down into the sand and brush" (line 9). What do their actions imply about the story's setting?**
   A   The hawks expect Hook to feed on wild wheat.
   B   The brush region is the perfect place for young hawks.
   C   The countryside is harsh but beautiful.
   D   Birds must change their lifestyles significantly to adapt to weather patterns.

Directions: Questions 6 and 7 refer to the following excerpt.

LIFE ON THE DIVIDE

Near Rattlesnake Creek, on the side of a little draw, stood Canute's shanty. North, east, south, stretched the level Nebraska plain of long rust-red grass that undulated constantly
(5) in the wind. To the west the ground was broken and rough, and a narrow strip of timber wound along the … muddy little stream that had scarcely ambition enough to crawl over its black bottom. If it had not been for the few
(10) stunted cottonwoods and elms that grew along its banks, Canute would have shot himself years ago. The Norwegians are a timber-loving people, and if there is even a turtle pond with a few plum bushes around it they seem
(15) irresistibly drawn toward it. …

As to the shanty itself, Canute had built it without aid of any kind, for when he first squatted along the banks of Rattlesnake Creek there was not a human being within twenty
(20) miles. It was built of logs split in halves, the chinks stopped with mud and plaster. The roof was covered with earth and was supported by one gigantic beam curved in the shape of a
(25) round arch.

From ON THE DIVIDE by Willa Cather, © 1910

6 Which statement best describes the view from Canute's house?
  A The house looks out on grassy plains.
  B Nothing but mud surrounds the house.
  C Canute can see the river on the eastern side.
  D The view in one direction is different from the others.

7 Which statement best describes the effect of the setting on Canute?
  A Everything but the trees makes him deeply depressed.
  B He enjoys living a rugged outdoor life despite the wind.
  C His house gives him a sense of comfort and accomplishment.
  D The bare, treeless landscape makes him miss city life.

Directions: Questions 8 through 10 refer to the following excerpt.

A CHILDHOOD REMEMBERED

A wigwam of weather-stained canvas stood at the base of some irregularly ascending hills. A footpath wound its way gently down the sloping land till it reached the broad river
(5) bottom; creeping through the long swamp grasses that bent over it on either side, it came out on the edge of the Missouri.

Here, morning, noon, and evening, my mother came to draw water from the muddy
(10) stream for our household use. Always, when my mother started for the river, I stopped my play to run along with her. …

I was a wild little girl of seven. Loosely clad in a slip of brown buckskin, and light-footed
(15) with a pair of soft moccasins on my feet, I was as free as the wind that blew my hair, and no less spirited than a bounding deer. These were my mother's pride—my wild freedom and overflowing spirits. She taught me no fear save
(20) that of intruding myself upon others.

From IMPRESSIONS OF AN INDIAN CHILDHOOD by Zitkala-Sa, © 1900

8 Which description best reflects the landscape?
  A hilly on the edge of a river
  B dry and flat with little water
  C rich, cultivated farmland
  D dense forests untouched by humans

9 The girl's home and clothing reveal that she most likely lives
  A in a small river town in Missouri.
  B near a big midwestern city in the 1880s.
  C in a rural Native American community.
  D in a windy area heavily populated by deer.

10 How does the girl's behavior reflect the setting?
  A The girl has no interest in the outdoors and prefers reading.
  B The mother is worried that the girl is too free to wander in the woods.
  C The girl is a free spirit, like the wind and the deer.
  D The girl's actions reflect the gentle flow of the river.

Directions: Questions 11 through 15 refer to the following excerpt.

THE BREAD LINE

The street was very dark and absolutely deserted. It was a district on the "South Side," not far from the Chicago River, given up largely to wholesale stores, and after nightfall was
(5) empty of all life. The echoes slept but lightly hereabouts, and the slightest footfall, the faintest noise, woke them upon the instant and sent them clamoring up and down the length of the pavement between the iron-shuttered
(10) fronts. The only light visible came from the side door of a certain "Vienna" bakery, where at one o'clock in the morning loaves of bread were given away to any who should ask. Every evening about nine o'clock the outcasts began
(15) to gather about the side door. The stragglers came in rapidly, and the line—the "bread line" as it was called—began to form. By midnight it was usually some hundred yards in length, stretching almost the entire length of the block.
(20) Toward ten in the evening, his collar turned up against the fine drizzle that pervaded the air, his hands in his pockets, his elbows gripping his sides, Sam Lewiston came up and silently took his place at the end of the line.
(25) He stood now in the enfolding drizzle, sodden, stupefied with fatigue. Before and behind stretched the line. There was no talking. There was no sound. The street was empty. It was so still that the passing of a cable-
(30) car in the adjoining thoroughfare grated like prolonged rolling explosions, beginning and ending at immeasurable distances. The drizzle descended incessantly. After a long time midnight struck.
(35) There was something ominous and gravely impressive in this interminable line of dark figures, close-pressed, soundless; a crowd, yet absolutely still; a close-packed, silent file, waiting, waiting in the vast deserted night-
(40) ridden street; waiting without a word, without a movement, there under the night and under the slow-moving mists of rain.

From A DEAL IN WHEAT by Frank Norris, © 1902

11 Which phrase best describes the setting in this passage?
  A poor and rural
  B poor and urban
  C wealthy and cosmopolitan
  D middle-class and residential

12 In this passage, how does the setting affect the feeling, or mood, of the story? The setting makes the mood
  A active and purposeful.
  B warm and inviting.
  C distant and other-worldly.
  D gloomy and forbidding.

13 To which location would a man in Sam Lewiston's condition be most likely to go?
  A a shelter
  B a park bench
  C a restaurant
  D another bakery

14 What can you conclude from the details about the South Side? The neighborhood is probably
  A a gritty business district.
  B an upscale warehouse district.
  C a suburban destination.
  D a performing arts district.

15 How does the description of the weather add to the overall effect of the passage?
  A It shows the gratitude of the men in line.
  B It heightens the difficulty of making the bread.
  C It emphasizes the discomfort of the characters.
  D It contrasts with the gloominess of the street.

Directions: Questions 16 through 19 refer to the following excerpt.

A SALESMAN GETS HELP WITH HIS CAR

"I done got your car out, mister," said Sonny's voice in the dark. "She's settin' a-waitin' in the road, turned to go back where she come from."

(5) "Fine!" said Bowman, projecting his own voice to loudness. "I'm surely much obliged—I could never have done it myself—I was sick…"

"I could do it easy," said Sonny.

Bowman could feel them both waiting in
(10) the dark, and he could hear the dogs panting out in the yard, waiting to bark when he should go. He felt strangely helpless and resentful. Now that he could go, he longed to stay. From what was he being deprived? His chest was
(15) rudely shaken by the violence of his heart. These people cherished something here that he could not see, they withheld some ancient promise of food and warmth and light. Between them they had a conspiracy. He thought of the
(20) way she had moved away from him and gone to Sonny, she had flowed toward him. He was shaking with cold, he was tired, and it was not fair. Humbly and yet angrily he stuck his hand into his pocket.

(25) "Of course I'm going to pay you for everything—"

"We don't take money for such," said Sonny's voice belligerently.

"I want to pay. But do something more. …
(30) Let me stay—tonight…" He took another step toward them. If only they could see him, they would know his sincerity, his real need! His voice went on, "I'm not very strong yet, I'm not able to walk far, even back to my car, maybe, I don't
(35) know—I don't know exactly where I am. …"

"You ain't no revenuer [tax collector] come sneakin' here, mister, ain't got no gun?"

To this end of nowhere! And yet he had come. He made a grave answer, "No."

(40) "You can stay."

From THE DEATH OF A TRAVELING SALESMAN by Eudora Welty, © 1936

16 Sonny says that Bowman's car is "settin' a-waitin' in the road" (line 2). Sonny's statement reveals that the story most likely takes place
   A at a shopping mall.
   B in a foreign country.
   C in a big city.
   D in the country.

17 What does Bowman's reaction to the setting reveal about his presence there (paragraph 4)?
   A Sonny has given Bowman travel directions.
   B Bowman is vacationing in the area.
   C Bowman is not there by choice.
   D Sonny has invited Bowman to the region.

18 The narrator says that Bowman could hear "the dogs panting out in the yard," waiting to bark at him. How is this detail about the setting significant?
   A It suggests that Bowman is in immediate danger.
   B It contributes to the unwelcome feeling that Bowman has.
   C It gives the image of a typical family's home and pets.
   D It adds to the feeling of the isolation of the location.

19 Bowman describes the setting as "this end of nowhere" (lines 37–38). What does this description reveal about Bowman's reaction to the setting?
   A Bowman finds the setting charming and relaxing.
   B The setting is remote and completely foreign to Bowman.
   C Bowman thinks his arrival in the setting is a fine adventure.
   D The setting reminds Bowman of the place in which he was raised.

LESSON 10

Tone

Fiction

1 Learn the Skill

When discussing short stories, the term **tone** means the feeling of the story. The tone can be, for example, happy, sad, condescending, encouraging, formal, or familiar. A story's tone expresses the author's attitude about the subject. Word choices and other details let readers know, for example, if the author is treating a subject seriously or is approaching it with irony or humor. A story's characters, setting, and some plot elements can affect the tone of the story.

2 Practice the Skill

By being able to interpret the tone of a literary work, you will improve your study and test-taking skills, especially as they relate to high school equivalency language arts/reading tests. Read the excerpt and strategies below. Then answer the question that follows.

WHAT DID THE YOUNG MAN DO LAST NIGHT?

A The man's tone in the paragraph indicates that he does not actually feel so good.

"Not feeling so well today?" she asked.

"<u>Oh, I'm great,</u>" he said. "<u>Corking, I am. Know what time I got up? Four o'clock this afternoon, sharp</u>. I kept trying to make it, and every time I took my head off the pillow, it would roll under the
(5) bed. This isn't my head I've got on now. I think this is something that used to belong to Walt Whitman. Oh, dear, oh, dear, oh, dear."

"Do you think maybe a drink would make you feel better?" she said.

B The woman's tone indicates that she is trying to make the man feel better about the events of the previous night. Think about how tone might help you understand the characters' interactions.

"The hair of the mastiff that bit me?" he said. "Oh, no, thank you.
(10) Please never speak of anything like that again. I'm through. I'm all, all through. Look at that hand; steady as a humming-bird. Tell me, was I very terrible last night?"

"<u>Oh, goodness,</u>" she said, "<u>everybody was feeling pretty high [good]. You were all right.</u>"

From Dorothy Parker's YOU WERE PERFECTLY FINE, © 1930

USING LOGIC

When reading for tone, determine whether characters' statements match the manner in which they are delivered. Serious statements delivered in a casual way tell readers the author is likely aiming for a particular effect.

1 The young man in the story is experiencing distress. How might you describe the author's tone in describing the young man?
   A uncaring
   B bitter
   C concerned
   D humorous

Apply the Skill

Directions: Questions 2 through 6 refer to the following excerpt.

HOW DOES THE FULL MOON AFFECT PEOPLE?

Up from the skeleton stone walls, up from the rotting floor boards and the solid hand-hewn beams of oak of the pre-war cotton factory, dusk came. Up from the dusk the full
(5) moon came. Glowing like a fired pine-knot it illuminated the great door and soft showered the Negro shanties aligned along the single street of factory town. The full moon in the great door was an omen. Negro women
(10) improvised songs against its spell. …

A strange stir was in her [Louisa]. Indolently she tried to fix upon Bob or Tom as the cause of it. … Separately there was no unusual significance to either one. But for
(15) some reason they jumbled when her eyes gazed vacantly at the rising moon. And from the jumble came the stir that was strangely within her. Her lips trembled. The slow rhythm of her song grew agitant and restless. Rusty
(20) black and tan spotted hounds, lying in the dark corners of porches or prowling around back yards, put their noses in the air and caught its tremor. They began to plaintively yelp and howl. Chickens woke up, and cackled.
(25) Intermittently, all over the countryside dogs barked and roosters crowed as if heralding a weird dawn or some ungodly awakening. The women sang lustily. Their songs were cottonwads to stop their ears. Louisa came
(30) down into factory town and sank wearily upon the step before her home. The moon was rising towards a thick cloud-bank that soon would hide it.

From Jean Toomer's BLOOD-BURNING MOON, © 1923

2 Which of the following best describes the tone of the excerpt?
- A humorous
- B cheerful
- C calm
- D threatening

3 Dogs and chickens are "heralding a weird dawn or some ungodly awakening" (lines 26–27). What does the animals' behavior imply?
- A The evening is completely normal.
- B Some misfortune is about to take place.
- C The sun is about to rise.
- D The moon is going down.

4 In the passage, a rising moon is an "omen" (line 9). What other type of writing might include an ominous moon?
- A a fairy tale
- B a sports account
- C a humorous piece
- D a mystery tale

5 In the passage, what is the women's response to the full moon?
- A They sing to guard against it.
- B They turn their heads and refuse to see it.
- C They admire it.
- D They howl at it.

6 Louisa has "agitant and restless" feelings about Bob and Tom (line 19). What do her emotions suggest? They suggest that
- A she loves only Bob.
- B she loves Bob, but not Tom.
- C she cares for both characters.
- D neither of the men care for her.

Directions: Questions 7 through 11 refer to the following excerpt.

HOW DOES BEN FEEL WHEN THE CARNIVAL COMES TO TOWN?

Carnival! In the vacant lot beyond the old ice plant! Trucks have been unloading all afternoon; the Whirlo-Gig has been unfolded like a giant umbrella, they assembled the baby
(5) Ferris wheel with an Erector Set. Twice the trucks got stuck in the mud. Straw has been strewn everywhere. They put up a stage and strung lights. Now, now, gather your pennies; supper is over and an hour of light is left in the
(10) long summer day. See, Sammy Hunnenhauser is running; Gloria Gring and her gang have been there all afternoon, they never go home, oh hurry, let me go; how awful it is to have parents that are poor, and slow, and sad!
(15) Fifty cents. The most Ben could beg. A nickel for every year of his life. It feels like plenty. Over the roof of crazy Mrs. Moffert's house, the Ferris wheel tints the air with pink, and the rim of this pink mixes in excitement
(20) with the great notched rim of the coin sweating in his hand. This house, then this house, and past the ice plant, and he will be there. Already the rest of the world is there, he is the last, hurrying, hurrying, the balloon is about to take
(25) off, the Ferris wheel is lifting; only he will be left behind, on empty darkening streets.

From John Updike's YOU'LL NEVER KNOW, DEAR, HOW MUCH I LOVE YOU, © 1960

7 How long has the carnival been in town?
  A one day
  B since the afternoon
  C one week
  D one night

8 Which of the following best describes the tone of this excerpt?
  A leisurely
  B argumentative
  C depressing
  D exciting

9 The character Ben thinks "how awful it is to have parents that are poor, and slow, and sad!" (lines 13–14). What do his thoughts indicate?
  A an acceptance of his parents' poverty
  B an understanding of the Erector Set
  C his knowledge of the Whirlo-Gig
  D his impatience to go to the carnival

10 Which of the following examples would be similar to Ben's character as described in the excerpt?
  A rewarding oneself with dessert
  B casually opening a familiar book
  C painstakingly explaining a math problem
  D running all the way to a new movie

11 The excerpt states "This house, then this house, and past the ice plant, and he will be there" (lines 21–22). What is Ben doing as he describes these things?
  A hurrying to the carnival
  B giving directions
  C telling his parents how to find the carnival
  D strolling to the ice plant

Directions: Questions 12 through 16 refer to the following excerpt.

WHAT'S WRONG WITH THIS PARTY?

At dinner the Lyntons were as hilarious as ever. … and my father and Mr. Lynton fairly crowed with delight. Phil and I looked at [Mrs. Lynton] with renewed wonder.
(5) And the whole party went off in that fashion. Never was a studio so consciously arty. There were no chairs at all—only black cushions on a scarlet floor—and we had to squat round the hearth and toast
(10) marshmallows at the wood fire (though it was a very warm night) and another lantern blazed up, and the sardines (what remained of them) were rancid—but everything was made into one huge, uproarious, continuous
(15) joke. Paintings were stacked everywhere; and it seemed to me that a little—perhaps commercial?—pressure was being put upon my poor ignorant father to look at every one of them. In fact, we all had to look at them.
(20) They were stood for us in every conceivable light: autumn trees, violet sunsets, marshes in moonlight, haystacks on Cape Cod, cranberry bogs, wharves, dories hauling up nets— watercolors, oils, crayons, every … kind of
(25) picture that I ever heard of. And all of them atrocious. We went through the vocabulary of praise till it was worn to a fiber.

From Conrad Aiken's O HOW SHE LAUGHED!, © 1934

12 What does the narrator mean by describing the studio as "consciously arty" (line 6–7)? The studio seems
 A natural.
 B comfortable.
 C artificial.
 D sturdy.

13 The narrator states that pressure was put on his father to "look at every one" of Mrs. Lynton's paintings (line 18). Which of the following words best describes the narrator's attitude toward this treatment of his father?
 A resentful
 B flattered
 C pleased
 D amused

14 Which of the following best describes the tone of the excerpt?
 A bewildered
 B annoyed
 C proud
 D excited

15 The narrator and his family use the "vocabulary of praise until it was worn to a fiber" (line 26–27). In what situation might people act similarly? Their experience is similar to people who
 A lavish praise on an animal to train it.
 B encourage children giving a performance.
 C write numerous thank-you notes.
 D must compliment an unattractive house.

16 The narrator says that the events of the evening are made into "one huge, uproarious, continuous joke" (lines 14–15). What does the author's tone imply? The tone indicates that the joke is
 A inexplicable.
 B complicated.
 C not actually funny.
 D hilarious.

Directions: Questions 17 through 21 refer to the following excerpt.

WHAT DOES THE REVEREND THINK OF HIS HOUSEKEEPER?

God smote the vines with hail, the sycamore trees with frost, and offered up the flocks to the lightning—but Mrs. Stoner! What a cross Father Firman had from God in Mrs.
(5) Stoner! There were other housekeepers as bad, no doubt, walking the rectories of the world, yes, but... yes. He could name one and maybe two priests who were worse off. One, maybe two. Cronin. His scraggly blonde of
(10) sixty—take her, with her everlasting banging on the grand piano, the gift of the pastor; her proud talk about the goiter operation at the Mayo Brothers', also a gift; her honking the parish Buick at passing strange priests
(15) because they were all in the game together. She was worse. She was something to keep the home fires burning. Yes sir. And Cronin said she was not a bad person really. ...
  For that matter, could anyone say that
(20) Mrs. Stoner was a bad person? No. He could not say it himself, and he was no freak. She had her points, Mrs. Stoner. She was clean. And though she cooked poorly, could not play the organ, would not take up the collection in
(25) an emergency, and went to card parties, and told all—even so she was clean. She washed everything. Sometimes her underwear hung down beneath her dress like a paratrooper's pants, but it and everything she touched was
(30) clean. She washed constantly. She was clean.

From J.F. Powers' THE VALIANT WOMAN, © 1947

17 Cronin's housekeeper is described as "something to keep the home fires burning" (lines 16–17). How might the tone of this description be described?
  A warm
  B lavish
  C depressed
  D sarcastic

18 The narrator describes Mrs. Stoner as a person who "went to card parties, and told all" (lines 25–26). What does this description mean? Mrs. Stoner is a person who
  A steals.
  B gambles.
  C gossips.
  D lies.

19 Which of the following best describes the tone of this excerpt?
  A proud
  B betrayed
  C livid
  D exasperated

20 The narrator repeatedly praises Mrs. Stoner by saying "she was clean" (line 22). What can we conclude from his praise?
  A He is pleased with Mrs. Stoner's service.
  B He likes Mrs. Stoner's cooking.
  C He has few complimentary examples to share.
  D Cleanliness is his most important job requirement.

21 Which example is most similar to the narrator's relationship with Mrs. Stoner?
  A Two partners work together and understand each other perfectly.
  B A person waits in line to get the best seats to a concert.
  C A person buys the fanciest appliance in the store, getting just what he or she wanted.
  D A person drives a car she hates because she cannot find a suitable substitute.

LESSON 11

Figurative Language

1 Learn the Skill

Authors use **figurative language**, such as **metaphors** and **similes**, to paint vivid pictures and create memorable images. A metaphor states that one thing is like another: *the baby's face was a rose*. A simile makes this comparison using the words *like, as,* or *similar to*: *the burned cake was like a brick*. Other types of figurative language include **hyperbole**, or extreme exaggeration, and **personification**, in which the author gives human qualities to animals or inanimate objects. Words such as *boom* and *splash* reflect the sounds they describe; they are examples of **onomatopoeia**.

2 Practice the Skill

By mastering the skill of identifying figurative language, you will improve your study and test-taking skills, especially as they relate to high school equivalency language arts/reading tests. Read the excerpt and strategies below. Then answer the question that follows.

A In this excerpt, the calf speaks to his mother just as a human child would.

B Numerous calves ask questions of the mother cow. Her patient response resembles that of a human mother.

WHAT HAPPENS TO ALL THE CATTLE?

A The calf ran up the hill as fast as he could and stopped sharp. "Mama!" he cried, all out of breath. "What is it! What are they *doing*! Where are they *going*?"
   Other spring calves came galloping too.
(5) They all were looking up at her and awaiting her explanation, but she looked out over their excited eyes. As she waited the mysterious and majestic thing they had never seen before, her own eyes became even more
B than ordinarily still, and during the considerable moment
(10) before she answered, she scarcely heard their urgent questioning.

From James Agee's A MOTHER'S TALE, © 1952

✓ TEST-TAKING TIPS

Authors use figurative language to help readers think about a subject in a different way. Look for comparisons that seem unusual or striking.

1 Which type of figurative language is used in this excerpt?
   A simile
   B metaphor
   C hyperbole
   D personification

③ Apply the Skill

Directions: Questions 2 through 5 refer to the following excerpt.

HOW DOES PAIN AFFECT THE PATIENT?

Blunderer that he was, Dr. Nicholas was an honorable enemy, not like the demon, pain, which sulked in a thousand guises within her head, and which often she recklessly willed
(5) to attack her and then drove back in terror. After the rout, sweat streamed from her face and soaked the neck of the coarse hospital shirt. To be sure, it came usually of its own accord, running like a wild fire through all the
(10) convolutions [complications] to fill with flame the small sockets and ravines and then, at last, to withdraw, leaving behind a throbbing and an echo. On these occasions, she was as helpless as a tree in the wind. But at other
(15) times when, by closing her eyes and rolling up the eyeballs in such a way that she fancied she looked directly on the place where her brain was, the pain woke sluggishly and came toward her at a snail's pace. Then, bit by bit,
(20) it gained speed. Sometimes it faltered back, subsided altogether, and then it rushed like a tidal wave driven by a hurricane, lashing and roaring until she lifted her hands from the counterpane, crushed her broken teeth into
(25) her swollen lip, stared in panic at the soothing walls with her ruby eyes, stretched out her legs until she felt their bones must snap. Each cove, each narrow inlet, every living bay was flooded and the frail brain, a little hat-shaped boat, was
(30) washed from its mooring and set adrift. The skull was as vast as the world and the brain was as small as a seashell.

From Jean Stafford's THE INTERIOR CASTLE, © 1969

2. The character is described as being "as helpless as a tree in the wind" (line 14). What type of figurative language is included in this description?
   A onomatopoeia
   B metaphor
   C simile
   D hyperbole

3. Why is pain compared to a wild fire (line 9)?
   A to reveal its heat
   B to indicate its speed
   C to prove its intensity
   D to show its size

4. Which of the following describes the writing of this excerpt? It contains
   A similes.
   B short sentences.
   C onomatopoeia.
   D metaphors.

5. Which part of the speaker's body is compared to a seashell?
   A the legs
   B the teeth
   C the eyeballs
   D the brain

Directions: Questions 6 through 10 refer to the following excerpt.

WHY IS THE HOUSE MAKING BREAKFAST?

In the living room the voice-clock sang *Tick-tock, seven o'clock, time to get up, time to get up, seven o'clock!* as if it were afraid that nobody would. The morning house lay empty.
(5) The clock ticked on, repeating and repeating its sounds into the emptiness. *Seven-nine, breakfast time, seven-nine!*

In the kitchen the breakfast stove gave a hissing sigh and ejected from its warm interior
(10) eight pieces of perfectly browned toast, eight eggs, sunnyside up, sixteen slices of bacon, two coffees, and two cool glasses of milk.

"Today is August 4, 2026," said a second voice from the kitchen ceiling, "in the city of
(15) Allendale, California." It repeated the date three times for memory's sake. "Today is Mr. Featherstone's birthday. Today is the anniversary of Tilita's marriage. Insurance is payable, as are the water, gas, and light bills."
(20) Somewhere in the walls, relays clicked, memory tapes glided under electric eyes.

Eight-one, tick-tock, eight-one o'clock, off to school, off to work, run, run, eight-one! But no doors slammed, no carpets took the soft
(25) tread of rubber heels. It was raining outside. The weather box on the front door sang quietly: "Rain, rain, go away; rubbers, raincoats for today. ..." And the rain tapped on the empty house, echoing.

From Ray Bradbury's THERE WILL COME SOFT RAINS, © 1950

6. What is the predominant type of figurative language used in the excerpt?
   A repetition
   B personification
   C simile
   D hyperbole

7. Which of the following contains an example of onomatopoeia?
   A "... seven o'clock, time to get up..."
   B "Today is August 4, 2026..."
   C "...the breakfast stove gave a hissing sigh..."
   D "It was raining outside"

8. Which of the following is most like the house described in the excerpt?
   A a computer program that schedules repairs
   B a mechanic who checks a car's computer
   C a car that needs an oil change
   D a car that drives itself

9. What is the effect of the statement that the clock sang "as if it were afraid" (line 3)? The statement
   A gives the house human feelings.
   B shows that the house is terrified.
   C makes the house owners seem lazy.
   D proves that the clock is accurate.

10. Which of the following items is repeated throughout the excerpt?
    A the date
    B the family's names
    C the time
    D the weather

Directions: Questions 11 through 15 refer to the following excerpt.

HOW DOES THE PATIENT COPE WITH PAIN?

The doctor…returned to her with another pack, pushing it with his bodkin doggedly until it lodged against the first. Stop! Stop! Cried all her nerves, wailing along the surface of
(5) her skin. The coats that covered them were torn off and they shuddered like naked people screaming, Stop! Stop! But Dr. Nicholas did not hear. …

The second nostril was harder to pack
(10) since the other side was now distended and the passage was anyhow much narrower, as narrow, he had once remarked, as that in the nose of an infant. In such pain as passed all language and even the farthest fetched
(15) analogies, she turned her eyes inward thinking that under the obscuring cloak of the surgeon's pain, she could see her brain without the knowledge of its keeper. … She was claimed entirely by this present, meaningless pain and
(20) suddenly and sharply, she forgot what she had meant to do. She was aware of nothing but her ascent to the summit of something; what it was she did not know, whether it was a tower or a peak or Jacob's ladder. Now she
(25) was an abstract word, now she was a theorem of geometry, now she was a kite flying, a top spinning, a prism flashing, a kaleidoscope turning.

From Jean Stafford's THE INTERIOR CASTLE, © 1969

11 Which of the following characterizes the writing in this excerpt?
- **A** extensive development of setting
- **B** complex dialog
- **C** elaborate descriptions and comparisons
- **D** short, abrupt sentences

12 The narrator's nerves "shuddered like naked people screaming, Stop! Stop!" (lines 6–7). What is the purpose of the comparison? Comparing nerves this way
- **A** shows the doctor's insensitivity.
- **B** highlights the speaker's pain.
- **C** emphasizes the speaker's emotional state.
- **D** diminishes the speaker's suffering.

13 When she is suffering, the narrator describes herself as "a kite flying, a top spinning" (lines 26–27). What does the comparison indicate? It shows that pain
- **A** makes the speaker feel removed from her body.
- **B** provokes the speaker's anger at the doctor.
- **C** helps the speaker concentrate on her operation.
- **D** will speed her recovery.

14 The narrator says she was "claimed entirely by this present, meaningless pain" (lines 18–19). Which of the following is most like her comparison?
- **A** Two rivals have a respectful dialogue.
- **B** A television plays in the background of a waiting room.
- **C** A person sings along with a car radio.
- **D** A barking dog demands its owner's attention.

15 Which of the following examples from the excerpt is a metaphor?
- **A** "as narrow…as that in the nose of an infant"
- **B** "now she was an abstract word"
- **C** "she turned her eyes inward"
- **D** "she forgot what she had meant to do"

Directions: Questions 16 through 19 refer to the following excerpts.

MEG'S WEDDING DAY

"You do look just like our own dear Meg, only so very sweet and lovely that I should hug you if it wouldn't crumple your dress," cried Amy, surveying her with delight when all was done.

(5) "Then I am satisfied. But please hug and kiss me, everyone, and don't mind my dress. I want a great many crumples of this sort put into it today," and Meg opened her arms to her sisters, who clung about her … feeling that the

(10) new love had not changed the old.

"Now I'm going to tie John's cravat for him, and then to stay a few minutes with Father quietly in the study," and Meg ran down to perform these little ceremonies, and then to

(15) follow her mother wherever she went, conscious that in spite of the smiles on the motherly face, there was a secret sorrow hid in the motherly heart at the flight of the first bird from the nest. …

JO'S LIFE AT PLUMFIELD

It never was a fashionable school … but it was just what Jo intended it to be—"a happy, homelike place for boys, who needed teaching, care, and kindness." Every room in the big house

(5) was soon full. … She had boys enough now, and did not tire of them, though they were not angels, by any means, and some of them caused … trouble and anxiety. But her faith in the good spot which exists in the heart … gave her patience,

(10) skill, and in time success, for no mortal boy could hold out long with [the Professor] shining on him as benevolently as the sun, and [Jo] forgiving him seventy times seven. Very precious to Jo was the friendship of the lads …

(15) Yes, Jo was a very happy woman there, in spite of hard work, much anxiety, and a perpetual racket. She enjoyed it heartily and found the applause of her boys more satisfying than any praise of the world, for now she told

(20) no stories except to her flock of enthusiastic believers and admirers. As the years went on, two little lads of her own came to increase her happiness—Rob, named for Grandpa, and Teddy, a happy-go-lucky baby, who seemed to

(25) have inherited his papa's sunshiny temper as well as his mother's lively spirit. How they ever grew up alive in that whirlpool of boys was a mystery to their grandma and aunts, but they flourished like dandelions in spring. …

From LITTLE WOMEN by Louisa May Alcott, © 1868

16 In the first excerpt, Meg's statement "I want a great many crumples of this sort put into it today" means that Meg
  A does not care whether her dress gets wrinkled.
  B cares more about love than about a wrinkled dress.
  C is concerned because she looks different in her wedding dress.
  D would rather stay with her sisters than get married.

17 The comparison in lines 15 through 18 indicates that Meg's mother
  A smiles but secretly disapproves of the man Meg will marry.
  B fears that Meg will not attend to the birds in the garden.
  C worries about the family's finances after Meg marries.
  D shows joy mixed with sorrow because her first child is leaving.

18 In the second excerpt, lines 10 through 13, the narrator says, "no mortal boy could hold out long with [the Professor] shining on him as benevolently as the sun, and [Jo] forgiving him seventy times seven." Which statement best explains the hyperbole?
  A The Professor and Jo treat the boys with a great deal of kindness and patience.
  B Troubled boys do well at Plumfield because of its strict behavior standards and academic focus.
  C Plumfield emphasizes permissiveness and shows little attention to academic standards.
  D The Professor is providing little academic training, and Jo is losing patience.

19 What does the metaphor "whirlpool of boys" in line 27 of the second excerpt suggest?
  A a group of boys at the beach
  B boys studying the movement of water
  C the boys' constant motion and activity
  D the movement of a top or spinning toy

LESSON 12

Symbols and Imagery

Fiction

① Learn the Skill

A **symbol** is another type of figurative language. Symbols are people, places, or things that stand for a larger idea. For example, a country's flag is a symbol that represents that country. In stories, characters' feelings or other attributes may be represented by a symbol. Symbols are often repeated throughout the text. **Imagery** is a type of figurative language that appeals to the reader's senses of taste, smell, vision, hearing, or touch. Images, like symbols, help readers understand important ideas.

② Practice the Skill

By mastering the skill of identifying symbols and images, you will improve your study and test-taking skills, especially as they relate to high school equivalency language arts/reading tests. Read the excerpt and strategies below. Then answer the question that follows.

WHAT DOES THE FLOWER MEAN TO THE MOTHER?

A The girl's reaction indicates the importance of the flower. This response tells readers to watch for a larger meaning associated with chrysanthemums.

"You've got a flower in your apron!" said the child, in a little rapture at this unusual event.
A "Goodness me!" exclaimed the woman, relieved. "One would think the house was afire." She replaced the glass
(5) and waited a moment before turning up the wick. A pale shadow was seen floating vaguely on the floor. …
Annie was still bending at her waist. Irritably, the mother took the flowers out from her apron-band.
"Oh, mother—don't take them out!" Annie cried,
(10) catching her hand and trying to replace the sprig. … The child put the pale chrysanthemums to her lips, murmuring:
"Don't they smell beautiful!"

B The mother's response is unhappy and she remembers bad times. This indicates that they symbolize past difficulties for the mother.

B Her mother gave a short laugh.
"No," she said, "not to me. It was chrysanthemums
(15) when I married him, and chrysanthemums when you were born, and the first time they ever brought him home drunk, he'd got brown chrysanthemums in his buttonhole."

From D. H. Lawrence's ODOUR OF CHRYSANTHEMUMS, © 1914

✓ TEST-TAKING TIPS

The meaning of a symbol might change slightly as it is repeated. A flower bud that blooms and dies in a story may represent the destruction of a character's ideals.

1 What might chrysanthemums symbolize to the mother?
A beauty
B happiness
C hope
D disappointment

Apply the Skill

Directions: Questions 2 through 5 refer to the following excerpt.

WHY IS THE AIRPLANE SO EXCITING?

We heard the plane come over at noon, roaring through the radio news, and we were sure it was going to hit the house, so we all ran into the yard. We saw it come in over the
(5) treetops, all red and silver, the first close-up plane I ever saw. Mrs. Peebles screamed.

"Crash landing," their little boy said. Joey was his name.

"It's okay," said Dr. Peebles. "He knows
(10) what he's doing." Dr. Peebles was only an animal doctor, but had a calming way of talking, like any doctor.

This was my first job—working for Dr. and Mrs. Peebles, who had bought an old house
(15) out on the Fifth Line, about five miles out of town. It was just when the trend was starting of town people buying up old farms, not to work them but to live on them.

We watched the plane land across the
(20) road, where the fairgrounds used to be. It did make a good landing field, nice and level for the old race track, and the barns and display sheds torn down now for scrap lumber so there was nothing in the way. Even the old
(25) grandstand bays had burned.

"All right," said Mrs. Peebles, snappy as she always was when she got over her nerves. "Let's go back in the house. Let's not stand here gawking like a set of farmers."

From Alice Munro's HOW I MET MY HUSBAND, © 1974

2 What does the excerpt suggest about the noise of the airplane? The noise
   A is pleasant.
   B hardly attracts attention.
   C is quieter than most planes.
   D is loud.

3 Based on the excerpt, what might the appearance of the plane symbolize?
   A the excitement of something new
   B the changing of the weather
   C the arrival of the fair
   D the destruction of the fairgrounds

4 Which of the following might be most similar to the appearance of the plane?
   A The sight of a bus leaving a station.
   B The smell of a car's exhaust.
   C The feel of a horse's warm nose.
   D The sight of a circus train arriving in town.

5 The speaker describes the old fairgrounds with "display sheds torn down now for scrap lumber so there was nothing in the way" (lines 22–24). How might the image of the old fairgrounds be described?
   A disappointed
   B weary
   C matter-of-fact
   D grieving

Directions: Questions 6 through 9 refer to the following excerpt.

WHAT HAPPENED TO THE HOUSE?

From that chamber, and from that mansion, I fled aghast. The storm was still abroad in all its wrath as I found myself crossing the old causeway. Suddenly there shot along the
(5) path a wild light, and I turned to see whence a gleam so unusual could have issued; for the vast house and its shadows were alone behind me. The radiance was that of the full, setting, and blood-red moon which now shone vividly
(10) through that once barely-discernible fissure of which I have before spoken as extending from the roof of the building, in a zigzag direction, to the base. While I gazed, this fissure rapidly widened—there came a fierce breath of the
(15) whirlwind—the entire orb of the satellite burst at once upon my sight—my brain reeled as I saw the mighty walls rushing asunder—there was a long tumultuous shouting sound like the voice of a thousand waters—and the deep and
(20) dark tarn at my feet closed sullenly and silently over the fragments of the "*House of Usher.*"

From Edgar Allan Poe's THE FALL OF THE HOUSE OF USHER, © 1845

6 What does the speaker find significant about the image described as a "full, setting, and blood-red moon which now shown vividly through that once barely-discernible fissure" (lines 8–10)? The speaker can
   A see the moon through a widening crack in the wall.
   B tell by the moon's color that the weather is changing.
   C recognize that the building is historic.
   D determine how to fix the crack in the wall.

7 How does the image of the moon in the storm affect the tone of the excerpt?
   A It shows the excitement of the house.
   B It shows the peacefulness of the house.
   C It makes the passage cheery.
   D It makes the passage eerie.

8 In the excerpt, the narrator watches "the mighty walls rushing asunder" as the mansion collapses (line 17). How might this situation be described in a different way?
   A Children tear down a sand castle.
   B The death of a tree.
   C A book with a family's history is ripped apart.
   D A frightening monster falls from a skyscraper.

9 Which of the following does the House of Usher most likely symbolize? It represents the
   A hope of a nation.
   B passing of a particular family.
   C growth of an industry.
   D birth of a child.

Directions: Questions 10 through 13 refer to the following excerpt.

WHY DOES THE AUTHOR DESCRIBE THE USES OF THE COLOR WHITE?

Though in many natural objects, whiteness refiningly enhances beauty, as if imparting some special virtue of its own, as in marbles, japonicas [flowering plants], and pearls; and
(5) though various nations have in some way recognised a certain royal pre-eminence in this hue; even the barbaric, grand old kings of Pegu [an ancient kingdom] placing the title of "Lord of the White Elephants" above all their other
(10) magniloquent [fancy language] ascriptions of dominion; and the modern kings of Siam unfurling the same snow-white quadruped in the royal standard; and the Hanoverian flag bearing the one figure of a snow-white charger;
(15) and the great Austrian Empire, Caesarian, heir to overlording Rome, having for the imperial color the same imperial hue; … for among the Romans a white stone marked a joyful day; and though in other mortal sympathies
(20) and symbolizings, this same hue is made the emblem of many touching, noble things—the innocence of brides, the benignity of age; … yet for all these accumulated associations, with whatever is sweet, and honorable, and
(25) sublime, there yet lurks an elusive something in the innermost idea of this hue, which strikes more of panic to the soul than that redness which affrights [scares] in blood.
    This elusive quality it is, which causes
(30) the thought of whiteness, when divorced from more kindly associations, and coupled with any object terrible in itself, to heighten that terror to the furthest bounds. Witness the white bear of the poles, and the white shark of the tropics;
(35) what but their smooth, flaky whiteness makes them the transcendent horrors they are? That ghastly whiteness it is which imparts such an abhorrent mildness, even more loathsome than terrific, to the dumb gloating of their aspect. So
(40) that not the fierce-fanged tiger in his heraldic coat can so stagger courage as the white-shrouded bear or shark.

From Herman Melville's MOBY-DICK, © 1851

10 Based on the excerpt, which of the following does the color white most likely symbolize?
   A sharks
   B ghosts
   C royalty
   D elephants

11 Earlier in the novel, Captain Ahab is hunting a white whale, called Moby-Dick. The whale had previously destroyed Captain Ahab's ship and bit off his leg. Based on this information, what might the whale symbolize to Captain Ahab? The whale might symbolize Captain Ahab's
   A destroyed ship.
   B obsession with getting revenge.
   C fear of bears.
   D wish to conquer the seas.

12 How does the author contrast the ideals associated with whiteness?
   A The author uses imagery to show how white can be both a royal color and a color associated with strength.
   B The author uses examples to show that white is a color of power and purity.
   C The author shows how white can make people happy as well as frighten them.
   D The author uses imagery to show how white can symbolize joyful and terrifying things.

13 Based on the excerpt, how might the author respond to a colorful painting in an art gallery?
   A The author might examine the painting for both positive and negative imagery.
   B The author might see positive imagery in the lighter colors of the painting, but associate negative imagery with the darker colors.
   C The author might believe that the artist chose specific colors to represent fear.
   D The author might give the painting a cursory glance and move on quickly.

Directions: Questions 14 through 17 refer to the following excerpt.

WHAT DOES THE MARK ON THE WALL MEAN TO THE SPEAKER?

And yet that mark on the wall is not a hole at all. It may even be caused by some round black substance, such as a small rose leaf, left over from the summer, and I, not being a
(5) very vigilant housekeeper—look at the dust on the mantelpiece, for example, the dust which, so they say, buried Troy three times over, only fragments of pots utterly refusing annihilation, as one can believe. …
(10) And if I were to get up at this very moment and ascertain that the mark on the wall is really—what shall we say?—the head of a gigantic old nail, driven in two hundred years ago, which has now, owing to the patient
(15) attrition of many generations of housemaids, revealed its head above the coat of paint, and is taking its first view of modern life in sight of a white-walled fire-lit room, what should I gain?—Knowledge? Matter for further
(20) speculation? I can think sitting still as well as standing up. …
I must jump up and see for myself what that mark on the wall really is—a nail, a rose-leaf, a crack in the wood?
(25) Here is nature once more at her old game of self-preservation. This train of thought, she perceives, is threatening mere waste of energy, even some collision with reality, for who will ever be able to lift a finger against Whitaker's
(30) Table of Precedency? …
I understand Nature's game—her prompting to take action as a way of ending any thought that threatens to excite or to pain. Hence, I suppose, comes our slight contempt
(35) for men of action—men, we assume, who don't think. Still, there's no harm in putting a full stop to one's disagreeable thoughts by looking at a mark on the wall.

From Virginia Woolf's THE MARK ON THE WALL, © 1921

14 The narrator describes the mark on the wall as possibly being "a nail, a rose-leaf, a crack in the wood" (lines 23–24). What might be the author's purpose in choosing this imagery to describe the mark?
   A to illustrate the different things that might have made the mark
   B to show the speaker's lack of imagination
   C to describe the speaker's cleaning habits
   D to emphasize the hideousness of the mark

15 The speaker believes that Nature is prompting her to take action (lines 31–33). Which action does she believe Nature wants her to take?
   A clean the wall
   B get up to figure out what made the mark
   C forget about the mark
   D stop having unkind thoughts about the mark

16 The speaker imagines many different things that could have made the mark on the wall. What does the mark seem to symbolize to the speaker?
   A The mark symbolizes the dirty house.
   B The mark is a symbol of destruction.
   C The mark symbolizes the speaker's attempts to gain knowledge.
   D The mark is a symbol of endless possibilities.

17 At the end of the story, the speaker gets up to examine the mark and discovers that it is a snail crawling up the wall. Based on the excerpt, how might the speaker react to this discovery?
   A The speaker might remove the snail from the wall and place it on a rose leaf in the garden.
   B The speaker might build a house for the snail.
   C The speaker might play a game with the snail.
   D The speaker might imagine many different ways in which the snail would have gotten into the house.

LESSON 13

Make Inferences

1 Learn the Skill

Like nonfiction writers, fiction writers do not explain all elements directly. As you learned in Lesson 8 of the Non-Fiction Unit, readers sometimes must **make inferences**, or educated guesses based on suggestions and clues found in the text. When making an inference, readers combine what they know about a subject with the information found in the text. Then they make a reasonable guess about what the author intended.

2 Practice the Skill

By practicing the skill of making inferences in fiction, you will improve your study and test-taking abilities, especially as they relate to high school equivalency language arts/reading tests. Read the passage below. Then answer the question that follows.

FIFTY DEGREES BELOW ZERO

A The first sentence suggests that the man is detached from his surroundings.

B From the explanation that this is the man's first winter in the area, you can infer that the man may lack experience in cold, rugged climates.

But all this—the mysterious, far-reaching hairline trail, the absence of sun from the sky, the tremendous cold, and the strangeness and weirdness of it all—made no impression on the man. It was not because he was long used to it. He was a new-comer in the land, a chechaquo, and this was his first winter. The trouble with him was that he was without imagination. He was quick and alert in the things of life, but only in the things, and not in the significances. Fifty degrees below zero meant eighty odd degrees of frost. Such fact impressed him as being cold and uncomfortable, and that was all. It did not lead him to meditate upon his frailty as a creature of temperature, and upon man's frailty in general, able only to live within certain narrow limits of heat and cold; and from there on it did not lead him to the conjectural field of immortality and man's place in the universe. Fifty degrees below zero stood for a bite of frost that hurt and that must be guarded against by the use of mittens, ear-flaps, warm moccasins, and thick socks. Fifty degrees below zero was to him just precisely fifty degrees below zero. That there should be anything more to it than that was a thought that never entered his head.

From TO BUILD A FIRE by Jack London, © 1916

✓ TEST-TAKING TIPS

Note that the passage suggests that the man's lack of imagination causes him trouble. Use the details in the passage and your knowledge of below-freezing temperatures to determine the possible effect of this cause.

1 **Why might the man's lack of imagination be a problem?**
   A Because the man considers only facts related to the cold weather, he does not contemplate the extent of the danger it poses.
   B Because the man is not impressed by the hairline trail and the absence of sun, he risks getting lost in the frozen wilderness.
   C Because the man does not think about being uncomfortable, he may not have packed the proper gear for his journey.
   D Because the man does not consider the significances of life, he is not intrigued by the strangeness of the frozen wilderness.

③ Apply the Skill

Directions: Questions 2 through 6 refer to the following excerpt.

AN INTERRUPTED STANDOFF

The two enemies stood glaring at one another for a long silent moment. Each had a rifle in his hand, each had hate in his heart and murder uppermost in his mind. The chance had
(5) come to give full play to the passions of a lifetime. But a man who has been brought up under the code of a restraining civilization cannot easily nerve himself to shoot down his neighbor in cold blood and without a word spoken, except for an
(10) offense against his hearth and honor. And before the moment of hesitation had given way to action a deed of Nature's own violence overwhelmed them both. A fierce shriek of the storm had been answered by a splitting crash over their heads,
(15) and ere they could leap aside a mass of falling beech tree had thundered down on them. Ulrich von Gradwitz found himself stretched on the ground, one arm numb beneath him and the other held almost as helplessly in a tight tangle of forked
(20) branches, while both legs were pinned beneath the fallen mass. His heavy shooting boots had saved his feet from being crushed to pieces, but if his fractures were not as serious as they might have been, at least it was evident that he could
(25) not move from his present position till someone came to release him. The descending twigs had slashed the skin of his face, and he had to wink away some drops of blood from his eyelashes before he could take in a general view of the
(30) disaster. At his side, so near that under ordinary circumstances he could almost have touched him, lay Georg Znaeym, alive and struggling, but obviously as helplessly pinioned down as himself. All around them lay a thick-strewn wreckage of
(35) splintered branches and broken twigs.

Relief at being alive and exasperation at his captive plight brought a strange medley of pious thank-offerings and sharp curses to Ulrich's lips. Georg, who was nearly blinded
(40) with the blood which trickled across his eyes, stopped his struggling for a moment to listen, and then gave a short, snarling laugh.

"So you're not killed, as you ought to be, but you're caught, anyway," he cried; "caught fast.
(45) Ho, what a jest, Ulrich von Gradwitz snared in his stolen forest. There's real justice for you!"

From THE INTERLOPERS by Saki, © 1919

2. Which is the most logical inference to make about the men's unwillingness to shoot each other?
   A Each man is unwilling to abandon a lifelong passion.
   B Human laws and traditions curb an inclination toward violence.
   C The act of murder requires a mental, not a heartfelt, hatred.
   D Before killing an enemy, an attacker must deliver a statement of wrongs.

3. The narrator states, "Nature's own violence overwhelmed them both." On the basis of this event, the most likely inference to make is that Nature
   A also holds hatred in its heart.
   B cares nothing for hearth and honor.
   C is not susceptible to the codes of civilization.
   D can reinforce the passions of a lifetime.

4. After the accident, Ulrich von Gradwitz cannot move until someone comes to release him, and Georg Znaeym is helplessly pinned down, as well. In this situation, the two men are most likely to
   A shoot each other.
   B appreciate the importance of their feud.
   C tend to each other's wounds.
   D stop being enemies.

5. What does the contrast between the men's potential violence and Nature's actual violence imply?
   A Nature is more deadly than humans because it lacks feelings.
   B Humans are more deadly than Nature because they have feelings.
   C Nature is the deadly enemy of humankind.
   D Humankind is the deadly enemy of Nature.

6. Which problem does the men's predicament most resemble?
   A carelessness resulting in forest fires
   B violent crime in urban settings
   C bullying among schoolchildren
   D neglect of storm warnings

Directions: Questions 7 through 11 refer to the following excerpt.

WHO WILL CARE FOR THE CHILDREN?

In the middle of an April night in 1919, a plain woman named Edith Fisk, lifted from England to California on a tide of world peace, arrived at the Ransom house to raise five half-
(5) orphaned children.

A few hours later, at seven in the morning, this Edith, more widely called Edie, invited the three eldest to her room for tea. They were James, seven; Eliza, six; and Jenny, four.
(10) Being handed cups of tea, no matter how reduced by milk, made them believe that they had grown up overnight.

"Have some sugar," said Edie, and spooned it in. Moments later she said. "Have
(15) another cup." But her *h*'s went unspoken and became the first of hundreds, then thousands, which would accumulate in the corners of the house and thicken in the air like sighs.

In an adjoining room the twins, entirely
(20) responsible for their mother's death, had finished their bottles and fallen back into guiltless sleep. At the far end of the house, the widower, Thomas Ransom, who had spent the night aching for his truant wife, lay across his
(25) bed, half awake, half asleep, and dreaming.

From Harriet Doerr's EDIE: A LIFE, © 1988

7 Which of the following can be learned about Edie from this excerpt?
  A She is from England.
  B She is from California.
  C She dislikes tea.
  D She dislikes children.

8 Based on the information in the excerpt, what has happened to Mrs. Ransom? She has
  A moved to England.
  B abandoned her children.
  C died in childbirth.
  D divorced her husband.

9 From the tone of the excerpt, what can we infer about Edie's character? She is
  A annoyed and bored.
  B stricken with grief.
  C nervous and fidgety.
  D kind and capable.

10 Which one of the following situations is most like that of the excerpt?
  A A mother-in-law arrives for a summer visit.
  B A niece lives with her aunt while attending school.
  C A grandfather teaches his grandchildren to whittle.
  D A grandmother arrives to care for a sick baby.

11 What we can conclude is Mr. Ransom's emotional state? He is
  A exhausted by his children.
  B stricken with grief.
  C annoyed with his new nanny.
  D overwhelmed by responsibility.

Directions: Questions 12 through 15 refer to the following excerpt.

THOUGHTS ABOUT MUSKETAQUID LAND

When I walk in the fields of Concord and meditate on the destiny of this prosperous slip of the Saxon family—the unexhausted energies of this new country—I forget that this
(5) which is now Concord was once Musketaquid and that the American race has had its destiny also. Everywhere in the fields—in the corn and grain land—the earth is strewn with the relics of a race which has vanished as completely as
(10) if trodden in with the earth.

I find it good to remember the eternity behind me as well as the eternity before. Where ever I go I tread in the tracks of the Indian—I pick up the bolt which has but just dropped at
(15) my feet. And if I consider destiny I am on his trail. I scatter his hearth stones with my feet, and pick out of the embers of his fire the simple but enduring implements of the wigwam and the chase—In planting my corn in the same
(20) furrow which yielded its increase to support so long—I displace some memorial of him. …

Nature has her russet [reddish-brown] hues as well as green—Indeed our eye splits on every object, and we can as well take one
(25) path as the other—If I consider its history it is old—if its destiny it is new—I may see a part of an object or the whole—I will not be imposed on and think nature is old, because the season is advanced. I will study the botany
(30) of the mosses and fungi on the decayed—and remember that decayed wood is not old, but has just begun to be what it is. I need not think of the pine almond or the acorn and sapling when I meet the fallen pine or oak—more than
(35) of the generations of pines and oaks which have fed the young tree."

From JOURNALS by Henry David Thoreau, © 1842

12 On the basis of the information in the first paragraph, of whom is Thoreau speaking when he refers to "relics of a race which has vanished"?
  A his deceased family members
  B settlers who worked the land before him
  C neighbors who moved far away from his cabin
  D Native Americans who first lived on the land

13 What does the author imply when he writes "In planting my corn in the same furrow which yielded its increase to support so long—I displace some memorial of him" (lines 18 through 21)?
  A He has planted corn in the same place as his ancestors.
  B As he plants his own corn, he is taking away traces of Native Americans.
  C He is acknowledging that others have planted in this spot before him.
  D He is claiming the land as his own through his planting ritual.

14 What is the most logical inference to make about the meaning of the statement "decayed wood is not old" (lines 30 to 31)?
  A There are much older forms of wood than decayed wood.
  B Decay is a natural process in the cycle of life.
  C Decayed wood is the start of a new cycle of life.
  D Decayed wood is young compared with mosses and fungi.

15 By focusing on the life cycle of plants, the author implies that
  A this cycle was important to his ancestors.
  B he has learned much by studying plant life.
  C the life cycle of plants is similar to that of humans.
  D the life cycle of plants explains the presence of relics.

Directions: Questions 16 through 19 refer to the following excerpt.

WHY IS PAULINE ON THE PORCH?

I don't know what to do about my husband's new wife. She won't come in. She sits on the front porch and smokes. She won't knock or ring the bell, and the only way I know
(5) she's there at all is because the dog points in the living room. The minute I see Stray standing with one paw up and his tail straight out I say, "Shhh. It's Pauline." I stroke his coarse fur and lean on the broom and we wait.
(10) We hear the creak of a board, the click of a purse, a cigarette being lit, a sad, tiny cough. At last I give up and open the door. "Pauline?" The afternoon light hurts my eyes. "Would you like to come in?"
(15) "No," says Pauline.
Sometimes she sits on the stoop, picking at the paint, and sometimes she sits on the edge of an empty planter box. Today she's perched on the railing. She frowns when she
(20) sees me and lifts her small chin. She wears the same black velvet jacket she always wears, the same formal silk blouse, the same huge dark glasses. "Just passing by," she explains.
I nod. Pauline lives thirty miles to the east,
(25) in the city, with Konrad. "Passing by" would take her one toll bridge, one freeway, and two backcountry roads from their flat. But lies are the least of our problems, Pauline's and mine, so I nod again, bunch my bathrobe a little
(30) tighter around my waist, try to cover one bare foot with the other, and repeat my invitation. She shakes her head so vigorously the railing lurches. "Konrad," she says in her high young voice, "expects me. You know how he is."

From Molly Giles's PIE DANCE, © 1985

16 Who does the speaker find on her porch?
A   her husband
B   her ex-husband
C   her husband's ex-wife
D   Konrad's new wife

17 The speaker describes Pauline as having a "high young voice" (lines 33–34). What does this tell us about Pauline? Pauline
A   is older than the speaker.
B   is younger than the speaker.
C   is the same age as the speaker.
D   and the speaker both have high voices.

18 What does the author's tone reveal about the speaker's relationship with Pauline?
A   Pauline threatens the speaker.
B   The speaker is amused by Pauline's behavior.
C   Pauline and the speaker hate one another.
D   Pauline and the speaker are good friends.

19 Which of the following examples is most like Pauline's situation in the excerpt?
A   Two enemies avoid one another on the street.
B   Two friends meet by accident at the mall.
C   Two acquaintances casually greet one another in passing.
D   Two people with a shared past visit awkwardly.

LESSON 14

Draw Conclusions

Fiction

1 Learn the Skill

As you learned in Unit 1, **drawing conclusions** is like solving a mystery. As a reader, you gather facts from your reading, combine it with what you know about the topic, and draw a conclusion about the significance of those facts. By drawing conclusions, readers discover connections between events and ideas as they read.

2 Practice the Skill

By mastering the skill of drawing conclusions, you will improve your study and test-taking skills, especially as they relate to high school equivalency language arts/reading tests. Read the excerpt and strategies below. Then answer the question that follows.

A Laird is in a wheelchair, and he is covered with blankets. What might the details indicate?

B The fact that "people who haven't seen him for a while" are shocked by Laird's appearance indicates that his illness is having a dramatic effect on him.

WHAT IS WRONG WITH LAIRD?

Her son wanted to talk again, suddenly. During the days, he still brooded, scowling at the swimming pool from the vantage point of his wheelchair, where he sat covered with blankets despite the summer heat. … After he was
(5) asleep, Janet would run through the conversations in her mind, and realize what it was she wished she had said. …
   A month earlier, after a particular long and grueling visit with a friend who'd come up on the train from New York, Laird had declared a new policy: no visitors, no telephone
(10) calls. She didn't blame him. People who hadn't seen him for a while were often shocked to tears by his appearance, and, rather than have them cheer him up, he felt obliged to comfort them.

From Alice Elliott Dark's IN THE GLOAMING, © 1994

✓ TEST-TAKING TIPS

Adding together details like "blankets despite the summer heat" and "people … were shocked by his appearance" let you know that Laird is very sick, even though the author never explicitly states this information.

1 Which of the following conclusions most accurately sums up the general situation described in the excerpt?
   A Laird is being treated for a rare disease.
   B Laird is indifferent about his medical treatment.
   C Janet has little background in current medicine.
   D Janet watches television news programs.

③ Apply the Skill

Directions: Questions 2 through 5 refer to the following excerpt.

WHAT'S WRONG WITH THE WOMAN ON THE PHONE?

She was in the airport, waiting for her flight to be called, when a woman came to the phone near her chair. The woman stood there dialing, and after a while began talking
(5) in a flat, aggrieved voice. Gloria couldn't hear everything by any means, but she did hear her say, "If anything happens to this plane, I hope you'll be satisfied." The woman spoke monotonously and without mercy. She was tall
(10) and disheveled and looked the very picture of someone who recently had ceased to be cherished. Nevertheless, she was still being mollified on the other end of the phone. Gloria heard with astounding clarity the part about
(15) the plane being repeated several times. The woman then slammed down the receiver and boarded Gloria's flight, flinging herself down in a first-class seat. Gloria proceeded to the rear of the plane and sat quietly, thinking
(20) that every person is on the brink of eternity every moment, that the ways and means of leaving this world are innumerable and often inconceivable.

From Joy Williams's THE LITTLE WINTER, © 1989

2. What conclusion can a reader draw from the description of the woman's voice as being "flat, aggrieved" in line 5?
   A   She feels nervous about flying on an airplane.
   B   She worries about the person on the other end of the phone.
   C   She thinks someone has mistreated her.
   D   She realizes that someone is listening to her phone call.

3. Which conclusion most likely can be drawn from the appearance of the woman on the phone in lines 9 through 12?
   A   The woman feels unloved.
   B   The woman feels carefree about her appearance.
   C   The woman feels calm about boarding the flight.
   D   The woman feels confident.

4. Which of the following conclusions does the speaker in the story draw about the woman on the phone?
   A   She should make friends with the woman during the flight.
   B   The woman on the phone is very unhappy.
   C   She should avoid listening to someone's private phone conversation.
   D   Traveling on airplanes is very dangerous.

5. Which of the following conclusions most accurately sums up the situation in the excerpt?
   A   A woman in the airport annoys Gloria.
   B   A woman at the airport takes Gloria's seat.
   C   Gloria watches a woman who is grieving for a dead parent.
   D   Gloria watches a woman who has recently ended a relationship.

Directions: Questions 6 through 9 refer to the following excerpt.

WHAT HAS HAPPENED TO ANGELA?

"For Sissy Miller." Gilbert Clandon, taking up the pearl broach that lay among a litter of rings and brooches on a little table in his wife's drawing-room, read the inscription: "For Sissy
(5) Miller, with my love."

It was like Angela to have remembered even Sissy Miller, her secretary. Yet how strange it was, Gilbert Clandon thought once more, that she had left everything in such
(10) order—a little gift of some sort for every one of her friends. It was as if she had foreseen her death. Yet she had been perfect health when she left the house that morning, six weeks ago; when she stepped off the curb in Piccadilly and
(15) the car had killed her.

He was waiting for Sissy Miller. He had asked her to come; he owed her, he felt, after all the years she had been with them, this token of consideration. Yes, he went on, as he
(20) sat there waiting, it was strange that Angela had left everything in such order. Every friend had been left some little token of her affection. Every ring, every necklace, every little Chinese box—she had a passion for little boxes—had
(25) a name on it. And each had some memory for him ... To him of course, she had left nothing in particular, unless it were her diary. Fifteen little volumes, bound in green leather, stood behind him on her writing table. Ever since they were
(30) married, she had kept a diary. Some of their very few—he would not call them quarrels, say tiffs—had been about that diary. When he came in and found her writing, she always shut it or put her hand over it. "No, no, no," he could
(35) hear her say, "After I'm dead—perhaps."

From Virginia Woolf's THE LEGACY, © 1944

6 What conclusion can you draw about Angela based on evidence in the excerpt?
  A She has treated Sissy Miller rudely.
  B She sold her jewelry for money.
  C She has been very ill.
  D She has recently died.

7 Gilbert Clandon says that Angela's diary caused, "he would not call them quarrels, say tiffs" (lines 31–32). What could you conclude from the tone of the excerpt? Gilbert
  A shared everything with Angela.
  B tried to minimize any marital problems.
  C kept his own diary.
  D learned about himself in Angela's diary.

8 Although she died suddenly, Angela left "a little gift of some sort for every one of her friends" (lines 10–11). What can you conclude from the facts surrounding Angela's death? Angela
  A told her secrets to Sissy Miller.
  B forgot to leave her husband a gift.
  C planned her own death.
  D was in poor health.

9 Which of the following is most like Gilbert's situation in the excerpt?
  A A husband and wife begin a new hobby together.
  B A stray note reveals a criminal's guilt.
  C A text message gives a clue to a mystery.
  D A friend deliberately leaves a message to be found after death.

Directions: Questions 10 through 13 refer to the following excerpt.

HOW DO THE GRANDPARENTS TREAT THEIR GRANDCHILDREN?

Whenever we children came to stay at my grandmother's house, we were put to sleep in the sewing room, a bleak, shabby, utilitarian rectangle, more office than bedroom, more
(5) attic than office, that played to the hierarchy of chambers the role of a poor relation. It was a room seldom entered by the other members of the family, seldom swept by the maid, a room without pride; the old sewing machine, some
(10) cast-off chairs. …There was nothing here to encourage us to consider this our home.

Poor Roy's children, as commiseration damply styled the four of us, could not afford illusions, in the family opinion. Our father had
(15) put us beyond the pale by dying suddenly of influenza and taking our young mother with him, a defection that was remarked on with horror and grief commingled, as though our mother had been a pretty secretary with
(20) whom he had wantonly absconded into the irresponsible paradise of the hereafter. Our reputation was clouded by this misfortune. There was a prevailing sense, not only in the family but in storekeepers, servants, streetcar
(25) conductors, and other satellites of our circle, that my grandfather, a rich man, had behaved with extraordinary munificence [generosity] in allotting a sum of money for our support and installing us with some disagreeable middle-
(30) aged relations in a dingy house two blocks distant from his own.

From Mary McCarthy's YONDER PEASANT, WHO IS HE?, © 1949

10 Based on the excerpt, what is the most reasonable conclusion that can be drawn about the relationship between the children's father and grandfather?
  A The grandfather loved his son very much but likely did not approve of his wife.
  B The father and the grandfather fought constantly.
  C The grandfather was the stepfather of the children's father.
  D When the children's father was a young boy, the grandfather shut him up in the old room.

11 What can you conclude about the children's stay in their grandparents' house?
  A They are made to feel welcome.
  B They are spoiled by generous grandparents.
  C They enjoy a relaxing visit.
  D They are treated as unwelcome guests.

12 The speaker says that her rich grandfather paid to "instal[l] us with some disagreeable middle-aged relations in a dingy house" (lines 29–30). What can you conclude from the speaker's tone?
  A The speaker loves her grandfather.
  B The grandfather is grieving over the death of his child.
  C The grandfather is not particular generous.
  D The speaker is very grateful.

13 Which of the following examples is most like the grandparents' situation in the excerpt?
  A A wealthy man gives money to support a home for unwanted pets.
  B Poor neighbors spend their last dime to feed stray animals in the neighborhood.
  C People on the block take up a collection to care for abandoned animals.
  D Well-off people pamper their own pets but ignore the hungry animals outside.

Directions: Questions 14 through 17 refer to the following excerpt.

WHAT IS LAIRD'S RELATIONSHIP WITH HIS FATHER?

"Dad ran off quickly," he said one night. She had been wondering when he would mention it.

"He had a phone call to make," she said (5) automatically.

Laird looked directly in her eyes, his expression one of gentle reproach. He was letting her know he had caught her in the central lie of her life, which was that she (10) understood Martin's obsession with his work. She averted her gaze. The truth was that she had never understood. Why couldn't he sit with her for half an hour after dinner, or, if not with her, why not with his dying son. …

(15) "I don't think Dad can stand to be around me."

"That's not true." It was true.

"Poor Dad. He's always been a hypochondriac—we have that in common. He (20) must hate this."

"He just wants you to get well."

"If that's what he wants, I'm afraid I'm going to disappoint him again. At least this will be the last time I let him down."

(25) He said this merrily with the old, familiar light darting from his eyes. She allowed herself to be amused. He had always been fond of teasing, and held no subject sacred. As the de facto authority figure in the house—Martin (30) hadn't been home enough to be the real disciplinarian—she had often been forced to reprimand Laird, but, in truth, she shared his sense of humor. She responded to it now by leaning over to cuff him on the arm.

(35) It was an automatic response, prompted by a burst of high spirits that took no notice of the circumstances. It was a mistake. Even through the thickness of his terrycloth robe, her knuckles knocked on bone. There was nothing (35) left of him.

"It's his loss," she said, the shock of Laird's thinness making her serious again.

From Alice Elliott Dark's IN THE GLOAMING, © 1993

14 What does Martin do after the meal is over?
  A He speaks to Laird.
  B He sits with his wife.
  C He makes a phone call.
  D He leaves quickly.

15 Laird refers to his father, saying that "at least this will be the last time I let him down" (lines 23–24). What can you conclude from this information?
  A Laird likes his mother better than his father.
  B Laird is Martin's best friend.
  C Laird does not get along well with his father.
  D Laird makes Martin proud of Laird's achievements.

16 The speaker observes that Martin cannot sit with his "dying son" (line 14). Which of the following examples is most like the one in the excerpt?
  A a shopper who admires a beautiful display of merchandise
  B a visitor to an art gallery who turns from an unattractive painting
  C a lawyer drawing up a will
  D a doctor conducting a painful operation

17 The speaker says that Martin's behavior is "his loss" (line 41). What could you conclude from her statement?
  A She thinks Martin is right to ignore Laird.
  B She thinks Martin is missing out by ignoring Laird.
  C She thinks Laird is too hard on Martin.
  D She loves Martin more than she loves Laird.

LESSON 15

Apply Ideas

① Learn the Skill

You have practiced making inferences (Lesson 13), and used that information to draw conclusions (Lesson 14). By gathering facts and thinking of reasonable explanations for those facts, you are **applying ideas** that can help you determine or predict unrelated events. For example, when you determine major elements of a character's personality, you can predict how he or she will act in a different situation. Applying ideas to a text can help you better understand the text as a whole.

② Practice the Skill

By mastering the skill of applying ideas, you will improve your study and test-taking skills, especially as they relate to high school equivalency language arts/reading tests. Read the excerpt and strategies below. Then answer the question that follows.

A The music has a particular effect on Paul. At first, the music appears to give him a kind of joy that he does not otherwise have.

B Paul's "struggl[ing]" spirit indicates that he may feel inhibited in his daily life.

HOW DOES THE SYMPHONY AFFECT PAUL?

A When the symphony began Paul sank into one of the rear seats with a long sigh of relief, and lost himself as he had done before the Rico. It was not that symphonies, as such, meant anything in particular to Paul, but the first
(5) sign of the instruments seemed to free some hilarious and potent spirit within him; something that struggled there like **B** the genie in the bottle found by the Arab fisherman. He felt a sudden zest of life; the lights danced before his eyes and the concert hall blazed into unimaginable splendor. When
(10) the soprano soloist came on, Paul forgot even the nastiness of his teacher's being there and gave himself up to the peculiar stimulus such personages always had for him.

From Willa Cather's PAUL'S CASE, © 1905

USING LOGIC

Consider how the character would react in a different set of circumstances. A character would probably act consistently, with the same personality traits. Use logic to imagine how these traits might be acted out in a different situation.

1 Based on his behavior in the excerpt, what can you infer about Paul?

 A He is great friends with his teacher.
 B He goes to the symphony daily.
 C He knows the soprano soloist.
 D He is deeply moved by the symphony.

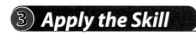

Directions: Questions 2 through 5 refer to the following excerpt.

WHAT MAKES LEO LOSE HIS TEMPER?

People born into the tradition of English country life are accustomed to eccentric owls. Mrs. Leslie and her daughter Belinda accepted the owl with vague acknowledging smiles. Her
(5) son-in-law, Leo Cooper, a Londoner whose contacts with nature had been made at the very expensive pleasure resorts patronized by his very rich parents, found midday hoots disconcerting, and almost said so. But did not,
(10) as he was just then in a temper and wholly engaged in not showing it.

He was in a temper for several reasons, all eminently adequate. For one thing, ... impelled by the nervous appetite of frustration he had
(15) eaten a traditional country breakfast and it was disagreeing with him; for yet another, he had been hauled out on yet another of his mother-in-law's picnics; finally, there was the picnic basket. The picnic basket was a family
(20) piece, dating, as Mrs. Leslie said on its every appearance, from an age of footmen. It was the size of a cabin trunk, built for eternity out of red wicker, equipped with massy cutlery and crockery; time had sharpened its red fangs,
(25) and however Leo took hold if it, they lacerated him. Also it caused him embarrassment to be seen carrying this rattling, creaking monstrosity, and today he had carried it farther than usual.

From Sylvia Townsend Warner's HEALTHY LANDSCAPE WITH DORMOUSE, © 1966

2 In the excerpt, where is Leo located?
 A in London
 B in a large house
 C in a large picnic basket
 D in the countryside

3 In the excerpt, Leo states he has been forced to go on "yet another of his mother-in-law's picnics" (lines 17–18). What could you predict about Leo, based on the tone of the excerpt? Leo will probably
 A love the next picnic.
 B dislike the next picnic, too.
 C tell his mother-in-law to stop having picnics.
 D ask to reschedule the picnic.

4 Leo's exposure to nature has been at "very expensive pleasure resorts" (line 7). His experience at the picnic is most like which of the following examples?
 A A person in New Jersey takes the train to watch a Broadway show.
 B A country couple drives to town for a dance.
 C A Chicago lawyer does not know how to saddle a horse on a trail ride.
 D A web designer knows a surprising amount of information about sheep.

5 Each time she uses the picnic basket, Mrs. Leslie tells people that it was first used in "an age of footmen" (line 21). Based on this knowledge of her character, what could you predict about Mrs. Leslie? She will
 A be generally modest about her accomplishments.
 B not announce an important award she has received.
 C give money to charities anonymously.
 D find excuses to brag about her family.

Directions: Questions 6 through 9 refer to the following excerpt.

HOW DOES MARGARET FEEL ABOUT HER APPEARANCE?

In the large Spanish-style house she and my father have shared for thirty-five of their nearly fifty years of marriage, a black-and-white Hollywood-style studio portrait of my
(5) mother as a wet-lipped ingénue, circa 1940, hangs framed on the stucco wall over the fireplace. Other than that, you would never guess what pride she once took in her beauty. No face lift or eye tuck for Margaret Pierce; at
(10) seventy-four, she would no sooner go under the knife for the sake of appearing five or six years younger than buy a dress simply because it was marked down. The same goes for reinforced undergarments, costly
(15) moisturizers holding out the promise of eternal youth, and hair rinses the various burnished hues of expensive luggage. "I'd rather look ancient," she'd sniff, "than pathetic."

Mother is a prime specimen of what most
(20) women claim to want even while desperately doing everything within their grasp to prevent it: growing old gracefully. Only traces remain of the ashy-lidded glamour queen over the fireplace that made a mockery of my
(25) own crabbed, self-conscious crawl toward womanhood. Her weathered beauty has taken on a kind of monolithic status more akin to Mount Rushmore than Rita Hayworth.

From Eileen Goudge's THE PRICE OF TEA IN CHINA, © 1998

6 What does the speaker say about her mother's appearance? Her mother
   A is vain.
   B is unaware of her beauty.
   C accepts her age.
   D refuses to buy new dresses.

7 The speaker says that her mother is "growing old gracefully" (line 22). From the author's tone, how can we predict she would describe her mother to her friends?
   A sad
   B practical
   C ugly
   D ridiculous

8 Margaret states that she would "rather look ancient…than pathetic" (line 17–18). Which of the following examples best illustrates that statement?
   A a car with hybrid technology
   B a minivan fully repaired after an accident
   C a 1950s sedan, restored to its original beauty
   D a functional, well-worn 1990s sub-compact

9 The speaker says that her mother does not use expensive moisturizers or hair rinses. Based on Margaret's preferences, what do you predict she would say to a department store clerk offering her a free sample?
   A "No, but thank you."
   B "This is just my color."
   C "I can't afford this."
   D "Great, I'll give this to my daughter."

Directions: Questions 10 through 13 refer to the following excerpt.

WHY DOES BELINDA WALK TO HER CAR?

"Belinda walks exactly like her father."
"She walks beautifully."
"Yes, doesn't she? I wonder where she's going."
(5) "She seems to be making for the car."
"Perhaps she has left something in it. Or perhaps she wants to move it into the shade. She has always been so fond of it. She learned to drive it when she was twelve. ..."
(10) Belinda was certainly walking towards the car. ...They watched her cross the cattle bridge and get into the car. They saw her start the car, turn it and drive away.
"So now they know." Belinda spoke in the
(15) tone of one who has achieved some stern moral purpose. "Or they soon will."
Belinda was one of those fortunate persons who fly into a rage as though into a refrigerator. Walking across the heath in the
(20) glaring post-meridian sun she had felt a film of ice encasing her, armoring her from head to foot in sleekness and invulnerability. She felt, too, the smile on her lips becoming increasingly rigid and corpselike. When she got into the car,
(25) though it was hot as an oven she seemed to be adjusting the hands of a marble effigy on the wheel. The car's smell, so familiar, so much part of her life, waylaid her with its ordinary sensuality, besought her to have a good cry.
(30) But righteousness sustained her. ...The whole afternoon was before her; she could go where she pleased. The whole afternoon was also before Leo and her mother, and a wide range of reflections; for there on the heath, with not a
(35) soul in sight, they would have to remain till she drove back to collect them.

From Sylvia Townsend Warner's HEALTHY LANDSCAPE WITH DORMOUSE, © 1966

10 Leo and Belinda's mother watch Belinda walk to the car. What do they not know? Belinda is
  A pleased with their outing.
  B moving the car to the shade.
  C going to leave them stranded.
  D going to practice walking.

11 Belinda observes that "righteousness sustained her" when she is tempted to cry (line 30–31). What is the author's purpose in including this information about Belinda?
  A to show how emotional she is
  B to show how much she hates her car
  C to show how easily she cries
  D to show how she has self-control

12 The excerpt states that Belinda's anger is like "a film of ice encasing her, armoring her from head to foot" (lines 20–22). Based on this description, how can we predict Belinda would react when confronted by an angry person?
  A She would discuss the person's anger.
  B She would yell back at the person.
  C She would refer the person to a counselor.
  D She would not respond.

13 Leo and Belinda's mother discuss Belinda as she drives away. Which of the following examples best illustrates their situation?
  A A person runs after a thief who has stolen his wallet.
  B A thief takes a person's wallet while talking to the victim.
  C A person drops a wallet on the ground without noticing the loss.
  D A clerk returns a purse that a shopper left on the counter.

Directions: Questions 14 through 17 refer to the following excerpt.

WHAT DILEMMA DOES LAURA FACE?

Laura's upbringing made her wonder for a moment whether it was quite respectful of a workman to talk to her of bangs slap in the eye.* But she did quite follow him.

(5) "A corner of the tennis-court," she suggested. "But the band's going to be in one corner."

"H'm, going to have a band, are you?" said another of the workmen. He was pale. He had (10) a haggard look as his dark eyes scanned the tennis-court. What was he thinking?

"Only a small band," said Laura gently. Perhaps he wouldn't mind so much if the band was quite small. But the tall fellow interrupted.

(15) "Look here, miss, that's the place. Against those trees. Over there. That'll do fine."

Against the karakas. Then the karaka-trees would be hidden. And they were so lovely, with their broad, gleaming leaves, and their (20) clusters of yellow fruit. They were like trees you imagined growing on a desert island, proud, solitary, lifting their leaves and fruits to the sun in a kind of silent splendour. Must they be hidden by a marquee [sign]?

(25) They must. Already the men had shouldered their staves and were making for the place. Only the tall fellow was left. He bent down, pinched a sprig of lavender, put his thumb and forefinger to his nose and snuffed (30) up the smell. When Laura saw that gesture she forgot all about the karakas in her wonder at him caring for things like that—caring for the smell of lavender. How many men that she knew would have done such a thing? Oh, (35) how extraordinarily nice workmen were, she thought. Why couldn't she have workmen for friends rather than the silly boys she danced with and who came to Sunday night supper? She would get on much better with men like (40) these.

*an old expression for "hit in the middle of the eye;" considered a crude expression used only by lower-class people.

From Katherine Mansfield's THE GARDEN PARTY, © 1922

14 How did Laura react to the workman smelling the lavender?
  A Laura was upset that the workman was not doing his job.
  B Laura is enthralled by his action and forgets about the party.
  C Laura thinks nothing of his action and continues setting up for the party.
  D The workman's action reminds Laura of some men that she forgot to invite to the party.

15 Which of the following is most likely the author's purpose in describing the karaka trees?
  A to show that Laura was proud of her garden
  B to give constructive gardening tips to readers
  C to indicate how important the trees are to Laura
  D to describe how Laura wanted to hide the trees from view

16 Based on the excerpt, how might Laura's attitude be described before the workman smells the lavender flower?
  A betrayed
  B lonely
  C rushed
  D resigned

17 Which of the following situations is most similar to Laura's situation?
  A A busy lawyer is distracted while walking down a street by a person painting a picture.
  B A band manager debates where to put a sign to promote his band.
  C A gardener watches a small child pick a flower from a flower bed.
  D A boy at a prom tries to decide with which girl he wants to dance first.

Unit 2 Review

The Unit Review is structured to resemble high school equivalency language arts/reading tests. Be sure to read each question and all possible answers carefully before choosing your answer. To record your answers, fill in the lettered circle that corresponds to the answer you select for each question in the Unit Review.

Do not rest your pencil on the answer area while considering your answer. Make no stray or unnecessary marks. If you change an answer, erase your first mark completely. Mark only one answer space for each question; multiple answers will be scored as incorrect.

Sample Question

For what does the speaker wish?
- A to read a new book
- B to travel to London
- C to leave Vera Cruz
- D to buy a drink at the bar

Directions: Questions 1 through 6 refer to the following excerpt.

WHAT TYPE OF VACATION DOES THE SPEAKER WANT TO TAKE?

I could not remember when last I had had a moment to myself. I had often amused my fancy with the prospect of just one week's complete idleness. Most of us when not busy (5) working are busy playing; we ride, play tennis or golf, swim or gamble; but I saw myself doing nothing at all. I would lounge through the morning, dawdle through the afternoon and loaf through the evening. My mind would (10) be a slate [chalkboard] and each passing hour a sponge that wiped out the scribblings written on it by the world of sense. Time, because it is so fleeting, time, because it is beyond recall, is the most precious of human (15) goods and to squander it is the most delicate form of dissipation in which man can indulge. Cleopatra dissolved in wine a priceless pearl, but she gave it to Antony to drink; when you waste the brief golden hours you (20) take the beaker in which the gem is melted and dash its contents to the ground. The gesture is grand and like all grand gestures absurd. That of course is its excuse. In the week I promised myself I should naturally (25) read, for to the habitual reader reading is a drug of which he is the slave; deprive him of printed matter and he grows nervous, moody and restless; then, like the alcoholic bereft of brandy who will drink shellac or (30) methylated spirit, he will make do with the advertisements of a paper five years old; he will make do with a telephone directory. …

But I had always fancied myself choosing my moment with surroundings to my liking, (35) not having it forced upon me; and when I was suddenly faced with nothing to do and had to make the best of it (like a steamship acquaintance whom in the wide waste of the Pacific Ocean you have invited to stay (40) with you in London and who turns up without warning and with all his luggage) I was not a little taken aback. I had come to Vera Cruz from Mexico City to catch one of the Ward Company's white cool ships to Yucatan; and (45) found to my dismay that, a dock strike having been declared over-night, my ship would not put in. I was stuck in Vera Cruz.

From W. Somerset Maugham's THE BUM, © 1929

1. What is the speaker's situation? He is
   A lost.
   B sick.
   C stranded.
   D homesick.

   Ⓐ Ⓑ Ⓒ Ⓓ

2. Why does the speaker want to do nothing? The speaker has
   A never been to Vera Cruz.
   B never been to Yucatan.
   C grown bored with reading.
   D not had time to himself.

   Ⓐ Ⓑ Ⓒ Ⓓ

3. The speaker says that "my mind would be a slate and each passing hour a sponge" (lines 9–11). How do these metaphors play a role in this excerpt?
   A They describe the speaker's restless feeling.
   B They explain how the speaker recovers from vacation.
   C They are metaphors for the speaker's desire to forget things.
   D They symbolize the speaker's profession.

   Ⓐ Ⓑ Ⓒ Ⓓ

4. Which word best describes the speaker's tone?
   A wishful
   B thankful
   C annoyed
   D angry

   Ⓐ Ⓑ Ⓒ Ⓓ

5. In the excerpt, the speaker says that Cleopatra dissolved a "priceless pearl" in wine (lines 17–18). Based on this excerpt, why might Cleopatra have done this?
   A to destroy an object of beauty
   B to show her love for Antony
   C to impoverish herself
   D to show the quality of the wine

   Ⓐ Ⓑ Ⓒ Ⓓ

6. The feeling expressed by the speaker in the last paragraph is most like which of the following people?
   A a diner whose meals is brought to his table
   B a person receiving a package at her doorstep
   C a commuter hopping on the last train
   D a customer told that a store is out of the product she wants

   Ⓐ Ⓑ Ⓒ Ⓓ

Unit 2 Review | Fiction

Directions: Questions 7 through 14 refer to the following excerpt.

THE HUNTERS RETURN

"My aunt will be down presently, Mr. Nuttel," said a self-possessed young lady of fifteen; "in the meantime you must put up with me."

(5) Framton Nuttel endeavoured to say the correct something. Privately he doubted whether formal visits to total strangers would help the nerve cure which he was undergoing.

"I know how it will be," his sister had said when he was preparing to migrate to this rural (10) retreat; "you will bury yourself down there and not speak to a soul, and your nerves will be worse than ever from moping. I shall just give you letters of introduction to all the people I know there. Some were quite nice."

(15) "Do you know many of the people round here?" asked the niece.

"Hardly a soul," said Framton. "My sister stayed at the rectory four years ago, and she gave me letters of introduction to some people (20) here."

"Then you know nothing about my aunt?"

"Only her name and address," admitted the caller. He was wondering whether Mrs. Sappleton was married or widowed. The room suggested (25) masculine habitation.

"Her great tragedy happened three years ago. You may wonder why we keep that window open on an October afternoon," said the niece, indicating a French window that opened on to a (30) lawn.

"It is warm for this time of year," said Framton; "but is it related to the tragedy?"

"Out through that window, three years ago her husband and her two brothers went off for their (35) day's shooting. They never came back. In crossing the moor they were engulfed in a bog. It had been that dreadful wet summer, and places that were safe gave way suddenly. Their bodies were never recovered. Poor aunt always thinks they will come (40) back someday, they and the little brown spaniel that was lost with them, and walk in at that window just as they used to do. That is why the window is kept open every evening. Poor dear aunt, she has often told me how they went out, her husband (45) with his white waterproof coat over his arm, and Ronnie, her youngest brother, singing. Sometimes on quiet evenings like this, I get a creepy feeling that they will all walk in through that window."

She broke off with a shudder. It was a relief (50) when the aunt bustled into the room.

"Don't mind the open window," said Mrs. Sappleton; "my husband and brothers will be home directly.

She rattled on cheerfully about the shooting (55) and the scarcity of birds. To Framton it was horrible. He made a desperate effort to turn to a less ghastly topic; he was conscious that his hostess was giving him only a fragment of her attention, her eyes straying past him to the open (60) window and the lawn.

"The doctors ordered complete rest, no mental excitement, and minimal physical exercise," announced Framton, deluded that strangers and chance acquaintances hunger for (65) details of one's ailments.

Then she suddenly brightened to attention, but not to what Framton was saying.

"Here they are at last!" she cried. "Just in time for tea."

(70) Framton shivered slightly and turned to the niece to convey comprehension. She was staring through the window with dazed horror in her eyes. Framton swung around and looked in the same direction.

(75) Three figures were walking across the lawn towards the window, all carried guns under their arms, and one was additionally burdened with a white coat hung over his shoulders. A brown spaniel kept close.

(80) Framton grabbed at his stick and hat; the hall door, gravel drive, and front gate were dimly noted stages in his headlong retreat.

"Here we are, " said the bearer of the white mackintosh, coming in through the window.

(85) "Who was that who bolted as we came up?"

"A Mr. Nuttel," said Mrs. Sappleton; "could only talk about his illnesses, and dashed off without a word. You'd think he had seen a ghost."

"I expect it was the spaniel," said the niece (90) calmly; "he told me he had a horror of dogs. He was once hunted into a cemetery and had to spend the night in a new grave with wild dogs snarling and foaming just above him.

Romance at short notice was her specialty.

Adapted from THE OPEN WINDOW by Saki, © 1914

7 From which point of view is this story told?
A the niece's
B the aunt's
C first-person
D third-person

ⒶⒷⒸⒹ

8 Which statement best explains how paragraphs 4 and 6 relate to the story?
A The niece must find out why Framton has come to the village before her aunt comes downstairs.
B The niece hopes that the conversation will encourage Framton to reveal details about his illness.
C His acquaintance with the neighbors and aunt is likely to determine whether Framton will believe the niece's story.
D These questions are usual topics of polite conversation, which the niece must continue until her aunt takes over.

ⒶⒷⒸⒹ

9 Which event occurs first in the story?
A Framton acts as though he has seen a ghost.
B The niece explains why the window remains open.
C Framton's sister stays at the rectory.
D The "tragedy" takes place.

ⒶⒷⒸⒹ

10 Which detail best indicates that the story takes place during the early 1900s, not at the present time?
A "Here they are at last!" she cried. "Just in time for tea."
B "Poor aunt always thinks that they will come back someday…"
C "It is quite warm for the time of the year," said Framton.
D "I shall just give you letters of introduction to all the people I know there."

ⒶⒷⒸⒹ

11 The aunt ironically describes Framton's departure by saying "One would think he had seen a ghost." This expression usually indicates that someone is
A pale.
B nervous.
C horrified.
D invisible.

ⒶⒷⒸⒹ

12 The most likely conclusion to draw about the niece is that she is
A visiting her aunt to recover from an illness.
B selfish and demands constant attention.
C highly imaginative and thinks quickly.
D well acquainted with Framton's sister.

ⒶⒷⒸⒹ

13 What causes Framton to leave the house suddenly?
A He cannot bear to be in a room with open windows because his illness makes him sensitive to chill.
B Mrs. Sappleton is rude to him because her attention is elsewhere as he discusses his illness.
C The arrival of the dog terrifies him, reminding him of an earlier incident in a cemetery.
D He believes the niece's story and thinks he is seeing dead men walk through the door.

ⒶⒷⒸⒹ

14 Which sentence best states a theme of this story?
A People with nervous conditions will believe whatever they are told.
B A convincing story may seem more believable than the truth.
C Children who make up tales eventually will be punished.
D Telling ghost stories to people in poor health can cause severe damage.

ⒶⒷⒸⒹ

Unit 3

Unit Overview

Poetry is a special kind of writing that appeals to people's emotions and senses through the use of descriptive language. Poets such as Henry Wadsworth Longfellow Emily Dickinson, and Georgia Douglas Johnson write poems to express their feelings or even to tell stories. You can read poems in books, magazines, or on the Internet. You also can hear a type of poetry—song lyrics—when you listen to music.

On high school equivalency language arts/reading tests, poetry makes up a part of the overall literature passages. Unlike fiction texts, which are written in sentences and paragraphs, poetry is often written in lines or groups of lines called stanzas. In Unit 3, the introduction of ideas such as rhythm and rhyme, analogies, and restatement will help you prepare for high school equivalency language arts/reading tests.

Table of Contents

Lesson 1: Rhythm and Rhyme 164
Lesson 2: Analogies 169
Lesson 3: Figurative Language 174
Lesson 4: Symbols and Imagery 179
Lesson 5: Make Inferences 184
Lesson 6: Restatement 189
Lesson 7: Theme 194
Unit 3 Review 199

Poetry

Frequently Confused Words

Some frequently confused words are homonyms. These are words that sound the same or nearly the same but are spelled differently and have different meanings. Sometimes the two words may be spelled alike but have different meanings. Below is a list of frequently confused words.

accept: *to receive; to endure; to approve*
except: *to exclude*

affect: *to influence*
effect: *a result*

ate: *past tense of eat*
eight: *the number 8*

be: *to exist*
bee: *an insect*

board: *a piece of wood*
bored: *uninterested*

brake: *to stop*
break: *to damage or destroy; a rest period*

buy: *to purchase something*
by: *near; according to*

capital: *city that is the seat of government; money to invest; very important*
capitol: *building in which the legislature meets*

cell: *a small room, as in a prison*
sell: *to offer for sale*

cent: *a penny*
scent: *to smell*
sent: *to cause to go or be transmitted*

close: *to shut; to finish*
clothes: *something to wear on the body, usually made of cloth*

complement: *to go with*
compliment: *flattering words*

dear: *much loved; sweet*
deer: *an animal*

desert: *a dry, barren, sandy region*
dessert: *the final, usually sweet, course of a meal*

flour: *ground grain used in making bread*
flower: *the bloom or blossom on a plant*

for: *to be used as; meant to belong to*
four: *the number 4*

hear: *to listen*
here: *in this place*

hole: *opening*
whole: *entire*

hour: *60 minutes*
our: *belonging to us*

its: *possessive of it*
it's: *contraction of it is*

knew: *was certain of*
new: *modern; recent*

leave: *to go away*
let: *to allow*

made: *created*
maid: *a person who cleans*

mail: *letters or packages delivered by the post office*
male: *the opposite of female*

main: *most important*
mane: *the hair of a horse or lion*

meat: *animal flesh that is eaten*
meet: *to get together*

one: *the number 1*
won: *past tense of win*

passed: *went by*
past: *a time before; opposite of future*

patience: *ability to wait*
patients: *plural of patient*

peace: *freedom from war; harmony; calm*
piece: *a part of something*

plain: *ordinary; simple*
plane: *airplane; a flat surface*

pole: *a long piece of wood or metal*
poll: *a listing of people; a vote*

principal: *first in rank; the head of a school*
principle: *a rule or belief*

right: *correct; opposite of left*
write: *to form visible words*

road: *a path or street*
rode: *past tense of the verb ride*

role: *a part played*
roll: *to turn over; a type of bread*

scene: *a view; part of a play or movie*
seen: *past participle of see*

sea: *the ocean*
see: *to look at*

set: *to put or lay something in a place*
sit: *to rest oneself on a chair or perch*

sight: *the ability to see*
site: *a place or location*

some: *a few*
sum: *the total amount*

their: *belonging to them*
there: *at or in that place*
they're: *a contraction of the words they are*

threw: *past tense of throw*
through: *in one side and out the other side*

to: *in the direction of*
too: *in addition; very*
two: *the number 2*

wait: *to stay until something happens; to serve food at a meal*
weight: *how heavy something is*

weak: *opposite of strong*
week: *seven days*

wear: *to have clothing on the body*
where: *referring to a place*

weather: *the climate*
whether: *in case; in either case*

who's: *contraction of who is or who has*
whose: *possessive of who*

wood: *what trees are made of*
would: *helping verb; also, the past tense of will*

you're: *contraction of you are*
your: *belonging to you*

LESSON 1

Rhythm and Rhyme

Poetry

1 Learn the Skill

Rhythm and **rhyme** are sound effects that influence a reader's understanding of poetry. Rhythm is a pattern of stressed syllables. In the phrase "'Twas the night before Christmas," for example, every third syllable is stressed—"'Twas the *night* before *Christ*mas." Rhythm can be created by the use of punctuation and line breaks. Words that rhyme may have similar vowel or consonant sounds, such as *teach* and *peach*. **Partial rhymes**, such as *teach* and *team*, include words that do not rhyme completely. To determine a rhyming pattern, assign a letter to the last word (the rhyming word) of a line of a stanza, as shown below. A **stanza** is a section of a poem, similar to a paragraph of fiction.

2 Practice the Skill

By mastering the skill of identifying a poem's rhythm and rhyme, you will improve your study and test-taking skills, especially as they relate to high school equivalency language arts/reading tests. Read the excerpt and strategies below. Then answer the question that follows.

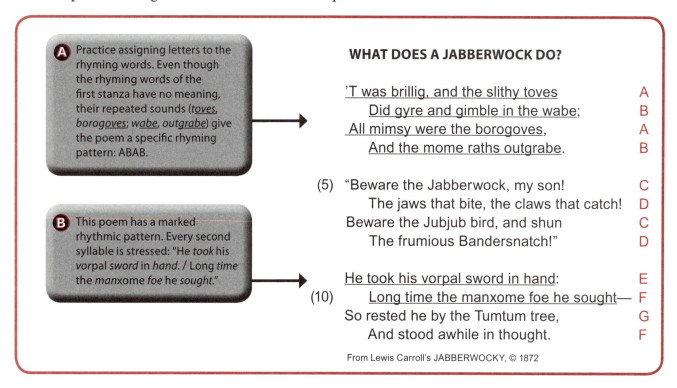

TEST-TAKING TIPS

Many poems were written to be read aloud. Softly saying a poem aloud can give you an idea of its rhythm and where the stressed syllables are.

1 How would you describe the rhythm in this poem?
   A surprising and offbeat
   B delicate and graceful
   C regular and reliable
   D lurching and unsteady

Apply the Skill

Directions: Questions 2 and 3 refer to the following poem.

WHAT MAKES THIS DESCRIPTION UNUSUAL?

The Panther

The panther is like a leopard,
Except it hasn't been peppered.
Should you behold a panther crouch,
Prepare to say Ouch.
(5) Better yet, if called by a panther,
Don't anther.

Ogden Nash's THE PANTHER, © 1940

2. What is the effect of the rhyme in the poem's last two lines (lines 5–6)? Readers are probably
    A amused by the rhyme of "panther" and "anther".
    B upset that "anther" is not a real word.
    C unsure how to pronounce "anther".
    D confused because answer is not spelled correctly.

3. "Don't anther" (line 6) is much shorter than the poem's other lines. What was the author's purpose in creating this type of rhythm?
    A to create a regular rhythm
    B to make the rhythm like a graceful panther
    C to emphasize that the poem ends abruptly
    D to show how a rhythm can be soothing

Directions: Questions 4 and 5 refer to the following poem.

WHAT GIFT DOES THE SPEAKER WANT?

One Perfect Rose

A single flow'r he sent me, since we met.
All tenderly his messenger he chose;
Deep-hearted, pure, with scented dew still wet—
(5) One perfect rose.

I knew the language of the floweret;
"My fragile leaves," it said, "his heart enclose."
(10) Love long has taken for his amulet
One perfect rose.

Why is it no one has ever sent me yet
One perfect limousine, do you suppose?
Ah no, it's always just my luck to get
One perfect rose.

Dorothy Parker's ONE PERFECT ROSE, © 1926

4. Which best describes the poem's rhythm?
    A bouncy
    B jerky
    C formal
    D pounding

5. Which of the following items would the speaker probably choose for a present?
    A a sentimental key chain
    B an inexpensive piece of costume jewelry
    C a puppy from an animal shelter
    D a jewelry store gift certificate

Unit 3 | Poetry

Directions: Questions 6 through 10 refer to the following poem.

WHAT DOES LOVE DO TO PEOPLE?

Song

The chimney sweepers
Wash their faces and forget to wash the neck;
  The lighthouse keepers
Let the lamps go out and leave the ships to
(5)   wreck;
  The prosperous baker
Leaves the rolls in hundreds in the oven to burn;
  The undertaker
Pins a small note on the coffin saying, "Wait till I
(10)   return,
  I've got a date with Love."

  And deep-sea divers
Cut their boots off and come bubbling to the top,
  And engine-drivers
(15) Bring expresses in the tunnel to a stop;
  The village rector
Dashes down the side-aisle half-way through a
    psalm;
  The sanitary inspector
(20) Runs off with the cover of the cesspool on his
    arm—
  To keep his date with Love.

W.H. Auden's SONG, © 1939

6 What is the rhyme pattern of the first stanza?
   A A, A, B, A, C, C, D, C, E
   B A, B, A, B, C, D, C, D, E
   C A, A, B, B, C, C, D, D, E
   D A, B, C, A, B, C, D, E, F

7 In the poem, which of the following word pairs contain a partial rhyme?
   A sweepers and keepers
   B burn and return
   C rector and inspector
   D psalm and arm

8 How does love affect the workers in this poem? Love makes the workers
   A work harder.
   B do their jobs better.
   C focus on their tasks.
   D abandon their jobs.

9 What is the author's purpose in repeating the phrase "date with Love" (lines 11 and 22)?
   A to indicate that not everyone can find love
   B to show that emotions are unreliable
   C to create a half rhyme
   D to emphasize the power of love

10 What would the speaker probably think if his meal arrived late at a restaurant? He would probably think the waiter
   A was lazy.
   B was untrained.
   C had too many customers.
   D was in love.

Directions: Questions 11 through 15 refer to the following poem.

WHAT DOES THE SPEAKER WANT FROM HER MOTHER?

The Courage That My Mother Had

The courage that my mother had
Went with her, and is with her still:
Rock from New England quarried;
Now granite in a granite hill.

(5) The golden brooch my mother wore
She left behind for me to wear;
I have no thing I treasure more:
Yet, it is something I could spare.

Oh, if instead she'd left to me
(10) The thing she took into the grave!—
That courage like a rock, which she
Has no more need of, and I have.

Edna St. Vincent Millay's THE COURAGE THAT MY MOTHER HAD, © 1954

11 Which of the following items would this speaker probably choose, if offered?
  A job security
  B an insurance policy
  C an expensive car
  D good advice

12 What is the main method the poet used to create rhythm?
  A a pattern of stressed syllables
  B repeating particular vowel sounds
  C repeating sounds at the beginnings of words
  D using common words

13 In stanza three, the words *grave* and *have* look alike, but are pronounced differently (lines 10 and 12). What is the effect of this partial rhyme?
  A It emphasizes the poem's rhyming lines.
  B It makes the poem upbeat.
  C It draws attention to the final line.
  D It makes the poem end smoothly.

14 What wish does the speaker express in the last four lines? She wants to have
  A her mother's brooch.
  B her mother's courage.
  C her mother's treasure.
  D New England granite.

15 In which line does the poem's rhythm differ from the rest of the poem?
  A "The golden brooch my mother wore" (line 5)
  B "I have no thing I treasure more:" (line 7)
  C "The thing she took into the grave!—" (line 10)
  D "Has no more need of, and I have." (line 12)

Directions: Questions 16 through 19 refer to the excerpt from the following poem.

WHAT ARE THE RIDERS PLANNING TO DO?

The Destruction of Sennacherib

The Assyrian came down like the wolf on the fold,
And his cohorts were gleaming in purple and gold;
And the sheen of their spears was like stars on
(5)   the sea,
When the blue wave rolls nightly on deep Galilee.

Like the leaves of the forest when Summer is green,
That host with their banners at sunset were seen:
(10) Like the leaves of the forest when Autumn hath blown,
That host on the morrow lay withered and strown

For the Angel of Death spread his wings on the blast,
(15) And breathed in the face of the foe as he passed;
And the eyes of the sleepers waxed deadly and chill,
And their hearts but once heaved, and for ever grew still!
…

(20) And there lay the steed with his nostril all wide,
But through it there rolled not the breath of his pride;
And the foam of his gasping lay white on the turf,
And cold as the spray of the rock-beating surf.

From George Gordon, Lord Byron's THE DESTRUCTION OF SENNACHERIB, © 1832

16 What is the main action described in this poem?
- A an army exercise
- B an angel's miracle
- C a military attack
- D a trip to Galilee

17 In the biblical story, the Angel of Death destroys Sennacherib's Assyrian troops as they attempt to capture the city of Jerusalem. How does this information affect the poem's message? It makes the Assyrian army appear
- A mighty.
- B small.
- C weak.
- D doomed.

18 What is the effect created by the poem's rhythmic pattern? The rhythm suggests a
- A casual stroll.
- B pounding movement.
- C relaxing chat.
- D baby's nap.

19 Which of the following is most like the fate of the Assyrians?
- A A good soccer team loses because of its pride.
- B An unforeseen event takes away a basketball team's sure win.
- C A lacrosse team is not prepared for a tough game.
- D A weaker swim team improves through practice.

LESSON 2

Analogies

Poetry

1 Learn the Skill

Poets often use **analogies** in their poems to compare two things to highlight similarities and differences. You learned about some forms of analogies in Unit 2. Analogies may take the form of **metaphors**, which describe one thing as being another: *My love is a rose*. **Similes** are another type of analogy that make comparisons by using the words *like* or *as*: *My street is as crooked as a maze* or *My love is like a rose*. Poets use similes and metaphors to make unusual comparisons that create memorable images.

2 Practice the Skill

By mastering the skill of analyzing analogies, you will improve your study and test-taking skills, especially as they relate to high school equivalency language arts/reading tests. Read the poem and strategies below. Then answer the question that follows.

HOW CAN THE SPEAKER GO SO MANY PLACES?

There Is No Frigate Like a Book

A In this analogy, the speaker compares a book to a frigate, which is a type of ship. This comparison uses the word *like*, which means it is a simile.

A There is no frigate [ship] like a book
  To take us lands away,
Nor any coursers [horses] like a page
  Of prancing poetry.

(5) This traverse [travel] may the poorest take
    Without oppress of toll;
B How frugal is the chariot
    That bears a human soul!

B The speaker says that a chariot carries away the human soul. Here, a chariot is a metaphor for the book that carries the speaker to far-away lands.

Emily Dickinson's THERE IS NO FRIGATE LIKE A BOOK, © 1924

 USING LOGIC

To analyze analogies, look for extended comparisons that may carry through the entire poem. Here the speaker compares books to different types of transportation that can carry her mind far away, even while her body remains in the same place.

1   In what way is a book similar to a sailing ship? It is
    A   available to people with little money.
    B   only found at the library.
    C   sold at the seaside.
    D   able to take readers to distant places.

Directions: Questions 2 through 5 refer to the following poem.

HOW DO OLD FRIENDS FEEL ABOUT SEEING ONE ANOTHER?

The Meeting

After so long an absence
   At last we meet again:
Does the meeting give us pleasure,
   Or does it give us pain?

(5) The tree of life has been shaken,
   And but few of us linger now,
Like the Prophet's two or three berries
   In the top of the uppermost bough.

We cordially greet each other
(10) In the old, familiar tone;
And we think, though we do not say it,
   How old and gray he is grown!

We speak of a Merry Christmas
   And many a Happy New Year;
(15) But each in his heart is thinking
   Of those that are not here.

We speak of friends and their fortunes,
   And what they did and said,
Till the dead alone seem living
(20) And the living alone seem dead.

At last we hardly distinguish
   Between the ghosts and the guests;
And a mist and shadow of sadness
   Steals over our merriest jests.

Henry Wadsworth Longfellow's THE MEETING

2. **What saddens the speaker about meeting his old friend?**
   A They have nothing in common.
   B They will not have a Merry Christmas.
   C Many of their friends have died.
   D They are no longer friendly.

3. **The speaker says that the friends are "Like the Prophet's two or three berries" in the top of a tree (line 7–8). What does this comparison reveal about the friends? The friends are**
   A hard to reach.
   B part of a prophecy.
   C like trees in a forest.
   D among a very few who still remain.

4. **Which word identifies the feeling of the poem?**
   A angry
   B disappointed
   C wistful
   D fearful

5. **The feelings expressed by the speaker in the last stanza (lines 21–24) are most like which of the following people?**
   A a person trying, but failing, to enjoy her birthday party
   B a host welcoming guests to a party
   C a child failing to blow out the candles on a cake
   D a helper distributing gift bags as guests leave

Directions: Questions 6 through 9 refer to the excerpt from the following poem.

WHY DOES THIS MAN WANT TO TRAVEL?

Ulysses

I cannot rest from travel: I will drink
Life to the lees: all times I have enjoyed
Greatly, have suffered greatly, both with those
That loved me, and alone; on shore, and when
(5)　Through scudding drifts the rainy Hyades
Vexed the dim sea: I am become a name;
For always roaming with a hungry heart
Much have I seen and known; cities of men
And manners, climates, councils,
(10)　　　governments,
Myself not least, but honoured of them all;
And drunk delight of battle with my peers;
Far on the ringing plains of windy Troy.
I am a part of all that I have met;
(15)　Yet all experience is an arch wherethrough
Gleams that untravelled world, whose margin
　　　fades
For ever and for ever when I move.
How dull it is to pause, to make an end,
(20)　To rust unburnished, not to shine in use!
As though to breathe were life. Life piled on life
Were all too little, and of one to me
Little remains: but every hour is saved
From that eternal silence, something more,
(25)　A bringer of new things; and vile it were
For some three suns to store and hoard
　　　myself,
And this grey spirit yearning in desire
To follow knowledge like a sinking star,
(30)　Beyond the utmost bound of human thought.

From Alfred Lord Tennyson's ULYSSES, © 1842

6 **What wish does the speaker express in the first six lines?**
   A to go to the Hyades
   B to avoid suffering
   C to rest and relax
   D to experience life through travel

7 **In lines 15 and 16, the speaker says that "experience is an arch wherethrough / Gleams that untravelled world." How does this comparison expand the meaning of the poem? The speaker**
   A does not want to walk under the arch.
   B wishes he enjoyed travel.
   C believes that experience is gained by travel.
   D is fearful of the untravelled world.

8 **The speaker wants "to follow knowledge like a sinking star, / Beyond the utmost bound of human thought" (lines 29–30). What mood does this comparison give to the poem? The comparison makes the search for knowledge seem**
   A uplifting.
   B petty.
   C dangerous.
   D ordinary.

9 **What would the speaker probably want to do on a day off?**
   A rake leaves
   B climb a mountain
   C read a book
   D watch a movie

Directions: Questions 10 through 13 refer to the following poem.

WHAT IS THE JOB OF A PARENT?

Ode on the Whole Duty of Parents

The spirits of children are remote and wise,
They must go free
Like fishes in the sea
Or starlings in the skies,
(5) Whilst you remain
The shore where casually they come again.
But when there falls the stalking shade of fear,
You must be suddenly near,
You, the unstable, must become a tree
(10) In whose unending heights of flowering green
Hangs every fruit that grows, with silver bells;
Where heart-distracting magic birds are seen
And all the things a fairy-story tells;
Though still you should possess
(15) Roots that go deep in ordinary earth,
And strong consoling bark
To love and caress.

Frances Cornford's ODE ON THE WHOLE DUTY OF PARENTS, © 1934

10 In this poem, what does the speaker say is a parent's responsibility to their children? Parents should provide
 A money.
 B education.
 C security.
 D discipline.

11 The poem compares children's spirits to "fishes in the sea" and "starlings in the skies" (lines 3–4). What does the comparison reveal about the speaker's belief about children? Children should be
 A free to explore.
 B guarded against danger.
 C kept healthy and well-fed.
 D allowed to swim.

12 The poem compares parents to a tree with "unending heights" and "roots that go deep" (lines 10 and 15). What kind of tone does this comparison set regarding the job of parenting?
 A joyous
 B exhausting
 C important
 D exciting

13 What does the speaker suggest by comparing children to fish and parents to the shore?
 A Children have more energy than their parents.
 B Parents must show children where to go.
 C Children are more adventurous than their parents.
 D Parents provide children a place to which they can return.

Directions: Questions 14 through 18 refer to the excerpt from the following poem.

WHAT CAN THE WIND DO?

Ode to the West Wind

O Wild West Wind, thou breath of Autumn's being
　Thou from whose unseen presence the leaves dead
(5)　Are driven like ghosts from an enchanter fleeing,

　Yellow, and black, and pale, and hectic red,
Pestilence-stricken multitudes! O thou
　Who chariotest to their dark wintry bed

(10)　The wingèd seeds, where they lie cold and low,
　Each like a corpse within its grave, until
Thine azure sister of the Spring shall blow

　Her clarion o'er the dreaming earth, and fill
(15)　(Driving sweet buds like flocks to feed in air)
　With living hues and odours plain and hill;

Wild Spirit, which art moving everywhere;
Destroyer and preserver; hear, O hear!

From Percy Bysshe Shelly's ODE TO THE WEST WIND, © 1819

14 How is the West Wind described in the excerpt's final stanza (lines 17–18)? The wind is a force that
  A moves leaves.
  B plants seeds.
  C wakes up the earth.
  D both preserves and destroys.

15 Lines 5 and 6 state that the wind makes dead leaves move "like ghosts from an enchanter fleeing." What kind of movement does this comparison imply?
  A leisurely and slow
  B awkward and gangly
  C smooth and elegant
  D skittish and fast

16 What is the effect of the speaker's comparison of seeds to "a corpse within its grave" (line 12)? The comparison makes the seeds seem
  A dead until warmed by the wind.
  B damaged by the wind's power.
  C to appear in a cemetery.
  D unable to ever grow.

17 The speaker's description of the West Wind is most like which of the following examples?
  A an artisan baker who creates elaborate breads
  B a teacher who passes his knowledge on to students
  C a mason who creates a wall that lasts for centuries
  D a potter who destroys pots and uses the clay to make new ones

18 Which word identifies the attitude of the speaker toward the West Wind?
  A resentful
  B fearful
  C admiring
  D indifferent

LESSON 3

Figurative Language

Poetry

1 Learn the Skill

As you learned in Unit 2, **figurative language** is the use of symbols, phrases, and ideas that give words a meaning beyond their ordinary meaning. Examples of figurative language may include **personification**, in which non-living objects are given human or animal qualities. For example: *The dirty dishes looked sullenly from the sink.* **Exaggeration**, also called **hyperbole**, is a type of figurative language used for emphasis or humor. *I told you a million times* is an example of exaggeration.

2 Practice the Skill

By being able to identify the figurative language in a literary work, you will improve your study and test-taking skills, especially as they relate to high school equivalency language arts/reading tests. Read the poem and strategies below. Then answer the questions that follow.

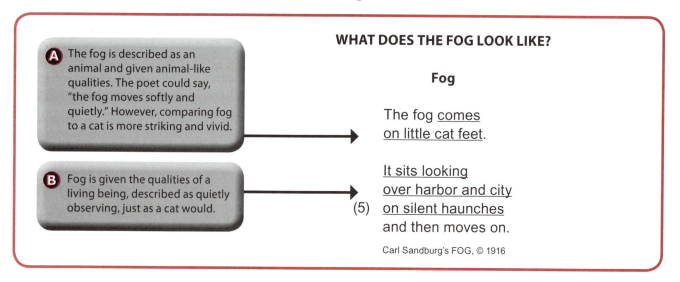

WHAT DOES THE FOG LOOK LIKE?

Fog

The fog comes
on little cat feet.

It sits looking
over harbor and city
(5) on silent haunches
and then moves on.

Carl Sandburg's FOG, © 1916

A The fog is described as an animal and given animal-like qualities. The poet could say, "the fog moves softly and quietly." However, comparing fog to a cat is more striking and vivid.

B Fog is given the qualities of a living being, described as quietly observing, just as a cat would.

✓ TEST-TAKING TIPS

When reading for personification, think about what similarities the poet would want a reader to see in the comparison he or she is making. In "Fog," for example, the poet asks readers to think about how a cat moves: smoothly, quickly, silently.

1. The fog is described as having "cat feet" (line 2). What can we tell about fog from this description?
   A It is furry.
   B It is quiet.
   C It has whiskers.
   D It purrs loudly.

2. Why might the poet have used personification?
   A to exaggerate
   B to remind readers of a sound
   C to set the feeling and tone of the poem
   D to symbolize fog

Apply the Skill

Directions: Questions 3 through 6 refer to the excerpt from the following poem.

HOW MUCH TIME DOES THE SPEAKER HAVE TO LOVE HIS LADY?

To His Coy Mistress

Had we but world enough, and time,
This coyness, Lady, were no crime
We would sit down and think which way
To walk and pass our long love's day.
(5) Thou by the Indian Ganges' [a river] side
Shouldst rubies find: I by the tide
Of Humber [a river] would complain. I would
Love you ten years before the Flood,
And you should, if you please, refuse
(10) Till the conversion of the Jews.
My vegetable love should grow
Vaster than empires, and more slow;
An hundred years should go to praise
Thine eyes and on thy forehead gaze;
(15) Two hundred to adore each breast,
But thirty thousand to the rest;
An age at least to every part,
And the last age should show your heart.
For, Lady, you deserve this state,
(20) Nor would I love at lower rate.
　　But at my back I always hear
Time's wingèd chariot hurrying near;
And yonder all before us lie
Deserts of vast eternity.

From Andrew Marvell's TO HIS COY MISTRESS, © 1919

3. **What does the speaker claim he would do if time permitted? He would**
   A love his mistress for hundreds of years.
   B stop loving his mistress.
   C visit the Ganges River.
   D prevent a flood.

4. **Time is a recurring theme in this poem. What does the speaker's description of time suggest?**
   A He does not have time for a relationship.
   B His mistress is running out of time.
   C He is exaggerating time for effect.
   D He knows that love is timeless.

5. **The speaker states that his love will grow "Vaster than empires" (line 11–12). Which of the following examples most resembles this statement?**
   A All's fair in love and war.
   B A penny saved is a penny earned.
   C Waste not, want not.
   D I'll give you the moon.

6. **The speaker says, "But at my back I always hear / Time's wingèd chariot hurrying near" (lines 21–22). What can you infer about the speaker? He knows that**
   A time travels on wings.
   B he has all the time in the world.
   C time continues to pass.
   D his mistress has a deadline.

Directions: Questions 7 through 10 refer to the following poem.

HOW DOES THE SIGHT OF THE FLOWERS AFFECT THE SPEAKER?

Daffodils

I wander'd lonely as a cloud
    That floats on high o'er vales and hills,
When all at once I saw a crowd,
    A host, of golden daffodils;
(5) Beside the lake, beneath the trees,
Fluttering and dancing in the breeze.

Continuous as the stars that shine
    And twinkle on the Milky Way,
They stretch'd in never-ending line
(10)   Along the margin of a bay:
Ten thousand saw I at a glance,
Tossing their heads in sprightly dance.

The waves beside them danced; but they
    Out-did the sparkling waves in glee:
(15) A poet could not but be gay,
    In such a jocund [cheerful] company:
I gazed—and gazed—but little thought
What wealth the show to me had brought:

For oft, when on my couch I lie
(20)   In vacant or in pensive mood,
They flash upon that inward eye
    Which is the bliss of solitude;
And then my heart with pleasure fills,
And dances with the daffodils.

William Wordsworth's DAFFODILS, © 1804

7 How are the flowers described in the opening stanza (lines 1–6)?
  A There are a few daffodils under the trees.
  B A few of the flowers are blowing in the wind.
  C None of the flowers are daffodils.
  D A large number of flowers are near the lake.

8 The speaker compares himself to a cloud (line 1). What does this comparison reveal about his feelings? The speaker
  A feels light-hearted.
  B is solitary.
  C likes to travel.
  D is unhappy when he is alone.

9 The flowers in the poem are "Tossing their heads in sprightly dance" (line 12). Which of the following examples is most like this description?
  A a bee gathering pollen from a flower
  B a dog rolling over
  C a cat talking to another cat
  D a bear scratching its back on a tree

10 The speaker says his heart "dances with the daffodils" when he remembers the flowers (line 24). What is the speaker's tone in this section of the poem?
  A lonely
  B grieving
  C joyful
  D annoyed

Directions: Questions 11 through 15 refer to the following poem.

DO THE OCEAN WAVES HAVE FEELINGS?

Once by the Pacific

The shattered water made a misty din.
Great waves looked over others coming in,
And thought of doing something to the shore
That water never did to land before.
(5) The clouds were low and hairy in the skies,
Like locks blown forward in the gleam of eyes.
You could not tell, and yet it looked as if
The shore was lucky in being backed by cliff,
The cliff in being backed by continent;
(10) It looked as if a night of dark intent
Was coming, and not only a night, an age.
Someone had better be prepared for rage.
There would be more than ocean-water broken
Before God's last Put out the Light was spoken.

Robert Frost's ONCE BY THE PACIFIC, © 1928

11 What scene is described in the poem?
  A a continent raging against the water
  B clouds causing rain
  C water making a cliff crumble
  D waves crashing on the shore

12 Which word identifies the speaker's mood?
  A excited
  B angry
  C admiring
  D afraid

13 The speaker says that the waves "thought of doing something to the shore / That water never did to land before" (lines 3–4). What feeling does the speaker attribute to the waves? The speaker thinks the waves are
  A helpful.
  B angry.
  C friendly.
  D afraid.

14 According to the speaker, the shore is "lucky in being backed by cliff" (line 8). Which of these examples most resembles that description?
  A Two small children help one another.
  B An older child takes a toy from a smaller one.
  C A big sister stands behind her smaller brother.
  D Two teenagers babysit a younger cousin.

15 Which one of the following examples gives human qualities to the ocean? The waves
  A look over other waves.
  B land on the shore.
  C crash against a cliff.
  D make a loud noise.

Directions: Questions 16 through 19 refer to the following poem.

WHAT KINDS OF TASKS DOES THE SPEAKER DESCRIBE?

Song

Go and catch a falling star,
    Get with child a mandrake root,
Tell me where all past years are,
    Or who cleft the Devil's foot;
(5) Teach me to hear mermaids singing,
    Or to keep off envy's stinging,
        And find
        What wind
Serve to advance the honest mind.

(10) If thou be'st born to strange sights,
    Things invisible to see,
Ride ten thousand days and nights
    Till Age snow white hairs on thee;
Thou, when thou return'st, wilt tell me
(15) All strange wonders that befell thee,
        And swear
        No where
Lives a woman true and fair.

If thou find'st one, let me know;
(20)   Such a pilgrimage were sweet.
Yet do not; I would not go,
    Though at next door we might meet.
Though she were true when you met her,
And last till you write your letter,
(25)   Yet she
        Will be
False, ere I come, to two or three.

John Donne's SONG

16 In the first stanza, the speaker asks the reader to do what types of actions? The speaker asks for acts that are
  A difficult.
  B humiliating.
  C embarrassing.
  D impossible.

17 What does the poet most likely mean when he says "Till Age snow white hairs on thee" (line 13)? The poet most likely means
  A a time when the subject of the poem is older and has gray hairs.
  B the subject of the poem enjoys standing still in the snow.
  C only Age has snow white hairs.
  D Age is the name of the subject's white horse.

18 In the second stanza, the speaker directs the reader to ride for "ten thousands days and nights" (line 12). What does the speaker expect the reader to find during this trip?
  A Most things are invisible.
  B There are many honest women.
  C No women are true and fair.
  D People's hair turns white.

19 What is the tone of this poem?
  A hopeful
  B bitter
  C uplifting
  D depressing

LESSON 4

Symbols and Imagery

Poetry

1 Learn the Skill

As you learned in Unit 2, people recognize many symbols in daily life. A flag, for example, symbolizes a country, while a mascot can symbolize a sports team. Poets use **symbols** to stand for important ideas and concepts. A huge tree, for example, might symbolize a family's home and heritage. **Imagery** in poetry describes the taste, touch, smell, sound, and appearance of objects to make them vivid to the reader.

2 Practice the Skill

By mastering the skill of identifying symbols and images, you will improve your study and test-taking skills, especially as they relate to high school equivalency language arts/reading tests. Read the poem and strategies below. Then answer the question that follows.

A The speaker describes the smell of whiskey on his father's breath. This sensory detail adds to the imagery of the boy and his father.

B The speaker includes details about the father's hands. How does the image of the father's hands affect your reading of the poem?

HOW WELL DOES THIS FATHER DANCE?

My Papa's Waltz

A The whiskey on your breath
Could make a small boy dizzy;
But I hung on like death:
Such waltzing was not easy.

(5) We romped until the pans
Slid from the kitchen shelf;
My mother's countenance
Could not unfrown itself.

The hand that held my wrist
(10) Was battered on one knuckle;
B At every step you missed
My right ear scraped a buckle.

You beat time on my head
With a palm caked hard by dirt,
(15) Then waltzed me off to bed
Still clinging to your shirt.

Theodore Roethke's MY PAPA'S WALTZ, © 1942

✓ TEST-TAKING TIPS

To find examples of imagery, look for examples that help you feel as if you are part of the poem. If the poem includes details that help you imagine particular sights, smells, sounds, feelings, or tastes, then those details are examples of imagery.

1. The poem describes the father's hands as "battered on one knuckle" (line 10). How does this imagery add to the poem? It shows that the father
   A has been in a fight.
   B is careless.
   C works in an office.
   D is vain about his appearance.

Unit 3 | Poetry

179

Apply the Skill

Directions: Questions 2 through 6 refer to the following poem.

WHERE DOES THIS ROAD LEAD?

Uphill

Does the road wind uphill all the way?
    Yes, to the very end.
Will the day's journey take the whole long day?
    From morn to night, my friend.

(5) But is there for the night a resting-place?
    A roof for when the slow, dark hours begin.
May not the darkness hide it from my face?
    You cannot miss that inn.

Shall I meet other wayfarers at night?
(10)   Those who have gone before.
Then must I knock, or call when just in sight?
    They will not keep you waiting at that door.

Shall I find comfort, travel-sore and weak?
    Of labour you shall find the sum.
(15) Will there be beds for me and all who seek?
    Yea, beds for all who come.

Christina Rossetti's UPHILL, © 1862

2. What conversation takes place in the first stanza (lines 1–4)? A traveler
   A asks about a journey.
   B gets supplies for a trip.
   C asks for directions.
   D makes reservations.

3. The first speaker predicts the journey will leave travelers "travel-sore and weak" (line 13). What does this tell us about the trip?
   A It will be easy.
   B It will be downhill.
   C It will be long.
   D It will be on horseback.

4. Based on the details in the poem, what might the road symbolize? The road is a symbol for
   A hope.
   B peace.
   C failure.
   D life.

5. The second speaker states that there will be "beds for all who come" (line 16). Which of the following statements is most like this statement?
   A Please knock before you enter.
   B The door is always open to you.
   C Do not disturb.
   D Checkout time is at noon.

6. In the poem, a second speaker answers questions with replies such as "They will not keep you waiting at that door" (line 12). Which word best describes the tone of these replies?
   A threatening
   B foreboding
   C disappointing
   D comforting

Directions: Questions 7 through 11 refer to the following poem.

WHAT HAPPENS WHEN DREAMS DO NOT COME TRUE?

Harlem

What happens to a dream deferred?
Does it dry up
like a raisin in the sun?
Or fester like a sore—
(5) And then run?
Does it stink like rotten meat?
Or crust and sugar over—
like a syrupy sweet?

Maybe it just sags
(10) like a heavy lead.

Or does it explode?

Langston Hughes's HARLEM, © 1959

7   What question does the speaker ask in this poem?
   A   What causes disappointments?
   B   How do you keep explosions from happening?
   C   How do people take care of their food?
   D   How do people respond when they are disappointed?

8   In the poem, what does the raisin symbolize?
   A   a broken dream
   B   a broken heart
   C   a new possibility
   D   a bright beginning

9   How does the question *"Or does it explode?"* (line 11) affect the poem's message? It makes the poem's final line appear more
   A   uplifting.
   B   hopeful.
   C   dangerous.
   D   depressing.

10   The poem compares an unattainable dream to a wound that "fester[s] like a sore" (line 4). That description is most like which of the following situations?
   A   Students at one school put off a trip to help students at another school.
   B   Neighbors vote to determine what problems in their area to address first.
   C   People combine their resources to solve a problem.
   D   A pothole that is not fixed gets deeper and deeper.

11   What is the poet's purpose in including sensory images such as "stink like rotten meat" (line 6)? The author wants to show
   A   the effects of poverty.
   B   how continued disappointments affect people.
   C   the need for culinary schools.
   D   the weather.

Directions: Questions 12 through 15 refer to the following poem.

WHERE ARE THE PEOPLE MARCHING?

The Parade

How exhilarating it was to march
along the great boulevards
in the sunflash of trumpets
and under all the waving flags—
(5) the flag of desire, the flag of ambition.

So many of us streaming along—
of all humanity, really—
moving in perfect sync,
yet each lost in the room of a private dream.

(10) How stimulating the scenery of the world,
the rows of roadside trees,
the huge blue sheet of the sky.

How endless it seemed until we veered
off the broad turnpike
(15) into a pasture of high grass,
heading toward the dizzying cliffs of mortality.

Generation after generation,
we shoulder forward
under the play of clouds
(20) until we high-step off the sharp lip into space.

So I should not have to remind you
that little time is given here
to rest on a wayside bench,
to stop and bend to the wildflowers,
(25) or to study a bird on a branch—

Not when the young
keep shoving from behind,
not when the old are tugging us forward,
pulling on our arms with all their feeble
(30)   strength.

Billy Collin's THE PARADE, © 2002

12 What does the speaker describe in the fourth stanza of the poem (lines 13–16)?
  A planners deciding to end a parade
  B people sightseeing in a pasture
  C a parade marching down a highway
  D a parade turning off a main street

13 What does the parade in the poem most likely symbolize?
  A a birth
  B a death
  C a lifespan
  D a parent's responsibility

14 The speaker observes "that little time is given here / to rest on a wayside bench" (lines 22–23). What is the tone of the speaker's statement?
  A bitterness
  B regret
  C acceptance
  D rebellion

15 The speaker describes individual marchers as "lost in the room of a private dream" (line 9). Which of the following situations is most like the speaker's description?
  A A class is bored by a film.
  B A person takes notes during a lecture to remember important details.
  C Two people whisper on the back of a bus.
  D A child listens politely to a parent while letting her mind wander.

Directions: Questions 16 through 20 refer to the following poem.

WHAT KIND OF STATUE DOES THE SPEAKER SEE?

The New Colossus

Not like the brazen giant of Greek fame
With conquering limbs astride from land to land;
Here at our sea-washed, sunset gates shall
(5)   stand
A mighty woman with a torch, whose flame
Is the imprisoned lightning, and her name
Mother of Exiles. From her beacon-hand
Glows world-wide welcome; her mild eyes
(10)   command
The air-bridged harbor that twin cities frame.
"Keep, ancient lands, your storied pomp!
   [splendor]" cries she
With silent lips. "Give me your tired, your poor,
(15) Your huddled masses yearning to breathe free,
The wretched refuse of your teeming shore,
Send these, the homeless, tempest-tost
   [tossed] to me,
I lift my lamp beside the golden door!

Emma Lazarus's THE NEW COLOSSUS, © 1883

16 What does the poem describe in lines 1 through 6? The poem describes a statue
   A called Mother of Exiles.
   B in Greece.
   C of a conqueror.
   D that stands astride two lands.

17 What does the statue represent to the speaker?
   A death
   B wealth
   C failure
   D hope

18 The statue in the poem cries, "Keep, ancient lands, your storied pomp" (line 12). What is the tone of this statement?
   A surrender
   B defiance
   C compassion
   D cooperation

19 The speaker describes the statue, saying "from her beacon-hand / Glows world-wide welcome" (lines 8–9). Which of the following examples is most like her description?
   A a hall light that conserves energy
   B a night light that comforts children
   C an airplane light that illuminates only one book
   D a lighthouse that guides people to safety

20 The statue states that the people who arrive are "huddled masses" who are "homeless, tempest-tost" (lines 15–17). What does this imagery reveal about these people? They are
   A sick.
   B needy.
   C talented.
   D wealthy.

LESSON 5

Make Inferences

Poetry

1 Learn the Skill

Readers **make inferences** when they make educated guesses about meanings that are unclear or incomplete. To make inferences, readers combine what they know about a topic with the evidence found in the poem. In addition, readers can use what they know about symbols and images, as discussed in Lesson 4, to help determine what ideas the poet has suggested or otherwise implied.

2 Practice the Skill

By mastering the skill of making inferences, you will improve your study and test-taking skills, especially as they relate to high school equivalency language arts/reading tests. Read the poem and strategies below. Then answer the question that follows.

WHAT KIND OF LIFE HAS THE WOMAN HAD?

When You Are Old

A From the description of the "soft look" the woman's eyes once had, readers can infer that she was a beautiful woman in her youth.

When you are old and gray and full of sleep,
And nodding by the fire, take down this book,
And slowly read, and dream of the soft look
Your eyes had once, and of their shadows deep;

B The description of "love false and true" implies that the woman has experienced sorrows, perhaps because men loved only her beauty.

(5) How many loved your moments of glad grace,
And loved your beauty with love false or true,
But one man loved the pilgrim soul in you,
And loved the sorrows of your changing face;

And bending down beside the glowing bars,
(10) Murmur, a little sadly, how Love fled
And paced upon the mountains overhead
And hid his face among a crowd of stars.

William Butler Yeats's WHEN YOU ARE OLD, © 1893

USING LOGIC

By examining the compassionate description of the woman, readers can infer that the speaker himself is the "one man" who loved the woman truly.

1 What can you infer about the woman based on her behavior?
 A No man ever loved her.
 B Her love has died.
 C She is pleased to have had many suitors.
 D She is sad that she was never beautiful.

Apply the Skill

Directions: Questions 2 through 6 refer to the following poem.

WHY IS THE MAN LOOKING AT THE FLOWER?

The Woodspurge

The wind flapp'd loose, the wind was still,
Shaken out dead from tree and hill:
I had walk'd on at the wind's will,—
I sat now, for the wind was still.

(5) Between my knees my forehead was,—
My lips, drawn in, said not Alas!
My hair was over in the grass,
My naked ears heard the day pass.

My eyes, wide open, had the run
(10) Of some ten weeds to fix upon;
Among those few, out of the sun,
The woodspurge flower'd, three cups in one.

From perfect grief there need not be
Wisdom or even memory:
(15) One thing then learnt remains to me,—
The woodspurge has a cup of three.

Dante Gabriel Rossetti's THE WOODSPURGE, © 1856

2 From the evidence in the poem, what can we infer about this man?
 A He is grieving.
 B He is studying flowers.
 C He loves nature.
 D He is monitoring the weather.

3 What is the man's position in lines 5 through 8? He is
 A walking up a hill.
 B sitting with his hands between his knees.
 C sitting with his head between his knees.
 D standing with his feet in the grass.

4 The speaker examines the flowers and states, "The woodspurge has a cup of three" (line 16). What might this observation mean? From the speaker's behavior, we can infer that this information
 A is important to him.
 B is all he can think about in his grief.
 C gives him wisdom he can share with others.
 D reminds him of something.

5 What is the tone of the poem?
 A confused
 B forgiving
 C indifferent
 D desolate

6 What does the first stanza tell us about the speaker?
 A He's in the middle of a storm.
 B He is sitting in a tree on the top of a hill.
 C His jacket flaps in the wind.
 D His movements have been dictated by the wind.

Directions: Questions 7 through 11 refer to the following poem.

WHAT IS RICHARD CORY REALLY LIKE?

Richard Cory

Whenever Richard Cory went down town,
    We people on the pavement looked at him:
He was a gentleman from sole to crown,
    Clean favored, and imperially slim.

(5) And he was always quietly arrayed,
    And he was always human when he talked;
But still he fluttered pulses when he said,
    "Good-morning," and he glittered when he
(10)   walked.

And he was rich—yes, richer than a king,
    And admirably schooled in every grace:
In fine, we thought that he was everything
    To make us wish that we were in his place.

(15) So on we worked, and waited for the light,
    And went without the meat, and cursed the bread;
And Richard Cory, one calm summer night,
    Went home and put a bullet through his
(20)   head.

Edwin Arlington Robinson's RICHARD CORY, © 1897

7. How does the speaker describe Richard Cory? Richard Cory is a person who is
   A despised.
   B feared.
   C admired.
   D mistrusted.

8. From the speaker's description, what can we infer about Richard Cory?
   A He was not concerned with outward appearances.
   B He had problems with money.
   C He was annoyed by the townspeople.
   D He did not share his troubles with others.

9. What is the author's purpose in the poem's last stanza (lines 15–20)?
   A to contrast the speaker's poverty with Richard Cory's wealth
   B to shock readers with Richard Cory's action
   C to show the speaker's resentment of Richard Cory
   D to explain Richard Cory's motivations

10. Which of the following examples is most like the description of Richard Cory?
    A A candidate rises from poverty to win high office.
    B A long-time neighbor hides a secret.
    C An official reveals his past in a memoir.
    D A well-loved father turns against his children.

11. Which of the following best describes the overall idea of *Richard Cory*?
    A Don't judge a book by its cover.
    B Don't judge people before walking in their shoes.
    C Be careful what you ask for.
    D A penny saved is a penny earned.

Directions: Questions 12 through 16 refer to the following poem.

OF WHAT DOES THE CROSS OF SNOW REMIND THE SPEAKER?

The Cross of Snow

In the long, sleepless watches of the night,
  A gentle face—the face of one long dead—
  Looks at me from the wall, where round its head
(5)   The night-lamp casts a halo of pale light.
Here in this room she died; and soul more white
  Never through martyrdom of fire was led
  To its repose; nor can in books be read
(10)   The legend of a life more benedight [blessed].
There is a mountain in the distant West
  That, sun-defying, in its deep ravines
  Displays a cross of snow upon its side.
(15) Such is the cross I wear upon my breast
  These eighteen years, through all the changing scenes
  And seasons, changeless since the day she died.

Henry Wadsworth Longfellow's THE CROSS OF SNOW, © 1879

12 According to the speaker, what has happened to his wife?
  A She died in a fire.
  B She was injured in a fire.
  C She traveled to a mountain in the West.
  D She gave him a necklace to wear.

13 Which of the following words best describes the speaker's wife in this passage?
  A misunderstood
  B forgotten
  C beloved
  D stern

14 From the details in the poem, what can we infer about the speaker? The speaker
  A was responsible for his wife's death.
  B continues to grieve for his wife.
  C has married another woman.
  D often travels to the West.

15 Longfellow's face was scarred from trying to save his wife. How does this information affect the poem's message? It makes the poem more
  A frightening.
  B touching.
  C gloomy.
  D uplifting.

16 What would this speaker probably want to do on the birthday of his dead wife?
  A forget the day entirely
  B try to ignore the day
  C honor her birthday quietly
  D visit the cross of snow

Directions: Questions 17 through 20 refer to the following poem.

WHAT LESSON DOES THE SNAIL TEACH THE MOTHER AND CHILD?

For a Five-Year-Old

A snail is climbing up the window-sill
into your room, after a night of rain.
You call me in to see, and I explain
that it would be unkind to leave it there:
(5) it might crawl to the floor; we must take care
that no one squashes it. You understand,
and carry it outside, with careful hand,
to eat a daffodil.

I see, then, that a kind of faith prevails:
(10) your gentleness is moulded still by words
from me, who have trapped mice and shot wild
    birds,
from me, who drowned your kittens, who
    betrayed
(15) your closest relatives, and who purveyed
the harshest kind of truth to many another.
But that is how things are: I am your mother,
and we are kind to snails.

Fleur Adcock's FOR A FIVE-YEAR-OLD, © 2000

17 What does the mother help her child do in the first stanza (lines 1–8)? She helps him
  A pick flowers.
  B crawl on the floor.
  C eat a daffodil.
  D rescue a snail.

18 The mother states that she has "purveyed / the harshest kind of truth to many another" (lines 15–16). What can we infer about the mother's character from her description? The mother
  A protects small animals from harm.
  B is always kind-hearted.
  C has had to perform difficult acts.
  D is a hypocrite.

19 The speaker says "I see, then, that a kind of faith prevails" (line 9). Which of the following is the best example of that "kind of faith"?
  A Children learn at an early age that they must study or fail school.
  B Grandparents are completely honest and tell their grandchildren all their faults.
  C Parents wait until their children are older to reveal unpleasant family truths.
  D Parents tell their children that there is no such thing as the tooth fairy.

20 What is the mother's tone when she states, "I am your mother, / and we are kind to snails" (lines 17–18)?
  A bossy
  B angry
  C impatient
  D tender

LESSON 6

Restatement

Poetry

① Learn the Skill

Identifying a poem's main idea can help you better understand and analyze what the poet is saying. One strategy to help identify a poem's main idea is **restatement**. Restating the poet's ideas in your own words can help you unlock the meanings of poems and identify a poem's most important message.

② Practice the Skill

By mastering the skill of restatement, you will improve your study and test-taking skills, especially as they relate to high school equivalency language arts/reading tests. Read the poem and strategies below. Then answer the question that follows.

WHAT MAKES THINGS DISAPPEAR?
Hidden

A. Read each stanza to determine the poet's meaning and restate it in your own words. The first stanza might be restated as "If you put a stone on top of a fern, the fern would disappear."

If you place a fern
under a stone
the next day it will be
nearly invisible
(5) as if the stone has
swallowed it.

If you tuck the name of a loved one
under your tongue too long
without speaking it
(10) it becomes blood
sigh
the little sucked-in breath of air
hiding everywhere
beneath your words.

B. Restating a section of a poem may involve reading through the line break, as in "hiding everywhere beneath your words."

(15) No one sees
the fuel that feeds you.

Naomi Shihab Nye's HIDDEN, © 1998

MAKING ASSUMPTIONS

When restating a poem, you may assume that many images are not describing a literal action.

1. **What is one way of restating lines 15 and 16?**
   A The people we love give us invisible strength.
   B We should not talk about loved ones.
   C People need fuel, just like machines.
   D We should not reveal the source of our fuel.

Unit 3 | Poetry   189

Apply the Skill

Directions: Questions 2 through 6 refer to the following poem.

WHAT DOES THE NEW YEAR BRING?

I Stood on a Tower

I stood on a tower in the wet,
And New Year and the Old Year met,
And winds were roaring and blowing;
And I said, "O years that meet in tears,
(5) Have ye aught that is worth the knowing?

"Science enough and exploring
Wanderers coming and going
Matter enough for deploring
But aught that is worth the knowing?"

(10) Seas at my feet were flowing
Waves on the shingle pouring,
Old Year roaring and blowing
And New Year blowing and roaring.

Alfred Lord Tennyson's I STOOD ON A TOWER, © 1868

2. What does the speaker mean by saying the "New Year and the Old Year met" (line 2)? The speaker
   A has been on the tower for a year.
   B wants the New Year to come.
   C is on the tower on New Year's Eve.
   D wants to celebrate the New Year.

3. What does the speaker imply by his description of "years that meet in tears" (line 4)?
   A The time is joyous.
   B It is a difficult time.
   C It has stopped raining.
   D Rain resembles tears.

4. Which of the following is the best restatement of the second stanza (lines 6–9)?
   A Which explorations should we know about?
   B How can we gather more scientific information?
   C How much of our new information is useful?
   D Why is so much information useless?

5. The feelings expressed by the speaker in the second stanza (lines 6–9) are most like which of the following people?
   A an engineer programming a new computer
   B a teenager text-messaging a friend
   C a teacher answering an instant-message question
   D a parent coping with rapidly changing technology

6. Which word identifies the tone of the poem?
   A complacent
   B uneasy
   C confident
   D romantic

Directions: Questions 7 through 11 refer to the following poem.

HOW DOES THE SPEAKER VIEW HIS OWN DEATH?

The Wish to Be Generous

All that I serve will die, all my delights,
the flesh kindled from my flesh, garden and
    field,
the silent lilies standing in the woods,
(5) the woods, the hill, the whole earth, all
will burn in man's evil, or dwindle
in its own age. Let the world bring on me
the sleep of darkness without stars, so I may
    know
(10) my little light taken from me into the seed
of the beginning and the end, so I may bow
to mystery, and take my stand on the earth
like a tree in a field, passing without haste
or regret toward what will be, my life
(15) a patient willing descent into the grass.

Wendell Berry's THE WISH TO BE GENEROUS, © 1970

7 The title of the poem suggests that the speaker wants to give something back. How do the last lines of the poem reinforce this point? The speaker
   A donates his farm to charity.
   B preserves his trees for his children.
   C gives his body back to the earth.
   D leaves his body to science.

8 To what does the speaker refer in the phrase "the flesh kindled from my flesh" (line 2)?
   A his farm
   B his children
   C his crops
   D his woods

9 What is the tone of the poem?
   A panic
   B acceptance
   C impatience
   D irritation

10 Which one of the following situations is most like that of the poem?
   A An elderly person plans a funeral.
   B Young lovers write their wills.
   C A pharaoh builds monuments that survive for thousands of years.
   D A plant dies and another takes its place.

11 To what does the speaker refer when he describes "the sleep of darkness without stars" (line 8)? He refers to his
   A sleeplessness.
   B nightmare.
   C death.
   D dream.

Directions: Questions 12 through 16 refer to the following poem.

WHAT IS THE SPEAKER HIDING?

We Wear the Mask

We wear the mask that grins and lies,
It hides our cheeks and shades our eyes,—
This debt we pay to human guile;
With torn and bleeding hearts we smile,
(5) And mouth with myriad subtleties.

Why should the world be over-wise,
In counting all our tears and sighs?
Nay, let them only see us, while
    We wear the mask.

(10) We smile, but, O great Christ, our cries
To thee from tortured souls arise.
We sing, but oh the clay is vile
Beneath our feet, and long the mile;
But let the world dream otherwise,
(15)   We wear the mask!

Paul Laurence Dunbar's WE WEAR THE MASK, © 1896

12 What action does the speaker express in the first five lines? The speaker is
   A dressing for a party.
   B voicing his complaints.
   C expressing his joy.
   D hiding his pain.

13 What would this speaker probably want to say to the public? He would probably
   A explain the reasons for his happiness.
   B give tips on wearing the mask.
   C encourage others to hide their emotions.
   D want to share his feelings.

14 From the final stanza (lines 10–15), what can we infer about the speaker's condition?
   A He accepts his plight.
   B His silence hides great suffering.
   C He is forced to walk great distances.
   D He is soothed by his mask.

15 Which of the following best restates the lines "We sing, but oh the clay is vile / Beneath our feet" (lines 12–13)?
   A We are singing because we like clay.
   B We look happy, but our condition is miserable.
   C We sing to keep our spirits high.
   D The soil here is too hard to grow crops.

16 How might the tone of the poem be best described?
   A angry
   B optimistic
   C sad
   D romantic

Directions: Questions 17 through 21 refer to the following poem.

WHAT MESSAGE DOES THE SPEAKER TAKE FROM THE TREE?

I Saw in Louisiana a Live Oak Growing

I saw in Louisiana a live-oak growing,
All alone stood it, and the moss hung down
　　from the branches;
Without any companion it grew there, uttering
(5)　　joyous leaves of dark green,
And its look, rude, unbending, lusty, made me
　　think of myself;
But I wonder'd how it could utter joyous leaves,
　　standing alone there, without its friend,
(10)　　　its
　　　　lover near—for I knew I could not;
And I broke off a twig with a certain number of
　　leaves upon it, and twined around it a
　　little
(15)　　　　moss,
And brought it away—and I have placed it in
　　sight in my room
It is not needed to remind me as of my own
　　dear friends,
(20) (For I believe lately I think of little else than of
　　them;)
Yet it remains to me a curious token—it makes
　　me think of manly love;
For all that, and though the live-oak glistens
(25)　　there in Louisiana, solitary, in a wide
　　flat
　　　space,
Uttering joyous leaves all its life, without a
　　friend, a lover, near,
(30) I know very well I could not.

Walt Whitman's I SAW IN LOUISIANA A LIVE OAK GROWING, © 1900

17 What does the speaker mean by saying that the tree is "uttering joyous leaves" (lines 4–5)? The tree is
　A singing loudly.
　B growing exuberantly.
　C shaking its leaves.
　D shedding leaves in the fall.

18 What does the description of the tree reveal about the speaker? The speaker craves
　A solitude.
　B order.
　C companionship.
　D money.

19 Which of the following is the best restatement of the poem's main idea?
　A The live oak tree can grow only with other trees.
　B My friends and I want to be with the live oak tree, but we also want to be alone.
　C I can stand with a live oak tree.
　D A tree can stand alone, but I cannot.

20 Which of the following items is most like the speaker's "curious token" (line 22)?
　A fresh-baked bread
　B a hand-made sweater
　C a generous gift
　D an inexpensive souvenir

21 Which of the following best describes the speaker's tone?
　A grateful
　B lonely
　C confused
　D admiring

LESSON 7

Theme

Poetry

① Learn the Skill

In Lesson 5, you practiced how to make inferences about meanings that were suggested but not explicitly stated in a poem. Making inferences is important when looking for the **theme**, or main idea, of a poem. A poem's theme reveals something about human nature, such as a lesson about life. Use what you know to make inferences about images, symbols, and figurative language; these inferences will help you identify the poet's opinions or beliefs on a larger topic.

② Practice the Skill

By mastering the skill of identifying a poem's theme, you will improve your study and test-taking skills, especially as they relate to high school equivalency language arts/reading tests. Read the poem and strategies below. Then answer the question that follows.

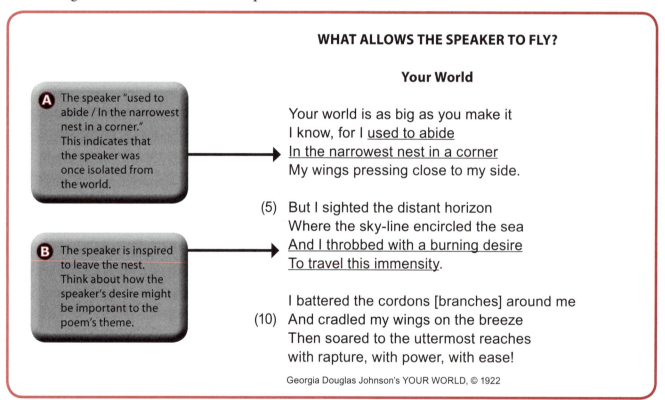

WHAT ALLOWS THE SPEAKER TO FLY?

Your World

Your world is as big as you make it
I know, for I <u>used to abide</u>
<u>In the narrowest nest in a corner</u>
My wings pressing close to my side.

(5) But I sighted the distant horizon
Where the sky-line encircled the sea
<u>And I throbbed with a burning desire</u>
<u>To travel this immensity</u>.

I battered the cordons [branches] around me
(10) And cradled my wings on the breeze
Then soared to the uttermost reaches
with rapture, with power, with ease!

Georgia Douglas Johnson's YOUR WORLD, © 1922

A The speaker "used to abide / In the narrowest nest in a corner." This indicates that the speaker was once isolated from the world.

B The speaker is inspired to leave the nest. Think about how the speaker's desire might be important to the poem's theme.

✓ TEST-TAKING TIPS

Remember that themes teach a larger lesson about ourselves or about humanity. The subject of this poem is flying through the world, but the theme of the poem shares a larger ideal.

1 Which of the following best describes the theme of the poem?
  A All birds like to fly along the shore.
  B People should stick to the places they know.
  C The world is not as big as we think it is.
  D A person can go anywhere and do anything if he or she only tries to do it.

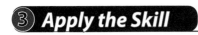

Directions: Questions 2 through 5 refer to the following poem.

WHAT EVENT IS THE SPEAKER DESCRIBING?

The Second Coming

Turning and turning in the widening gyre [spiral]
The falcon cannot hear the falconer;
Things fall apart; the centre cannot hold;
Mere anarchy is loosed upon the world,
(5) The blood-dimmed tide is loosed, and everywhere
The ceremony of innocence is drowned;
The best lack all conviction, while the worst
Are full of passionate intensity.

(10) Surely some revelation is at hand;
Surely the Second Coming is at hand.
The Second Coming! Hardly are those words out
When a vast image out of Spiritus Mundi
(15) Troubles my sight: somewhere in sands of the desert
A shape with lion body and the head of a man,
A gaze blank and pitiless as the sun,
Is moving its slow thighs, while all about it
(20) Reel shadows of the indignant desert birds.
The darkness drops again; but now I know
That twenty centuries of stony sleep
Were vexed to the nightmare by a rocking cradle,
(25) And what rough beast, its hour come round at last,
Slouches towards Bethlehem to be born?

William Butler Yeats' THE SECOND COMING, 1921

2. **What does the speaker mean when he says "The falcon cannot hear the falconer; / Things fall apart; the centre cannot hold" (lines 2–3)? The speaker**
   A believes the falcon is holding onto the center of a ball.
   B believes that events in the world are out of control.
   C has taken up falconry, but is not very good at controlling the bird.
   D thinks birds should not fly in circles.

3. **What word best describes the tone of the poem?**
   A hopeful
   B blank
   C worried
   D untroubled

4. **This poem was written at the end of World War I as a protest against the political events of the time, such as the war and the Russian Revolution. Based on this information, what might the speaker be implying when he says, "The best lack all conviction, while the worst / Are full of passionate intensity" (lines 8–9)?**
   A People with the worst intentions are those who speak the loudest.
   B All the great thinkers are convicted of crimes.
   C The worst falcons fly with the most passion.
   D People are neither good nor bad, though some are more intense than others.

5. **Which of the following best states the theme of this poem?**
   A Birds are omens of bad luck.
   B The world ends not with a bang, but a whimper.
   C Innocence is lost.
   D The evil of men will bring about the end of the world.

Directions: Questions 6 through 9 refer to the following poem.

HOW DOES THE SPEAKER RESPOND TO GROWING OLD?

Awake to Smile

When I blink sunshine in my eyes
    And hail the amber morn,
Before the rosy dew-drop dries
    With sparkle on the thorn;
(5) When boughs with robin rapture ring,
    And bees hum in the may,—
Then call me young, with heart of Spring,
    Though I be grey.

But when no more I know the joy
(10)   And urgence of that hour,
As like a happy-hearted boy
    I leap to land aflower;
When gusto I no longer feel,
    To rouse with glad hooray,—
(15) Then call me old and let me steal
    From men away.

Let me awaken with a smile
    And go to garden glee,
For there is such a little while
(20)   Of living left to me;
But when star-wist I frail away,
    Lord, let the hope beguile
That to Ecstatic Light I may
    Awake to smile.

Robert Service's AWAKE TO SMILE, © 1954

6 What does the speaker express in the first eight lines?
   A Morning is the most beautiful time of day.
   B He is becoming older and cannot appreciate nature.
   C He is young as long as he has a joyful spirit.
   D Birds' songs make the morning special.

7 Which of the following words best describes the mood of the speaker?
   A weary
   B ungrateful
   C accepting
   D resentful

8 Which of the following most resembles the speaker's situation? The speaker is like a person who
   A fears going into a dark cave alone.
   B wishes he was healthy.
   C studies the flight patterns of bees.
   D looks forward to a big party.

9 Which of the following best states the theme of the poem?
   A People should plan for their old age.
   B People should not try to increase their life expectancy.
   C Life is worth living only when done with joy.
   D When you have lived life to the fullest, you can accept the inevitably of death.

Directions: Questions 10 through 14 refer to the following poem.

WHAT MAKES A PERSON HAPPY?

Happiness

So early it's still almost dark out.
I'm near the window with coffee,
and the usual early morning stuff
that passes for thought.
(5) When I see the boy and his friend
walking up the road
to deliver the newspaper.
They wear caps and sweaters,
and one boy has a bag over his shoulder.
(10) They are so happy
they aren't saying anything, these boys.
I think if they could, they would take
each other's arm.
It's early in the morning,
(15) and they are doing this thing together.
They come on, slowly.
The sky is taking on light,
though the moon still hangs pale over the
    water.
(20) Such beauty that for a minute
death and ambition, even love,
doesn't enter into this.
Happiness. It comes on
unexpectedly. And goes beyond, really,
(25) any early morning talk about it.

Raymond Carver's HAPPINESS, © 1985

10 What scene does the speaker see outside?
 A the moon rising
 B a company delivering the newspaper
 C two boys walking together
 D boys shivering in the cold

11 The speaker says that the boys "if they could, they would take / each other's arm" (lines 12–13). What does this detail imply about the boys? The boys
 A appreciate one another's company.
 B stay together for safety.
 C are brothers.
 D huddle together for warmth.

12 Which of the following best states the theme of the poem?
 A Happiness grows from friendship.
 B Happiness comes from simple things.
 C Early morning is the happiest time.
 D Part-time jobs make young people happy.

13 How might you describe the speaker's tone?
 A wistful
 B envious
 C appreciative
 D melancholy

14 Which person does the speaker most resemble? A person
 A admiring a piece of art
 B laughing at a joke
 C preserving an artifact
 D educating a student

Directions: Questions 15 through 18 refer to the following poem.

HOW DOES A CHILD GROW UP?

To a Daughter Leaving Home

When I taught you
at eight to ride
a bicycle, loping along
beside you
(5) as you wobbled away
on two round wheels,
my own mouth rounding
in surprise when you pulled
ahead down the curved
(10) path of the park,
I kept waiting
for the thud
of your crash as I
sprinted to catch up,
(15) while you grew
smaller, more breakable
with distance,
pumping pumping
for your life, screaming
(20) with laughter,
the hair flapping
behind you like a
handkerchief waving
goodbye.

Linda Pastan's TO A DAUGHTER LEAVING HOME, © 1998

15 What happens when the speaker's daughter rides away?
   A The daughter falls.
   B The daughter comes back.
   C The daughter laughs.
   D The daughter leaves home.

16 The title of the poem suggests that the speaker is recalling an earlier experience. How does the bike ride relate to the poem's title?
   A The bike ride is a failure, but the daughter can still leave home.
   B The bike ride is successful, but the daughter cannot leave home.
   C Both are examples of success.
   D Both are examples of the daughter's independence.

17 Which of the following best states the theme of the poem?
   A Learning new skills is part of growing up.
   B The process of growing up is both exciting and frightening.
   C Bike-riding builds family relationships.
   D Leaving home is a lot like learning to ride a bicycle.

18 What is the author's purpose in describing the daughter's hair as flapping "like a / handkerchief waving / goodbye" (lines 22–24)? The description
   A emphasizes that maturity brings separation.
   B draws attention to the daughter's flowing hair.
   C uses the handkerchief image to symbolize weeping.
   D shows the daughter's wish to stay with her mother.

Unit 3 Review

The Unit Review is structured to resemble high school equivalency language arts/reading tests. Be sure to read each question and all possible answers very carefully before choosing your answer. To record your answers, fill in the lettered circle that corresponds to the answer you select for each question in the Unit Review.

Do not rest your pencil on the answer area while considering your answer. Make no stray or unnecessary marks. If you change an answer, erase your first mark completely. Mark only one answer space for each question; multiple answers will be scored as incorrect.

Sample Question

How does the poet view the setting?
A The poet considers the location to be dirty.
B The poet sees it as beautiful as he remembered.
C The poet wishes he was somewhere else.
D The poet wants winter to be over.

Directions: Questions 1 through 6 refer to the following poem.

HOW CAN THE POET'S ATTITUDE BE DESCRIBED?

**Lines Composed a Few Miles Above Tintern Abbey
On Revisiting the Banks of the Wye During a Tour. July 13, 1798**

      Five years have passed; five summers, with the length
      Of five long winters! and again I hear
      These waters, rolling from their mountain-springs
      With a soft inland murmur.—Once again
(5) Do I behold these steep and lofty cliffs,
      That on a wild secluded scene impress
      Thoughts of more deep seclusion; and connect
      The landscape with the quiet of the sky.
      The day is come when I again repose
(10) Here, under this dark sycamore, and view
      These plots of cottage-ground, these orchard-tufts,
      Which at this season, with their unripe fruits,
      Are clad in one green hue, and lose themselves
      'Mid groves and copses. Once again I see
(15) These hedge-rows, hardly hedge-rows, as little lines
      Of sportive wood run wild: these pastoral farms,
      Green to the very door; and wreaths of smoke
      Sent up, in silence, from among the trees!
      With some uncertain notice, as might seem
(20) Of vagrant dwellers in the houseless woods,
      Or of some Hermit's cave, where by his fire
      The Hermit sits alone.

From William Wordsworth's TINTERN ABBEY

1. What information does the speaker share in the first four lines? The speaker tells readers
   A   he is leaving for five years.
   B   he has been away for five years.
   C   the land has been dry for five years.
   D   the river has flooded this land for five years.

2. Which of the following best describes the speaker?
   A   friendly
   B   sporty
   C   solitary
   D   uncertain

3. The speaker says "The day is come when I again repose / Here, under this dark sycamore" (lines 10–11). What can you infer about the speaker from these lines?
   A   The speaker has never been here before.
   B   The speaker believes that he is a sycamore tree.
   C   The speaker will return to this spot another time.
   D   The speaker has been to this location before.

4. For what reason might the speaker have described his surroundings?
   A   to demonstrate that he remembered this place
   B   to explain how new everything seems
   C   to show how feeling so alone, he cannot even connect with the beauty around him
   D   to tell readers about his home

5. Tintern Abbey, the abbey near which the poet wrote this poem, was abandoned in the 1500s when the religious climate in England was changing. How might this additional information affect the reader's understanding of the poem? The speaker of the poem may now appear
   A   to be very religious.
   B   as an orphan.
   C   to be lost.
   D   to be writing about history.

6. Where would this speaker probably want to go on a holiday?
   A   to the beach
   B   to an amusement park
   C   to the country
   D   on a train ride

Directions: Questions 7 through 12 refer to the excerpt from the following poem.

FOR WHAT IS THE POET ARGUING?

Aurora Leigh

      Truth, so far, in my book;—the truth which draws
      Through all things upwards,—that a twofold world
      Must go to a perfect cosmos. Natural things
(5) And spiritual,—who separates those two
      In art, in morals, or the social drift
      Tears up the bond of nature and brings death,
      Paints futile pictures, writes unreal verse,
      Leads vulgar days, deals ignorantly with men,
(10) Is wrong, in short, at all points. We divide
      This apple of life, and cut it through the pips,—
      The perfect round which fitted Venus' hand
      Has perished as utterly as if we ate
      Both halves. Without the spiritual, observe,
(15) The natural's impossible,—no form,
      No motion: without sensuous, spiritual
      Is inappreciable,—no beauty or power:
      And in this twofold sphere the twofold man
      (For still the artist is intensely a man)
(20) Holds firmly by the natural, to reach
      The spiritual beyond it,—fixes still
      The type with mortal vision, to pierce through,
      With eyes immortal, to the antetype
      Some call the ideal,—better call the real,
(25) And certain to be called so presently
      When things shall have their names. Look long enough
      On any peasant's face here, coarse and lined,
      You'll catch Antinous somewhere in that clay,
      As perfect featured as he yearns at Rome
(30) From marble pale with beauty; then persist,
      And, if your apprehension's competent,
      You'll find some fairer angel at his back,
      As much exceeding him as he the boor,
      And pushing him with empyreal disdain
(35) For ever out of sight. Aye, Carrington
      Is glad of such a creed: an artist must,
      Who paints a tree, a leaf, a common stone
      With just his hand, and finds it suddenly
      A-piece with and conterminous to his soul.

From Elizabeth Barrett Browning's AURORA LEIGH

7 Which idea does the speaker express in lines 3 through 9?
  A spiritual things and natural things should not be divided
  B spiritual things are greater than natural things
  C natural things are greater than spiritual things
  D natural things and spiritual things should be separated in art
  Ⓐ Ⓑ Ⓒ Ⓓ

8 Which of the following best describes the overall meaning of the poem?
  A Carrington paints wonderful nature scenes.
  B Life is like an apple which must remain whole.
  C Life must be a balance between the natural and the spiritual.
  D Peasants are naturally more inclined to appreciate art.
  Ⓐ Ⓑ Ⓒ Ⓓ

9 The speaker refers to an apple in Venus' hand in lines 10 and 11. What does this apple represent to the speaker? The apple represents
  A beauty.
  B art.
  C love.
  D life.
  Ⓐ Ⓑ Ⓒ Ⓓ

10 How might the poet's tone best be described?
  A sad
  B determined
  C angry
  D hurt
  Ⓐ Ⓑ Ⓒ Ⓓ

11 The speaker says, "Look long enough / On any peasant's face here, coarse and lined, / You'll catch Antinous somewhere in that clay" (lines 25–27). Antinous was an ancient Greek who was considered very beautiful. Why might the poet have used an analogy to Antinous in the poem? The poet wanted to
  A encourage people to closely look at their environment.
  B emphasize the clay-like fragility of human life.
  C tell readers how she admires Antinous.
  D demonstrate that something beautiful can come from an ordinary background.
  Ⓐ Ⓑ Ⓒ Ⓓ

12 Which of the following might the poet do for a hobby?
  A create art from natural objects, such as wood carving
  B travel around the world to modern cities
  C explore famous military battle sites
  D harvest and can fresh fruits
  Ⓐ Ⓑ Ⓒ Ⓓ

Answer Key

UNIT 1 NON-FICTION

LESSON 1, pp. 2–6

1. D, The phrase "finds that its teachers are in fact more effective than those with traditional training" supports the idea that Teach for America teachers are valuable.
2. D, The subject line of the memo and the second paragraph tells us that the human resources director wants to clarify dress code for the upcoming summer season.
3. B, Based on the list of the bulleted items, an office manager could ask employees not to wear shirts with offensive slogans.
4. B, The last sentence of paragraph one explains that animals can conserve energy while hibernating.
5. C, The main idea is that hibernation is a seasonal state of inactivity.
6. C, All of the supporting details are about the main idea that tortoises have well-defined mating habits.
7. D, The number of eggs a female tortoise lays is a detail that supports the main idea.
8. C, The first paragraph describes the history of the gopher tortoise in North America and tells where it lives.
9. A, The Lines 15 through 18 state that the tortoise stays underground during the heat of the day, coming out only at dawn and dusk to feed.
10. B, The third paragraph says the different factors have made the tortoises' food supply scarce.
11. D, The reduction in the tortoises' food supply is the only answer option that is supported by the excerpt.
12. C, The author clearly believes that all wildlife, especially birds, should be protected from harm.
13. B, The letter addresses a group called the Audubon Society. If you are not sure as to what that group represents, you can determine from reading the rest of the letter that It is likely an organization of people who are concerned with the conservation and protection of wildlife.
14. D, The author is obviously fond of outdoor activities and observing wildlife in its natural habitat. The author would most likely enjoy doing an activity during times in which animals are out and active. Hiking is one such activity.
15. A, The author's main idea is that all harmless wildlife, and especially birds, should be protected. This detail supports that idea.
16. D, Given the author's focus on protecting species of wild animals, he most likely would vote for a bill to pass a law that would make it more difficult for people to hunt in national parks.

LESSON 2, pp. 7–11

1. D, The question asks you to use the summary to evaluate Bruce Wayne as a young adult. Answer D best summarizes how Wayne feels about formal education.
2. D, In lines 3 through 5, the speaker says he has been "granted the role of defending freedom in its hour of maximum danger."
3. A, The speaker is asking his listeners to think about what they can do to help their country. Answer A best summarizes this statement.
4. D, In lines 4 through 6, the speaker states that the "political thing to do … is to either ignore them or deny them."
5. C, The speaker concludes his speech by saying that he believes "that the people have got to have confidence in the … men who run for office." Answer C best summarizes this statement.
6. D, Lines 4 through 7 state that the country is "well into our fifth year" of a policy that was started to end slavery agitation. The policy began five years before this excerpt was written.
7. B, The author is saying that the country is like a house. If the country is divided over an important issue, such as slavery, the country will fall apart.
8. D, The first part of the paragraph lets us know that the country is currently half free (meaning half the states do not allow slavery) and half slave (meaning half the states allow slavery). The author later says that he believes it will be "all one thing, or all the other," meaning that all the states will either allow or not allow slavery.
9. B, At the end of the first paragraph, the author states "I need the help of all Americans, and all America."
10. C, In lines 17 through 19, the author is encouraging people to "derive … strength" and to act upon that strength.
11. A, *Rededicate* means to "dedicate again, or renew a pledge or an agreement." A contract is an agreement, and to renew a contract is to sign it again or agree to it again.
12. D, The author encourages the American people to continue doing what they had done with a new resolve, or persistence; therefore answer D best describes the overall message of the excerpt.
13. D, The last few lines of the first paragraph explain why the author felt the "Muselmanner" were the most tragic.
14. C, Lines 28 through 30 state that "indifference is always the friend of the enemy, for it benefits the aggressor."
15. D, The author is saying that when people do not offer hope to those in need, they are choosing indifference and betraying their humanity.
16. B, Lines 38 and 39 state, "Indifference, then, is not only a sin, it is a punishment."

LESSON 3, pp. 12–16

1. D, The passage states that the Mazda 6 matches up with "rivals in the mid-size segment."
2. B, Eric Jackson would be best placed in the category of option B because his salary falls within the approved salary range.
3. D, The letter states that a condition such as a down payment may lower the required monthly payments.
4. C, The author writes mostly about the nursing leaves of the oak tree.
5. D, The line reads, "while foliage and twig and trunk are busy in catching sunbeams, air, and thunderstorms."
6. B, The author explains how the leaves use the oxygen to turn starches into food. Answer is the only answer option that deals with an organism (the baby) taking in nutrients (the milk in the bottle).
7. D, Line 17 states that "Phosphates and all the delicacies of plant-food are brought in." These nutrients are gathered by the rootlets mentioned in line 15.

UNIT 1 (continued)

8. D, The beginning of the paragraph says, "From television, the child will have learned. ..." Therefore you know that the paragraph is describing those skills a child has learned from television.
9. B, Answer B best addresses what the author is saying in the paragraph. He says that this period is one "during which the child learns that success comes from telling testers what they want to hear."
10. A, The author is basing all of his arguments on students' test-taking abilities. Therefore, if someone was not able to pass a test required to go onto graduate school, the author would likely describe that person as a poor test taker.
11. C, The last paragraph lists all the things that a person with a good record of test taking might have, but it ends by saying that person would then begin to get an education. The author believes that doing well in school is only part of what someone needs to have a good education.
12. C, The text states that the Census Bureau discovered that older citizens "vote more regularly than younger citizens. ..."
13. B, The texts states that one reason for the difference in voting patterns between older and younger citizens is that younger citizens move more often.
14. A, The author states "voter registration for older citizens remains the same" while "younger voters must think about ... registering in their new place of residence." So the author associates living in one place for a long time with not having to think about voter registration before every election.
15. C, The second paragraph describes the situations of younger voters that results in their lower election-day turnout.

LESSON 4, pp. 17–21

1. C, The speaker says that his work week begins on Thursday, and that on Thursdays, he patrols the roads and walks the trails.
2. B, The author explains in paragraph 3 that he began to teach poetry as a way to get the attention of a new fourth grade class in April. The passage states that the teacher was working in a segregated school in Boston that was crowded and poor, which indicates that it was not a suburban school. And while the teacher was fired in the spring, it was for teaching poems that were not approved. "Teaching poetry" alone was not enough of a reason to fire the teacher.
3. A, In paragraph 4, the author explains that the poem he read to his students was not on the list of approved "fourth grade poems."
4. B, The author means that the results of the first tests gave him an idea about how the constant change of teachers affected the students. In lines 15 through 17, the author gives details showing how poorly the students were doing.
5. C, Because the author is a teacher, it is logical to assume that he most likely went on to teach at a different school.
6. D, The author is very agitated that people were riding their motor vehicles, so it is most likely that the author called to report the violation.
7. D, Line 25 states, "Smiling thoroughly at peace, I turned back to my drink."

8. B, If you can not immediately recognize that the story is being told in chronological order, examine the other options. The excerpt is not taking place in the present, so option A is incorrect. The excerpt is not being told backwards, so option 3 is incorrect. The narrative has a clear, constant direction, so answer C is incorrect. The author says "only a few days ago," so option D is incorrect.
9. B, The first step in Jenner's investigation began with his interest in a dairymaid's observation that her having cowpox meant she would never have small pox.
10. B, Jenner's first test was to infect Phipps with cowpox.
11. C, Jenner needed to allow time for the cowpox vaccine to become effective.
12. C, Finally, Jenner published a report of his findings.
13. B, The excerpt progresses by date, as the author gives us the time: October 1987, spring of 1988, March 1989.
14. D, The first sentence ends by letting us know that "the backyards of residents have been employed as dump sites." Reading further in the passage, we know that city health officials believe this is hazardous because flies and rodents may be attracted to the waste.
15. B, The stories presented in this excerpt are alarming and are told from the perspective of the people who gave interviews for the story.
16. C, The excerpt explains that "Raw sewage... overflowed into a playground just behind the housing project, which is home to 187 children." It also gives an example of how two of the children were affected by the raw sewage flowing into their homes.

LESSON 5, pp. 22–26

1. D, The first paragraph explains that global warming has many effects, such as hunger, thirst, floods, and disease. The author lists all of the effects before the cause.
2. B, The first line of the article explains that scientists who conducted the study found that high- fructose corn syrup was a potential cause of weight gain.
3. D, The third paragraph explains how the process in which sugars are turned into fat increased significantly in those people who drank fructose drinks.
4. A, Lines 28 and 29 state that dieters should not eliminate fruit because it contains many beneficial nutrients.
5. A, Lines 1 through 4 of the excerpt tell us that both Republicans and Democrats feel as though the $90 million spent on the study would be a "government waste," but no other plan is suggested.
6. C, The beginning of the third paragraph shares the outcome of the study: "He found that … children exposed to virtual bloodshed shows greater 'short-term' increases."
7. C, Lines 2 and 3 of the excerpt state that "rising energy bills, public health concerns, and a general desire to adopt eco-friendly principles" are the reason why classrooms are going green.
8. A, Lines 21 through 25 state that children "generally fared better" on tests because natural light "improved student focus and achievement."
9. A, Answer option A is the only effect that is implied. All the other answer choices are directly stated effects.

UNIT 1 (continued)

10. D, Lines 15 through 17 state that Ohio plan to save $1.4 billion in energy costs over 40 years.
11. B, Lines 7 through 10 explain that the urushiol from the poison ivy plant causes poison ivy rash.
12. D, Lines 18 through 20 state "The greater the contact, the more urushiol sticks to a person's skin, causing a more severe rash."
13. C, Lines 12 through 14 explain that the cause of a poison ivy rash spreading is touching other parts of the body can after touching anything with urushiol.
14. B, Lines 20 through 24 state that scratching a rash caused by poison ivy can lead to a skin infection from the bacteria in someone's fingers.
15. A, Lines 26 through 29 state that doctors recommend immediately washing the area to get rid of as much urushiol as possible.

LESSON 6, pp. 27–31

1. A, The author states that "at first there is no discrimination in the eye," meaning that nothing stands out or calls attention to itself. Then he says that smaller things caught his attention.
2. B, The old policy allowed people to enter the building using different types of photo identification and allowed them to phone a supervisor if they forgot their badge. The new policy requires that people show a company badge to enter the business.
3. D, A child care facility is most likely to be interested in controlling the access of people entering a building, since its managers would be particularly interested in the safety of the children there.
4. B, Line 9 explicitly states that "Black bears are smaller than brown grizzly bears." There is no mention of grizzly bears' diet or habitat, and black bears have longer, less furry ears than brown bears.
5. D, Lines 1 though 17 state that black bears are smaller than polar and grizzly bears. While the weight of a polar bear is not is provided, it is reasonable to assume based on the comparison to these larger bears that polar bears probably compare in weight to grizzly bears.
6. A, The author predominately discusses black bears first, before contrasting them with grizzly and polar bears.
7. D, Line 16 calls polar and grizzly bears "American giants."
8. B, The passage indicates that Lincoln and radical Republicans in Congress had differing views about how the nation should be rebuilt and lists aspects of each side's plan.
9. A, The information in the passage indicates that Lincoln hoped to rebuild the nation and keep peace by extending forgiveness to the Confederates.
10. C, Both documents were created to govern the states. When the Articles of Confederation proved insufficient, American leaders had to establish another kind of government.
11. B, The reason for creating the U.S. Constitution was the failure of the Articles of Confederation to provide a strong national government. Therefore, answer B is correct.
12. D, Answer D is correct, according to the information in paragraph 3 which mentions both legislatures. Whereas the U.S. Constitution provided for two.
13. D, Only answer D would have been possible because under the Articles of Confederation, states collected taxes. The U.S. Constitution gave this power to the national government.

LESSON 7, pp. 32–36

1. C, Answer C is the only option that gives insight into the author's beliefs about the subject. The other options are phrases that describe what happens in the movie.
2. B, This passage most clearly demonstrates the kinds of eating habits that are associated with country living. In the first paragraph, the author explains that the rural area that was studied had more convenience stores than grocery stores or supermarkets, and that those typically do not stock the healthy food found in grocery stores or supermarkets.
3. A, The author uses many facts and statistics throughout the excerpt, such as the percentage of convenience stores in Orangeburg County, and the percentage of stores in that county that carry fruits and vegetables.
4. D, The author uses the phrase "food desert" to make a comparison. She says that, in the way that a desert has limits on the amount of water and resources it provides, a "food desert" has limits on the amount of healthy foods that are readily available to buy in that area.
5. C, Based on the phrase "one of the most amazing public dining rooms I have ever seen," answer C is the only opinion of the answer options.
6. B, In lines 16 through 29, the author states, "I felt dismal about the state of bread in Paris, and had not yet found that it would be almost as bad everywhere." As a result she decided that the food at the restaurant was the best she had had lately.
7. A, The author enjoys her food very much, but makes no comparison to any other kind of food.
8. D, In lines 19 through 22, the author states that the bread she had at that restaurant was the best she had ever had, and then adds the note that it still is, which indicates that this restaurant is still better than any other restaurant.
9. C, The dates and locations of Mr. Ellison's birth and death are facts. All other answer options are opinions.
10. A, The last two sentences of the first paragraph applaud Ellison's intellectual mind, and then say that such a mind seems unappreciated today.
11. C, The second paragraph tells us that Ellison often wrote about "race, racism, and African-American identity." Ellison's novel most likely examines the problems of identity that might affect African-Americans.
12. A, Based on lines 3 through 5, the author's opinion is that the actor who plays the Phantom does an excellent job and is extremely talented.
13. D, Watching a movie is similar to watching a play. From the review, the reader can gather that the author enjoys watching performances and therefore apply that he or she would also enjoy watching performers in a movie.
14. D, Answer D is the only answer that offers an opinion. All of the other answers are facts.
15. C, to the nature of his job, the conductor enjoys spending time and working with young people. Therefore, it is logical to think that the conductor would enjoy volunteering at a summer camp as a potential hobby.

UNIT 1 (continued)

LESSON 8, pp. 37–41

1. D, The author states that, "While Dudley has everything, including a spare bedroom for his toys, Harry is forced to live in a tiny space under the stairs" (lines 4–6). This line implies that Harry's Aunt Petunia and Uncle Vernon do not treat their nephew the same way they treat their son. In fact, they give him very little love and support as he is forced to live under the stairs while his cousin has an entire extra bedroom just for his toys.

2. B, Lines 11 and 12 refer to a "colorized version of The Maltese Falcon." Given that the author is writing about people who watch too much television, it can be implied based on these facts that The Maltese Falcon is a black-and-white movie.

3. A, Answer A is the only option which is fully expressed in the excerpt.

4. A, The author discusses how people used to be "fond of the outdoors" but now are content to stay inside.

5. D, Earlier in the passage, the author mentions the Musketaquid, which was a group of Native Americans who lived in the area around Concord. The relics mentioned are those left behind by the Musketaquid.

6. B, Again, the author refers to the Musketaquid, who used to live in the area. The author is noting the fact that everything he does to the land erases something the Musketaquid might have left behind.

7. A, We know the author enjoys being outside and working with the land, and has a great appreciation for nature. Gardening is the most likely hobby for the author.

8. D, Lines 6 through 12 explain that Alfred Nobel was upset he had been labeled "The Merchant of Death," so he chose to "serve the cause of peace" and honor other people who did the same.

9. B, The speaker says "Seven years ago tomorrow, I read my own political obituary." From the byline at the end of the passage, you can infer that the event occurred in the year 2000. Since he "read his own political obituary," you can assume that his political hopes were "killed" seven years ago.

10. A, As you read the entire excerpt, you learn that the author is concerned about environmental problems.

11. B, The author is saying that young writers must accept the fear that is inspired by strong emotions and move on. He believes that people should be fearless when writing about things such as love, honor, and pity.

12. A, The last sentence of the third paragraph indicates that because of man's soul and "spirit capable of compassion and sacrifice and endurance," the author believes mankind will prevail or carry on. The other answer options do not reflect the author's optimistic beliefs.

13. D, Lines 48 through 51 state, "The poet's voice…can be one of the props, the pillars to help him endure and prevail." The author believes that the poet and the writer have a duty to write and share their gifts of compassion and endurance (lines 40–44).

LESSON 9, pp. 42–46

1. D, The excerpt explains that gas is cheaper in Venezuela than it is in the United States. It also explains that in "most other industrialized nations," gas is more expensive than it is in the United States. So gas in the United States is more expensive than in some areas, but less expensive than in others.

2. B, In lines 18 and 19, the author clearly states that sometimes separate is better. In the excerpt, she explains her belief that girls who are in a separate education system are more likely to do well on standardized tests and perform better in math and science. Answer B most accurately restates the author's words in the excerpt.

3. D, Line 29 says "The evidence, though scant, is promising." The rest of the paragraph goes on to say that the evidence includes higher test scores and better performance from the girls in the all-girls' classes.

4. A, Answer A is the only option that provides support for a conclusion.

5. B, The second paragraph gives an example of someone who missed office life so much that he became depressed.

6. C, The second paragraph quotes Ron Glover as saying that some people need to work "close together so they can be supported and developed . …'

7. A, The first paragraph and beginning of the second paragraph state that the majority like being able to work remotely when technology allows people to colloborate from anywhere in the world.

8. D, The passage gives both the pros and the cons of some people working remotely, so answer D is the most logical conclusion.

9. C, After the author states that she is glad her vote did not change anything, she explains throughout the rest of the excerpt why she believes that separate education is more beneficial for women.

10. D, Lines 15 through 18 state that the test "does ask about math and science, though, and that's where the differences between boys and girls are most pronounced."

11. A, The author believes that girls receive better education when they are given the same opportunities to learn that boys are given. The author believes boys receive more attention from teachers, especially in difficult math and science classes.

12. D, Since the author wants to "cement the friendship of the races," you can assume that there is a gap, or a break, which needs to be fixed, or cemented. The author also wants to bring about a "hearty cooperation between them."

13. A, It is unlikely that people would invite the author to speak if they were angry about what he said, so answer 2 is incorrect. The text makes no mention of a debate stemming from his speech, so answer C is incorrect. The author was striving to bridge the gap between the races and seemed to be well received, so answer D is incorrect. If the author's speech had little success, it is unlikely he would be asked to speak elsewhere, so answer A is correct.

14. D, The language the author uses is serious and calm. The author does not boast about his achievements; he merely presents them as facts. His manner in the excerpt is humble.

15. D, Based on the excerpt, the author's speech was well received, so answers A and B are incorrect. The author was greeted by people and "hearty congratulations" after his speech, so people did not accept his speech quietly, which means answer D is correct.

LESSON 10, pp. 47–51

1. D, All of the answers relate to the flu or flu shots, but answer D states in the clearest and strongest terms why readers should get a flu shot—"Flu shots are the most effective way to prevent influenza."

UNIT 1 (continued)

2. D, The author argues that education and other social institutions, such as churches and families, are the most important factors in determining whether a person will rise out of poverty. The author begins by noting how much the government spends fighting poverty through social services. However, he goes on to write that these programs alone do not succeed in lifting people out of poverty. Answer D accurately summarizes the author's viewpoint.

3. A, The author argues that education is a key factor in determining whether a person will overcome poverty. He argues that social services and government programs have not succeeded in reducing or eliminating poverty. Answer A best summarizes this opinion.

4. C, Answer C is correct because the author acknowledges the liberal viewpoint and then presents his own logical counterargument.

5. B, Answer B is correct because it supports the author's viewpoint, explained in the previous paragraph: that education, employment, and mediating institutions are keys to upward mobility.

6. A, The author states that he wants to confirm the plans for evacuating Atlanta. This information appears in paragraph 1.

7. C, Sherman's implicit purpose is to justify his invasion of Atlanta, which he does by countering Hood's argument—most likely part of an earlier correspondence—claiming that such destruction has recent precedents.

8. C, The passage discusses the increasing desire for possessions, for which people create needs, thus confusing what they want with what they need. Therefore, answer C best explains the author's overall purpose.

9. A, In contrasting the tyranny of things with oppression by another person, the author notes that when people are oppressed by others, people are quick to react to protect their freedom. The tyranny of things happens slowly, and people are willing participants. People realize only gradually that they have given up their freedoms to their things.

10. C, The author writes, "Our opulent friends are constantly demonstrating by example how indispensably convenient the modern necessities are, and we keep buying such things until we either exceed our incomes or miss the higher concerns of life." This statement suggests that the author's implied purpose is to persuade readers to be more thoughtful about the things they purchase. Answer C best expresses this idea.

11. B, The second-to-last sentence states that a person "goes on having things and imagining that he is richer for owning them." The last sentence reverses this wording to state, "it is the things that own him." This reversal emphasizes the way things can come to dominate a person's life, limiting that person's freedom as he or she must work to pay for and maintain the things. Answer B best expresses this idea.

12. A, The purpose, summarized in answer A, appears in the first paragraph with the statement that the IRS is announcing "that it is providing a new, simpler option for calculating the home office tax deduction . . . ."

13. B, The passage notes that the change to the home office tax deduction is "part of ongoing efforts by the Administration" and then uses favorable language to explain these efforts, such as "reduce paperwork burdens," "streamline and simplify," and "make interacting with the federal government easier and more efficient for businesses of all sizes." This positive language is intended to encourage support for the changed deduction and the Administration, which enacted it. Answer B best expresses this implicit purpose.

14. C, The evidence in answer C best supports the claim because it indicates that a significant percentage of the workforce owns or works for small businesses.

15. C, General readers are unlikely to need to see a sample calculation of the deduction, but owners of home businesses would likely benefit from such information.

16. A, At the end of the passage, the authors note that many businesses are going virtual and hiring employees who might live far away. These employees use technology to work from home. This situation implies that the authors believe employees must be flexible (answer A) because they may not work in a traditional office setting.

LESSON 11, pp. 52–56

1. B, The author ends the passage by encouraging readers to support legislation for developing mass transit. Answer B best states this call to action. The passage does not encourage readers to take public transportation whenever possible (answer A), nor does it suggest that getting a job in mass transit will lead to a secure future (answer C). The passage argues that mass transit benefits even those who do not live in areas that have mass transit, so answer D is incorrect.

2. A, In the question "Why does this matter?" the word *this* refers to the extension of Medicaid. After this question, the author begins exploring the reasons and evidence that support his argument about the importance of extending Medicaid coverage for former foster youth. Answer A is correct. Answers B, C, and D do not make sense in the context of the passage.

3. A, The author argues that education is a key factor in determining whether a person will overcome poverty. He argues that social services and government programs have not succeeded in reducing or eliminating poverty. Answer A best summarizes this opinion.

4. D, That author cites many of the difficulties former foster youths face, but focuses specifically on only one way society can help—by extending Medicaid to these people.

5. B, Answer B is correct because it supports the author's viewpoint, explained in the previous paragraph: that education, employment, and mediating institutions are keys to upward mobility.

6. A, Answer A is the only option that makes a claim, or a statement about an issue. Answers B and C provide evidence to support this claim through examples. Answer D is a conclusion.

7. B, Answer options A, C, and D give opinions (using words such as "ought to be" in A and "should" in C). Only answer B presents an example as evidence.

8. D, Answer D asks people to think about something in a particular way and therefore is a conclusion.

UNIT 1 (continued)

9. C, The author lists reasons and evidence that build to the conclusion that violent personalities are not caused by violent media. The author does not include true stories, so answer A is incorrect. Although several paragraphs are numbered, the author does not present steps in a process of any kind (answer B). Although the author disagrees with the thesis, or claim, that violence in the media contributes to violent behavior, the passage does not compare and contrast different arguments about violence in the media.

10. A, As stated in answer A, the author believes that violent video games tend to attract people who have violent personalities. He does not believe that video games cause violence, so answer B is incorrect. He believes that video games and violent personalities do have a connection (violent people are attracted to violent games), so answer C is incorrect. Answer D is incorrect because the author does not state or imply that playing video games prevents a person from acting violently.

11. D, The author counters the claim that people copy crimes they see on television by stating that the people who copy the crimes already have violent personalities. Answer D is correct. The author does not argue that some crimes are too violent to show on television (answer A), nor does he present statistics (answer B) nor suggest that people who commit the crimes were likely victims themselves (answer C).

12. D, The author presents his reasons for believing that violence in the media does not contribute to violent personalities, but he does not present any data or cite any sources in his evidence. He assumes that his credibility as a respected psychologist makes him a reliable source who readers will trust. Answer D best states this assumption. The author does not include details about what he considers violent media. Instead, he assumes that readers will understand what he means when he talks about violent video games and television, so answer A is incorrect. The passage does not indicate whether the author assumes readers will be in favor of reducing violence in media (answer B). The author agrees with the verdict in the Florida case, and because he mentions the case at the end of the passage, he likely assumes that readers will have understood his argument and also agree. Answer C states that the author assumes readers will disagree, which is incorrect.

13. B, Paragraph 1 provides background information to help readers better understand Roberts's decision and argument. Although paragraph 1 does explain the government's claim, the rest of the passage does not give evidence to support it (answer A). Paragraph 1 does not provide evidence to support Roberts's claim, which appears in paragraph 4 (answer C). Paragraph 1 does explain the position of those opposed to the act, but the rest of passage does not counter this position—the passage supports it. Answer D is incorrect.

14. D, Answer A indicates a choice and its classification as a transition word is questionable. Answer B indicates an opposing or contrasting idea. Answer C indicates additional information or ideas. The word consequently indicates a causal relationship—the consequence, or result, of a cause.

15. A, The word therefore indicates a cause-and-effect relationship. In this passage, therefore shows how Roberts's understanding of the Commerce Clause led him to believe that the individual mandate is unconstitutional (answer A). The other answer choices are inaccurate because they do not relate to details connected in a cause-and-effect relationship by the word therefore. Answer C is also incorrect because it relates to information not included in the passage.

16. C, Answer C best summarizes the steps of Roberts's argument. Answer A is incorrect because Roberts was making a decision about the individual mandate, not the act as a whole, and because Roberts decided the individual mandate was unconstitutional under the Commerce Clause. Answer B is incorrect because it does not relate to Roberts's decision. Likewise, answer D is incorrect because it does not relate to Roberts's argument.

LESSON 12, pp. 57–61

1. D, Language such as greatest threat and imperil appeal to readers' emotions and make readers fearful about the threat that butterflies face. This language does not show that the author is a credible source, so answer A is incorrect. Language indicating a credible source would be an appeal to ethics. The author does not attempt to mislead readers and provides facts to show that butterflies do face threats, so answer B is incorrect. This language does not relate to butterflies' migration, so answer C is incorrect.

2. B, The fact that intelligence agencies never uncovered disloyal activities, such as espionage, by Japanese Americans shows that Japanese Americans did nothing to deserve evacuation and thus were evacuated without cause. The other answer choices reflect facts the author provides in the letter, but none of these facts supports the idea that Japanese Americans were evacuated without cause. Answer A notes how many Japanese Americans were evacuated. Answers C and D explain consequences of the evacuation.

3. D, The author discusses the outstanding service of Japanese Americans to show that Japanese American troops were brave and patriotic. Although the passage implies that evacuees may have made greater sacrifices than other Americans, this implication does not relate to Japanese Americans' record of service (answer A). Although the author appreciates what the Armed Forces did, he does not mention Japanese Americans' service to express appreciation (answer B). Answer C is incorrect because the passage does not mention of the number of men among the evacuees.

4. A, The evidence in paragraph 3 shows that the evacuation was hasty, and, as a result, Japanese Americans suffered financial losses (answer A). The evidence does not suggest that more planning would have helped the evacuation run more smoothly (answer B) or that Japanese Americans had trouble determining the value of their possessions (answer D). Although one sentence suggests that evacuees might have been forced to leave their property with people they did not trust, accepting "inadequate arrangements" is only one fact among the evidence presented, so answer C is incorrect.

5. C, The author presents facts that build to the claim that the United States should "offer some degree of compensation for the losses the evacuees suffered." Answer C, therefore, is correct. The author does not mention his position as Secretary of the Interior to persuade readers (answer A). Answer B is incorrect because he does not begin by stating a claim or use personal stories. The author uses facts, so answer D is incorrect.

UNIT 1 (continued)

6. C, Each electoral vote in Alaska is equivalent to approximately 112,000 people. Each electoral vote in New York is equivalent to approximately 404,000 eligible people. The detail is logical because it can be proved or disproved and thus is considered an appeal to reason.

7. D, Answers A, B, and C state fact. In contrast, D gives a detail in strong language that could arouse readers' feelings of fear ("crisis of confidence").

8. A, The ethical appeal is the speaker's identification as the League's representative, which lends authority.

9. A, The author appeals to ethics by quoting credible sources—a NASA historian and an astronomy teacher and writer who have in-depth knowledge about the space program (answer A). Although the author describes inventions that came about in part because of the space program (answer B) and provides an account of astronauts' activities during the moon landing (answer C), these details are not appeals to ethics. Answer D is incorrect because the author does not use particularly strong language to discuss the moon landing itself.

10. B, Answer B is correct because paragraph 1 supports the claim by providing an example of a new technology mentioned in paragraph 1. Answer A is incorrect because nothing in the example restates or summarizes the claim. The information is additional. To counter the claim, answer C would have to say that the Apollo program did not lead to new technologies. Answer D is incorrect because the example narrows rather than broadens the claim. To broaden the claim, the author would have to include something in addition to technology, not provide an example of one of the technologies mentioned in paragraph 1.

11. B, Answer B is correct because the statement cannot be proved true or false. On the other hand, the information in answers A, C, and D can be investigated and verified as accurate or inaccurate.

12. D, The evidence shows that the Apollo program led to technological advances beyond the invention of technology required to reach the moon. This evidence shows that scientific projects can bring unexpected and far-reaching benefits. Answer D is correct. The evidence in the passage does not suggest that politicians get in the way of technological advancements and scientific discovery (answer A). Nor does the evidence suggest that the United States will lose the technology race (answer B). No evidence discusses government funding of the space program, so answer C is incorrect.

13. D, The author's implicit claim is that prairies are important habitats that should be conserved. The evidence does not suggest that park rangers should use controlled fires to keep prairie habitats healthy (answer A). Answers B and C are facts that the author states directly in the passage and thus cannot be implied claims.

14. A, This opinion is supported by the fact that diversity of prairie species is important to agriculture and medicine. Answer B addresses the variety of plant and animal life prairie once supported but does not explain the value prairie holds for people now. The facts in answers C and D are not related to the opinion.

15. A, The percentages are an example of data. Percentages are classified as fact (can be proved true or untrue); thus this statement is an appeal to logic. Answer B might be possible, and some readers might see it as an appeal to patriotism, but it is not the best answer because authors appeal to emotions through strong language or visuals, not data. Answer C is incorrect because the information does not contain an opinion. Answer D is incorrect because no authorities are named.

16. C, Answer C states a claim not supported by evidence in the passage. The author does not discuss how much conservation efforts might cost or whether they will be successful. The claims expressed in the other answer choices are supported by evidence in the passage. Evidence supporting answer A appears in paragraphs 4 and 5. Evidence supporting answer B appears in paragraph 4. Evidence for the claim made in answer D is in the details that describe the loss of prairie throughout the passage.

LESSON 13, pp. 62–66

1. D, The author says that there is a clear need to look into a mining disaster. Later, the author implies that the mine operators could have prevented the disaster, but that they "concealed danger warnings and…chiseled underground pillar supports to the point of breaking." These statements show that the author believes people need to be aware of and try to change the way mine operators work.

2. C, The excerpt's initial focus is on the National Park Service Centennial Initiative and the money that it would cost to enact it. At the end of the excerpt, the author encourages the legislature to provide the money for this initiative. Answer C best states the author's beliefs.

3. B, Answer B best conveys the sense of urgency for immediate, positive action that the author expresses in the excerpt.

4. A, In lines 11 and 12, the author states "the parks need all the help they can get." Throughout the excerpt, the author discusses ways in which the federal government could help the parks. Answer A best restates the author's point of view.

5. A, Lines 16 through 20 state that most of the Katrina survivors "see recovery moving in the right direction."

6. C, The last sentence of paragraph 2 says, "Smaller majorities see little or no progress in making medical services available… or rebuilding neighborhoods."

7. A, In lines 2 and 3, the author says students are turning to "second-rate schools abroad."

8. D, The third and fourth paragraphs list problems with the Board of Regents plan.

9. C, Answer C is the only option that presents someone being trained improperly. This most closely matches with the author's concerns about improperly trained doctors.

10. C, The author uses language that indicates his or her opinion while describing the facts that were researched and presented in the excerpt.

11. B, Line 34 states that the judge "seemed particularly annoyed" at the situation. "Annoyed" is not quite as strong as "angry," so answer B best fits the scenario, as presented from the author's point of view.

UNIT 1 (continued)

12. D, Based on the author's language, one can assume the author sides with the judge against the states and the Fish and Wildlife Service's policies.

LESSON 14, pp. 67–71

1. B, The author is emphasizing that her party is "the instrument of the people" and that people have turned to her party in times of need. She's encouraging people to do so again.
2. B, The author gives many facts and details about the financial state and the impact of taxes on the country. He delivers these details in a very straightforward, calm manner.
3. D, The first paragraph explains how the national budget is facing difficulties and gives specific examples about those problems. The author is not asking people for money, and his uncomfortable feeling concerns the good luck, or prosperity, the country is facing. He never mentions that people should begin to save money.
4. C, Answer C is the only option that advises readers to take action, specifically to re-examine and determine if they are acting in a manner in which the Founders encouraged.
5. A, The author uses straightforward, factual wording, so he is not writing in an ambiguous manner. While this excerpt does not advocate fighting of any kind, it does encourage action and change, so it is not peaceful. The author very clearly supports the people and ideals of his country, so the excerpt is not unpatriotic. Finally, the author does not provide insights from other points of view, so the excerpt is not balanced. The author does provide much information, so answer A is the best choice.
6. B, As you read the excerpt, you can understand the author has a deep respect and love for his country, and he is very honored to have been recognized for his service to his country.
7. C, The author uses two repetitive structures to make his point. The first is to describe the "hallowed words," as the author says "what you…" three times. The second is a repetitive structure which shows the reasons the words are rallying points: to do something important. This structure is used four times.
8. A, Line 29 states that the ideals "build your basic character."
9. A, In the first paragraph, the speaker describes how he is "deeply moved" to be given the award and lets readers know how grateful he is to be receiving it.
10. B, Words such as honored in the last paragraph indicate the writer's respectful tone.
11. A, The restaurant hopes to appeal to children with a playscape and child-appropriate food. Similarly, a grocery store that gives away children's snacks would also appeal to the people of the neighborhood.
12. C, The author is attempting to inspire the reader to feel the same way he does about the way the representative referred to the people as "the masses."
13. D, By using the phrase "Founding Fathers," the author is attempting to evoke patriotic feelings in his readers and to get them to see his side by using those feelings.
14. A, In the third paragraph, the author begins to list figures that could be confirmed by research. The term "factual" best describes the style of the last paragraph.

LESSON 15, pp. 72–76

1. C, Lines 10 and 12 state that "[pit bulls] bite, hold, shake, and tear." Answer C is the only option that accurately rephrases the text into a generalization.
2. A, The second paragraph indicates that the company has operated for 25 years.
3. B, The first paragraph of the pamphlet sets out the company's attitude, which is that trees should be maintained in order to provide shade and comfort.
4. C, Removing limbs prevents future damage, just as a flu vaccination prevents future illness.
5. A, The social worker assumed that because the boy had dark spots on his body, he had been beaten. Rather than listen to the family, the social worker based her assumption and her report on the idea that the boy was being abused.
6. D, Lines 11 through 15 state that "black, Hispanic, and other minority children…are far more likely than white youngsters to be … placed in foster care."
7. B, The excerpt says that "stereotyping on the part of social workers is just one factor in the racial gap," so you can generalize and assume that the cultural-awareness training is to prevent stereotyping by social workers.
8. B, Lines 12 through 14 state that custody proceedings in which men are accused of being abusers "tap into age-old stereotypes about men and ensure that Mom becomes the primary guardian."
9. D, The first sentence of the second paragraph indicates that men are often assumed to be abusive because of stereotypes.
10. A, Answer A is the only option that addresses a stereotype about something that women enjoy, like the stereotype that men enjoy violent movies.
11. A, The last sentence of the excerpt states that "Much of what's wrong with family law today lies in warmed over stereotypes of men as fundamentally unsuited to caring for children."
12. B, The first paragraph attributes the increased sales to the traffic from Farmers' Market Days.
13. A, The fourth paragraph details how the store will cut back on luxury items and feature lower-priced items.

UNIT 1 REVIEW, pp. 77–80

1. A, The author states a problem, gives details, and uses some emotional language, such as "magnitude of these cuts," "no place to turn," and "radical cuts." It concludes with a call to action for readers to protest. Answer A is the only option that fully explains that the author's purpose is to persuade.
2. C, The author does not state that there will be fewer items to check out from the library or that people might pay more for services. The author does not suggest readers wait until after the budget is reduced to increase protests. The letter focuses on C, the effect of the proposed budget cuts.
3. B, The author gives examples of how different age groups use the library, from children to teens, adults, and the elderly, allowing readers to generalize that people of all ages use the library.
4. B, Only answer B presents an opinion. The other answer options are statements of fact.

UNIT 1 (continued)

5. D, The author is indirectly suggesting that if many people protest cuts to the library's budget, the city council will be swayed to vote against those cuts.
6. C, The author states "I am writing to introduce myself to you and your associates" in line 1.
7. D, The use of the phrase "preferred guests" indicates that the recipient is a special client of the hotel.
8. B, The letter is addressed to "Mr. Frank Thomas, CEO" of "Thomas Building Supplies."
9. D, The previous sentence refers to an event that Mr. Thomas's company is organizing in September and hints at other possible events in the future. The author wants to make sure that Mr. Thomas knows he can rely on her for assistance with those events.
10. C, The tone of the letter is professional and courteous, indicating that the author cares about her job and helping other people in ways related to that job.

UNIT 2 FICTION

LESSON 1, pp. 83–87

1. C, Lines 4 through 7 explain that nothing about the man's narrative changes. From this context, you can assume that the tone stays the same.
2. C, If you did not already know that deserted means "empty," you could guess its meaning from context clues. The narrator says "I remained alone in the bare carriage" (lines 13–14), so no other answer option fits.
3. D, From the information that precedes the narrator "handing a shilling to a weary looking man," you can guess from context clues that the narrator is going through the gate to the bazaar. Based on this information, you can assume that a shilling is the price of entry to the bazaar.
4. A, The excerpt tells us that a town (hamlet) called Barry's Ford began where a river was "fordable" and that there is now a bridge there. From this information, you can assume that a ford is a "place to cross a river."
5. C, The phrase "inherent with the existence" lets you know that something that is inherent goes along with the existence. If the phrase had said "inherent against" or "inherent from," you could assume that the inherent object would work against the existence. So something that is inherent is not similar to something else in the existence or separate but equal to the existence. It is also not removed from the whole of existence, or replacing a previous element. Answer 3 is the best option.
6. A, The speaker states that "a man…must be prepared to forget many of the things he has learned" and to acquire the customs of the new land. The speaker is advocating that people give up their previous habits to learn the customs of a new place.
7. B, The excerpt describes a land that is torn apart by a war. Answer 2 is the only option that describes the destruction that war can cause.
8. A, Lines 6 through 8 describe branches and trunks that lie tangled in the mud. From the context, you can assume the trees that are "shattered upright forms" are still standing but look sad.
9. C, The beginning of the excerpt describes the husband's health, saying that his voice had grown very weak.
10. D, The narrator describes how the husband gets irritated when his wife cannot hear what he is saying. She says his "irritability, this increasing childish petulance" describes their relationship at this point. From this context, you can assume that one who is petulant would be difficult to get along with.
11. B, Lines 7 through 10 describe the estrangement in the relationship: "Like two faces looking at one another through a sheet of glass they were close together, almost touching, but they could not hear or feel each other." They are no longer physically close.
12. D, The narrator says that the woman's "self-reproachful tenderness was tinged with the sense of his irrationality." From this context, you can assume that the woman still cares about her husband and wishes she could take care of him (her self-reproachful tenderness) but is irritated and does not know how to deal with his "helpless tyrannies" (lines 17–20).
13. C, *Conductivity* is "the ability to transfer energy from one thing to another," such as electricity from an outlet to a power cord, much the same way that a light bulb socket transfers energy to the light bulb.
14. A, The excerpt describes Zelig as someone who does not fit in with the rest of his co-workers. From this context, you can assume that *alien* means "different."
15. C, "Mister" is a term that implies respect; it is a formal way to address someone. In the excerpt, we learn that "Mr." is similar to "Reb;" therefore, you can assume that "Reb" is a courtesy title, giving someone the courtesy of one's respect.
16. D, Based on the excerpt, you can assume that a stave is something required to keep a barrel together or whole. The phrase "a barrel with a stave missing" indicates that the neighbors think Zelig is not entirely whole, or not mentally stable.
17. B, You learn that Zelig's hair is long, and that his clothes are shabby and hang loosely on him. Based on these clues, you can assume that Zelig's grooming habits are not very good.

LESSON 2, pp. 88–92

1. B, In lines 5 through 7, the narrator explains the strange feeling she gets from the house. She tells John about the feeling, but he believes she is simply cold.
2. C, Line 15 states that her "treatment taught him at least the power of living alone."
3. C, Lines 5-6 describe Mrs. Jennett's behavior toward Dick as coming "partly through a natural desire to cause pain."
4. D, Lines 9-12 describe Mrs. Jennett's making Dick unhappy through her lack of love or even a little sympathy for him.
5. A, Lines 2-4 state that Mrs. Jennett's money came from "allowances supposed to be expended on his clothes."
6. B, Lines 19 and 20 state that because of his early arrival, the narrator "could find no porter."
7. D, The newspapers reported that "trains had been stalled in the snow and fishing villages cut off," meaning that no one could get to the villages. This is most like a small island town with no bridge for people to cross.

UNIT 2 (continued)

8. A, The narrator describes everything he has packed and is wearing: a heavy coat over two sweaters, and warm underwear. This underlines the severity of the weather conditions at his destination.

9. B, The narrator says that he intends to read "an optimistic report on the future of the Yiddish language" (lines 15–16). You can assume that, based on the additional information about the narrator's time as a prisoner in a concentration camp, the most likely effect of the reminder of his past is that the narrator will feel less optimistic about the future of the Yiddish language.

10. D, Lines 18 and 19 tell us that Sylvia does not tell the location of the heron and that her grandmother rebukes or yells at her for not telling.

11. D, Lines 12 and 13 describe the dress as a "worn old frock" that is "torn and tattered, and smeared with pine pitch." Sylvia has not taken care of her dress.

12. D, The guest likely guesses that Sylvia has been near the white heron. Her dress is torn and "smeared with pine pitch," which indicates she has climbed up a tree where the heron might be.

13. C, Sylvia does not tell the guest where to find the heron, so the guest cannot hunt the heron and kill him.

14. B, The woman has traveled in airplanes many times and knows her preferences. She has the knowledge to select the best seats.

15. C, The excerpt tells us that the woman makes herself comfortable and does not look at the man when he tries to talk to her. Based on this information, you know that she wants to be left alone for the duration of the flight. She will most likely try to ignore him when he attempts to talk to her.

16. D, The woman most likely increased the distance between herself and the man to give him more room.

17. B, The woman makes negative judgments: she's afraid of being on the plane, she dislikes the night sky, and she assumes the man next to her is going to snore. She also makes herself appear messy and untidy, which indicates that she does not encourage people to engage her in discussion.

LESSON 3, pp. 93–97

1. D, Lines 9 through 11 explain that Susan tells jokes and riddles to get attention, while Emily is quiet and does not draw attention to herself. Thus, Susan is less confident in public.

2. C, The excerpt explains that the couple do not enjoy the same kinds of music, so answer A is incorrect. The narrator likes bluegrass music, while Gloria does not, so answer B is incorrect. Gloria says she could see the narrator might like bebop music, in contrast to bluegrass, so answer D is incorrect. Thus, the husband must be the only one who likes hillbilly music.

3. A, In lines 7 and 8, Gloria explains that hillbilly music and the New York Stock Exchange change quickly in a negative way: "If you see a sharp rise in it, you better watch out."

4. B, Earlier in the excerpt, the narrator says that his "perceptions were shaped in South Carolina." The author is showing the difference between Gloria's upbringing in the North and his own childhood in the South.

5. D, You can assume from the author's description that the Ibo and Yoruba are very different from one another. Answer D is the only option that lists two very different things.

6. A, The Kelveys are not welcome to play with many of the other children, so answer B is incorrect. There is no indication that the Burnells like wildflowers, so answer C is incorrect. Only the Kelveys are shunned by the other children, so answer D is incorrect.

7. B, The second paragraph describes how all the children of the area go to the same school, so children from families of different classes mingle together. The narrator goes on to say that "the line had to be drawn somewhere" and that the Kelvey children were on the other side of the line, indicating that the Kelveys are not as well off as many of the other families of the area.

8. D, Lines 24 through 29 state that "the Kelveys were shunned by everyone. Even the teacher" responds to them negatively, with a "special" voice and a "special smile to the other children" when Lil gives her flowers. The teacher treats the poorer Kelveys differently from the other children.

9. A, Readers learn about the families of the children who make up Isabel's circle of friends in the second paragraph, and that information along with the fact that Kelveys are not allowed to play with Isabel and her friends emphasizes the differences in social status between the Kelvey children and the others.

10. C, Based on the term "mixture," you know that the narrator's beliefs are a blend of "Yankee and Confederate folkways."

11. D, Lines 10 and 11 identify Yankees as "penny-pinching," meaning they are careful with their money. The author uses this description to show one difference he sees between Yankees and Confederates.

12. D, The author does not seem to favor one side over the other, so answer A is incorrect. The author indicates that some schools were named after Southerners while others were named after Northerners, so the term "most" in answer B makes that option incorrect. The author contrasts Northern and Southern cultures, so answer C is incorrect. The narrator has obviously learned both Northern and Southern ideas, so answer D is incorrect.

13. B, Lines 20 through 25 state that the "schoolbooks, … required classroom songs, … songs, … [and] very relation to the statues and monuments in public parks" made it seem as though people from the North had never come to the South.

14. B, Many of the narrator's descriptions of her daughter's early life indicate that there was not enough money to give her daughter the security and attention she needed.

15. A, The narrator describes her daughter as "a child of her age, of depression, of war, of fear," but says that "[h]er younger sister seemed all that she was not" (lines 15–19). This indicates that the older sister has dealt with more difficult times than her younger sister.

16. C, As the narrator grew older and had more children, she understood and knew more about raising children. She gained insight as the years went by.

17. A, The narrator describes the older daughter as being very different from how she "should" have been: "dark and thin and foreign-looking in a world where the prestige went to blondness and curly hair and dimples, she was slow where glibness was prized" (lines 7–10). This description, placed immediately before the line about proud versus anxious love, emphasizes the daughter's strangeness and indicates that the anxious love had an effect on her daughter.

UNIT 2 (continued)

LESSON 4, pp. 98–102

1. B, In line 14, Mrs. Wright tells Mr. Hale that he cannot speak to John because John is dead.

2. D, A person would have a "word of comfort" for someone who is going through a difficult time. However, Goodman Parker does not have a word of comfort for Mary, who is also described as "a young woman in trouble," so he has no good news for her.

3. A, The beginning of the excerpt describes Margaret as a widow, so we know that her husband is believed dead. At the end of the excerpt, Goodman Parker tells Margaret that her husband was among a number of men who were reportedly killed but are actually alive.

4. D, Delaying the announcement makes the tension and suspension of the plot increase. Readers are likely sympathetic to Margaret's case, and want the news just as badly as she does.

5. C, You know Margaret has received the happy news that her husband is not dead. However, Mary is "a young woman in trouble," so it is likely she does not have good news. This plot element is likely to be a source of conflict between Margaret and Mary.

6. D, The tension of the excerpt rises up until the point that the women decide to act. After the decision is made, events play out based on that decision that lead to the resolution of the excerpt.

7. C, Lines 22 through 24 let us know there is a bird in the box. However, neither Martha Hale nor Mrs. Peters reacts to finding the bird in the box, so we can assume the women previously knew that the bird was in the box.

8. D, The end of the second paragraph tells us that what is in the box could lead to the conviction of another woman. By snatching the box away from Mrs. Peters, and presumably hiding the box from the sheriff and county attorney, Martha Hale is resolving the conflict of whether the other woman will be convicted.

9. A, In this excerpt, Martha Hale and Mrs. Peters are acting together. Based on this information, they would most likely cheer on the same team at a sporting event.

10. A, The explanation gives you background about two characters, Stephen and Mary. This is part of the exposition. Because Stephen is trying to help Mary and give her good news, the information about Stephen having tried to date Mary in the past is not a complication.

11. D, The reader is told that Stephen has come to cheer up Mary, and that she is a widow. Mary misunderstands Stephen's intent and assumes that he is attempting to date her so soon after her husband's death. This is a source of conflict for Mary.

12. B, Stephen's message is stated in lines 25 through 33, when he tells her that he sees her husband standing on the deck of a ship. From this information, you can assume the resolution of this excerpt would be that Mary's husband comes home.

13. D, Stephen is described as having been an "unsuccessful wooer" and "rejected lover." The speed with which he appears at Mary's house, so soon after she has been notified of her husband's death, leads Mary to believe that Stephen is once again attempting to win her affections.

14. D, Mrs. Penn lists what is wrong with the house: the lack of carpet and the dirty wallpaper.

15. B, Mr. and Mrs. Penn have been married for a while and have a daughter about to be married, so answer A is incorrect. Mrs. Penn is very irritated about the changes she wants made, more than she would be in a light-hearted tiff, so answer C is incorrect. Mr. and Mrs. Penn are not discussing finances, so answer D is incorrect.

16. C, You can assume that, based on Mrs. Penn's forceful personality, she will push to have improvements to the house done in time for Nanny's wedding.

17. D, In lines 6 and 7, Sarah Penn states, "I 'ain't never complained, an' I ain't goin' to complain now, but I'm goin' to talk plain." The statement that she's never complained before lets us know that up to this point she's been patient when dealing with her husband.

18. B, Lines 18 through 22 let us know that Nanny is getting married and Mrs. Penn is upset about the state of the room in which Nanny is getting married.

LESSON 5, pp. 103–107

1. D, Line 9 says that Mrs. Whipple "couldn't stand to be pitied." This indicates she is a proud woman who does not want other people to feel bad for her.

2. B, The narrator relates that at one time, Tiny set off for Alaska after hearing miners' "wonderful stories" and lived in the wilds. That "daring" is an example of an adventurous life.

3. D, The narrator relates that after Tiny had taken "desperate chances" in the Klondike, "nothing interested her much now but making money."

4. C, The narrator reveals Tiny's character by describing her actions, responses, and statements, but does not give an account of her appearance.

5. D, The narrator states that another character now helps keep her from becoming too miserly, indicating that she has a tendency to hold on to her money. This detail leads to the inference that her sense of adventure has given way to a need for security.

6. B, The narrator describes going into the old man's bedroom each morning to ask how he got along during the night, so it is logical to infer that he takes care of the old man. No details from the passage suggest that the old man is the narrator's father or employee; rather, it seems that the narrator works for, or at least helps, the old man. It is clear that the narrator and old man are not enemies because the narrator states in the first paragraph of the passage that he loved the old man and that the old man had never wronged him.

7. C, In the first paragraph, the narrator explains that he decided to kill the old man so that he no longer would have to see the old man's eye, which frightened the narrator. The narrator also makes it clear that he has no desire to have the old man's money and that the old man has never done anything to harm him, so he does not resent the old man's wealth or think that the old man has been cruel to him. Although it may be inferred that the old man is not well, the narrator gives no indication of wanting to end the old man's suffering.

UNIT 2 (continued)

8. A, In paragraph 2, the narrator acknowledges that readers will judge him to be mad and then argues against this judgment. He uses words such as wisely and cunningly to show that his actions result from wisdom and intelligence, not mental illness. His choice of words relates to proving only that he is rational; he seems unconcerned about whether readers think him educated, blameless, or organized.

9. D, Common sense suggests that taking an hour to thrust one's head through a doorway to look into a room is not an action that a reasonable person would take. Therefore, the narrator's actions are not reasonable or sensible; rather, he is irrationally cautious and methodical as he makes preparations to kill the old man. Because the narrator is taking steps to kill the old man, it is unlikely that he is concerned about the old man's need for rest. No evidence in the passage suggests that the narrator is exaggerating his own actions.

10. D, The narrator believes that the old man's eye is a threat, and he is obsessed with killing the old man when the eye is open. Although the narrator may have been a dependable and helpful caregiver for the old man at one time, he now merely feigns concern for the old man to keep his plan of murder a secret. The secretive and elaborately practiced steps the narrator is taking to kill the old man, based on his fear of the old man's eye, prove that the narrator is not innocent, trusting, fearless, or arrogant.

11. B, Lines 27 and 28 let us know that Nick has an appeal to women the narrator cannot understand.

12. D, The hands of a surgeon have to be exact, and a surgeon has to be good at what he or she does in order to save a person's life. Based on this information, the narrator is saying that Nick is a good mechanic.

13. B, Nick would be considered a working-class man, and his unexplainable appeal to women could be generalized as all working-class men appeal to women.

14. B, The narrator does not speak poorly of Nick, as he describes him in polite and positive terms. However, he does not understand the attraction Nick has to women, so his attitude is best described as affectionate disbelief.

15. A, Based on the attention the women constantly give Nick, you can assume they have crushes on him.

16. C, Mrs. Whipple is irritated with her husband's inability to provide for the family, after Mr. Whipple buys a new horse that then dies.

17. D, Mrs. Whipple's attitude is angry and irritable. She holds a grudge against her husband and is unwelcoming to Him. Her attitude is best described as bitter.

18. B, At first, Mrs. Whipple provides the bare necessities for Him, as she states that "there are things you can't cut down on, and they cost money" (lines 13–14).

19. C, The fact that Mrs. Whipple feels ashamed when she tells the doctor why He does not have His blanket leads us to believe that she is hiding the real reason that the blanket was taken off.

LESSON 6, pp. 108–112

1. C, Based on line 12, in which we learn that Martha sees her mother "savoring…the vengeful triumph," we can assume that the mother does not want the children to get the family records and belongings.

2. C, The last paragraph explains that Greenspahn is mad at Siggie for selling him bad cheese. He believes Siggie is doing this on purpose.

3. B, Wholesalers would most likely throw away food that has gone bad, which would mean that they would take a loss on the product. However, if they sold a product that had gone bad, they would not lose that money.

4. A, Siggie's sale of bad cheese to Greenspahn indicates that he is likely trying to avoid talking to Greenspahn about the products. There is no mention of Siggie's work habits, and he does not say that he is going to be late. Siggie and Shirley were talking before Greenspahn tried to get Siggie's attention. Siggie already gave Greenspahn a good deal if he was previously cheaper than the dairy (lines 33–35).

5. D, In line 15, Greenspahn tells Siggie, "I been getting complaints."

6. B, The speaker is telling the story as though the audience already knows what happened in the end. He most likely believes that the audience knows what he planned to the old man.

7. D, The speaker gives no indication that the old man may have booby-trapped the door, so answer A is incorrect. The speaker deliberately only opened the door wide enough to fit himself through, so answer B is incorrect. The speaker states that he spoke with the old man the next morning, not at night, so answer C is incorrect.

8. A, The speaker explains that "it was not the old man that vexed [him], but his Evil Eye." He did not want to harm the old man; instead, he wanted to destroy the eye. However, with the eye closed, the speaker did not follow through on his plan.

9. D, If you do not know that meticulously means "with great care," you can eliminate the other answer options. The speaker very carefully and deliberately goes about sneaking into the old man's room, so he shows great care and attention to detail. The speaker praises his cunning at sneaking into the room, but that does description only emphasizes the details and sophistication of his plan. In this excerpt, "mad" is a synonym for insane, not angry. The speaker's confessional language indicates that he is telling someone about what he did, but he is delighted with his plan, and does not show any sense of guilt.

10. D, Lines 1 through 4 state that she had sold Marlcrest and "momentarily righted the wrong of her life by taking from someone else what she felt had been taken from her."

11. D, Martha is reluctant to tell her mother about Rowdy's death. If she were a nurse, she would probably want to avoid giving patients bad news.

12. D, The mother did not care for her children's feelings when she sold Marlcrest and did not tell them, but she was very upset to not see her dog.

13. B, Martha and Perry Jr. know that their mother loved the dog, so they most likely want to spare her feelings as she is ailing.

14. B, Greenspahn claims that Frank "shook [the woman] down," meaning he charged her extra money to not tell Greenspahn about her attempted theft. Frank most likely would have kept the money for himself, so answer B best describes his likely motivation.

UNIT 2 (continued)

15. D, Jake is very angry with Frank, but does not seem to be very angry with the woman at all. If Jake were a judge, he would most likely believe that someone who overcharges a hungry person is worse than a shoplifter.
16. C, Frank is very angry that Greenspahn fired him for blackmailing the shopper.
17. B, Again, Frank is very angry about being fired. He most likely mentioned Greenspahn's dead son to hurt Greenspahn.

LESSON 7, pp. 113–117

1. C, The author states that Connie "check[s] other people's faces to make sure her own was all right" and tells us that the mother "noticed everything and knew everything."
2. D, The narrator explains that she is still in school, and that she lives with her parents.
3. A, The pronoun "I" can only be used to tell the thoughts of one person. It also indicates first-person point of view.
4. D, Readers do not learn anything about the rest of the family's feelings, so answer A is incorrect. There is no analysis of the father's bathing habits, so answer B is incorrect. There is no indication that the mother resents anything, so answer C is incorrect. Readers know only the thoughts and feelings of the narrator, so answer D is correct.
5. B, The narrator presents ordinary facts about her daily life, in much the same way that a person would write in his or her diary.
6. C, The narrator refers to Jo and Meg by their names, so the narrator is not either of them. The narrator is not using first-person pronouns, so the author did not use first-person point of view. There is no indication that the narrator is an expert on young girls. The narrator does give readers insights into memories and thoughts that Jo and Meg have, so the narrator is omniscient.
7. B, In lines 33 and 34, Meg states that "Mother wants [the girls] to read and love and mind these books, and we must begin at once." Meg believes that their mother wants the girls to enjoy reading the books and to pay attention to the lessons they might learn from reading the books.
8. D, The narrator is omniscient and knows all the thoughts and feelings of the characters. The author most likely chose this point of view to present the thoughts of all the characters.
9. A, Meg speaks with an authoritative voice, and in a tone that is meant to guide the other girls. Meg would most likely enjoy teaching.
10. D, The narrator describes the little girl and the actions in strong, bold tones, and tells readers the thoughts of both the girl and Dexter.
11. B, The narrator knows what the girl is thinking, if she is described as being blatantly artificial or fake and convincing.
12. D, This excerpt does not give readers descriptions of the motives, so answer A is incorrect. Nothing about the excerpt indicates the narrator is describing the girl in a false or unreliable manner, so answer B is incorrect. The narrator has shown Dexter's thoughts in the excerpt, so answer C is incorrect.

13. C, The narrator is making a judgment about the girl's personality (ungodly) based on her appearance. This is most like a psychological profile.
14. C, The first sentence tells readers that the narrator is a poor student. Later in the first paragraph, he says that he was "on [his] way to [his] senior year in college."
15. C, The story is told from the first-person point of view, so readers will only get the thoughts and feelings of the main character. That character may describe the actions of the other characters as he sees them.
16. B, The narrator tells readers a little bit about each of the four men he tutors. This is most like a host introducing guest speakers.
17. A, The narrator emphasizes his youth by telling readers his age, describing himself as a young man, and describing his excitement "to get going" (lines 13–14). Because he is young, he likely does not have a lot of experience, so answer B is incorrect. His eagerness indicates that he is not cynical so answer C is incorrect. Nothing in the text indicates that the narrator is very worldly, so answer D is incorrect.
18. C, The narrator states that he "gave English lessons to recently arrived refugees" (lines 4–5). You might know that Adolf Hitler began invading Germany's neighboring countries in 1939 and that many German citizens were leaving Germany. Based on this information, you could assume that the narrator's pupils only spoke German.

LESSON 8, pp. 118–122

1. Synthesis: (1), The narrator describes the different ways the children are able to entertain themselves throughout the afternoon, so the theme of this excerpt could be "Children are able to find ways to have fun in different situations."
2. C, Donald is sparing people his bad moods and trying to cope with his memories of serving in the Vietnam War. He is haunted by his memories of what was done to the land and the people of Vietnam. These memories disrupt his life.
3. B, Lines 4 through 7 state, "Vietnam had never seemed such a meaningful fact until a couple of years ago, when he grew depressed and moody."
4. A, Donald goes on to say that the war stripped off "the best part of the land and the country." This statement indicates he believes both the war and the strip mining are destructive actions.
5. D, Donald's memories of Vietnam haunt him in the same way that a ghost might haunt a house.
6. D, At the end of the second paragraph, Donald is satisfied that coal companies have to plant trees and bushes to replace what they have taken from the land.
7. A, Before Ray asks "Why should I pay?" he says, "She went into the woods with him because she wanted to go. What he wanted she wanted." Ray feels he is being held responsible for something that was not his responsibility.
8. B, Prior to raging "against everything that makes life ugly," Ray is protesting his own and all life, indicating that he feels as though his life has not been as rich as it could have been.
9. C, Ray is disappointed with his life and with the events that have taken place prior to this excerpt, and wants to make sure Hal does not follow down that path.

UNIT 2 (continued)

10. D, The theme of this excerpt is best stated as "disappointed people want to stop others from making their mistakes." Based on the things that Ray says as he's running (lines 11–19), you know that Ray disagrees with a decision Hal has made or is about to make.

11. D, From reading the excerpt, you know that Hadleyburg is "an incorruptible town" and that the offended stranger has a plan to corrupt it somehow.

12. D, Something that happened in the town offended the passing stranger. This information implies that the stranger felt he was treated poorly in some way.

13. B, Hadleyburg is known for being honest and upright, but the stranger wants to prove that it is not as wonderful as the people believe. His plan to corrupt the town is most like someone wanting to expose the greed in a company that is known for its charity.

14. C, To maintain its honor, the town of Hadleyburg is going to have to prove its honesty and uprightness and withstand the stranger's efforts to corrupt the town.

15. A, The fourth paragraph describes Donald simulating a helicopter blade with the blade of the food processor.

16. C, Donald keeps reliving the horrors he saw in the war, much like a shark-attack survivor would have nightmares about sharks.

17. B, Donald's experiences in the war have not been properly handled and processed, and so they remain unresolved. They are problems for him in the present.

18. C, Donald relies on Jeannette to stay with him, as is described at the end of the excerpt. He's emotionally fragile, as evidenced by his crying because he thought she was afraid he was going to hurt her. The author wanted to emphasize Donald's state of mind.

LESSON 9, pp. 123–127

1. C, The author's description of the setting includes tall waves crashing against a boat smaller than a "bath-tub," so the boat ride is not calm, and the boat is not seaworthy. He also mentioned the horizon and the sea, so readers know the men are at sea, not on a lake.

2. D, The end of the excerpt tells us that Hook can hear the Pacific Ocean from his location, so we know he must live near the ocean.

3. C, Hook's parents left to find a new place where they could get the resources they need to feed and take care of themselves. This is most like human parents moving to a new town to find a job.

4. B, In this excerpt, the author is demonstrating how Hook is affected by his parents' abandonment of him. Describing Hook's environment in words that show the difficulty of finding food and fending for himself emphasizes the effect.

5. D, Hook's parents make him change his location sooner than usual so that he can be closer to any food source that might be present. This is brought on by the lack of water and the potential lack of food that might result.

6. D, Answer D is correct because the landscape looks the same on three sides only, as stated in paragraph 1. The west is different. Answer A is incorrect because grass cannot be seen to the west. Answer B is incorrect because mud is mentioned only in describing the stream. Answer C misinterprets information in the passage; there is a stream, but no river, which is on the western side.

7. A, Answer A is correct because the narrator states in paragraph 1 that Canute would have shot himself except for the trees. Answer B is incorrect because the implication is that Canute does not enjoy much about life nor does the narrator say or imply anything that shows Canute's feelings about the wind. Answer C is incorrect because he is deeply depressed; although he built his house by himself, nothing is stated or implied about his attachment to or feelings about it. Answer D is incorrect because nothing is mentioned about Canute's earlier life.

8. A, The landscape is described in paragraph 1. The wigwam is situated at "the base of some irregularly ascending hills. A footpath wound its way gently down the sloping land till it reached the broad river bottom. ..." Therefore, answer A is correct. Answer B is incorrect because the landscape is the opposite. Answer C is incorrect because no farms are mentioned. Answer D is incorrect because there is a path to the river.

9. C, Answer C is correct because the girl's buckskin slip and moccasins and her teepee home reflect the dress and living quarters of many Native American people living in the Midwest at the time in which the story takes place. Answer A is incorrect because there is no indication of a small town. Also, Missouri names the river, not the state. Answer B is incorrect because no big cities are mentioned. Answer D does not answer the answer the question about the girl's clothing and home.

10. C, Answer C is correct because the girl is described as being as free as the wind and as spirited as the deer. Answer A states the opposite of the correct answer; the girl is at one with the outdoors. Nothing is mentioned about her enjoyment of reading. Answer B is incorrect because her mother pays close attention to her and encourages her spirit. Answer D is incorrect because the girl is shown as wild and free, not calm.

11. B, The setting describes a neighborhood in a city. The neighborhood is populated with "outcasts." The neighborhood is clearly not rural or wealthy. It is most likely not residential, as the text indicates that it comprised mostly of wholesale stores.

12. D, The description of the rain in paragraph 2 and the description of the neighborhood create a feeling of gloom and forbidding. Answers A and B are incorrect because nothing in the description of the rain, the bleak neighborhood, and huddled figures in a bread line suggests these feelings. Answer C may be more likely than A and B, but the setting is very worldly and not distant.

13. A, Readers can infer that he is homeless. On the basis of this assumption, and that Sam is tired and cold, a shelter would be the most likely place a person in his position would go. Answer B is incorrect because the weather is too bad for staying outdoors. Answer C might be correct if the restaurant were distributing food, but no mention is made of this. Answer D, too, would be logical if another bakery were mentioned, but neither answer choice indicates a more likely decision.

14. A, The description of the desertion and the iron shuttered fronts of the wholesale stores makes answer A the best choice. The area is not upscale, judging by the residents, nor does anything indicate that it features warehouses. The South Side of Chicago is not suburban, nor is there evidence that the area is a performing arts district.

UNIT 2 (continued)

15. C, Most people would not want to stand outside in line late on a cold night to wait for food, so the characters already would be uncomfortable. The weather, "a fine drizzle that pervaded the air," emphasizes the characters' discomfort. The rain would have no effect on the characters' gratitude, so answer A is incorrect. No connection is mentioned between rain and making bread, so answer B is incorrect. Answer D is incorrect because the rain would emphasize the gloom, not contrast with it.
16. D, Sonny's language and reference to the car in the road indicate that it is in the country, not in a city. Because they are clearly outside on a road, they cannot be in a shopping mall. There is no indication that the setting is anywhere other than in the United States, most likely in the South.
17. C, Sonny has fixed Bowman's car. The conversation is about the car, payment, and a request to stay the night. Answer A is incorrect because neither Sonny nor Bowman is giving directions. Answer B is incorrect because Bowman does not seem to be vacationing. The title of the passage indicates that Bowman is a salesman and is probably in the area because of his work, despite his illness. Answer C is correct because the setting in which Bowman finds himself indicates that he is not there by choice, wanting to leave and wanting to stay at the same time. Answer D is a misreading of the text. Sonny has consented to let Bowman lodge in his house, given the situation. Sonny and Bowman are not acquainted.
18. B, The author likely includes this detail to emphasize that Bowman is unwelcome in this place. The dogs are waiting to bark when he leaves. Their panting reminds him that they want him to leave. Although panting dogs might suggest danger in some situations, this interpretation is not supported as strongly by the passage. The dogs do not seem to suggest the isolation of the location or the typical home.
19. B, The setting emphasizes distance from familiar surroundings and emphasizes Bowman's discomfort, so answer B is the best choice. Nothing indicates that Bowman likes his surroundings—in fact they seem inhospitable and forbidding, so answer A is incorrect. Answer C is incorrect because Bowman's illness and discomfort indicate displeasure, not a fine adventure. Nothing is mentioned about the place in which Bowman grew up, so answer D is incorrect.

LESSON 10, pp. 128–132

1. D, The young man is described in funny, sympathetic terms. The author's tone is humorous.
2. D, The author describes the scene in ominous and frightening terms. The tone is threatening.
3. B, The words "weird dawn" and "ungodly awakening" imply that something bad is likely to take place soon.
4. D, An omen is something which hints that something else will happen. A mystery tale is the most likely kind of story to have some sort of hint or foreshadowing of what is to come.
5. A, Lines 28 and 29 state that the womens' songs "were cottonwads to stop their ears." People use cottonwads to muffle or avoid sounds, so the women were singing to drown out the affect of the dogs barking and roosters crowing in response to the full moon.
6. C, Earlier in the passage, the narrator says that Louisa was thinking about Bob and Tom, and that neither character alone had any "unusual significance." However, when she combined her thoughts of each man, she became agitated and restless.
7. B, Lines 2 and 3 state that the "[t]rucks have been unloading all afternoon," which indicates the carnival had just arrived that afternoon.
8. D, The author uses language that shows the excitement Ben experiences at the idea of going to the carnival. Readers get a sense of the excitement from the exclamation point after "Carnival," and the quick pace with which the author goes through all the things to do and see at the carnival are indicators of the tone.
9. D, Ben is extremely impatient to get to the carnival. He sees Sammy running to the carnival, knows that Gloria has been there all afternoon, and is aggravated that his parents are slowing down his progress to the carnival.
10. D, Ben is very excited for the carnival. The last paragraph describes him running past different parts of his neighborhood, in much the same way that someone might run to the theater to see a new movie about which he or she is excited.
11. A, Ben is anticipating rushing past these different parts of his town on his way to the carnival.
12. C, The word "consciously" indicates that the studio was decorated with a lot of thought and effort into making it appear a certain way. The narrator's tone indicates that he believes whoever decorated the studio was trying especially hard to make the studio look arty and thus it comes across as artificial.
13. A, The narrator's tone in lines 15 through 19 indicates that he resents being forced to look at every painting.
14. B, The narrator is not confused or bewildered, so answer A is incorrect. The narrator is also not proud, as he seems very irritated, so answer C is incorrect. He is not excited to be at the party, so answer D is incorrect.
15. D, Lines 25 through 27 state that the narrator believed that every painting was "atrocious," but that he and his father "went through the vocabulary of praise until it was worn to a fiber." This is most similar to someone feeling that he or she must compliment an unattractive house.
16. C, The narrator is uncomplimentary to everything going on at the party. The line about the continuous joke seems insincere and sarcastic, indicating that the narrator did not find the joke funny at all.
17. D, From the information in the excerpt, you can assume the phrase "something to keep the home fires burning" means something to keep people at home or in a present situation. The narrator has described Cronin's housekeeper and expressed that she was worse than Mrs. Stoner, so he would rather keep his own housekeeper than get another one.
18. C, The narrator indicates that Mrs. Stoner tells a lot of gossip at her card parties.
19. D, The narrator is exasperated with Mrs. Stoner's behavior, but does not know how to make a change.
20. C, The only nice thing the narrator can say about Mrs. Stoner is that she is clean. This indicates he feels as though she does not have many good qualities.

UNIT 2 (continued)

21. D, The narrator complains about Mrs. Stoner throughout the excerpt but is concerned that he would not be able to find a suitable replacement. He fears getting a worse housekeeper, as can be seen by his complaints against Cronin's housekeeper. This situation is most like a person driving a car he or she hates because a suitable substitute cannot be found.

LESSON 11, pp. 133–137

1. D, Cows do not speak, but in this excerpt they are given dialogue, like humans. This is an example of personification.
2. C, The character is comparing herself to a tree in the wind. The use of the phrase "as helpless as" indicates this is a simile.
3. B, The author is trying to describe how quickly the pain sets in—"running like a wildfire." The simile of the wildfire indicates its burning speed, as wildfires are prone to spread quickly.
4. A, The author frequently uses figurative language to describe the feelings her character is experiencing, and she most frequently uses similes to do so.
5. D, Lines 31 and 32 state, "the brain was as small as a seashell."
6. B, The author has given human-like qualities to the appliances around the house. This is an example of personification.
7. C, The word "hiss" creates a noise when it is said. This is an example of onomatopoeia.
8. D, The house is able to do things on its own, such as reminding the inhabitants of important events of the day. This is most like a car being able to drive itself.
9. A, The story uses personification to give human qualities to inanimate objects. Houses do not have feelings, but the personification lends human feelings, such as fear, to the house.
10. C, The "voice-clock" tells the time at the beginning and end of the first paragraph, and then again at the beginning of the fourth paragraph.
11. C, The sentences of the excerpt are long and very detailed. The author shows the feelings of the narrator in elaborate descriptions and comparisons.
12. B, People who are naked and screaming are most likely in pain. This comparison emphasizes the pain the speaker feels.
13. A, The author uses the comparisons of a kite to show that the speaker feels as though she is in the air and not on the ground, and a top spinning to show that the speaker does not feel in control of her own motions, as though she is removed from her body.
14. D, The speaker's pain has taken control of her attention, much the same way a barking dog might demand its owner's attention.
15. B, A person is not a word, but in this line, the speaker is compared to a word. The comparison does not use the words "like" or "as," so this comparison is a metaphor, describing the way the speaker's pain affects her and makes her feel abstract or undefined.

16. B, Answer B is correct because the metaphor indicates that hugging and kissing the bride might cause wrinkles, or "crumples," in her dress. Meg welcomes such wrinkles, as she states in paragraph 2, as signs of love.
17. D, Answer D is correct, suggesting the term empty nest. Parents often feel mixed emotions at a son's or daughter's wedding. Answers A and C are unsupported by the text. Nothing indicates disapproval or concern about finances. Answer B is a misinterpretation of the reference to a bird's nest; the meaning is figurative, not literal, nor does it indicate that Meg attends to the birds.
18. A, Answer A best explains the two examples of hyperbole in the sentence. The first example emphasizes that the Professor's kindness has a positive effect on many boys. The second emphasizes that Jo has an extremely forgiving nature.
19. C, Answer C is the best choice because a whirlpool moves in circles and suggests constant motion. Although boys at the beach might see whirlpools, the metaphor does not suggest a beach setting. The boys are at the school, not at the shore. Answer B is not the best choice because nothing is suggested about studying the movement of water. The boys themselves, not their studies, are the subject of the comparison. Answer D seems more plausible but is not as good a choice as answer C because it omits mentioning the boys and brings in additional objects—a top and a toy.

LESSON 12, pp. 138–142

1. D, The last paragraph indicates that the mother does not have happy memories about chrysanthemums. For her, the chrysanthemums symbolize disappointment.
2. D, The noise of the plane is described as "roaring through the radio news," which implies that it was so loud the radio could not be heard.
3. A, The narrator describes the scene in exciting terms, as the characters rush out of the house to watch the plane, and says it was "the first close-up plane I ever saw" (lines 5–6). The plane symbolizes the excitement of something new.
4. D, Many people are intrigued by the sight of the plane and rush out to gawk. This is most like the arrival of a circus to town.
5. C, The description of the fairgrounds explains why it is a good place for the plane to land. This image is best described as matter-of-fact.
6. A, The speaker describes the moon, and then says that it is "now shown vividly" through a crack in the wall that used to be very small. This indicates the crack is becoming larger, so that now the speaker can see the whole full moon.
7. D, The dark night, the lightning flashing through the storm, and the appearance of a full, "blood-red moon" all make the passage eerie and creepy.
8. C, The House of Usher belonged to the Usher family and was likely the location for many family events. The destruction of the house is much like a book containing a family's history being ripped apart.

UNIT 2 (continued)

9. B, Readers are given no indication that any particular event caused the house to fall apart quickly, so you can assume it has been falling apart for a while. This indicates the family has likely not lived in the house for many years, and may in fact be dead.

10. C, In most cultures, the color white is a symbol for purity and truth, which would be important to royalty. The excerpt lists numerous royal families that used the color white in their family symbols.

11. B, Captain Ahab is likely very angry with the whale for destroying his ship and taking his leg. He most likely is hunting the whale to get his revenge.

12. D, The first paragraph is full of imagery that shows how white can symbolize good things, such as flowers and pearls. The second paragraph contains imagery that shows how white can be associated with scary things, such as polar bears and sharks.

13. A, The author gives weight to both positive and negative imagery in the excerpt. He would likely apply this same thoroughness to a colorful painting in an art gallery.

14. A, The speaker's imagination runs wild as she thinks about all the different things that might have made the mark on the wall.

15. B, Lines 27 and 28 state that the speaker's train of thought "threaten(s) mere waste of energy, even some collision with reality" indicating that the time the speaker takes to imagine all the different possibilities about the mark are preventing her from getting up and walking to the wall to find out what really made it.

16. D, Throughout the excerpt, the speaker keeps thinking of new events that could have left the mark on the wall. As each idea comes to her, she imagines the situation which surrounded each event, with seemingly limitless possibilities.

17. D, Based on the speaker's behavior throughout the story, she is most likely to spend more time imagining how the snail got into the house and why it would crawl up the wall.

LESSON 13, pp. 143–147

1. A, The details and final sentence of the passage suggest that the man does not think about the reality that it is fifty degrees below zero—that humans are especially frail and even vulnerable to death in such extreme conditions. The man is aware of where the trail is and where the sun should be, so there is no indication that he may get lost. Also, the man is aware of how uncomfortable a person can be in cold weather and understands that special gear is required to guard against such discomfort and protect oneself from frostbite.

2. B, The two men do not shoot each other because they have been "brought up under the code of a restraining civilization," meaning that they have been taught to act against base instincts. In each man's case, murder would be the fulfillment, not the abandonment, of a lifelong passion. The act of murder requires a disregard for the restraining code of civilization, not necessarily hatred of any kind or a statement of wrongs.

3. C, While the men restrain themselves because they adhere to human codes of conduct, Nature has no such limitations. Nature does not have feelings, so it does not feel hatred or care about honor, for example. Although nature may reinforce—or, for that matter, diminish—someone's passion, the statement that Nature's violence overwhelmed both men is intended to emphasize the physical results of Nature's violence.

4. D, The situation is likely to change the relationship between the men. They must help each other or die. They are not likely to shoot each other now that they need each other. In fact, they are likely to realize the foolishness of their feud, not elevate its significance. Although they may wish to tend to each other's wounds, it is unlikely that either man will be able to do so, given that both are held captive under the tree.

5. A, The men do not kill each other because they care about a code of propriety. Nature cares nothing for such codes; it simply acts without regard for feelings or consequences, making it more deadly than humans. Nature and humankind are deadly enemies, but they rely on each other for survival, as well.

6. D, The men are single-mindedly focused on their feud, so they ignore the storm, which endangers them. This situation is similar to the problem of people putting themselves and others in danger by ignoring storm warnings in favor of their own interests. The men are not in their current situation because of careless actions or a violent crime; they are the victims of a natural phenomenon. Although one man has more land than the other, the men seem to regard each other as equal partners in their feud; one is not bullying the other.

7. A, Lines 2 and 3 indicate Edie has just come from England to California.

8. C, Lines 19 through 22 state that the twins, who were "entirely responsible for their mother's death," are sleeping in another room. This indicates Mrs. Ransom died while giving birth to the twins.

9. D, Edie has come to live with the Ransoms to help take care of the children after their mother has died. She treats the children kindly and takes care of them while their father is grieving over his wife's death.

10. D, Edie's job is to take care of the children, just like a grandmother might arrive at her child's house to take care of a sick grandchild.

11. B, Thomas Ransom is described as having spent the night aching for his wife, and lying in bed half awake, half asleep, and dreaming. He is grief-stricken over his wife's passing.

12. D, Thoreau mentions the Musketaquid, a Native American people who lived in the area around Concord, Massachusetts. The relics mentioned are those left by the Musketaquid. Answer A is incorrect because the Native Americans who settled the land earlier may have died, but their "race" has not vanished. Animals are not mentioned in reference to relics, nor are former neighbors.

13. B, The passage is about Thoreau and the Native Americans who worked the land; it is not about the author's direct ancestors. Thoreau implies that everything he does to the land erases memories of the Musketaquid. Although Thoreau does mention that others worked the land before him, the implication is explained in answer B and goes beyond the statement in answer C. No claims on the land are mentioned or implied.

14. C, The author suggests that decayed wood is part of an eternal cycle of life. The end of one piece of a tree's life is the beginning of life for "mosses and fungi." Generations have come before the decayed tree and generations will come after it. Although decay is a natural process, this information is not the author's suggestion in the paragraph. He does not imply that there are older forms of wood, but rather that this is a stage in an eternal cycle. Mosses and fungi are not older than decayed wood; instead they are the next stage in the cycle.

UNIT 2 (continued)

15. C, Answer C is the most specific. Answer B may be true, and even evident in the passage, but it is not the best choice because it is so general. Answer A is not addressed in the text, and no evidence supports it. Answer D reflects a misreading of the passage; the life cycle of plants and the existence of relics are not connected.
16. D, Lines 1 and 2 state that the person on the front porch is the new wife. The end of the excerpt gives the husband's name, Konrad.
17. B, The speaker is likely comparing Pauline's voice to the way her own voice sounds. You can infer that Pauline is younger than the speaker.
18. B, The speaker allows Pauline to sit outside on her front porch as long as she wants. The speaker describes Pauline's behavior with a slight bit of humor, so she's likely amused at Pauline's behavior.
19. D, The women are awkward around one another but do have something in common. They were both married to Konrad at one point. This situation is most like one in which two people with a shared past visit awkwardly.

LESSON 14, pp. 148–152

1. A, Readers are told that Laird is cold, despite the heat of the day, and that his appearance has changed greatly. This indicates he is most likely suffering from a rare disease.
2. C, Someone who is aggrieved has cause for complaint. If readers don't know the word *aggrieved*, the woman's feelings become clear when she is described as speaking without mercy and slamming down the phone. This is the behavior of someone who feels mistreated.
3. A, Readers are told that the disheveled appearance is the "picture of someone who recently ceased to be cherished." Thus, she must feel unloved.
4. B, Gloria's thoughts turn dark as she starts thinking about death after she observes the woman on the phone. It's reasonable to conclude that she thinks the woman is very unhappy.
5. D, Gloria watches the woman's behavior. She acts as someone who "recently had ceased to be cherished," meaning that she is no longer considered important or dear to someone else. From this information, you can conclude that she has just gotten out of a relationship.
6. D, Gilbert is going through Angela's belongings and sorting them out. This information, combined with the statement that Angela may have "forseen her death," indicates that she has died recently.
7. B, The narrator describes Gilbert as being very selective in his choice of words about the marital fights he had with Angela. He downgrades them from quarrels to tiffs, indicating that he likely minimized or did not give importance to any fights they might have had.
8. C, The narrator tells readers that Angela's death was sudden, yet Angela had time to label each of her objects to instruct her husband to whom they should go. From this information, you can conclude that Angela likely planned her death.
9. D, After reading the excerpt, you know Gilbert has found notes from Angela that she must have written prior to her death. You can conclude that this situation is like one in which a friend has deliberately left messages to be found after he or she died.
10. A, The children's father is referred to as "Poor Roy" (line 12), which tells us that the father was likely well-loved by his family and within this society. However, the children are not treated as family, and their mother is compared to a "pretty secretary" (line 19), which indicates that she may have been considered beneath Roy in social status. This is the only reasonable conclusion based on the details provided in the excerpt.
11. D, The beginning of the excerpt tells you that whenever the grandchildren visited their grandparents, they were put in the sewing room, "a bleak, shabby, utilitarian rectangle." Based on this information, you can conclude that the grandparents treated the children as unwanted guests.
12. C, The grandfather is described as having money, but chooses to put the children up with disagreeable relations in a "dingy" house, and not spend the time or money on them.
13. D, The children's father, Roy, is grieved by the grandparents and the townspeople alike, but his children's reputation is "clouded by misfortune," and they are treated poorly. This situation is most like one in which well-off people take great care with their own pets but ignore any hungry animals that might be outside.
14. D, In the middle of the excerpt, Martin is identified as Laird's father. The first line tells us that Martin has left the house quickly.
15. C, Laird's tone and words indicate that he feels as though he disappoints his father often. From this information, you can conclude that Laird and his father Martin do not get along well.
16. B, The speaker is aggravated with Martin for not staying to sit with his sick and dying son. You can assume that Martin likely feels as though he has other things to attend to, or that it pains him to see his son in such a state. Martin's situation is most like that of a visitor to an art gallery who turns away from a painting he or she finds unappealing.
17. B, Despite her son's failing health, the speaker still loves him and enjoys spending time with him. You can conclude that the speaker feels Martin is losing out on the joys of spending time with his family.

LESSON 15, pp. 153–157

1. D, Most of the excerpt describes how Paul reacts to the music.
2. D, The beginning of the excerpt explains that Mrs. Leslie and Belinda are used to country life, and then describes different aspects of country life. From this description and Leo's discomfort, you can assume that Leo is in the country.
3. B, The phrase "yet another" picnic lets us know that Leo has attended more than one of the picnics, and indicates his impatience with them. Leo will most likely dislike the next picnic to which he is invited.
4. C, Leo is out of his element and does not know entirely what to do, as he has no prior experience in this sort of situation. He is most like a big city lawyer on a trail ride who does not know how to saddle his horse.

UNIT 2 (continued)

5. D, You may know that some people take pride in having artifacts that have been passed down through their families for generations. Mrs. Leslie's constant references to the age of the picnic basket indicate that she likes to brag about her family.

6. C, The narrator tells us that her mother would rather appear her age than look silly trying to appear younger, and that she has grown old gracefully.

7. B, In addition to admiring her mother for aging gracefully, the narrator says that her mother "would no sooner go under the knife for the sake of appearing five or six years younger than buy a dress simply because it was marked down" (lines 10–13). She would most likely describe her mother as being practical.

8. D, Margaret is aging, but she still has a lot of pride in her appearance and chooses to appear and act her age rather than hide it. A simile for her state of mind could be that she runs as well as a functional, well-worn 1990s sub-compact, indicating she is older but still has grace.

9. A, Based on the information that Margaret would likely not accept or buy anything just because she can, she would most likely turn down an offer for a free sample.

10. C, Belinda's mother and Leo are distracted by Belinda's similarity to her father. They do not realize that Belinda plans to leave them stranded, as indicated by her statement "so now they know. … or they soon will" in lines 14 through 16.

11. D, The author is giving readers an insight into Belinda's self-control. The author tells us that Belinda wants to cry, but her righteousness or belief that she should not cry helps her hold her emotions in check.

12. D, Based on the description of Belinda, the reader can infer that she would likely enter a similar state of mind, as though she were covered in ice and armored against emotions, if an angry person were to confront her.

13. B, Belinda was talking with Leo and her mother before the beginning of the excerpt, and then she left them where they were, without any means of getting to any other place. This situation is most like one in which a thief talks to his or her victim before stealing a wallet.

14. B, Laura forgets about all the other things that have to happen before the party and wishes she knew more men who would stop to appreciate something as simple as the way a flower smelled.

15. C, The author describes the trees as "lovely, with their broad, gleaming leaves, and their clusters of yellow fruit" (lines 18–20). This indicates that Laura is very fond of the trees, and does not want them blocked from view by the marquee.

16. C, You might not know that a person who is resigned has given into the demands or needs of someone or something. However, you can eliminate the other answers, based on Laura's acceptance of the fact that her trees must be hidden by the marquee (line 25).

17. A, Laura is quite busy as she plans for the garden party, but her attention is distracted by the small action of the workman admiring the lavender. This is most like a busy lawyer stopping to watch a painter.

UNIT 2 REVIEW, pp. 158–161

1. C, The last sentence of the excerpt states that the speaker is "stuck in Vera Cruz." While he has accepted his fate, he is quite annoyed with it, which makes "stranded" the best answer option.

2. D, Lines 1 through 4 of the excerpt let us know that the speaker has been busy for a while and that the idea of having nothing to do is amusing.

3. C, A slate is like a chalkboard that can be erased, and a sponge is often used to wash down and erase a slate or a chalkboard. Based on this information, you can assume that the speaker wants his mind to be erased.

4. A, The speaker wishes to not be stuck in Vera Cruz and that he were able to forget things. He also wishes he could choose his moment of laziness and have his surroundings exactly as he would want them. However, he has apparently accepted the fact that he is stuck for the time being and does not seem to be annoyed. His tone is best described as wishful.

5. B, The pearl is described as being "priceless," but rather than ingest it herself, Cleopatra gave the drink with the pearl to Antony. This action shows she cared for him more than for herself.

6. D, The speaker has a wish: to continue his trip and leave Vera Cruz; but his wish is not fulfilled because of the dock strike. His situation is most like that of a customer who wants to buy an item that is not available to her.

7. D, Answer D is correct because the narrator uses third-person pronouns to tell the story. Answers A and B are incorrect because both characters are referred to in third-person pronouns, by name, or by relationship. Answer C is incorrect because the narrator is not a character in the story.

8. C, Answer C is the best choice. If Framton knew the aunt or many people in the town, he would know that the story the niece is about to tell him could not be true.

9. C, The sequence of events is as follows, as indicated in the text: Framton's sister stays at the rectory. The "tragedy" takes place. The niece explains why the window remains open. Framton acts as though he has seen a ghost.

10. D, Answer D is the best choice because it refers to letters of introduction, which were written as a way to introduce people, particularly when one moved to a new location. In this case, Framton's sister provides him with such letters so that he will meet people while he rests and be invited to social events. At the time the story takes place, telephones were not in wide use, particularly in rural areas.

11. C, Answer C is correct because the expression describes the shock and fear that someone would experience upon seeing something unbelievable. Although someone might turn pale, the pallor would come as a result of shock.

12. C, Answer C is correct. She has just frightened an adult guest with a highly detailed and believable story and continues, at the end, to improvise another tale explaining Framton's departure.

UNIT 2 (continued)

13. D, Answer D best explains Framton's reasons for leaving as he does. The niece's story is vivid and accurately detailed; when Framton sees the men arrive, they are exactly as the niece has described them. In his fragile state of mind, Framton is likely to be frightened easily. The niece invents the tale in lines 89–93 to explain Framton's sudden departure and perhaps to avoid explaining her role in causing it.

14. B, Answer B is correct because the accuracy and detail of the niece's story, as well as her self-possession, convince Framton that the men actually disappeared. He has no reason to doubt her and continues to believe her even when the men return. In fact, he believes her tale more than he believes what he sees. The story causes Framton to believe he has seen ghosts and to flee the house in a panic.

UNIT 3 POETRY

LESSON 1, pp. 164–168

1. C, If you read the poem out loud, you should notice that your speech patterns fall into a steady, regular pattern of stressed and unstressed syllables.

2. A, The poet was most likely attempting to make readers laugh at the sudden and unexpected rhyme.

3. C, Lines 1 through 3 each contain eight syllables, and line 5 has nine syllables. These lines of similar lengths create a predictable rhythm that is thrown off slightly by line 4, and is completely thrown off by the abrupt ending.

4. C, The poet chose a formal rhythm that matches her very proper language to contrast with the ending of the poem, in which she asks for one perfect limousine.

5. D, The poem suggests that the speaker would prefer a more useful or material object, such as a limousine. The poem also indicates that the speaker has particular tastes, so she would probably most like a jewelry store gift certificate.

6. B, Remember that the rhyme pattern is determined by the last word in each line. The words *sweepers* and *keepers* rhyme, as do *neck* and *wreck*, and these words set up the beginning of an ABAB rhyming pattern. *Baker* and *undertaker* rhyme with one another, but not with *sweepers* or *keepers*, so the rhyming pattern becomes ABABCDCD. The word *love* does not rhyme with any other word in the first stanza, so the final rhyming pattern for the first stanza is ABABCDCDE.

7. D, The words *psalm* and *arm* form a partial rhyme because they have similar "a" sounds and both end with an "m."

8. D, All of the workers mentioned in the poem stop doing their jobs when they are in love.

9. D, The speaker describes the things that happen and the jobs that people stop doing because of a date with love. This emphasizes the importance of and the power that love has over people.

10. D, The speaker seems to believe that people in love abandon their jobs, so he would likely think that a waiter who served a meal late was in love.

11. D, The speaker states that she could spare the jeweled brooch her mother left for her, which tells us that the speaker is not concerned with material things. The speaker would most likely choose good advice.

12. A, Every other syllable in the poem is a stressed syllable. This creates the rhythm of the poem as it is said aloud.

13. C, The change in rhyme scheme makes the reader pay particular attention to the last line and its rhyme, which is different than the previously established rhyme.

14. B, The speaker is sad that her mother took her courage with her, even though the mother has no need for it anymore, because the speaker feels she needs it now.

15. D, The stressed and unstressed syllables in the last line make the rhythm different than in the other lines.

16. C, Line 3 alludes to the spears of the Assyrian soldiers. A *cohort* is "a military unit." These indicate that the poem is about an attack by the Assyrian army.

17. D, In line 13, the Angel of Death attacks the Assyrian army. With the additional information about the Biblical story, the poem describes the Assyrian army as being doomed.

18. B, The pattern of stressed and unstressed syllables reflects a pounding rhythm, such as one that would be created by an army on the march.

19. B, The Assyrian army is described as a wolf descending on the fold, or flock of sheep. This description implies that the Assyrian army was stronger and faster than its opponent. However, it was defeated, much in the same way that an unforeseen event might take away a basketball team's sure win.

LESSON 2, pp. 169–173

1. D, The poet states that books "take us lands away" (line 2). The comparison means that a book can take its readers on adventures, much like a ship can take passengers on adventures.

2. C, Lines 15 through 20 explain that the speaker and his friend are thinking of the people they both knew who are no longer living.

3. D, Typically, it is easier to pick or gather fruit that hangs toward the bottom of the tree, so the fruit at the top of the tree is usually there the longest. In this poem, the two or three berries refer to the few members of the speaker's circle of friends who are still alive.

4. C, *Wistful* means "wishing or longing for something." In the poem, the speaker is wishing that more of his friends were still alive. The poet is not angry or disappointed, so answers 1 and 2 are incorrect. The speaker does not indicate that he is afraid of anything, so answer 4 is incorrect. The poem does end with merry jests, but there is a hint of sadness present, so the speaker is not joyous; therefore, answer 5 is incorrect.

5. A, The meeting is some sort of celebration, but the people there are constantly remembering the people who are no longer with them. This is most like a person trying, but failing, to enjoy her own birthday party.

6. D, A garden would likely bring beauty to a desert, which is a harsh environment. The speaker believes that prairies bring beauty to a harsh environment.

UNIT 3 (continued)

7. D, The first two lines state that the speaker cannot rest from travel and wants to drink life to the lees, or the fullest. This implies that the speaker wants to experience life through travel.
8. C, These lines compare experience to an arch, or a gateway. The speaker says that on one side of the arch is the known or traveled world, and on the other side is the untraveled or unknown world. By going through the arch, or traveling to the unknown world, a person can gain experience.
9. A, The speaker wants to learn as much as possible and expand upon his own knowledge. This sentiment is uplifting.
10. B, The speaker is an adventurous man who enjoys the idea of traveling far and wide to gain new experiences. He would most likely enjoy climbing a mountain on a day off.
11. C, The poem says that children should be allowed to roam far and wide and try different things, but that parents should be waiting to provide security and "become a tree" (line 9) in the event that a child becomes afraid of something.
12. A, The speaker believes that children "must go free" (line 2) and explore the world.
13. C, Comparing a parent to a tree that stands tall and has a strong support system of roots makes parenting seem very important.
14. D, Some fish live in shallow waters and come near shores on the tide or currents. By comparing parents to the shore and the children to the fish, the speaker says that parents must be the steadfast, constant shore of support to which children occasionally return.
15. D, The speaker states the West Wind is both destroyer and preserver in line 18.
16. D, You can imagine that ghosts would fear an enchanter, and would quickly and skittishly run away from the enchanter.
17. A, The beginning of the poem tells us that the West Wind happens in autumn, when the weather gets colder. Most plants do not grow in colder weather, so the seeds of the plants would not grow during autumn. This metaphor says the seeds are dead, until the warmer winds of spring come to blow over them.
18. D, The West Wind is described as a destroyer and preserver, which is most like a potter who destroys pots and uses the clay to make new pots.
19. C, The poet does use some frightening images in describing the West Wind. However, the speaker's overall attitude seems to be one of admiring the wind's strength.

LESSON 3, pp. 174–178

1. B, Cats are known for being quiet, so the poet uses the image of the fog walking like a cat to emphasize its quiet appearance.
2. C, Fog cannot sit, and it has no haunches, but describing the fog in this manner gives readers an idea of how it appears to the poet and helps them to identify with the feeling and tone of the poem.
3. A, Lines 13 through 16 tell us that the speaker would spend hundreds and even thousands of years devoted to his mistress.

4. C, No person could live for the amount of time that is described in the passage, yet the speaker insists that he would love this woman for ages.
5. D, The speaker uses hyperbole to emphasize the depth of his love for his mistress. Love cannot physically grow, so it cannot be vaster than an empire, in much the same way that a person cannot give the moon to another person.
6. C, The speaker knows that for all the time he would spend with his mistress, he cannot escape time, and it will continue to pass.
7. D, A *host* is "a large group of things." The speaker describes many daffodils standing by the lake.
8. D, The speaker says that he is lonely like a cloud, and the tone of the first stanza indicates that he is unhappy until he sees the flowers.
9. C, The line in the poem uses personification. Flowers do not actually dance, but they appear to be dancing like a person would. Cats communicate, but do not actually talk as humans do. This example also uses personification, just like the poem.
10. C, The speaker refers to the daffodils in a happy, upbeat tone that is best described as joyful.
11. D, Lines 1 and 2 describe the ocean waves shattering against the shore.
12. D, The speaker is afraid of the ocean's shattering waves and believes they are a danger to him.
13. B, The speaker describes the ocean in violent terms, and line 12 explains that someone needed to be prepared for rage. The waves are best described as angry.
14. C, The cliffs stand behind the shore and support it as it is repeatedly attacked by the ocean waves. This is most like a big sister standing behind her smaller brother as a support.
15. A, Waves do not have eyes, or any other organ with which to see. The poet gave the waves the human-like ability to see.
16. D, All of the tasks that the speaker asks readers to do are impossible. A person cannot catch a falling star. A root cannot be pregnant. Past years do not physically go anywhere.
17. A, The poet says "Ride ten thousand days and nights" in line 13. This statement, along with line 14, indicate that the subject of the poem to whom the speaker is referring will be older and have white hair.
18. C, The end of the stanza says the speaker suspects the traveler will not be able to find any woman who is true and fair.
19. B, The speaker of the poem is very bitter. He believes that people, especially women, are not honest.

LESSON 4, pp. 179–183

1. A, The image of the battered knuckle gives readers the idea that the father has probably recently punched someone or something, like a wall.
2. A, In line 3, the traveler asks about the day's journey.
3. C, An easy trip would not leave people feeling travel-sore and weak, so answer A is incorrect. The poem states that the journey is uphill all the way to the end, so answer B is incorrect. There is also no indication that the traveler is on horseback; D is incorrect as well.
4. D, In poetry, a road is often a symbol of life's journey. The first stanza gives a hint—the road only goes one way, uphill, and it will take an entire day, or one lifespan.

UNIT 3 (continued)

5. B, The second speaker indicates that travelers are always welcome at this inn, in much the same way that someone might say "the door is always open."

6. D, The first speaker asks if he must knock or call when he approaches the door, and the second speaker lets him know that he will not even have to wait. This is a comforting thought to someone who has traveled a long time.

7. D, A dream deferred might be something that a person has been looking forward to but is not able to attain. That person would be disappointed. The poem is asking what happens when people are disappointed.

8. A, The speaker compares the dream deferred to a raisin that is left out in the sun.

9. C, The first ten lines of the poem are rather sad, but the idea of an explosion creates a dangerous image.

10. D, A sore that festers becomes more and more infected and painful and can ultimately be dangerous. This description is most like a pothole that is not fixed and gets deeper and deeper, which can cause damage to a car.

11. B, The descriptions the poet uses are things that have been allowed to sit around and become dangerous or gross. These comparisons show that disappointment can have a negative effect on people.

12. D, A turnpike is a major road. In this stanza, the parade is veering off the major road and heading into a field of grass.

13. C, In the beginning of the poem, the parade is very exciting and new to the speaker, much like the world would be to a small child. The parade continues to travel down the road, with many people marching alongside the speaker. The parade then turns off the main road and heads into a grassy field, towards the "dizzying cliffs of mortality." The parade in this poem symbolizes a person's lifespan.

14. C, The speaker seems to accept that he does not have time to stop and rest on the bench, as he later explains that this rush is because the young are pushing him forward and the old are tugging on him.

15. D, The speaker describes the things that are going on around him, but states that his mind is lost in a private dream. This description is most like that of a child whose mind wanders while listening to a parent talk.

16. A, Lines 7 and 8 tell us that the statue is called the Mother of Exiles.

17. D, Lines 8 and 9 describe the statue as holding a light that glows with a world-wide welcome. This best symbolizes hope for people coming to the new land.

18. B, The poet gives the statue these words to show her defiance towards the old countries and their "storied pomp," or snobbishness.

19. D, The statue is described as holding a lamp that acts as a guiding light for immigrants, who are leaving the safety or familiarity of their homelands for new starts. This is most like the way that a lighthouse guides sailors to safety.

20. B, The "huddled masses" the poet describes have no homes and have been tossed about by ocean waves and perhaps political struggles in their homelands. This description tells us that these people are in need.

LESSON 5, pp. 184–188

1. B, From the last stanza, you can infer that the speaker's love has likely died.

2. A, Line 13 indicates that the speaker is experiencing "perfect grief."

3. C, The speaker says, "between my knees my forehead was." If you rearrange this phrase to read "my forehead was between my knees," you will understand that he is sitting with his head between his knees.

4. B, The speaker is on a hilltop staring at some weeds (lines 9 and 10). He is so blinded by his unconsoled grief (lines 13 and 14) that the only thing that holds his attention is the woodspurge.

5. D, You might know that the word *desolate* means "extremely empty or sad," which would describe the poem's tone. If you did not know the meaning of desolate, you can make inferences to rule out the other answer options. The tone is not confused, nor forgiving. A feeling of grief is an extreme feeling, while indifference is a lack of interest. The speaker does not want to fight anyone, so the tone is not combative.

6. D, Lines 3 and 4 state that the speaker walked at the wind's will. He was paying no attention to where he was walking, simply moving as the wind pushed him.

7. C, The first three stanzas of the poem describe Richard Cory as a person who is admired by the other people in town.

8. D, From the description of Richard Cory in the poem, no one in town knew he had any problems that might make him want to commit suicide.

9. B, The last stanza is shocking in its abrupt shift in tone and subject matter.

10. B, The people of the town knew Richard Cory well and admired him, but his feelings were apparently hidden from the townspeople, in much the same way that a long-time neighbor might hide a secret.

11. A, The overall idea of this poem is that a person cannot assume he or she knows everything about another person, as that other person might be hiding something. This is best summed up as "Don't judge a book by its cover."

12. A, Lines 6 through 8 state that "soul more white/never through martyrdom of fire was led," indicating that the subject, the speaker's wife, died in a fire.

13. C, The speaker describes his deceased wife in loving terms.

14. B, Lines 15 and 16 tell us that the speaker has grieved for his wife for the last 18 years.

15. B, Knowing that the poet was injured while trying to save his wife from the fire makes the poem more touching to readers.

16. C, The speaker quietly remembers his wife with a simple cross around his neck. He would most likely observe her birthday quietly and privately.

17. D, The speaker tells the child that it is unkind to leave the snail where it is and carries it outside with a careful hand.

18. C, The speaker admits that she has done some things that were difficult and unkind, but her tone is remorseful, indicating that she did them because she felt she had to.

19. C, After this line, the speaker goes on to list unpleasant truths about life that she has witnessed and acts she has performed. She wants to shield her child from these facts, in the same way that another parent might wait until his or her child is older to reveal unpleasant family truths.

UNIT 3 (continued)

20. D, The speaker very tenderly tells her child that he or she should be kind to snails.

LESSON 6, pp. 189–193

1. A, The second stanza describes what happens "if you tuck the name of a loved one / under your tongue," or keep that person in your thoughts. Lines 15 and 16 imply that the fuel or energy a person "feeds" on comes from a person he or she loves.
2. C, Line 1 tells us the speaker is standing on a tower. You can infer that the speaker is implying the time is New Year's Eve, when an old year and a new year "meet."
3. B, From this line, you can assume that the speaker has had a difficult year and is in tears as the years change over.
4. C, In lines 6 and 7, the speaker states that there's been enough science and exploration. "Aught" is an old term for "anything." From this information, you can restate the stanza as "Have we learned anything that is useful and worth knowing?"
5. D, The speaker is concerned about the amount of information that has become available, and questions whether it is worth knowing. This is similar to the way that a parent might try to cope with rapidly changing technology.
6. B, The speaker of the poem questions whether things are worth knowing, and the descriptions in the poem are uncomfortable, with the storm and the wind roaring. The tone of the poem is best identified as "uneasy."
7. C, Lines 10 through 15 tell us that the speaker wishes to be part of nature. He wants to return to earth as a seed and become a tree.
8. B, The speaker is referring to his children in this line.
9. B, The speaker accepts that he will one day die and return to the earth.
10. D, The speaker refers to his eventual death and return to earth, followed by his rebirth. This is most like a plant dying and then being replaced by another.
11. C, The speaker refers to his death when he describes "the sleep of darkness without stars."
12. D, The mask the speaker refers to is hiding the "torn and bleeding hearts" of the people (line 4).
13. D, The poem describes what the speaker feels and what he needs to keep behind the mask. If given the opportunity to speak to the public, he would most likely want to articulate his feelings.
14. B, The last stanza tells us that the speaker's soul is tortured and crying out, although he will let the world dream otherwise.
15. B, The subjects of the poem sing along with the rest of the world and appear to be happy, but they are secretly in pain and are miserable.
16. A, The tone of the poem is best described as angry. The speaker is upset that he and others have been forced to hide their true feelings.
17. C, The speaker says that the trees are shaking their leaves, which makes a sound or utterance of joy.
18. C, Lines 8 through 11 tell us that the speaker is wondering why the tree can be so happy when it is all alone. This tells us that the speaker likely craves companionship himself.
19. D, The main idea of the poem is in lines 24 through 30. The speaker says that he knows he could never be happy without companionship, even though the tree can.
20. D, The speaker's curious token is a twig with leaves and some moss on it. The speaker has it in remembrance of the happy tree, much like someone would have an inexpensive souvenir from a trip.
21. B, The speaker is jealous of the tree's happiness while being alone, because the speaker himself is lonely.

LESSON 7, pp. 194–198

1. D, The theme of the poem can be inferred from the first line: "Your world is as big as you make it." The speaker means that people can limit themselves to a small area or small ideas, or they can dream big.
2. B, The speaker says, "[m]ere anarchy is loosed upon the world" in line 4. The speaker believes that events in the world are creating an unstable environment, in which the center is falling apart and cannot hold together.
3. C, The tone of the poem indicates that the speaker is worried about how events of the time will lead to the destruction of world.
4. A, These lines can be restated as "The people who have the best intentions lack the conviction to speak up, while the people who have the worst intentions are shouting at the tops of their lungs." The speaker is most likely implying that people with the worst intentions are those who speak the loudest, so answer 1 is the best, most complete option.
5. D, The first stanza explains how everything is falling apart and the speaker feels that mankind is to blame: "anarchy is loosed upon the world," "the ceremony of innocence is drowned," and "the worst / Are full of passionate intensity." The second stanza discusses the Second Coming, which is a reference to an apocalypse that will end the world. The theme of this poem is best stated as "The evil of men will bring about the end of the world."
6. C, The last two lines of the first stanza indicate that the speaker feels young, even though he is gray and old.
7. C, The speaker is very accepting of his inevitable mortality and the life he has led.
8. D, The speaker has accepted his life and its eventual end and is looking forward to it in a way, as a final journey to the "Ecstatic Light." This is most similar to a person who is looking forward to a party.
9. C, The poem describes a life that has been full of joy and happiness. The poet is accepting of his inevitable death because he has lived his life fully.
10. C, Line 5 states that the speaker sees a boy and his friend walking up the road.
11. A, The description indicates that the boys are happy to have each other as company.
12. B, The speaker describes the simple scene of the two boys walking up the road and the happiness they seem to be experiencing, which brings him happiness in return.
13. C, The speaker is appreciative of the simple happiness the boys represent.
14. A, The speaker stands at his window watching the two boys walk up the road but does not interact with them, and this scene makes the speaker happy. This is most like someone admiring a piece of art.

UNIT 3 (continued)

15. C, Lines 19 and 20 tell us that the child is "screaming with laughter."

16. D, The daughter is leaving home and becoming independent, much like she did when she took off on her bicycle.

17. D, The poet uses the imagery of the child learning to ride the bicycle as an analogy of how her child will likely proceed with leaving home and becoming independent. The child shows now fear while riding her bike. She is only excited and laughing, so answer 3 is incorrect.

18. A, The image of the handkerchief waving goodbye implies a departure or a separation. The speaker is sad about the inevitable separation that comes when a child leaves the home.

UNIT 3 REVIEW, pp. 199–202

1. B, The speaker implies that he has been gone for five years and has missed the sound of the water trickling through the river bed.

2. C, The speaker indicates that he is alone at the site, saying that his thoughts lean towards more seclusion (lines 5–7) and comparing himself to a hermit (lines 21–22).

3. D, These lines can be restated as "I'm sitting here, under this sycamore tree, again." This tells readers that the speaker came to this location previously.

4. A, The speaker tells readers that he has been to this place before, and describes all the things he remembers about the place and their current appearance.

5. D, The speaker does not tell readers about any religious ideas he may follow, so answer 1 is incorrect. The speaker also gives no indication that his family is dead, so answer 2 is incorrect. The speaker describes the setting as a place he has been before and likely knows his way around, so answer 3 is incorrect. Nothing in the poem indicates that the speaker is writing about history, so answer 5 is incorrect.

6. C, The speaker shows a great appreciation for the natural beauty of the countryside around him, and indicates that he has been to this location before. He would most likely enjoy a visit to the country while on a holiday.

7. A, The speaker says, "Natural and things / and spiritual, — who separates those two…[t]ears up the bond of nature and brings death." This indicates that the speaker believes that the natural and the spiritual should not be divided.

8. C, The poet uses symbolism and imagery to show how life must be balanced between the natural and the spiritual. For instance, the image of the apple, which in this poem represents life ("This apple of life," line 10), is destroyed when it is cut in half and divided: "The perfect round which fitted Venus' hand / Has perished as utterly as if we ate / both halves" (lines 11–13).

9. D, In line 10, the author says, "This apple of life."

10. B, The poet firmly argues her case for the union of the natural and the spiritual parts of life, but does so through the use of examples of beauty and art. This indicates that she is most likely determined to get her point across to her readers.

11. D, From the context of the poem and the information provided in the question, you can assume that Antinous was a beautiful Greek man who was born into the lower classes of society. The poet's reference to Antinous indicates that she believes something beautiful can come from an ordinary background.

12. A, The poet believes that beautiful art can and should come from natural objects that have a sort of spirituality. Given her examples of marble and clay statues, the author would most likely choose to take up wood carving as a hobby.

Index

Note: Page numbers in **boldface** indicate definitions or main discussion with examples. Page numbers in *italic* indicate a visual representation. Page ranges indicate practice.

A

Analogies, **169**, 170–173
Analogy, 82
Analyze elements of persuasion, 52, 53–56
Analyzing elements of persuasion, 52, 53–56
Appeal to emotions, 57
Appeal to ethics, 57
Appeal to logic, 57
Applying ideas, **153**, 154–157
Arguments, 52
Audience, 47
Author's point of view, 47, **62**, 63–66
Author's position, 52
Author's purpose, **47**, 48–51, 62, 72

C

Categorizing, **12**, 13–17
Cause, 82
Cause and effect
   determining to draw conclusions, 42
   elements in fiction, 89–92
   identifying in fiction, **88**
   identifying in nonfiction, **22**, 23–26
   signal words for, 22, 88
Characters
   motivation of, **108**, 109–112
   traits and actions of, **103**, 104–107
Claims, 52
Climax, 82, 98
Compare, 82
Comparing and contrasting
   in fiction, **93**, 94–97
   in nonfiction, **27**, 28–31
   signal words for, 27
Comparisons, 93
Complications, 82, 98
Conclusion, 52
Conclusions, drawing
   from fiction texts, **148**, 149–152
   from nonfiction texts, **42**, 43–46
   from persuasive texts, 53–56
   using to apply ideas, **153**, 154–157
Context clues, 82, **83**, 84–87

Contrast, 82
Contrasting. *See* Comparing and contrasting
Contrasts, 93
Counterclaim, 52

D

Details, 143, 148
Determining author's purpose, **47**, 48–51
Distinguishing facts from opinions, **32**, 33–36, **57**, 58–61
Drawing conclusions
   application of ideas using, **153**, 154–157
   from fiction texts, **148**, 149–152
   from nonfiction texts, **42**, 43–46
   from persuasive texts, **52**, 53–56

E

Effect, 82
   See also Cause and effect
Emotions, 57
Ethics, 57
Evidence
   analyzing in opposing arguments, 52
   identifying in persuasive texts, **52**, **57**, 58–61
Exaggeration, 174
Exposition, 82, 98

F

Facts, **32**, 33–36, **57**, 58–61, 82
Fiction, 82
   apply ideas, **153**, 154–157
   cause and effect, **88**, 89–92
   characters, **103**, 104–107
   compare and contrast, **93**, 94–97
   context clues, **83**, 84–87
   draw conclusions, **148**, 149–152
   figurative language, **133**, 134–137
   make inferences, **143**, 144–147
   motivation, **108**, 109–112
   plot elements, **98**, 99–102
   point of view, **113**, 114–117
   review, 158–161
   setting, **123**, 124–127
   symbols and imagery, **138**, 139–142
   theme, **118**, 119–122
   tone, **128**, 129–132
   types of, 81
Figurative language
   in fiction, **133**, 134–137, **138**, 139–142

   in poetry, **169**, 170–173, **174**, 175–178, **179**, 180–183
   using to identify theme, **194**, 195–198
First-person point of view, 113
Frequently confused words, 163
Frequently misspelled words, 1

G

Generalizations, **72**, 73–76

H

Hyperbole, 82, 133, 174

I

Ideas, applying, **153**, 154–157
Identifying evidence, **57**, 58–61
Imagery, 82
   in fiction, **138**, 139–142
   in poetry, **179**, 180–183
   using to identify theme, **194**
   using to make inferences, 184
Inferences, 82
   application of ideas using, 153
   making from fiction, **143**, 144–147
   making from nonfiction, **37**, 38–41, 42
   making from poetry, **184**, 185–188, **194**
Information
   categorizing, **12**, 13–16
   comparing and contrasting, **93**, 94–97
   distinguishing facts from opinions, **32**, 33–36
   identifying evidence, **57**, 58–61
   making inferences using, 37

L

Logic, 57

M

Main ideas
   definition, **2**
   details and, **2**, 3–6
   identifying in poetry, **189**, 190–193
   summarizing, 7
Making Assumptions
   comparing and contrasting, 27
   determining author's purpose, 47
   determining validity of generalizations, 72

distinguishing fact from opinions, 32
identifying theme, 118
making inferences and draw conclusions, 42
restating a poem, 189
supporting details, 27

Making inferences
application of ideas using, 153
from fiction, **143**, 144–147
from nonfiction, **37**, 38–41, 42
from poetry, **184**, 185–188, **194**, 194–197

Metaphors, 82, 133, 169
Mood, 82
Motivation, 82, **108**, 109–112

N

Narrator's point of view, 113
News articles, 7
Nonfiction, 82
analyze elements of persuasion, **52**, 53–56
categorize, **12**, 13–16
cause and effect, **22**, 23–26
compare and contrast, **27**, 28–31
determine author's purpose, **47**, 48–51
determine point of view, **62**, 63–66
distinguish facts from opinions, **32**, 33–36
draw conclusions, **42**, 43–46
generalize, **72**, 73–76
identify evidence, **57**, 58–61
importance of understanding, xii
main idea and details, **2**, 3–6
make inferences, **37**, 38–41
review, 77–80
sequence, **17**, 18–21
style and tone, **67**, 68–71
summarize, **7**, 8–11

O

Omniscient point of view, 82, 113
Onomatopoeia, 133
Opinions, 32, 33–36, 57, 82
Opposing point of view, 52

P

Partial rhymes, 164
Personification, 82, 133, 174
Persuasive texts
analyzing elements of, **52**, 53–56
author's purpose, 47

distinguishing facts from opinions in, 57, 58–61
Plot, 98
Plot elements, **98**, 99–102
Poetry
analogies, **169**, 170–173
defined, 162
figurative language, **169**, 170–173, **174**, 175–178
make inferences, **184**, 185–188
restatement, **189**, 190–193
review, 199–202
rhythm and rhyme, **164**, 165–168
symbols and images, **179**, 180–183
theme, **194**, 195–198
Point of view, 82
author's in nonfiction, **62**, 63–66
narrator's in fiction, **113**, 114–117
opposing, 52
Prior knowledge, 42
Protagonist, 82
Purposes for writing, 47
See also **Author's purpose**

R

Reliable sources, 47
Resolution, 82, 98
Restatement of poems, **189**, 190–193
Rhyme, **164**, 165–168
Rhythm, **164**, 165–168

S

Sequencing, **17**, 18–21
Setting, 82, **123**, 124–127
Signal words
for cause and effect, 88
for compare and contrast, 27
Similes, 82, 133, 169
Stanza, 164
Stories. See **Fiction**
Style, determining, **67**, 68–71, 72
Summarizing, **7**, 8–11
Supporting details, **2**, 27, 37
Symbol, 82, 138, 179
Symbolism
in fiction, **138**, 139–142
in poetry, **179**, 180–183
using to identify theme, **194**
using to make inferences, **184**
Synonym, 83

T

Test-Taking Tips
analyze questions, 52

author's purpose and point of view, 62
compare and contrast with Venn diagrams, 93
draw conclusions, 148
figurative language, 133
finding imagery, 179
identify character's personality, 103
make inferences, 143
organize setting details, 123
pronouns indicating narrator's point of view, 113
read for character's motivation, 108
read for personification, 174
read poetry aloud, 164
sequence, 17
summarize, 7
theme, 194
think of complications as roadblocks, 98
use context clues, 83
Theme, 82
identifying in fiction, **118**, 119–122
identifying in poetry, **194**, 195–198
Tone, 82
of fiction, **128**, 129–132
of nonfiction, **67**, 68–71, 72

U

Unit Reviews, 77–80, 158–161, 199–202
Using Logic
analyze analogies, 169
apply ideas, 153
categorize, 12
determine cause and effect, 88
determine tone of nonfiction, 67
identify valid claims, **57**
main idea or supporting detail, 2
make inferences, 37, 184
read for tone in fiction, 128
signal words for cause and effect, 22
understand symbols, 138

V

Venn diagram, 93
Viewpoint. See **Point of view**

W

WH questions, **7**, 8–11